# PREVENTING CHILD TRAFFICKING

# PREVENTING CHILD TRAFFICKING

A Public Health Approach

Jonathan Todres, JD *&* Angela Diaz, MD

JOHNS HOPKINS UNIVERSITY PRESS | *Baltimore*

Johns Hopkins University Press
2715 North Charles Street
Baltimore, Maryland 21218-4363
www.press.jhu.edu

Library of Congress Cataloging-in-Publication Data

Names: Todres, Jonathan, author. | Diaz, Angela, MD, author.
Title: Preventing child trafficking : a public health approach / Jonathan Todres, JD,
   and Angela Diaz, MD.
Description: Baltimore : Johns Hopkins University Press, 2019. | Includes
   bibliographical references and index.
Identifiers: LCCN 2019007919 | ISBN 9781421433011 (hardcover : alk. paper) |
   ISBN 142143301X (hardcover : alk. paper) ISBN 9781421433028 (electronic) |
   ISBN 1421433028 (electronic)
Subjects: | MESH: Human Trafficking—prevention & control | Child Abuse, Sexual—
   prevention & control | Child | Adolescent | Physician's Role | Nurse's Role | Human
   Trafficking—legislation & jurisprudence
Classification: LCC HV6570 | NLM WA 325 | DDC 362.76/4—dc23
LC record available at https://lccn.loc.gov/2019007919

A catalog record for this book is available from the British Library.

*Special discounts are available for bulk purchases of this book. For more information,
please contact Special Sales at 410-516-6936 or specialsales@press.jhu.edu.*

Johns Hopkins University Press uses environmentally friendly book materials,
including recycled text paper that is composed of at least 30 percent post-consumer
waste, whenever possible.

*To the children around the globe who have survived human trafficking or other forms of exploitation. Their courage, strength, humanity, and intellect inspire us to work harder to create a world in which no child suffers human rights violations.*

We are grateful to everyone who supported us and this book project. We want to begin by thanking trafficking survivors who have shared their stories over the years. Their courage and strength inspire us, and their insights have guided our thinking. We also want to thank all the professionals and advocates working to address all forms of human trafficking. We have learned from colleagues and benefited from their partnership for many years. Many individuals contributed to and helped support this book. We are particularly grateful to the following individuals for their important feedback at various stages in the development of this book: Tonya Chaffee, Janie Chuang, Jordan Greenbaum, Anita Ravi, Nirej Sekhon, Hanni Stoklosa, and Martina Vandenberg. Librarians and staff at Georgia State University College of Law helped us track down many hard-to-find sources; we thank in particular Pamela Brannon, Meg Butler, Trina Holloway, Gerald Perriman, David Rutland, and Juanita Wheeler. In addition, a number of graduate research assistants at Georgia State University College of Law provided valuable research support; we are grateful to Brea Croteau, Caitlin Fox, Christina Scott, and Jordan Whitaker for their assistance. We also thank the following individuals at Mount Sinai Adolescent Health Center who provided assistance along the way: Mia N. Campbell, Jessica Halper, Pratima Maharjan, and Anthony Salandy. We extend an extra special thank-you to Monica Laredo Ruiz, also a graduate research assistant at Georgia State University College of Law, who provided both excellent research assistance and invaluable assistance during the production process. We also want to thank the JHU Press editorial and production team, particularly Robin Coleman, for their support of this book. Our thanks also to Joanne Allen for her keen eye in copyediting. Completing a book project while sustaining full-time jobs requires institutional support; our thanks to Dean Wendy Hensel, Georgia State University College of Law. Our ideas on a public health approach to child trafficking, and in particular the discussion in chapter 4, derive from an article previously published in the *North Carolina Law Review*; see Jonathan Todres, "Moving Upstream: The Merits of a Public Health Law Approach to Human Trafficking," *North Carolina Law Review* 89, no. 2 (2011): 447–506.

Finally, each of us would like to thank the individuals below.

*Jonathan*: Most of all, I want to thank Alison, Benjamin, and Desmond. The three of you have brought indescribable joy to my life. I am grateful for your love and support and for the opportunity to spend time with you every day.

*Angela*: Special thanks to Gabriel, Adriana, and Daniela Diaz. I also would like to thank the twelve thousand amazing young people we serve every year at Mount Sinai Adolescent Health Center, who share their lives with us and give us the gift to serve them, and the wonderful staff who have the privilege to work with them.

*Case studies.* In this book we draw on our experiences interacting with and serving trafficking survivors over many years. In a number of chapters, we include stories of particular trafficking survivors to humanize the experience of survivors, to illustrate the challenges they confront, and to show their strength and resilience. The names of these individuals and other potential identifying information have been changed to protect their identity.

*Terminology.* Language matters. The anti-trafficking movement comprises diverse views, backgrounds, expertise, and agendas, resulting in different opinions on terminology. Indeed, the fact that the definitions of human trafficking used by various organizations differ (see chapter 1 for a discussion of this) speaks to the range of perspectives in the field. We clarify here how we use selected terms in this book.

We use *child* or *children* to mean any individual(s) under eighteen years of age (consistent with how *child* is defined in international law; see UN Convention on the Rights of the Child, art. 1). We recognize that childhood is a spectrum, however, and that young people do not change overnight simply because they turn eighteen years old. Many interventions we discuss are needed not only for those under eighteen but also those eighteen years of age and older. In addition, we recognize that many adult trafficking survivors were first trafficked as children. Their needs merit attention as well. Although this book focuses on children and child trafficking, we believe all forms of trafficking of all individuals must be addressed.

When speaking about those who have been harmed in human trafficking, we use *survivor*, as opposed to *victim*, wherever possible because *victim* can be misconstrued to suggest a passive individual without agency.

We have seen the strength and resilience of young people who endured trafficking, and *survivor* much more aptly describes their courage. In some cases, however, such as where we are speaking of crime victims or situations in which human trafficking victimizes children, we use *victim*, but otherwise we support the use of *survivor*. Ultimately, as dialogue on terminology continues to evolve, we believe that survivors themselves should decide the term(s) the field uses.

Finally, this book is foremost about child trafficking, but it references both child trafficking and human trafficking. We use *human trafficking* (which includes the trafficking of adults and children) to reflect what is discussed in the law, policy, or research we are reviewing.

In the end, we recognize that word choice is not an exact science, but we hope the above clarifies the intent of this book.

# PREVENTING CHILD TRAFFICKING

# Child Trafficking in Our Communities

I T'S 2:20 A.M. on a cold winter's night. A young emergency room physician is well into another twelve-hour shift at the end of a long week. The waiting area is nearly full. A young woman walks through the entrance doors. She is dressed inappropriately for the cold weather, not wearing a winter coat. A man accompanies her, and he does almost all of the talking. During registration, the hospital clerk learns that the young woman does not have health insurance. The clerk also finds that the woman and the man with her struggle somewhat to give a straight answer when asked for their address. Eventually they provide an address. After registration, a nurse triages the young woman. The nurse takes her vital signs and records the patient's concerns. The man with the patient still does most of the talking. Finally, the physician enters the exam room, reviews the chart, talks with the young woman about her concerns, and examines her. The physician ultimately confirms a diagnosis of bacterial vaginosis—a vaginal infection, though not one considered a sexually transmitted disease— and treats the patient accordingly. He also tells the young woman that she will be contacted if any of the tests indicate that further treatment is needed. With that, the young woman is discharged, and she walks through the hospital doors and out into the cold night, accompanied by the man who arrived with her.

Ask them about that patient, and the clerk, nurse, and doctor are all likely to say that it was a fairly straightforward case. Perhaps the young woman was with her boyfriend and they had just been out for the night. Her coat could be in the car, and many young people dress the way they want to, regardless of weather or context. That's all certainly plausible. As for the man with the young woman answering most of the questions asked by hospital personnel, each provider might say that although it is better to hear directly from the patient, there are many situations in which another person does the talking, especially when the patient is young or where there are language barriers. In short, nothing about this case suggested anything unusual to the people who encountered the woman in the ER, and her condition did not necessitate a significant investment of time.

Yet if the nurse or doctor had probed further, they might have discovered that the young woman was actually underage. They might have noticed other red flags: not only was the young woman dressed inappropriately for the winter weather but she had a tattoo commonly used by traffickers on victims. Had they known the signs to look for, these health care providers might have figured out that the young girl was a sex trafficking victim.

Scenarios like this are occurring in hospitals throughout the United States. This scenario presents an arguably more stereotypical case of sex trafficking, but in fact many trafficked young persons—including those trafficked for labor as well as those trafficked for sex—show up at health care facilities. Often they are dressed as any other youth might be and are not necessarily accompanied by someone who might raise suspicions. In other words, although particular details might differ, this young girl's situation is not unique; trafficked cisgender and transgender girls and boys regularly pass through the health care system, as well as many other systems, including education, social services, and criminal justice. Similarly, the experiences and responses of the people who interact with them, including the health care professionals who crossed paths with this adolescent girl, are not uncommon. Adults working in the health care system frequently miss the signs and fail to identify trafficking victims and survivors.

Sex trafficking is a widespread form of exploitation and abuse of children. And sex trafficking is only part of an even bigger global problem:

human trafficking. Too often *human trafficking* is used as synonymous with *sex trafficking*, but that overlooks the enormous problem of labor trafficking. Human trafficking encompasses not only exploitation in the commercial sex industry but also exploitation of labor in almost every sector of society.

Victims of human trafficking pass through the health care system on a daily basis. One study found that 87.8 percent of sex trafficking victims reported having contact with the health care system during their trafficking experience but were not identified as a result of these encounters.[1] Hospital emergency rooms, hospital clinics, and community health centers are frequently visited by trafficking victims. Though emergency rooms may be the health care facilities that trafficking victims most commonly frequent, survivors and victims also report visiting health care professionals in other settings, including primary care physicians, OB/GYNs, pediatricians, traditional or alternative medicine practitioners, dentists, and others.[2] And although the care provided to these individuals may well be medically appropriate, a window of opportunity is missed each time such patients are not identified as trafficking victims but instead are left to return to their violent and harmful situations.

Identification of trafficking victims is challenging, but it is a task that health care professionals are well positioned to facilitate. Yet lack of awareness and lack of training currently hamper such efforts. A study examining emergency room personnel's understanding of human trafficking found that although 76 percent of health care professionals in the study knew what human trafficking was, only 29 percent understood human trafficking to be a problem among their emergency room population.[3] Further, only 13 percent felt confident or very confident that they could identify a trafficking victim, and less than 3 percent had been trained in victim identification.[4] A lack of training increases the chances that a person being trafficked will be misidentified as a "willing" prostitute, troubled youth, runaway, sexual assault victim, domestic violence victim, or struggling immigrant.[5]

Although human trafficking occurs across many sectors and systems, the health care system offers a critical opportunity to fight against human trafficking, and child trafficking in particular. It can help to identify victims and survivors and to ensure that they receive the assistance they need. Health care delivery systems also offer opportunities to educate and empower at-risk youth to recognize the red flags that can increase their vulnerability to exploitation in the first place. But policymakers, government agencies, health care professionals, and communities have a lot of work to do if the health care system is to maximize its potential to contribute to the prevention of and response to human trafficking.

Ending human trafficking—or even child trafficking—is not a task that any sector can achieve on its own. It will require efforts from all sectors of society and all walks of life. How can all of us play a role in preventing human trafficking? We believe it is possible, but it will require rethinking our approach to the problem and developing a comprehensive, integrated response. This book shows how a public health approach to trafficking can help build a more effective response and lead to genuine progress on this issue. Public health methodologies and strategies offer a roadmap for advancing efforts to *prevent* human trafficking and *reduce* harm. And the health care sector is a critical component of that response. Thus we focus in depth on the health care sector to uncover the opportunities that exist there to strengthen responses to child trafficking.

Drawing on our experience, which has focused primarily on sex trafficking of children and adolescents, we aim to show how health care professionals can facilitate positive interventions in the lives of children and youth at risk of, and victimized by, human trafficking. And in modeling ways in which public health and health care can advance anti-trafficking efforts, we hope to provide insights into how other individuals and entities —in areas from education and social services to the private sector—can also contribute to this vital endeavor of stopping human trafficking and related forms of exploitation.

In the United States, January is now recognized annually as National Slavery and Human Trafficking Prevention Month. In 2017, President Barack Obama issued a proclamation before leaving the Oval Office urging all Americans to play a role in "ending all forms of slavery," including human trafficking.[6] Health systems are a key partner in this effort and can help advance efforts to end this exploitation of children. Furthermore, in deciding how best to intervene, public health has a wealth of experience that is relevant to the fight against child trafficking.

## Human Trafficking Explained

Simply put, human trafficking involves the exploitation of another individual. Although existing legal definitions of human trafficking differ across various jurisdictions, broadly speaking, the crime of human trafficking has three elements: an act, a means, and a purpose:

- *Act* includes "recruitment, transportation, transfer, harbouring or receipt of persons" (some jurisdictions also include "obtains" and other similar terms).
- *Means* includes "the threat or use of force or other forms of coercion, of abduction, of fraud, of deception, of the abuse of power or of a position of vulnerability or of the giving or receiving of payments or benefits to achieve the consent of a person having control over another person."
- The *purpose* is exploitation, including "the exploitation of the prostitution of others or other forms of sexual exploitation, forced labour or services, slavery or practices similar to slavery, servitude or the removal of organs."[7]

In other words, if an individual uses force, fraud, or coercion to recruit or obtain a person for the purpose of exploitation through forced labor or sexual exploitation, that individual has committed the crime of human trafficking. When the victim is a minor, however, the means employed are irrelevant.[8] That is, it does not matter whether force, fraud, or coercion was used, because a minor cannot legally consent to such an act. Thus, when children are the victims, proving the crime of human trafficking requires only that the prosecutor establish that the perpetrator engaged in one of the above acts for the purpose of exploiting the child.

To many, human trafficking sounds like the type of crime that happens in the dark recesses of society, far away from where most of us live our

daily lives. Although the crime is by its nature hidden, in fact human trafficking touches all of us. The clothes we wear and the food we buy may
have been produced by trafficked or forced labor. Human trafficking occurs in a breadth of industries, including agriculture, construction, domestic service and other care and cleaning work, fishing, food processing and
packaging, forestry, garment and textiles, hair and nail salons, hospitality
and catering, logging, manufacturing, mining, pornography, prostitution,
quarrying, transportation, and other areas.[9]

Given human trafficking's reach, it is not surprising that the scale of the
problem is significant. Global estimates on human trafficking victims vary
greatly, but when human trafficking and forced labor are viewed as two
related forms of exploitation with overlapping definitions, the number
of victims is estimated to be in the millions annually. (See chapter 1 for a
discussion of the scale of the problem and difficulties in estimating prevalence.) Even using more narrow definitions of human trafficking, the
number of victims—whether we count in millions, hundreds of thousands,
or thousands—far exceeds anything acceptable. The only acceptable number of victims is zero. Until then, governments and civil society need to
continually explore ways to build comprehensive, effective responses to
human trafficking that foremost prevent the harm from occurring and
subsequently ensure needed services and assistance for survivors and accountability for perpetrators of these human rights violations.

## The Consequences of Human Trafficking

Human trafficking has both short- and long-term impact on health and
well-being. It can lead to physical, psychological, and developmental issues throughout life. It also leaves survivors confronting social and legal
issues, and it creates broader issues for communities and countries.

Human trafficking exacts a significant toll on its victims. Survivors of
human trafficking suffer a wide variety of physical injuries. Physical consequences include broken bones, bruises, lacerations, traumatic brain injury, as well as unhealthy weight loss, chronic headaches, pervasive body
aches, dizziness, gastrointestinal issues, neglect of chronic illness, derma-

tological problems, and dental issues.[10] Poor nutrition, overcrowded and substandard housing, and exposure to toxic chemicals and other harmful substances add to the health consequences of human trafficking.[11]

Sexual and reproductive health issues include sexually transmitted infections (STIs), which can progress to pelvic inflammatory disease with associated inflammation and scaring that can cause chronic pelvic pain and/or pain during intercourse.[12] Female victims frequently get pregnant, which can lead to pregnancy- and abortion-related complications. Victims can also experience anal trauma. And victims—male and female, cisgender and transgender—are at risk of contracting HIV/AIDS.

No less substantial, victims and survivors of human trafficking suffer severe psychological and emotional trauma.[13] This includes post-traumatic stress disorder (PTSD), anxiety, emotional blunting, depression, suicidal ideation, low self-esteem, excessive guilt or shame, anger, irritability, hostility, poor interpersonal relationships, mistrust and suspicion of authorities and service providers, disassociation, somatization, and sleep problems, as well as memory loss, traumatic bonding with traffickers, minimization and denial, and drug and alcohol abuse.[14] These health consequences are dramatic, and many survivors suffer multiple harms simultaneously.

When the harms and scale of human trafficking are considered together —some estimates of trafficking and forced labor victims suggest more than 20 million victims globally (see chapter 1)—its population-level consequences become clear. This is a public health issue. By comparison, a 2017 World Health Organization report indicated that there were 10.4 million new cases of tuberculosis in the world in 2015.[15] In the United States, there were 9,272 reported cases of tuberculosis in 2016, far fewer than the estimated number of trafficking victims.[16] Of course, human trafficking is very different from an infectious disease. While not classified as a disease itself, it leads to many adverse health consequences. In this regard, it parallels another issue that receives significant attention from public health officials: obesity. In other words, public health's mandate is not merely to address narrowly defined diseases but rather to study and work to prevent phenomena that produce adverse health consequences for the population. For years, public health researchers have studied the effects of violence on human health.[17] Human trafficking is another form of violence. Like obesity and like other forms of violence, human trafficking leads to wide-ranging adverse consequences for many people. Public health offers important insights into how to develop an effective response to human trafficking.

## What Are We Doing about It?

Although the problem of human trafficking is not new—indeed such exploitation has occurred for centuries, if not millennia—the modern response to human trafficking is only about two decades old. In 2000, two major achievements sparked renewed commitment to addressing human trafficking. In the United States, Congress passed the Trafficking Victims Protection Act (TVPA), which has been reauthorized five times since 2000 and serves as the cornerstone of the US response. The mandate of the TVPA includes the production of an annual State Department report—the *Trafficking in Persons Report*—that reviews all countries' practices. The *Trafficking in Persons Report* has become highly influential in other countries, and thus the TVPA arguably has had a global impact. Also in 2000, the international community adopted two major treaties related to the trafficking of children: the Protocol to Prevent, Suppress and Punish Trafficking in Persons, Especially Women and Children, Supplementing the United Nations Convention Against Transnational Organized Crime (Trafficking Protocol), and the Optional Protocol to the Convention on the Rights of the Child on the Sale of Children, Child Prostitution and Child Pornography (Sale of Children Protocol). Both treaties and the TVPA established a similar three-pronged mandate to address human/child trafficking that requires governments to (1) criminalize and prosecute acts of trafficking; (2) assist victims and survivors; and (3) implement prevention programs. Although broadly speaking these three areas capture what is needed, a more nuanced analysis of these laws reveals that they all emphasized criminal justice responses.[18] In the early years, law enforcement responses dominated the anti-trafficking landscape.

As concerns grew that survivors' needs were not being met, many called for a shift to a victim-centered approach. That push helped increase support for shelters for trafficking survivors and an array of services to help survivors recover from the trauma they had experienced and rebuild their lives. Though protections and services for victims and survivors have expanded significantly in the last decade, they are still well short of what is needed. Too many survivors go without services to address both short- and longer-term needs.

Finally, prevention, which is the ultimate goal, has been largely overlooked. Law enforcement initiatives provide a limited deterrent effect. Similarly, billboards and other media campaigns help raise general awareness, but they do not necessarily provide individuals with the tools to prevent exploitation or take other relevant actions. The lack of prevention measures further highlights the value of a public health perspective, as the field of public health has a wealth of experience in working to *prevent* an array of harms and promote health.

Although the United States has relied most heavily on law enforcement and social services to address human trafficking, in the past few years we have witnessed an emerging understanding of the importance of creating a comprehensive multisector response to the problem. Today, there is growing emphasis on engaging individuals and organizations in sectors that have historically been underutilized. Health care, education, child welfare, the private sector, media, transportation, and others are being challenged to figure out how to contribute to the effort to stop human trafficking. We believe that all sectors must be involved and that health care offers critical opportunities and resources for the fight against human trafficking.

## About This Book

This book has four aims. First, we want to raise the profile of public health methodologies and help bring them into mainstream discourses on trafficking of children. Public health frameworks offer important insights into the problem of human trafficking and potentially valuable models for building effective responses to the problem. A limited number of stakeholders have expressed support for public health–oriented responses to human trafficking,[19] but public health methodologies remain largely unknown and underutilized by governments and the majority of anti-trafficking entities.[20] Second, we seek to highlight the vital role that the health care system can, and in some case already does, play in responding to child trafficking and, more broadly, human trafficking. Health care is a major component of the US economy (17.9 percent of gross domestic product in 2016).[21] Health care's size and stature necessitate that it play a role in addressing human trafficking. And it has the capacity to do so. In detailing how the health care system and health care professionals intersect with human trafficking, we hope to spur all health care entities and professionals to explore how they and their organizations can implement and strengthen responses to this exploitation of human beings. Third, we believe that developing best practices for health care's response to child trafficking can inform health care responses to youth who may be vulnerable to other forms of harm and exploitation. Working with vulnerable and trafficked youth is challenging. However, we believe that learning how to respond effectively in this context can provide a foundation for a more constructive response to other at-risk and maltreated children. Fourth and finally, in exploring how health care systems can improve their responses to child trafficking, we hope to offer a starting point for other sectors to think about how their core capabilities can be employed to prevent trafficking.

This book draws heavily on our years of working on human trafficking. Our own work has focused primarily on sex trafficking of children and adolescents. However, all forms of human trafficking—including labor and sex—must be prevented. And labor trafficking has been overlooked for far too long. But we believe that by focusing primarily on sex trafficking of children, which enables us to draw on our experience, we can offer a more nuanced analysis of the problem and potential solutions. Furthermore, throughout the book, but particularly in the chapters on identification and treatment of children in health care settings, we draw primarily on the approach of Mount Sinai Adolescent Health Center, which Angela Diaz has led for thirty years. In doing so, we aim to incorporate insights from working directly with trafficking survivors. We also recognize that there are many other entities in the health care sector and other sectors that are doing important work with child trafficking survivors.

We begin, in chapter 1, by providing an overview of the nature and scope of child trafficking. We start by discussing the question on everyone's mind: How big a problem is this? After the "numbers discussion," we step back to explicate the definitions of human trafficking and child trafficking and situate trafficking in the broader context of exploitation of human beings. The chapter then looks at who is involved in trafficking, the different types of trafficking, and the breadth of sectors implicated. Finally, the chapter ends by discussing briefly the root causes of the problem.

In chapter 2, we examine the consequences of child trafficking. The primary focus is on the physical, mental, and emotional health consequences for youth victims of trafficking. Victims of human trafficking, including child survivors of sex trafficking, experience an array of adverse health consequences, ranging from physical injuries and sexually transmitted infections to depression, anxiety, PTSD, and other psychological harms. The chapter also briefly discusses other important consequences of trafficking, including educational, financial, housing, and legal harms. Examining the consequences of child trafficking, in particular the health consequences, highlights the limitations of criminal justice frameworks and reinforces the importance of public health methodologies and health care professionals in preventing, identifying, and responding to these acts of child exploitation.

We then look at the prevailing responses to human trafficking in chapter 3. Human trafficking, including child trafficking, garnered renewed interest among policymakers in the late 1990s, leading to the adoption of the Trafficking Victims Protection Act in 2000. Since then, the federal government has revised its anti-trafficking laws multiple times and promulgated numerous policies and programs. All fifty states have adopted anti-trafficking laws and policies. This chapter reviews the legal and programmatic responses to child trafficking. It provides an overview of the legal framework on human trafficking and special provisions addressing child trafficking. The chapter also highlights gaps in current responses, showing that current responses are not equipped to address all the consequences of child trafficking or to prevent the harm from occurring in the first place.

Having discussed the problem of child trafficking and the shortcomings in responses to date, we then shift in part II to the public health response. Chapter 4 examines the value of employing public health methodologies to address the root causes of trafficking and to reorient reactive responses to focus on preventing the harm from occurring. The chapter discusses the socio-ecological model and the relevance of public health strategies in the trafficking context. The chapter focuses on four key themes in public health: its emphasis on evidence-based research; its prevention focus; its experience addressing underlying causes of adverse health outcomes; and its strategic approach to engaging stakeholders. Finally, the chapter discusses how public health perspectives can help foster greater understanding of the complexities of the problem of human trafficking to help facilitate the development of more effective responses. Chapter 4 provides the public health framework for the other chapters in part II and also for the concluding chapter.

Chapter 5 details the risk factors associated with child trafficking. What makes certain young people more vulnerable to exploitation? We use the socio-ecological framework to detail the individual, relationship, community, and societal factors that increase vulnerability to trafficking. This detailed look at the complex interplay among risk factors sets up and informs later chapters on identification and treatment of child trafficking survivors and the concluding chapter on building a comprehensive response to the problem. More broadly, this mapping of risk factors is relevant to all professionals and volunteers who work with children, as they are in a position to recognize and address vulnerability.

In chapter 6, we focus on identification of children and adolescents at risk of and exploited through trafficking. In particular, we explore strategies for identifying at-risk and trafficked youth in health care settings. Clinicians can play a critical role in identifying and treating at-risk and exploited children and adolescents. These youth visit a range of health care settings, including emergency departments, primary care clinics, adolescent medicine clinics, school-based health centers, community health centers, health department clinics, family planning clinics, mental health clinics, and dental clinics. The chapter discusses how to create an environment conducive to identification, screening techniques that health care professionals can employ to identify victims and survivors of these abuses, and barriers that need to be overcome.

Chapter 7 shifts to the treatment of trafficked youth. Topics covered include case management systems, survivor-led or survivor-informed programming, youth-friendly services, trauma-informed care, and the need for comprehensive, integrated services. While the chapter focuses on the health care setting, it identifies connections with other sectors in order to help not only health care professionals but also others working to address child trafficking who might need or want to partner with health care professionals.

The conclusion explores ways to improve responses to child trafficking and human trafficking more generally. It pulls together themes from earlier chapters and examines what a comprehensive public health approach to child trafficking would look like. It provides a "public health toolkit" for health care professionals and other professionals who work with vulnerable youth or work on human trafficking. This toolkit offers a starting point for exploring how to respond more effectively to child trafficking and how to begin to prevent it from occurring. Finally, the concluding chapter discusses how we can build a comprehensive, integrated response to this exploitation of children and adolescents. Ultimately, if as a community we are successful in reducing the prevalence of child trafficking, we could develop a roadmap for addressing other harms that affect children.

## Conclusion

The demands confronting the young emergency department physician described at the beginning of this introduction are significant. Long hours, high numbers of patients, limited time to talk with each person who comes to the emergency room, and other factors work against her and other health care professionals in similar settings. The limited engagement with the health care sector on the issue of human trafficking—one study found that only 3 percent of emergency department clinicians had been trained to identify trafficking victims—has exacerbated the problem.[22] It is not surprising, then, that at-risk and exploited youth are missed even though they are in plain sight. But what if this did not occur? What if that physician had been well trained to identify potential trafficking situations and had helped connect that teenage girl with needed services? And what if providers helped educate and empower youth, families, and their communities about risky situations before children were harmed? We are seeing the beginnings of such work, but much more is needed. Health care professionals in numerous settings have opportunities to help forge a strong response to human trafficking, to reduce risk, and to facilitate earlier interventions. Similarly, professionals in other sectors—law enforcement, social services, education, media, the private sector, and so on—can play an important role. What if they, too, were well trained to identify and respond effectively to vulnerable and exploited youth? Constructing a comprehensive, integrated response to trafficking is not easy, but guided by insights from public health, we have the capacity to respond more effectively and even to prevent the trafficking of children and adolescents.

PART I **CHILD TRAFFICKING AND CURRENT RESPONSES**

# Understanding Child Trafficking

## The Nature and Scope of the Problem

Human trafficking has been reported in nearly every country in the world.[1] Although there are wide-ranging estimates of the prevalence of human trafficking, experts broadly agree that substantial numbers of people are exploited globally through human trafficking and its attendant forms of exploitation. A significant component of this exploitation is the victimization of children.

This chapter explores the nature and scope of the problem of human trafficking, with a particular emphasis on child trafficking. Given the state of the research on human trafficking—notably, that many studies do not disaggregate by age, making it difficult to determine whether they address trafficking of adults, children, or both—we draw on research that focuses on children as well as on more general studies of human trafficking to explicate the problem. We begin by examining the scale of the problem and the parameters of human trafficking. Next, we address who is involved in human trafficking, the types of trafficking, and the sectors implicated by human trafficking. Finally, we end this chapter by taking a step back to explore the conditions under which child trafficking occurs and the underlying causes of this exploitation.

## Scale of the Problem

Inquiries about human trafficking frequently start with the "numbers question": how many people are trafficked? For many people, when they first learn about human trafficking, the horrors of the practice prompt them to ask that question, expecting or hoping that such exploitation is rare. After all, the idea that human beings are bought and sold in the twenty-first century is both disturbing and hard to comprehend. Policymakers, who often must decide on priorities amid numerous compelling social issues, often ask a similar question: how significant is this problem? Embedded in this question are two related queries: First, as a threshold matter, is the problem big enough to merit a response? Second, what will it take to respond effectively?

In deciding whether the issue merits a response, one might argue that if even one child is trafficked, that is too many. Of course, that is true. No child should suffer in indentured servitude, be exploited for labor, or be forced to have sex with strangers for someone else's financial gain. However, resources are always limited, and at the policy level tough choices must be made. Should a government invest more in preventing harm caused by sharks or in preventing harm caused by jellyfish?[2] In preventing harm from infectious diseases or in preventing harm from road accidents? The answers depend, in part, on the prevalence of each issue and the magnitude of harm that can result. Governments typically act on specific issues only if the scale of the problem and the magnitude of the harm meet a minimum threshold. The field of public health constantly grapples with these questions of where and how best to allocate resources.

Once policymakers determine that a problem merits a response, reliable estimates of the scale of the problem and where it occurs are needed so that governments and advocates can determine the amount of resources necessary to respond effectively and how best to allocate those resources. Finally, knowing the scale of the problem is critical to measuring the impact of responses. That is, we need both baseline data and ongoing data collection so that agencies and organizations can evaluate how effective their responses are.

That brings us back to the question of how big a problem child trafficking, or human trafficking more generally, is.

Here is what we know: We know that human trafficking, including the trafficking of children, occurs across the globe.[3] We know that it takes place in urban, suburban, and rural areas.[4] We know that it occurs in numerous sectors of society, from agriculture to retail operations to the sex industry (see "Where Trafficking Occurs," below). Within the United States, we know that human trafficking has occurred in all fifty states, the District of Columbia, and the US territories.[5] In short, we know that it affects a breadth of communities around the world.

How significant is the impact? In other words, how many people are affected across the globe, and more specifically, how many are affected within each country or region? Precisely how many people are victimized by human trafficking and how many children are exploited is unknown. However, there are estimates of the scale of the problem. An often-cited 2012 International Labour Organization (ILO) study found that at any point in time there were 20.9 million victims of human trafficking and forced labor, of whom 68 percent were exploited for labor, 22 percent were sexually exploited, and 10 percent were exploited in state-imposed forced labor.[6] Of the 20.9 million human trafficking victims overall, an estimated 5.5 million are children.[7] According to the ILO report, the Asia-Pacific region had the highest number of exploited individuals (56 percent of the global total), but trafficking and forced labor were most prevalent in the Central and South-Eastern Europe and Commonwealth of Independent States (CSEE & CIS) and Africa (AFR) regions (4.2 and 4.0 per 1,000 individuals, respectively).[8]

Another frequently cited study, a 2017 report coauthored by the International Labour Organization and the Walk Free Foundation, determined that 40.3 million individuals were victims of "modern slavery."[9] Unlike the prior study, this study included forced marriages in the total numbers, which accounts for much of the gap between the two estimates. If we exclude the estimated 15.4 million victims of forced marriages, the 2017 study found that 24.9 million individuals were in forced labor, including human trafficking.[10] It bears noting that the different numbers—24.9 million in the 2017 report versus 20.9 million in the 2012 ILO report—are not proof of an increase in trafficking; rather, they primarily reflect differences in methodologies used.[11] Although efforts were made to develop the best possible estimates, the ILO and the Walk Free Foundation acknowledge that "no single source provides suitable and reliable data for all forms of modern slavery," and therefore "a combined methodology [was] adopted, drawing on a variety of data sources as required."[12] This acknowledgment echoes what many scholars have expressed: uncertainty surrounds global estimates of human trafficking.[13]

That is, while the various models for estimating the prevalence of human trafficking have all determined that significant numbers of people are harmed by this form of exploitation, these studies use different methodologies, and all of them have limitations. Indeed, some researchers have been highly critical of existing estimates, asserting that "they are often based on biased sampling methods and nebulous extrapolation techniques —not to mention they remain susceptible to politicization."[14] Because of these limitations and the hidden nature of human trafficking generally, precise numbers remain elusive at this stage. Thus, we cannot be sure of the exact magnitude of the problem globally.

Given the limited resources and infrastructure in many countries, the quality of data collection systems varies across the globe. Readers might assume, however, that while data collection issues in low-resource countries might hamper global studies, a reliable estimate of the scale of human trafficking or child trafficking would be possible in wealthier countries like the United States. Yet in the United States the reality is similar: we do *not* know the precise number of trafficking victims. The state of human trafficking research in the United States is captured in a two-sentence explanation by Michelle Stranksy and David Finkelhor. Reviewing estimates of sexually exploited children in the United States, Stransky and Finkelhor reported: "These estimates range from 1,400 to 2.4 million, although most fall between 300,000 and 600,000. BUT PLEASE DO NOT CITE THESE NUMBERS."[15] These two sentences reflect where we are in determining the prevalence of human trafficking. First, estimates vary widely according to definitions and methodologies used, the quality of data collection, and other issues. Second, we do not have reliable numbers. As Stransky and Finkelhor urge, advocates should not repeat these numbers because "none are based on a strong scientific foundation."[16] And keep in mind that they were looking at sex trafficking of children in the United States, a subset of human trafficking cases for one country. In other words, there is at best a very limited evidence base from which to determine the prevalence of human trafficking.

Given the above, what conclusions can we make about the numbers of victims? As noted above, cases of human trafficking and child trafficking have been documented across the globe. And new cases are regularly being identified. In short, while acknowledging that current global—and even national—estimates have significant limitations, we believe there is sufficient evidence to indicate that the problem is substantial. And as discussed in chapter 2, the harms inflicted are significant. Recall that when policymakers decide whether to prioritize an issue, they typically want to know both the prevalence of the problem and the magnitude of the harm. Although precise numbers do not exist, research to date suggests that the scale of the problem and the magnitude of harm should lead us to conclude that human trafficking merits a response.

### Further Unpacking the Uncertainty Surrounding the Numbers

As noted above, determining the prevalence of human trafficking involves significant challenges. These include the hidden nature of the crime, the lack of definitional consistency, poor methodology and data collection, and bias and broader agendas.

First, as with other illicit activities, the hidden nature of human trafficking makes it difficult to identify victims and determine overall prevalence. This is a problem that policymakers and child advocates have confronted in others areas, notably child abuse and neglect. When C. Henry Kempe and his coauthors published "The Battered Child Syndrome" in the *Journal of the American Medical Association* in 1962, they identified 749 cases of physically abused children in the United States.[17] That publication sparked interest in the issue, leading to state mandatory reporting laws for child maltreatment. By 1969 there were 60,000 reported cases. The number of reported cases steadily increased over the years, and in 1990 there were more than 3 million reports of child maltreatment and 1.2 million confirmed cases.[18] Today, there are still significant numbers of child maltreatment cases; in 2016 there were nearly 3.5 million reports of child maltreatment and 676,000 confirmed cases.[19] In other words, as concern about and attention to the issue of child abuse grew, as a society we started to look for it. And when we did, we found that we had an epidemic on our hands. It is important to recognize that although we now look for and do a better job identifying child maltreatment, the number of reported cases still underrepresents the true nature of the problem as many child abuse cases are never reported or confirmed.[20]

Although we do not claim that child trafficking will have the same trajectory or scale as child abuse, the point is that as we have started to try to identify cases, we have uncovered more instances of both adult and child trafficking. For example, globally 77,823 human trafficking victims (including both adults and children) were identified in 2015, compared with 30,691 identified in 2008.[21] And we should expect to find more cases as we direct more efforts to identifying and addressing all forms of human trafficking. Trafficking victims are often hidden from plain view—in underground sex trafficking rings, in sweatshops, or in remote labor settings. The clandestine nature of the activity is a major obstacle to identifying victims. Yet the history of child abuse identification and reporting offers two important reminders: that it is possible to identify and measure hidden criminal activity and that we should not assume either that a problem doesn't exist because it is difficult to find cases or that the number of identified cases represents the full scale of the problem.

Second, the lack of definitional consistency across studies and agencies adds to the challenge of determining prevalence. For example, the widely reported Global Slavery Index employs a definition that it developed that differs from definitions of human trafficking used by the United Nations and other international organizations.[22] Such differences also exist in legal definitions. For example, child trafficking is defined differently under US federal law than under international law; the former requires proof of force, fraud, or coercion for child labor trafficking, though not child sex trafficking, whereas the latter establishes that children cannot consent to any form of trafficking.[23] These two examples show some of the variation in definitions of human trafficking and child trafficking used by different organizations and legal regimes.

Adding to the complexity, the definition of human trafficking has changed over time in some locales. Since 2000 the definition of human trafficking used by many governments, including the United States, has expanded to include all forms of forced labor.[24] Estimates of human trafficking, which once counted only cases in which the victim was transported or moved to a different location, now include individuals in forced labor settings, even if they have not been moved.[25] More subtly, decisions at the local level can also affect the numbers. For example, if relying on law enforcement data, it matters how local prosecutors and law enforcement officers view every case. If a prosecutor decides for strategic reasons to charge a defendant with other related crimes, but not human trafficking, that case may not be recorded as a human trafficking case even if it meets the definition. In other words, a case could be a human trafficking case in terms of the victims' experience or the elements of the crime but not be prosecuted and recorded as one. Different approaches in different jurisdictions might result in numbers that are inaccurate or do not allow for helpful comparisons. In short, if different definitions are used across jurisdictions and by different entities, such variations will make it impossible to obtain reliable global estimates and will impede efforts to compare responses across regions or progress over time.

Third, on top of definitional issues, there are methodological issues in various studies to date. Not only can the use of different methodologies produce different prevalence numbers (as discussed above) but some methodologies significantly limit the generalizability of findings. For example, one study of methodologies used in estimating human trafficking found that "much antislavery research is based on a relatively small sample of survivors, usually identified by law enforcement agencies or persons assisted by NGOs or international organizations."[26] Already identified victims may or may not be representative of the larger population of those vulnerable to human trafficking or even representative of all trafficking survivors. Important questions exist—and are sometimes overlooked in media coverage of human trafficking research—as to whether and how much one can extrapolate from small sample sizes. Some studies have used data from "representative" countries to determine estimates for other countries nearby or with similar attributes, but it is unclear whether those assumptions or estimates are accurate.[27] In short, there are important methodological limitations in human trafficking research, and global or national estimates should be understood in the context of such limitations.

Fourth, human trafficking research is not immune to biases and the pressures of broader agendas. As Janie Chuang wrote in reference to the US government response to human trafficking, "With broad support from a motley alliance of neo-abolitionist feminists, neoconservatives, and evangelical Christian groups, the [George W.] Bush administration pressured states worldwide to target prostitution as a key anti-trafficking measure. . . . Despite inclusion of non-sex-sector trafficking in both the international and U.S. legal definitions of trafficking, the Bush administration maintained an almost-exclusive focus on the sex sector."[28] The Obama administration then took a different tack, "ma[king] a concerted effort to spotlight the problem of non-sex-sector trafficking."[29] While recognizing that non–sex-sector trafficking was consistent with the definition of human trafficking, the Obama administration also "significantly expanded" the definition of human trafficking by "recast[ing] (1) all forced labor as trafficking and (2) all trafficking as slavery."[30] Whether or not one considers any of these decisions valid, the point is that as long as political or ideological agendas influence the scope of what is included in "human trafficking," it will be difficult to determine prevalence of the harm and compare numbers across locations or time.

Given the challenges of measuring the prevalence of human trafficking accurately, it is fair to ask how important global estimates of human trafficking really are. A moral or human rights–based response would insist that we work to prevent such exploitation irrespective of the scale of the problem. However, knowing the scale of the problem or at least having reliable estimates would advance efforts in several ways. First, having reliable estimates, particularly at the local level, can help ensure that we do not overlook victims. For example, if we identify and assist five hundred trafficking victims in a particular city, without reliable estimates we simply do not know whether we have missed others or how many we have missed.

Second, knowing the scale of the problem, the types of cases, and the geographical distribution of cases will help enable governments and other organizations to direct resources where they are most needed. As Andrew Guth and his coauthors explain,

> Effective creation and monitoring of antislavery policies requires more focused and disaggregated numbers. Worldwide estimates do little more than suggest that the issue is worth addressing, but the enormity of resources used to attempt such aggregates is more efficiently spent developing and monitoring targeted projects and policies. Focused and replicable studies that use similar definitions and methodologies more accurately examine patterns and trends and regional or national studies that are sector or theme based lead to more effective policies.[31]

Third, we have limited, if any, reliable baseline data on human trafficking or child trafficking. We need good data so that we can evaluate the effectiveness of interventions. Without evidence-based research on the scope of the problem, public health professionals cannot assess whether particular primary, secondary, and tertiary interventions are having any positive impact.

How do we move forward? We need to acknowledge the flawed nature of current estimates. That said, the harms inflicted on trafficking victims are too great to declare a moratorium on action until we have precise numbers. We need to move forward with action. As we do, we must develop better estimates so that we (1) ensure that no victim is overlooked; (2) allocate resources to where the need is; and (3) make it possible to evaluate law, policy, and programs aimed at reducing the prevalence of, and ultimately ending, human trafficking.

## Returning to the Definition of Child Trafficking

This chapter, like many conversations, opens with the question on the minds of many: the scale of the problem. But as noted above, one of the barriers to developing accurate estimates of human trafficking or child trafficking is inconsistency in the definitions used. Thus, it is helpful to return to the definition of human trafficking (first explained in the introduction).

There is significant ambiguity in definitions of human trafficking.[32] Even the Trafficking Protocol—which includes the most widely accepted definition under international law—"left key aspects of the legal definition intentionally vague" in order to reach consensus.[33] In general terms, human trafficking involves the exploitation of another individual. Of course, there are a variety of crimes that involve the exploitation of another human being. Reduced to its core—and as enshrined in international law[34]—the crime of human trafficking has three elements: an act, a means, and a purpose:

- *Act* includes "recruitment, transportation, transfer, harbouring or receipt of persons" (some jurisdictions also include "obtains" and other related terms);
- *Means* includes "the threat or use of force or other forms of coercion, of abduction, of fraud, of deception, of the abuse of power or of a position of vulnerability or of the giving or receiving of payments or benefits to achieve the consent of a person having control over another person";
- The *purpose* is exploitation, including "the exploitation of the prostitution of others or other forms of sexual exploitation, forced

labour or services, slavery or practices similar to slavery, servitude or the removal of organs."[35]

If an individual uses force, fraud, or coercion to recruit or obtain a person in order to exploit that person through forced labor or sexual exploitation, he or she has committed the crime of human trafficking. Under international law, when the victim is a minor, the means employed are irrelevant. (As discussed in chapter 3, US law differs on this point with respect to child labor trafficking.)[36] That is, it does not matter whether the perpetrator used force, fraud, or coercion, because a minor cannot legally consent to being recruited, transported, or harbored for purposes of being exploited. When the victim is a child, the crime of human trafficking requires only that the perpetrator engaged in one of the above acts for the purpose of exploiting the child.

As noted above, even among individuals who work on human trafficking, different definitions are used. Often trafficking and smuggling of persons are confused and even conflated, but there are important differences between the two. Smuggling involves procuring the illegal entry of another person into another country for the purpose of financial or material gain.[37] Although smuggled migrants can become trafficking victims, and traffickers might engage in both smuggling and trafficking operations, trafficking and smuggling are not the same. First, smuggled migrants typically consent to being smuggled, whereas trafficking occurs without the victim's consent.[38] Second, smuggling involves crossing an international border and entering another country, but trafficking does not require crossing an international border (or movement).[39] Indeed, intracountry trafficking accounts for a substantial percentage of human trafficking cases.[40] Third, smuggling involves a financial transaction that ends once the person has been taken across the border, whereas trafficking is ultimately about exploitation of a person rather than a crime against a border.[41] These distinctions do not mean that smuggling does not involve situations with pronounced power imbalances and vulnerable individuals. However, it is important to distinguish between smuggling and trafficking in order to be able to measure prevalence accurately and develop appropriate interventions.

## Trafficking as a Form of Exploitation

Fidelity to the above definitions of human trafficking and child trafficking would leave some acts of exploitation excluded. That does not mean that those acts should not be addressed. To the contrary, we believe that all forms of exploitation should be prevented, and where we fail to prevent harm, we should ensure that all survivors of exploitation have the resources and support needed. But definitions matter—for prosecutions, for determining access to specialized services for survivors, for measuring prevalence, and for developing and evaluating responses to the problem. Continually expanding the definition of human trafficking to encompass an ever-broader range of crimes runs the risk of both weakening the definition and creating other unintended consequences.

Still, having a clear definition of human trafficking and child trafficking does not mean ignoring the broader context of exploitation. Human trafficking must be understood in both its historical context and in the context of the spectrum of labor settings that exist today. And that means understanding it as a form of exploitation.

First, despite the increased attention to human trafficking in the past two decades, human trafficking and its attendant forms of exploitation are not new phenomena. Historical references to the trade date back at least to the 1400s.[42] Slavery and exploitation have existed for centuries.[43] A range of factors helped create the conditions under which exploitation could thrive, including poverty, gender-based and racial discrimination, armed conflicts, economic crises, and social instability.[44] Even though current law prohibits slavery, millions of individuals live and work in circumstances akin to slavery.

The recent focus on human trafficking can be attributed to circumstances unique to today's world. The globalization of trade and commerce and the increased movement of people across borders have helped foster conditions in which human trafficking can thrive.[45] Increased global competition, as well as the desire to continually maximize profits, puts pressure on producers and distributors of goods to find cheaper means of production.[46] Added to that, natural disasters, armed conflicts, and civil unrest have all led to the displacement of millions of individuals, leaving them more vulnerable.[47] In other words, although human trafficking has recently emerged in the national consciousness, it is part of a centuries-old dynamic in which vulnerable individuals are exploited.

Second, trafficking and, more generally, labor are best understood on a spectrum. At one end of the spectrum are safe, secure employment opportunities for individuals that provide a living wage or better. At the other end are trafficking, forced labor, and other exploitative labor settings, in which rights of workers are blatantly violated and workers are at risk of significant harm.[48] In between these two poles are a range of employment settings, some of which creep closer to the type of exploitation that we often find in human trafficking. That said, although these settings are similar to human trafficking and harmful to workers, we do not have to label them trafficking. We can understand them as exploitation that must be addressed, without expanding the definition of human trafficking. And by seeing labor on a spectrum, we can also understand how economically vulnerable individuals who are compelled to accept risky employment opportunities that fall short of human trafficking can subsequently end up in a situation of human trafficking. Those individuals, like any other trafficking victim, should be seen as victims and survivors, regardless of how they end up in that situation.

In the end, all forms of exploitation should be prohibited and prevented. However, by using a consistent, focused definition of human trafficking, we can develop a more precise understanding of the nature and scope of the problem and develop more responsive policies and programs that make a difference.

## Who Is Involved

Understanding human trafficking and child trafficking also means recognizing the range of roles played, by those directly engaged in the crime and by others in the communities where trafficking occurs. Broadly speaking, trafficking involves five types of individuals: traffickers, victims (or survivors), purchasers, facilitators, and bystanders.

## Traffickers

In trafficking schemes, individuals can play a range of different roles. Some traffickers are engaged in a single task, such as recruiting or transporting, as part of a larger trafficking enterprise, while other traffickers play multiple roles, from initially recruiting a victim to engaging in the end exploitation.[49]

A report published by the Organization for Security and Co-operation in Europe (OSCE) Office of the Special Representative and Co-ordinator for Combating Trafficking in Human Beings provides a useful map of the various roles in one type of trafficking scheme. For example, in a large-scale operation for trafficking migrants the following actors might be involved:

- *investors*: those who put forward funding for the operation, and oversee the entire operation. These people are unlikely to be known by the everyday employees of the operation, as they are sheltered by an organizational pyramid structure that protects their anonymity; they may be separate from the organization;
- *recruiters*: seek out potential victims and secure their commitment. These people may be members of the culture and the community from which victims are drawn;
- *transporters*: assist the migrants/potential victims in leaving their country/place of origin, either by land, sea or air;
- *corrupt public officials or protectors*: may occur throughout the trafficking process; officials may assist in obtaining travel documents, or accept bribes to enable migrants to enter/exit illegally, or to cover up any investigation and obstruct any prosecution;
- *informers*: gather information on matters such as border surveillance, immigration and transit procedures, asylum systems, law enforcement activities;
- *guides and crew members*: are responsible for moving trafficked persons from one transit point to the other or helping them to enter the destination country;

- *enforcers*: are primarily responsible for policing staff and trafficked persons, and for maintaining order;
- *debt collectors*: are in the destination country to collect fees;
- *money launderers*: launder the proceeds of crime, disguising their origin through a series of transactions or investing them in legitimate businesses;
- *supporting personnel and specialists*: may include local people at transit points who might provide accommodation and other assistance.[50]

It is important to note that the above list represents a larger-scale operation. Not every trafficking scheme includes all the individuals named above; in many cases, individuals might play multiple roles and have differing levels of knowledge of their role in exploitation.[51] But an understanding of the different roles can aid identification of opportunities to disrupt existing trafficking networks and prevent new ones from emerging. Take the example of recruiters and recruitment agencies. Recruiters work for both sex trafficking and labor trafficking rings. Labor brokers, who facilitate employment opportunities for migrant workers, play a key role in many trafficking operations.[52] In some cases, labor brokers can facilitate legitimate employment opportunities. In the human trafficking context, they recruit vulnerable workers and make arrangements for their travel to the place where they will be employed/exploited.[53] Fake modeling agencies serve a similar purpose in enticing primarily young women and girls into the sex industry.[54] In some locales, a substantial percentage of recruiters are women.[55] Recruiters can also be peers; in the United States, for example, some trafficked children are recruited by other young persons.[56] Understanding the roles of recruiters and who they are helps us to identify opportunities to intervene more effectively. In addition, it is important to understand that some perpetrators have been victims as well (such as in the case of trafficked young women who then help recruit new victims for their traffickers),[57] or they may have suffered some of the same prior trauma as victims, including child abuse, discrimination, and other harms (see chapter 5).[58] The breadth of roles and the varied profiles and backgrounds of perpetrators highlight the complexities of human trafficking and child trafficking. They also underline the importance of understanding how trafficking operations work, the different profiles of traffickers, their incentives, and how governments can identify and disrupt existing networks and prevent new ones from forming.[59]

## Victims/Survivors

The victims and survivors of trafficking include men, women, boys, and girls; they include both cisgender and transgender adults and children. Victims come from urban centers and rural areas.[60] They are often young. And they are frequently targeted because traffickers recognize their vulnerability. In Chapter 5, we discuss in detail the risk factors associated with child trafficking and the profile of child trafficking victims and survivors.

## Purchasers

Although traffickers prey on and exploit victims, they do so because there is demand for the goods and services provided by trafficked individuals. Purchasers are one of the root causes of the problem. In sex trafficking contexts, the purchaser is arguably easier to identify, as that individual typically directly interacts with traffickers and victims.[61] However, in the labor trafficking context, the purchaser is made up of a much broader population. It includes all of us, as we buy the goods produced and the services provided by trafficked labor.[62] We help sustain the demand for low-cost goods and services. As we discuss in chapter 4, it is critical to understand the motivations and interests of purchasers so that we can develop law, policies, and programs that mitigate demand for exploited individuals.

## Facilitators

Many descriptions of trafficking focus on the binary trafficker-victim dynamic or at best also include a discussion of purchasers. Such a characterization overlooks the fact that many more individuals and institutions play a role in fostering the conditions that allow trafficking to thrive. When we first started thinking about others involved, we began by breaking this category down into facilitators and bystanders. Facilitators play some active role in helping trafficking flourish or at least fostering the conditions in which it can. Bystanders, in contrast, include individuals who do nothing when presented with potential scenarios involving trafficking victims, unknowingly end up enabling trafficking, or chose not to learn about their role or the role of their organization in supporting human trafficking.

As noted in the OSCE report, corrupt public officials can play a variety of roles. In some countries and localities, prosecutors and law enforcement officials may overlook exploitation or even enable human trafficking to occur.[63] Some police officers moonlight as security guards in establishments where trafficking victims are exploited.[64] This participation "mak[es] them potentially complicit with traffickers and reduc[es] the likelihood victims would trust police enough to report such crimes."[65] In addition, in certain locations, customs and immigration officials accept bribes to allow illegal crossings of trafficking victims or to produce fraudulent documents for trafficking enterprises.[66] And in some cases, as the US State Department reports, "still other government officials are culpable for using their positions to facilitate or commit trafficking crimes for their own financial gain or even exploit victims themselves, such as by subjecting their household workers to domestic servitude or knowingly purchasing commercial sex from trafficking victims."[67]

It is not only public officials who facilitate trafficking; the private sector is also complicit in some cases. Companies that do not adequately review and assess their own supply chains for potential trafficking victims and forced labor also foster the conditions for exploitation. As they compel suppliers and other subcontractors to lower production costs, they increase pressure on the supply chains and foster the conditions under which trafficking might occur. Other companies tolerate their employees —whether they are managers traveling to trade conferences or long-distance truckers on the road—contributing to the demand without penalizing them.

*Bystanders*

Finally, bystanders play a role. Bystanders include a variety of individuals who might be positioned to intervene in appropriate cases but either choose not to say something or lack awareness about human trafficking. Those who own or work in transportation networks—including airlines, trains, buses—might sit on the sidelines as traffickers use their transportation to facilitate the exploitation of human beings.[68] In contrast, some airlines now train employees to recognize potential signs of human trafficking.[69] Hotel employees might fail to recognize the signs as trafficked individuals walk through the hotels where they work, although some hotel chains now have agreed to train their employees.[70] Visitors to hair and nail salons might fail to ask questions about the employees.[71] Investors in multinational corporations might choose to avoid learning about a company's supply chains, instead choosing profits and maximization of return on investment over the well-being of workers.[72] And the list goes on. Across many sectors where trafficking thrives, there are individuals who encounter trafficking victims and fail to recognize the signs, choose not to say anything, or do not know what can be done. These bystanders do not actively facilitate trafficking, but their silence allows the exploitation to continue.

## Where Child Trafficking Occurs

Children (as well as adults) are trafficked for both labor and sexual exploitation. Trafficking occurs in a wide range of sectors. A representative list of the sectors includes the following: agriculture; construction; domestic service and other cleaning work; fisheries; food processing and packaging; hospitality and catering; logging; mining and extractives; restaurants; the sex industry; the textile industry; tourism; and transportation.[73] In addition to these and other sectors in which children are trafficked, trafficking also occurs in situations involving bonded labor (including in many of the abovementioned sectors) and in the context of recruitment and use of child soldiers.[74]

In the United States, sex trafficking receives the lion's share of attention, but labor trafficking is prevalent as well.[75] Labor trafficking occurs in industries across the United States and its territories. Labor trafficking victims have been identified in agriculture in Hawaii and Washington, the health and beauty industry in New Jersey, the hospitality industry in South Dakota, domestic work in Georgia, construction in Louisiana and California, the garment industry in American Samoa, and forced peddling and begging rings in New York City, to name just a few examples.[76]

And, more broadly, human trafficking—including the trafficking of children—likely occurs in every country in the world. The sectors in which trafficking is prevalent differ from country to country, but what is clear is that it touches almost, if not every, sector of society.

## The Drivers of Child Trafficking

We know that traffickers exploit children and adults in human trafficking. But to say that trafficking is the fault of only traffickers is to fall short of a conception of the problem that might lead us to address the harm. As we discuss in chapter 4, a public health approach seeks to identify and address the underlying causes of a disease or other harm. In similar fashion, we ultimately need to examine the underlying causes of the problem of human trafficking. What drives this exploitation?

Human trafficking is sometimes described in terms of supply and demand.[77] On the supply side, a seemingly endless number of vulnerable individuals are available to traffickers. Marginalized children and young adults supply the labor and services that are exploited, and in the process these lives are exploited as well.[78] Individuals who ultimately are exploited through human trafficking "often find themselves in vulnerable situations, which include precarious circumstances in different aspects of their lives, especially in the area of employment, housing conditions and the family configuration. These situations can consist of insecure working conditions, low quality accommodations and residential area and unstable family structures."[79]

The demand side is also relevant. Individuals engage in trafficking because it is profitable. And it is profitable because there is demand for the goods and services produced by trafficked individuals. Demand for commercial sex drives sex trafficking. And labor trafficking, as noted above, implicates all of us. Businesses that seek to maximize profits at all costs drive demand for exploited labor. As consumers, we are responsible too; we create the demand for goods and services provided by exploited labor.

Although describing the root causes of human trafficking in terms of supply and demand may make it easier to understand human trafficking, doing so is problematic in two ways. First, using such economics terminology runs the risk of furthering the commodification of human lives. Commodification of human beings and its attendant devaluation of certain human lives is a cause of human trafficking,[80] so we want to move away from language that reinforces that idea.

Second, and equally important, while the supply-and-demand model is easy to understand, it does not capture the full range of drivers of human trafficking. Public health offers a better approach. As discussed in more detail in chapter 5, public health employs the socio-ecological model to understand the full range of factors that foster the conditions under which child trafficking, and human trafficking more broadly, can thrive. The socio-ecological model examines individual, relationship, community, and societal factors that operate—and interact with one another—to leave children (and others) vulnerable to harm.[81] This model can help enhance understanding of the complex factors that affect who is trafficked. It also can help us understand the factors that drive demand, from the local level to broader societal factors—for example, the sexualization of youth, especially girls, that spurs demand for young victims in the commercial sex industry, consumerism that thirsts for affordably priced goods and services, capitalist ideas of profit maximization that spur labor exploitation, and more. Using the socio-ecological model not only helps us to look at individual, relationship, community, and societal factors but also reveals how different factors at each of these levels interact with one another. As we discuss later in the book, the insights from the socio-ecological model can point us in the right direction in terms of developing more effective responses to the trafficking of children (and adults).

## Conclusion

Human trafficking and the trafficking of children are complicated issues. Definitional issues, politics, and other issues cloud the picture. However, as researchers study the problem and anti-trafficking advocates work to address the issue, two themes become apparent: First, we continue to identify new cases. This does not mean that the crime is increasing or that the numbers of trafficking victims in various studies have been validated. Rather, the more we look for trafficking, the more cases we identify. Second, in so many of these cases, survivors have suffered significant harm. As with other public health issues, as more cases of harm are identified, there is increased pressure to respond more effectively so that we can not only address the impact of the harm that has occurred but also prevent the harm from occurring in the future. With child trafficking, and human trafficking more generally, the scale of the problem and the magnitude of the harm lead to the conclusion that a more strategic, comprehensive response is required. Public health methodologies can help point the way.

# The Consequences of Child Trafficking

ISABELLA, A sex trafficking survivor, first came to Mount Sinai Adoles-cent Health Center (MSAHC) as a teenager with her daughter. She has been part of the center's Teen Parent Program ever since. In conjunction with this program, patients receive integrated medical, sexual and repro-ductive health, dental, optical, and behavioral and mental health services, as well as social services. The scope of services offered reflect the wide-ranging needs of survivors who are working to recover from and overcome the consequences of human trafficking.

When Isabella first came to MSAHC, she was found to have a history of trauma and post-traumatic stress disorder (PTSD). She initially was very challenging to engage, suspicious of any questions staff asked of her. She had a difficult time interacting with other people, preferring to be alone with her daughter, and even got into several verbal altercations with oth-ers at the center. She worried that her daughter might end up in a similar situation.

Over time, as trust has built, Isabella has been able to access the ser-vices she needs. Like other young parents and children in the Teen Parent Program, Isabella and her child receive health care and other services during the same visit to make it easier for these young parents to care for their children without neglecting their own health needs. The young par-ents participate in parenting classes and with their children participate in attachment work. Isabella also regularly calls her social worker when she has questions about parenting and meets with her for counseling whenever she comes to MSAHC for medical services for her and her daughter. In this way, the center has become a source of much broader support for Isabella as she works to build a healthy life for herself and her daughter.

As Isabella's case illustrates, human trafficking consequences are significant and lasting, requiring sustained commitment to overcome.[1] The enduring and intergenerational impact of these consequences is directly attributable to the physical, sexual, and emotional violence carried out by perpetrators of human trafficking on their victims.[2] Because of the many health, social, legal, and other consequences of human trafficking, it is essential for survivors to receive wraparound services and/or have access to a multidisciplinary team of service providers to help them recover and thrive (see chapter 7).

In this chapter, we map the extent of consequences of child trafficking. We begin by examining the health consequences, including physical, sexual and reproductive, psychological/mental, and other health and social consequences. Trafficking victims experience an array of harms, including but not limited to (*a*) deprivation of food, shelter, and sleep; (*b*) extreme stress; (*c*) poor sanitation or conditions that cause poor hygiene; (*d*) hazardous travel and working conditions; and (*e*) physical, sexual, and psychological violence.[3] All these conditions can cause health problems. Trafficking victims also often lack preventive health care or have neglected chronic conditions. Additional consequences of trafficking include emotional harm; traumatic bonding/Stockholm Syndrome; psychosomatic symptoms; substance use and abuse; intimate partner violence; sexual violence, including sexual assault; and other adverse impacts on victims' well-being and development.[4]

Although this chapter focuses primarily on health consequences of child trafficking, trafficking-related harms reach well beyond health and well-being. Trafficking also has adverse consequences for educational attainment, work opportunities, and financial security. And given the criminal nature of trafficking, children who are trafficked often suffer legal consequences. These consequences in other domains, such as educational and legal consequences, in turn increase vulnerability to adverse health consequences. Together, all of these issues combine to levy both immediate and, in many cases, lifelong harm.[5]

As we discuss the consequences of human trafficking, it is important to keep in mind that although human trafficking may cause all the negative consequences listed above, these consequences may be bidirectional; that is, trafficking victims and survivors may have experienced some of these harms prior to being trafficked, and such harms may have left them more vulnerable to being trafficked. For example, prior physical, sexual, and psychological violence, lack of shelter, financial insecurity, lack of educational attainment, substance abuse, and other issues can increase the risk of trafficking (see chapter 5). In turn, human trafficking can cause further adverse consequences in all of these areas.

## Health Issues

### Physical Health Consequences

Both sex trafficking and labor trafficking inflict a range of harms, causing numerous adverse health consequences. Because the research on child trafficking is more limited—in part because of the more significant barriers to research involving children, an inherently vulnerable population[6]—we include in this chapter literature on trafficking of adults and children to provide more detailed evidence of the trafficking experience and its impact on the health status of those victimized by the trade.

The negative health repercussions of trafficking are pervasive and extensive. Minors who are sex trafficking victims suffer many direct physical injuries, including bruises; mutilations; scars from cigarette burns; lacerations; broken bones/fractures; dental injuries, including broken teeth; hearing loss resulting from injury to the ears; and head trauma, concussions, and in some cases traumatic brain injury.[7] Because of the nature of human trafficking, some injuries may not be readily visible, as some trafficked children are beaten or otherwise injured in such a way as to preserve their physical appearance. For example, cigarette burns in areas such as the lower back or feet can cause significant pain while preserving the victim's outward appearance.[8]

A systematic review of nineteen studies investigating health consequences of human trafficking found that all nineteen studies reported high prevalence of violence and physical health symptoms (as well as adverse mental health consequences) among trafficking survivors.[9] One study on women trafficked in Europe found that 95 percent had experienced physical or sexual violence while in their trafficking situation and 71 percent had experienced both.[10] Fifty-seven percent of women in the study had between twelve and twenty-three concurrent physical health symptoms when they entered care; the most frequent and severe symptoms included headaches, fatigue, dizzy spells, back pain, stomach/abdominal pain, and memory problems.[11] More than 60 percent of women reported sexual health problems, and the majority reported symptoms consistent with PTSD.[12] In another study of trafficked women in Europe, all of the women reported being sexually abused and coerced into involuntary sex acts, and the vast majority reported being harmed intentionally, resulting in symptoms and injuries including "broken bones, contusions, pain, loss of consciousness, headaches, high fevers, gastrointestinal problems, undiagnosed pelvic pain, complications from abortions, dermatological problems (e.g., rashes, scabies, and lice), unhealthy weight loss, and dental and oral health problems."[13]

The research on health consequences of labor trafficking is even more sparse. However, the small number of published studies are consistent in reporting significant adverse health implications of labor trafficking.[14] There are health consequences for victims both while being trafficked and subsequently at their end destination. During the journey, trafficked individuals may be hidden among cargo shipments and in danger of "injury or death by drowning, freezing, or suffocating, or by being crushed or exposed to toxic materials."[15] Additionally, overcrowded and unsanitary conditions, food and water shortages, and environmental extremes worsen their situation, further increasing the risk of illness and injury.[16]

Upon arriving at their destination, individuals trafficked for labor most commonly are placed into agriculture, construction, fishing, manufacturing, and mining, as well as domestic service.[17] In many countries, these sectors are subject to minimal oversight even though these types of work expose employees to a range of health and safety risks.[18] Individuals trafficked for labor purposes report "living and working conditions that are overcrowded, poorly ventilated and lack adequate sanitation. Long working hours and little rest time may be punctuated with poor or inadequate nutrition and prolonged exposure to extremes of heat or cold."[19] The potential public health risks from overcrowding, inadequate sanitation, and poor nutrition, among other issues, are numerous and often severe.[20] These are settings where infectious diseases flourish.[21]

Trafficked laborers also often suffer physical abuse and are exposed to a variety of harms, "frequently suffer[ing] physical injuries, infectious and communicable disease and, not least, post-trauma mental health symptoms including, anxiety, depression, post-traumatic stress disorder, feelings of low self-esteem and isolation."[22] One study found a high incidence of "violence-related injuries associated with forced labor includ[ing] bruises, broken bones, head wounds, stab wounds, and mouth and teeth injuries."[23] The US government's Office of Refugee Resettlement reported that labor trafficking victims experience physical abuse and health impacts including "scars, headaches, hearing loss, cardiovascular/respiratory problems, limb amputation . . . [and] chronic back, visual and respiratory problems."[24] The violence and deprivation of labor trafficking settings often leave victims malnourished and suffering from numerous physical and mental health issues.[25]

Exposure to environmental hazards in various industries presents another health risk for trafficked laborers. For example, in the construction industry, "exposure to irritants and carcinogens from construction sites is associated with acute and chronic respiratory disease, poisoning, certain cancers, and irritant and allergic dermatitis."[26] Other industries, such as mining, agriculture, and manufacturing, expose trafficked adults and children to similar harms, as well as to the risk of workplace injuries.[27]

Trafficking victims may also suffer scarring. For example, tattoos are found on some sex trafficking victims, as certain traffickers have victims under their control tattooed either with their street name or with some other phrase that communicates that the victim "belongs to" the trafficker.[28] These tattoos are commonly located on the neck.[29] Any tattoo that states or symbolizes "Property of . . . ," "Daddy," or something similar is suspicious.[30] Although tattoos might not be seen as injury in general, in addition to the temporary pain inflicted, they violate the person's bodily integrity when done without consent and provide a visual reminder to victims of their trauma.

In addition to inflicting physical injuries, trafficking presents a barrier to accessing needed health care. Trafficked youth may not feel empowered to seek out care or know where to go for care. In some cases, traffickers may not allow young people under their control to access care when needed, or they may delay seeking care, preferring to wait to see whether they can avoid the health care visit. As a result, trafficking victims often lack preventive health care[31] and in many instances access care very late in the course of an illness. This delay in seeking care exacerbates their health issues.

When trafficking victims and survivors do access care, they may also have signs of neglect such as weight loss, malnourishment, or neglected chronic illnesses (e.g., diabetes, hypertension, arthritis, and other conditions) that have not been well managed.[32] They may also have chronic maladies such as back and stomach pain and pain from old fractures.[33] Or they may have dental caries and missing teeth or eye injuries, eye strain, or poor vision from working in prolonged low-light conditions.[34] Victims may present with infectious diseases such as tuberculosis or dermatological problems including rashes, scabies, and lice from poor and crowded living conditions.[35] Victims may report sleep-related difficulties such as insomnia and disrupted sleep patterns, as some trafficking victims tend to sleep during the day and work primarily at night.[36]

Finally, it bears noting that in some cases the consequences of human trafficking include loss of life. Suicide and homicide often are overlooked in human trafficking discourses. Yet they are significant issues. In one study, 46.2 percent of the trafficking victims interviewed reported suicidal ideation during their trafficking experience, and 41.5 percent had attempted suicide.[37] Other studies have also found high rates of suicidal ideation.[38] In addition, some trafficking victims tragically end up victims of homicide. We need to consider and address these most severe trafficking-related harms when we contemplate the health consequences of human trafficking. (For more on physical health consequences and symptoms of human trafficking, see the resources listed in the appendix.)

### Sexual and Reproductive Health Consequences

For many trafficking survivors, the array of physical health consequences of human trafficking often occur simultaneously with sexual and reproductive health issues. Sex trafficking victims suffer dozens and often hundreds of incidents of sexual violence.[39] Some labor trafficking victims are also subjected to sexual violence.[40] Moreover, while women and girls are frequent victims of sexual violence, men and boys are also targeted.[41] And LGBTQ youth are also at high risk of sexual violence.[42]

Trafficking also has significant reproductive health consequences. Female victims are at risk of pregnancy.[43] The risk of unwanted pregnancies is exacerbated when traffickers deny victims access to preventive care, including contraceptive care. These pregnancies may result in unwanted births, abortions, or threatened or incomplete miscarriages. Trafficking victims may experience complications of pregnancy such as severe blood loss or acute pelvic infection.[44] Trafficking victims rarely have access to proper or timely prenatal care.[45]

In one study, researchers interviewed more than one hundred trafficking survivors ranging in age from fourteen to sixty years old about the health consequences of their trafficking experience.[46] Of those women who responded to the question regarding the number of pregnancies, 71.2 percent of women had had at least one pregnancy and 21.2 percent reported more than five.[47] For women who responded to the question on miscarriages, 54.7 percent reported at least one miscarriage and almost 30 percent reported more than one.[48] More than half (55.2%) of the sixty-seven trafficking survivors who responded to the question about abortions reported at least one abortion, and twenty women (29.9%) reported multiple abortions.[49] Although only thirty-four of the women in the study responded to questions about whether their abortions had been their choice, more than half of those who responded stated that their abortions had been forced upon them.[50] Although there are limitations to this study, the results indicate that pregnancies and related complications are a real concern for many female trafficking victims. The study also suggests that delay in accessing care—such as when traffickers refuse to allow victims to access health services—can have both physical and mental health consequences.

In addition to these reproductive health issues, both cisgender and transgender trafficking survivors commonly report sexual health symptoms.[51] Trafficked youth are at risk of various sexually transmitted infections, including chlamydia, gonorrhea, herpes, syphilis, and HIV/AIDS.[52]

In a study by Lederer and Wetzel, more than two-thirds of trafficked women reported having contracted at least one sexually transmitted infection, with chlamydia, gonorrhea, and hepatitis C being the most common.[53] Survivors in this study also frequently reported other urogenital/gynecological symptoms, including pain during sex (46.2%), urinary tract infections (43.8%), and vaginal discharge (33.3%).[54] Sexually transmitted infections can progress to pelvic inflammatory diseases, with the associated inflammation leading to scar formation and chronic pelvic pain and/or pain during intercourse (dyspareunia) resulting from pelvic adhesions.[55] These conditions may result in associated damage to sexual, reproductive, and urogenital systems, sometimes leading to infertility.[56]

HIV infection is also a risk. A Harvard School of Public Health study conducted in Nepal found that 38 percent of repatriated Nepalese women and girls who were sex trafficking survivors were HIV-positive.[57] These trafficked women and girls who were HIV-positive also had a higher incidence of other sexually transmitted infections (e.g., syphilis and hepatitis B).[58]

Male victims similarly face sexual health risks. Sexual violence is inflicted on men and boys, and they suffer negative physical health consequences, including sexually transmitted infections.[59] Shame, stigma, and homophobia all contribute to male victims being overlooked in sex trafficking settings.[60] Similarly, in labor trafficking settings, where sexual violence may be employed as part of psychological coercion, such violence often goes unseen because the binary construct of human trafficking portrays the issue as consisting of two distinct forms: sex trafficking and labor trafficking.[61]

Trafficking victims may also experience anal trauma from forced anal penetration during sex and in some cases from being forced to smuggle drugs anally.[62] This may lead to anal tissue tears from insertion or systemic poisoning from the drugs rupturing inside them.[63] This happens to cisgender and transgender boys and girls. And finally, victims often are raped by their traffickers, exploiters, purchasers, and others, which can lead to suicidal ideation.[64]

### Psychological and Mental Health and Related Consequences

Trafficking victims experience a breadth of emotional and psychological harms. Rates of mental health problems are high among survivors of labor and sex trafficking.[65] And girls and boys experience similar rates of mental health issues.[66] "Victims of human trafficking have been described as exhibiting symptoms and needs for service similar to torture victims, victims of domestic violence/sexual assault, battered immigrant women, migrant workers, refugees, and asylum seekers."[67] Both labor and sex trafficking survivors suffer PTSD, depressive disorder, and anxiety disorders.[68] As Heather Clawson and her coauthors found, "Specific symptoms exhibited by victims can include nightmares, difficulty concentrating, becoming easily upset, and having difficulty relaxing. Victims can frequently feel sad or angry, have difficulty thinking, experience feelings of hopelessness, and demonstrate sleep disorders. The trauma itself also may manifest as physical symptoms, such as headaches, chest pain, shaking, sweating, and dizziness."[69]

Trafficking survivors also report substance use and abuse,[70] which may be an attempt to self-medicate or a result of being forced by their traffickers to take drugs in order to provide sex or engage in work or services they are coerced to perform. Substance use and abuse may also predate—and increase vulnerability to—human trafficking, as some young people with addiction issues may end up in trafficking situations as a result of seeking ways to support their drug habit.

Additionally, the psychological impact of subordination to coercive control has many common features. These can include anxiety, emotional blunting, numbness, flat affect, excessive guilt or shame, low self-esteem, poor interpersonal relationships, depression, suicidal ideation, disassociation, hostility, anger, irritability, and memory loss.[71]

Trafficking victims often exhibit symptoms of PTSD owing to the chronic trauma.[72] For example, nearly three-fourths of participants in a five-country study of prostituted children and adults met the diagnostic criteria for PTSD.[73] The consequences are significant, as "PTSD can limit an individual's ability to function effectively, decreasing the likelihood that he or she can take advantage of available resources and possibly minimizing any likelihood of leaving prostitution."[74] The presence of social support can modify the long-term mental health consequences,[75] though many trafficking survivors lack such support.

Some trafficking victims experience a more severe form of post-traumatic stress disorder known as complex PTSD.[76] Complex PTSD results from and encompasses the sequelae of multiple, persistent, prolonged, or repeated trauma. Complex PTSD occurs in persons exposed to extreme, chronic, and usually relational forms of trauma and changes the individual's affect regulation, consciousness and perceptions of self, the perpetrator, relationships, and systems of meaning.[77]

Trauma inflicts more than psychological harm. A growing body of evidence, particularly in research on the consequences of child abuse, shows that trauma can adversely affect brain development. The type of traumatic stress faced by trafficking victims can lead to dysregulation of normal neurochemical and hormonal responses. In short, severe trauma "can damage the brain and body's ability to respond to stress or to distinguish neutral versus threatening situations and can cause long-lasting changes in the brain, which in turn can have behavioral consequences."[78] Although more research is needed to understand the impact of trafficking experiences on brain development and regulation, research on trauma's impact on the brain and behavior offers evidence of its significant and long-term consequences. Trauma has also been found to impact physical health, including the immune system.

Finally, it is important to remember that many trafficking survivors have had previous adverse life traumas (e.g., sexual abuse, homelessness, gang violence, living in violent communities, or emigrating from war-torn countries). In some cases, psychological harms reported, including PTSD, may predate survivors' trafficking experiences. Research has shown that child trafficking victims have higher adverse childhood experiences (ACEs) scores than the general population.[79] These prior histories of trauma not only increase vulnerability to exploitation (see chapter 5) but also compound the trafficking-related trauma. Higher ACEs scores also have implications for many long-term adult health consequences, such as obesity, diabetes, hypertension, and other conditions.[80] In other words, the trauma trafficking survivors have experienced, both during their trafficking situation and earlier in life, can result in a wide range of short- and long-term adverse health consequences.

### Other Health and Social Issues and Consequences

Human trafficking is associated with other adverse consequences and social situations. We briefly highlight two issues—substance abuse and intimate partner violence—to demonstrate the breadth of intentional and unintentional harm that can occur as a result of trafficking and to highlight the range of opportunities to assist and support youth who are at risk of or exploited through human trafficking.

#### Substance Abuse

A number of studies indicate high rates of disorders that co-occur with substance abuse among adolescents.[81] A cross-sectional study of 9,154 adolescents discharged from adolescent units at psychiatric inpatient hospitals throughout the United States found that 25 percent had mental health and substance use comorbidity.[82] Conversely, among youth in the substance abuse system, an even higher percentage (up to 75-90%) suffer from a mental health disorder.[83]

Substance abuse tends to co-occur with sex trafficking.[84] Many youth who are trafficking victims have prior substance use and abuse issues.[85] Others commence drug use once they enter their trafficking situation, either as a way to cope with the circumstances or because drugs have been forced upon them by traffickers as a means of controlling them.[86] In some trafficking settings, drugs may be easily accessible and part of the day-to-day environment.

## Intimate Partner Violence

Many trafficked youth experience intimate partner violence. In the sex trafficking context, traffickers often play roles in which lines are blurred; many victims refer to their traffickers as their boyfriends. In one study of prostituted young women and girls in Chicago, 64 percent of participants said they considered their pimp to be their boyfriend.[87] The study also reported that the majority of these young women had experienced force and coercion during recruitment and reported that the force and coercion had increased over time.[88] In an international study on prostitution in nine countries, 71 percent of study participants had been physically assaulted in prostitution and 63 percent had been raped.[89]

The research on substance abuse and intimate partner violence in trafficking situations highlights the breadth and depth of adverse consequences for trafficking victims. It also shows both the range of services survivors need to recover fully and the opportunities for positive interventions.

## Developmental Issues

The trauma inflicted in trafficking situations can disrupt the normal, healthy development of children and adolescents.[90] As a National Academies of Sciences, Engineering, and Medicine study committee reported, "Disrupted transitions can be defined as life events that interrupt normative developmental patterns or occur prematurely."[91] Examples of such disruptions include premature sexual activity, which can lead to teenage pregnancy, and early cohabitation or marriage.[92] These early life disruptions can have a ripple effect. As Thulitha Wickrama and her coauthors explain, "Certain early life events may create 'damages' that may multiply and continue into the young adult years."[93]

Trafficking victims are socialized in an environment that is not conducive to healthy development. Trafficked youth tend to be disconnected from families, schools, community, and other traditional social structures. Like other consequences, this disconnect may have occurred earlier in life, increasing their vulnerability to being trafficked. Whether it predated a young person's trafficking experience or resulted directly from being trafficked, disconnection from family and other supportive social structures makes it difficult for trafficked youth to develop the skills that typically are developed in these settings. They may miss critical developmental milestones.[94] This has important long-term implications. Adverse behavioral outcomes, including attachment difficulties, mistrust of adults, antisocial behaviors, and difficulties relating to others have been reported among children who were trafficked.[95]

In summary, there are short- and long-term adverse consequences and negative impacts of human trafficking. Human trafficking affects physical health, sexual and reproductive health, mental health, and substance use, and it puts a young person at higher risk for intimate partner violence and other types of violence. These adverse consequences have a significant negative impact, as the trauma interrupts normal child and adolescent development. The negative impact on health and the interrupted development interfere with young persons' ability to leave their trafficking situations, reintegrate into communities, and ultimately develop to their fullest potential.

## Educational Issues

Trafficking has significant consequences for children's educational opportunities and development. Trafficked youth often experience higher absenteeism.[96] The lifestyle and health consequences of trafficking can make it difficult for trafficked children to regularly attend school.[97] In some cases, traffickers prevent children under their control from attending school.[98] Higher absenteeism adversely affects school performance and may lead to falling behind peers. Some trafficked children drop out of school.[99] Even those who maintain regular attendance may see a decline in school performance as a result of physical exhaustion, the effects of psychological trauma, or the attendant higher absenteeism.[100]

Although some trafficked youth report many of the above disruptions in education prior to their trafficking experience—which increases their vulnerability to exploitation—others point to trafficking as causing or exacerbating barriers to education. The consequences of such an impact on education are felt in both the short and the long term. Research shows that educational deprivation among trafficking victims has a range of adverse outcomes, including "developmental delays, language and cognitive difficulties, deficits in verbal and memory skills, poorer academic performance, and grade retention."[101] With developmental delays, higher absenteeism, and falling behind classmates, trafficked youth become further marginalized in education settings. Those who miss significant schooling or drop out are at heightened risk of further exploitation because of their youth, vulnerability, and limited skills.[102] Interference with education has long-term consequences as well. Trafficked children are often deprived of completing their education and, in turn, of the opportunity to access better jobs and improve their future economic situation over their life span.

## Financial Issues

One sign of a possible trafficking situation is that an individual is not paid directly for their services or has no access to his or her earnings.[103] "Trafficked persons rarely have control over what they earn and are frequently subjected to deceptive accounting practices and usurious repayment obligations, such as [for] housing, food, clothing, and inflated debts related to travel costs."[104] Whatever sector they are forced to serve in, trafficking victims are robbed of the economic value of their labor.

And the value of their labor is significant. The International Labour Office (ILO) has estimated that illegal profits from trafficked and forced labor amount to more than $150 billion annually.[105] Such global numbers can be overwhelming and make it difficult to appreciate how much is taken from individual trafficking victims. However, individual cases highlight the extent of the economic harm suffered. In 2015, Signal International, a marine services company, agreed to a $20 million settlement to resolve a labor trafficking lawsuit that had argued that the company had exploited more than two hundred workers from India.[106] In *United States v. Webster*, a sex trafficking case involving eleven victims, including some minors, the court adopted what it called "the most conservative approach possible" to valuation of the victims' services and still found that "$3,615,750.00 is a fair and reasonable estimate of the gross income to the defendant as a result of the victims' services."[107] In cases of mandatory restitution, trafficking victims rarely collect anything close to these amounts, which underscores the economic losses suffered.[108]

Adding to the loss, research has found that "defendants who traffic children appear to be far *less* likely to be ordered to pay restitution than those who traffic only adults."[109] The failure to order restitution in many cases underlines the importance of civil lawsuits such as the ones against Signal International, especially for cases involving children.

In short, human trafficking denies its victims the economic value of their labor. In addition, as noted above, trafficked victims endure interruptions in education that make it less likely that they will complete school. This denial of education has lifelong consequences in terms of job opportunities and financial well-being. Moreover, the health consequences for trafficking victims can have consequences for their short- and long-term job prospects. Ultimately, the trafficking experience exacts a significant economic toll, both during the time the individual is being exploited and in the years that follow.

### Housing Issues

Housing insecurity has a bidirectional relationship with trafficking. As a threshold matter, housing insecurity heightens vulnerability to trafficking; homeless children are often at increased risk of exploitation (see chapter 5).[110] And runaway and thrownaway youth are among the highest risk populations for human trafficking, as many of them end up homeless. The trafficking experience itself can also disrupt children's access to stable housing. After extricating themselves from human trafficking, many survivors need safe emergency housing as well as assistance in transitioning to stable permanent housing.[111]

Emergency shelters for trafficking survivors are few and far between. According to a national survey study conducted by the Polaris Project in 2012, there were 1,644 shelter beds available in the United States for human trafficking survivors, both adults and children.[112] One study found that prosecutors working on human trafficking cases reported that the lack of emergency shelters is a "huge problem."[113]

In addition, trafficking survivors may not be able to access certain emergency shelters because they do not qualify. For example, trafficking survivors might be ineligible to stay at a domestic violence shelter because they cannot prove that a domestic partner abused them.[114] Other shelters present additional barriers. For example, some LGBTQ trafficking survivors report being denied access to services offered by some faith-based entities.[115] Given the heightened vulnerability of LBGTQ youth—who account for up to 40 percent of runaway and homeless youth[116]—this has potentially significant consequences. In addition, the vast majority of the available shelters for trafficking victims serve girls.[117] As a result, cisgender and transgender males of all ages often have no emergency shelter options.[118]

Emerging research shows the significant gap between housing needs and availability. One study found that only 3.9 percent of trafficking survivors who needed long-term housing actually were able to secure it.[119] As Gregory Maney and his coauthors found, "Providers [who serve trafficking victims] reported that although over 86% of survivors would benefit from long-term housing, less than 4% of these clients have actually received long-term housing through referrals from providers."[120] According to another report, in 2013 there were thirty-three residential programs in the United States exclusively designed for trafficking victims, with a total of 682 beds.[121] That means that many parts of the country have no shelter specifically designed for trafficking survivors.

Even when housing is available for trafficking survivors, it frequently is not available for a sufficient amount of time to meet survivors' needs.[122] And often the housing is unsuitable for trafficking survivors because of safety concerns, lack of appropriate services, and insufficient training for staff.[123]

Children and adolescents are particularly vulnerable. As Maney and his coauthors found in their study of New York City, "Age is the strongest predictor as to whether or not a survivor will be eligible for housing. Minors are the least likely sub-population to be eligible for housing services, with two-thirds of housing providers reporting that survivors under the age of eighteen are ineligible for their programs. Only 18.1% of foreign-born survivors under the age of eighteen were supplied emergency housing— the form of housing most readily available but least suited to trafficking survivors."[124]

In its Federal Strategic Action Plan on Services for Victims of Human Trafficking in the United States, the Department of Health and Human Services acknowledged that housing is "a significant issue in achieving long-term recovery and self-sufficiency for human trafficking survivors."[125] Despite its importance, access to suitable housing remains challenging.

In some states, child welfare services often are not involved in securing housing for child survivors of human trafficking because human trafficking is not considered a form of child abuse and thus is not within their mandate. When child welfare services cannot take on the responsibility of ensuring safe housing for young trafficking survivors, the task often falls to local nonprofit organizations. Beyond these barriers and the fact that there is insufficient housing for trafficking survivors, the research on housing assistance in the trafficking context is very limited, so that our knowledge about which housing options work best for which survivors is also limited.[126]

Ultimately, housing needs are connected with other survivor needs, including health care, education, job training, employment opportunities, access to counseling, legal assistance, and other support.

## Legal Issues

Prior to the emergence of "safe harbor" laws (see chapter 3), survivors of trafficking and commercial sexual exploitation were often arrested and charged with prostitution or other offenses.[127] In certain instances, law enforcement reported arresting children because they viewed detainment as a protective mechanism for removing children from a dangerous situation. Law enforcement faces a difficult challenge in these cases, but as the Supreme Court of Texas explained in *In re B.W.*, arrest is not the only way to protect these children (and it actually inflicts further harm).[128]

Although "safe harbor" laws aim to reduce arrest and criminal punishment of prostituted and exploited children, such practices still occur, even in jurisdictions that have safe harbor laws.[129] The immediate and longer-term consequences of arrest and punishment are significant. In the immediate term, arrest and detention can be a traumatic experience.[130] In addition, when a trafficking victim is charged with a crime (prostitution or another offense), "the circumstances around the arrest and the overtaxed criminal court system create tremendous pressure on the victim to plead guilty, rather than contesting the charge or revealing the trafficking situation."[131] In some instances, with the intention of helping or giving the young person a break, charges will be reduced from prostitution to a status offense, but this well-intentioned step covers up the trafficking situation (both for that individual and more broadly for measuring trafficking prevalence) and can leave the youth with a record of having violated the law.

A conviction from a trafficking situation can produce both short- and long-term adverse consequences. Having a criminal record can be a barrier to employment, educational, and housing opportunities as well as other benefits, making it that much harder for survivors to rebuild their lives.[132] For noncitizens, a conviction can lead to the Department of Homeland Security issuing a Notice to Appear instructing them to appear before an immigration judge, which can lead to the commencement of deportation proceedings.[133]

Recognizing the problem with criminalizing children who are victims of human trafficking, in 2007 selected states began to develop safe harbor laws. The goal was to ensure that trafficking victims were treated not as criminals but as crime victims. A number of states now have safe harbor laws, although they vary considerably in the protection they offer human trafficking victims. And as noted above, trafficking victims continue to be arrested by law enforcement.[134]

Moreover, even positive steps by prosecutors and law enforcement can potentially expose trafficking victims to further harm. As cases proceed against traffickers, in some instances prosecutors may ask victims to cooperate with law enforcement and potentially to testify against their traffickers. In some cases, trafficking victims may be reluctant or unable to assist owing to the trauma they have suffered. Being pressured to testify against their trafficker can cause victims to relive the trauma, further scarring them. It can also put the trafficking survivor and potentially his or her family at risk of harm.[135] Although under federal law minors are not required to testify in order to access the benefits intended for human trafficking victims,[136] the way a prosecution is handled can still create difficult, often painful choices for trafficked youth that do little to assist in healing. Understanding the consequences of human trafficking and its impact on children and adolescents who survive the experience means appreciating and responding to the range of short- and long-term legal consequences for these young people.[137]

## Resilience

The extent of human trafficking's consequences can appear overwhelming. When confronting social ills and harms such as human trafficking, there is a tendency to focus on risk factors, adverse outcomes, and what individuals are unable to do as a result of their traumatic experience. Too often, all of us—policymakers, service providers, and researchers—fail to pay enough attention to protective factors, resilience, positive outcomes, and the many things that survivors are capable of doing. Although the harmful consequences of human trafficking are unmistakable, it is also true that survivors demonstrate tremendous strength and resilience and that they have their own dreams and aspirations, which merit full consideration and support.

Studies on young people's experience with trafficking find that many youth demonstrate self-reliance and other strengths that enable them to survive and persevere in the face of the trauma of trafficking and significant barriers to housing, education, and other vital resources.[138] Our own experience listening to and interacting with survivors compels us to reject any construct of human trafficking that suggests that trafficked youth are victims without agency. They are survivors. They are individuals with numerous strengths and varied talents. And many of them overcome their trafficking experience to thrive and succeed. Indeed, when one considers the breadth of adverse consequences detailed in this chapter, confronting all of that—and in many cases traumatic experiences prior to being trafficked—is itself evidence of strength and resilience that should not be overlooked.

## Conclusion

The consequences of trafficking are significant. Not only are there dramatic health consequences but trafficking also has educational, employment, financial, housing, legal, and other consequences. Addressing those consequences requires sustained, integrated responses that ensure meaningful assistance to trafficking survivors. The scale of the consequences across all these domains should also serve as a reminder of how much is lost—by individuals, their families and communities, and their countries—when trafficking is allowed to persist. Awareness of the harms caused by trafficking should spur more concerted efforts not only to assist trafficking survivors but also to prevent the trafficking of children and adolescents. Moreover, given the breadth of health and other consequences—both immediate and long-term—it is critical that we develop comprehensive, integrated responses that meet the needs of human trafficking survivors.

# Current Responses to Child Trafficking

I N THE PAST two decades, human trafficking has captured the attention of government leaders, the media, and the public. Former president Barack Obama referred to it as "one of the great human rights causes of our time."[1] Media coverage of the issue has continued to increase, and human trafficking is now regularly in the news. And public awareness has grown. In response to this emerging awareness of the horrors of human trafficking, numerous countries, including the United States, have taken significant steps to address human trafficking.[2] The US response, like that of other countries, developed largely out of a criminal justice approach to the issue.[3] Only more recently has recognition of the value of other frameworks and the importance of a multisector response emerged.[4] This chapter reviews current responses to child trafficking. It analyzes the legal framework on child trafficking, explores the evolution of anti-trafficking efforts, and discusses the limitations of current responses.

## The Current Legal Framework for Child Trafficking

The late 1990s marked a renewed interest in human trafficking among governments. This interest spurred the passage of three significant legal instruments at the beginning of the twenty-first century. In 2000, the international community adopted two key treaties: the Protocol to Prevent, Suppress and Punish Trafficking in Persons, Especially Women and Children, Supplementing the United Nations Convention Against Transnational Organized Crime (Trafficking Protocol)[5] and the Optional Protocol to the Convention on the Rights of the Child on the Sale of Children, Child Prostitution and Child Pornography (Sale of Children Protocol).[6] That same year, the United States adopted the Trafficking Victims Protection Act (TVPA), which would serve as the cornerstone of US anti-trafficking efforts and simultaneously influence efforts in many other countries.

The law on human trafficking—in these three landmark legal instruments as well as subsequent legal initiatives—can be understood as organized around a three-pronged response. First, law and policy must criminalize all acts of human trafficking, and perpetrators must be held accountable. Second, law and policy must ensure protection of and assistance to victims and survivors. Third, law and policy should advance prevention efforts.[7]

This 3 P's framework—prosecution, protection, and prevention—was first advanced in 1998 by the Clinton administration, which then pressed for the Trafficking Protocol to be structured along these lines.[8] The Clinton administration first described the three prongs as "prevention, victim assistance and protection, and enforcement."[9] That is notable in two respects: first, it gave first priority to prevention, which should be the ultimate goal but has been relegated to the margins (as discussed below); and second, by including "assistance" along with protection of victims, it more clearly recognized the agency of trafficking survivors, rather than viewing them solely as victims in need of protection.

Since the Clinton administration, the United States has been a leader in the response to human trafficking. Not only did it help to shape the development of the international framework but its subsequent law and policy have significantly influenced the development of anti-trafficking strategies in many other countries.[10] The discussion that follows begins with the international framework and then provides an overview of federal and state responses to human trafficking. It traces the 3 P's framework, following the order in which most work has been undertaken to date. As the discussion reveals, that has left prevention behind.

### International Law Framework

The 3 P's (Prosecution, Protection, Prevention)

The Trafficking Protocol and the Sale of Children Protocol, both of which the United States has ratified, emerge out of two distinct frameworks. The Trafficking Protocol, which has been ratified by 173 countries, is situated in a criminal justice framework and overseen by the UN Office on Drugs and Crime.[11] In contrast, the Sale of Children Protocol, which has been ratified by 175 countries, is part of the international human rights law framework and monitored by the UN Committee on the Rights of the Child.[12] Despite these disparate origins, both treaties employ the familiar three-pronged mandate: prosecution, protection, and prevention. Although this tripartite approach provides the framework for an effective response in theory, there are important distinctions in the legal mandate for each prong, as well as other key differences between the two treaties.

To begin, the two treaties impose the strongest obligations on governments with respect to the criminalization of human trafficking. The criminal law provisions of the Trafficking Protocol and the Sale of Children Protocol employ mandatory language.[13] For example, article 5 of the Trafficking Protocol requires that governments that ratify the treaty "*shall* adopt such legislative and other measures as may be necessary to establish as criminal offences the conduct set forth in [the Trafficking Protocol's definition of 'trafficking in persons']."[14] Similarly, article 3 of the Sale of Children Protocol requires that governments "*shall* ensure that, as a minimum, the following acts and activities are fully covered under its criminal or penal law."[15] Reflecting the serious nature of crimes against children, the Sale of Children Protocol also demands that states deem such forms of exploitation of children extraditable offenses.[16] The Trafficking Protocol supplements its criminalization requirements with additional provisions requiring that states provide relevant training for law enforcement and immigration officials and adopt appropriate border security measures.[17] The mandate created by both treaties imposes a definitive obligation requiring the criminalization and prosecution of all acts of child trafficking.

In contrast, both treaties' provisions on assistance to trafficking victims and prevention of trafficking are comparatively weaker. To begin, the Trafficking Protocol identifies a number of important means of assisting victims' recovery by calling on states to provide appropriate housing, counseling and information to victims about their rights, physical and mental health services, education and training, employment opportunities, and material assistance.[18] However, the mandate is only that states "consider implementing" such measures.[19] Similarly, the Sale of Children Protocol requires that states "take all feasible measures with the aim of ensuring all appropriate assistance to victims."[20] Other, more specific requirements to assist child victims are limited for the most part to the context of the criminal justice process (e.g., special protections if the child serves as a witness for the prosecution).[21] In short, the mandate for assisting child survivors of trafficking is both more limited and employs more permissive language, allowing states to "consider" taking steps or limit their efforts to what is merely "feasible" under the circumstances.

Prevention, which should be the ultimate goal, similarly receives less priority in both treaties. Although article 9 of the Trafficking Protocol requires that states parties "shall establish comprehensive policies, programmes and other measures" to prevent human trafficking, it immediately weakens that obligation by setting forth that "States Parties shall endeavour to undertake measures such as research, information and mass media campaigns and social and economic initiatives to prevent and combat trafficking in persons."[22] In other words, the obligation is not that a government take those steps to prevent trafficking but only that it "endeavour to undertake" such measures. Similarly, the Sale of Children Protocol provides little in the way of specific requirements: "States Parties shall adopt or strengthen, implement and disseminate laws, administrative measures, social policies and programmes to prevent the offences referred to in the present Protocol. Particular attention shall be given to protect children who are especially vulnerable to such practices."[23] Acknowledging the value of a multifaceted approach—including not only laws but also social policies and programs—is important, but absent any specific requirements the resulting obligation is vague and of limited impact.

## Other Key Components

Although as the above discussion reveals, there are many parallels between the two treaties, there are also important distinctions, both in their approach and in their impact.

First, the Trafficking Protocol covers trafficking of adults and children, whereas the Sale of Children Protocol applies only to trafficking of children (individuals under eighteen years of age). Second, the Trafficking Protocol is more limited in scope: it covers only those acts of trafficking that are "transnational in nature and involve an organized criminal group."[24] In contrast, the Sale of Children Protocol imposes a broader obligation to criminalize child trafficking crimes "whether such offences are committed domestically or transnationally or on an individual or organized basis."[25] This broader scope of the Sale of Children Protocol is critical, given that most trafficking is intracountry and that both individuals and groups perpetrate such criminal acts. Third, the Trafficking Protocol requires states to criminalize human trafficking "when committed intentionally," whereas no such limiting language is included in the Sale of Children Protocol, and a prosecutor would need to prove only that the perpetrator committed the crime, not that he or she did it intentionally.[26]

These differences might lead one to conclude that the Sale of Children Protocol offers greater promise in addressing child trafficking. Although it is true that the Trafficking Protocol has several key limitations, it has garnered significant support since its adoption in 2000. It is recognized as arguably the cornerstone of anti-trafficking law at the international level. In that respect, and because it also establishes an internationally agreed-upon definition of human trafficking (see chapter 1), the Trafficking Protocol remains a key component of any effort to address child trafficking. Likewise, the Sale of Children Protocol, with its more specific focus on children and its broader scope of application, is an important tool. In the end, both treaties create important mandates to address child trafficking.

## US Legal Framework

### Federal Law: 3 P's and More

Since first advancing the idea of the 3 P's in the late 1990s, the US government has been a strong proponent of this approach, and federal law reflects that framework. In recent years, the federal government discussed a fourth P—partnerships—to reflect the importance of collaborative responses.[27] While partnerships have not achieved the same level of recognition as the 3 P's, they are relevant to public health approaches and offer a foundation upon which more effective responses can be developed. This section provides an overview of the federal response in all four areas: prosecution, protection, prevention, and partnerships. It does not detail every law and regulation relevant to human trafficking. Rather, the aim is to provide readers with an overview so that they can consider the role of law in responding to child trafficking. Ultimately, while good law is critical to an effective response, law alone will not address the problem.

*Prosecution*  Unlike international law, which treats all forms of trafficking of children equally, federal law treats sex trafficking and labor trafficking of children differently. Distinctions between the two types of trafficking under federal law are embedded in both the elements of the crime and the penalties for violating the law. First, under US federal law, evidence of force, fraud, or coercion is not required when a child is a victim of sex trafficking.[28] Consent is irrelevant when a minor is a victim of sex trafficking; in other words, a child cannot "volunteer" or choose to participate. Moreover, federal law on sex trafficking does not require that the prosecution prove that the defendant knew the victim was under eighteen years of age if the defendant had "a reasonable opportunity to observe the [victim]."[29] In contrast, federal law makes it harder to prosecute a perpetrator for labor trafficking or forced labor involving children by requiring evidence of force, fraud, or coercion.[30] This two-tiered approach conflicts with international law, which establishes that a child cannot consent to trafficking and thus force, fraud, or coercion does not need to be proven for *any* type of trafficking in which a child is the victim.[31]

Second, federal law also establishes more significant penalties for child sex trafficking than for child labor trafficking. Sex trafficking of children carries a minimum sentence of fifteen years if the child was under fourteen years of age, ten years if the child was at least fourteen but under eighteen, and a maximum of a life sentence in either case.[32] For labor trafficking of children, there is no minimum sentence, and the maximum sentence is twenty years unless the trafficking results in the death of the victim, in which case the perpetrator can receive a life sentence.[33]

The greater weight given to sex trafficking as compared with labor trafficking is also reflected in the prosecution of trafficking cases. In fiscal year 2015 (October 1, 2014, to September 30, 2015), the US Department of Justice initiated 257 federal human trafficking prosecutions, resulting in charges against 377 defendants.[34] Of these 257 cases, 248 involved primarily sex trafficking, while 9 involved primarily labor trafficking.[35] Some cases involved both sex trafficking and labor trafficking.

In recent years, in addition to enhancing penalties for traffickers, Congress has expanded the federal definition of trafficking. In 2015 Congress adopted the Justice for Victims of Trafficking Act. Among other things, it added *patronizes* and *solicits* to the definition of trafficking, so that purchasers and traffickers can be held equally culpable for trafficking crimes.[36]

In recognition of the pathways into trafficking, federal law also criminalizes a number of acts that heighten vulnerability to and facilitate the core crimes of sex trafficking and labor trafficking. For example, confiscation of identification documents with intent to engage in sex trafficking is a crime punishable by a fine, a sentence of up to five years, or both.[37] Federal law also covers any attempt to commit an act of trafficking or forced labor or any conspiracy to commit trafficking.[38]

While anti-trafficking law represents a more recent legislative development, federal law on commercial sexual exploitation of children has a much longer history. Dating back to the Mann Act of 1910,[39] federal law has criminalized travel in interstate or foreign commerce for the purpose of sexually exploiting a minor.[40] Although the Mann Act has been subjected to significant criticism historically for its biased enforcement,[41] today it is employed to punish sex tourism and commercial sexual exploitation of children. Transporting a minor in interstate or foreign commerce "with intent that the individual engage in prostitution or in any sexual activity for which any person can be charged with a criminal offense" is punishable by a fine and a sentence of ten years to life in prison.[42] In a related provision, persuading, inducing, enticing, or coercing a minor to travel in interstate or foreign commerce to engage in prostitution is subject to a fine, a sentence of up to twenty years, or both.[43] Both of these provisions cover acts perpetrated by sex traffickers. Two additional provisions address sex tourism, which in many cases exploits child sex trafficking victims. First, travel in interstate or foreign commerce "for the purpose of engaging in illegal sexual conduct with another person" is subject to a fine, a sentence of up to thirty years, or both.[44] And addressing sex tour operators and others who profit from sex tourism, federal law establishes that any individual who "arranges, induces, procures, or facilitates" such travel for "commercial advantage or private financial gain" shall be subject to a fine, imprisonment of up to thirty years, or both.[45] In both trafficking cases and Mann Act cases, courts must order forfeiture of any proceeds obtained by the defendant and of any property used in commission of the crime.[46]

Overall, federal law establishes expansive coverage and significant penalties for sex trafficking of children. It also covers labor trafficking and labor exploitation, but because federal law still requires proof of force, fraud, or coercion when minors are victims and has lesser penalties associated with it, the law on labor trafficking of children is not as strong as the provisions on sex trafficking. This differential treatment fails to recognize fully that child victims of labor trafficking also suffer significant trauma and harms.

*Protection and Assistance* The US government reports that it provides a broad range of services for human trafficking survivors: "Federally-funded victim assistance includes case management and referrals for medical and dental care, mental health and substance abuse treatment, sustenance and shelter, translation and interpretation services, immigration and legal assistance, employment and training, transportation assistance, and other services such as criminal justice advocacy."[47] These services are provided by and through a number of federal agencies, including the Department of Justice and the Department of Health and Human Services. Federal agencies are responsible for both service provision and funding of state and local services to address the needs of child trafficking victims and survivors. Although the list of services provided appears fairly comprehensive, it is difficult to determine how many trafficking survivors are able to access the full range of needed services in their recovery and reintegration. A 2013 National Academies of Sciences, Engineering, and Medicine study committee highlighted the challenges associated with the disperse services available:

> The committee identified no resource that provides a comprehensive detailing of all federal programs or federally funded programs available to minors who are victims of commercial sexual exploitation and sex trafficking. . . . It appears that such a source either does not exist or has not been made available to key stakeholders. The committee observes that this difficulty in ascertaining services and programs available to child victims presents potential obstacles for children and adolescents seeking to access services after the trauma of sexual exploitation or sex trafficking and for professionals and caregivers attempting to help them.[48]

One of the most prominent challenges is that many of these services are available through general social services programs established and supported by the federal government. Therefore, they may not explicitly identify as programs for minors or programs for trafficking victims. Furthermore, there is little or no evaluation of anti-trafficking programs, which makes it very difficult to assess whether survivors' needs are met or whether there are gaps in services—including, for example, health care, mental health, and substance abuse services—for some or all trafficking survivors.

In the past several years, Congress has adopted new legislation to strengthen the federal government's protection measures. The Preventing Sex Trafficking and Strengthening Families Act of 2014 imposes requirements on states to develop policies and procedures for identifying and responding to children in the foster care system who might be at risk or victims of sex trafficking.[49] And the Justice for Victims of Trafficking Act of 2015 amended the federal Child Abuse Prevention and Treatment Act to require that states train child welfare case workers in identification, assessment, and provision of services to child sex trafficking victims.[50]

Through the Justice for Victims of Trafficking Act, the federal government bolstered its support of grants for providers serving child survivors of human trafficking and added a grant to be awarded to a school of medicine or nursing to develop best practices for identification of and response to victims of trafficking in health care settings.[51] In addition, the Justice for Victims of Trafficking Act also incentivizes the Department of Justice to select grant awardees in states that have "safe harbor" laws, which aim to provide additional protections for trafficking victims (for more on safe harbor laws, see below under "States").[52]

Beyond direct services and financial support of state and local programs, federal law offers two other vehicles that can assist trafficking survivors in securing resources to rebuild their lives. First, federal law provides that in human trafficking cases courts must order mandatory restitution for trafficking victims for the "full amount of the victim's losses."[53] Under federal law, victims are entitled to two types of damages: compensation for their personal losses (including costs of health care services in their recovery) and compensation for the economic value of their services. Despite often significant losses, in many cases restitution is not awarded. A study by the Human Trafficking Pro Bono Legal Center and the Wilmer Hale law firm found that over a four-year period, courts awarded restitution in only 27 percent of cases.[54] Even in cases in which restitution is awarded, the convicted trafficker often has few assets to pay any restitution, and garnishing of prison wages results in only a fraction of the amount of losses being recovered. For example, in one sex trafficking case involving eleven victims, the court awarded a total of $3,615,750 in restitution but acknowledged the limitations of mandatory restitution: "The court doubts that any significant amount of restitution will ever be paid in this case. The court assumes that the victims will become aware of the entry of this restitution order. The court believes it is only fair that the victims should know that, as discussed above, the defendant's circumstances are such that it is highly unlikely he will ever actually pay any significant amount of restitution."[55]

Second, federal law also provides a civil remedy for trafficking victims.[56] Survivors are now able to pursue civil lawsuits against their traffickers and anyone else who profited from participating in their exploitation. While some survivors might find pursuing a civil remedy to be empowering, others might be reluctant to relive the experience.[57] This latter concern reinforces the importance of ensuring that mandatory restitution is awarded, because it does not require a trafficking survivor to request damages or actively participate in the legal proceedings.

Overall, federal law appears to cover a range of options and services that offer potential benefit to trafficking survivors. How effective they are in reaching all human trafficking survivors remains unclear because of the very limited evaluation of policies and programs.

*Prevention* Prevention efforts have lagged behind work on prosecution and protection. The lack of prevention-related work might be a result of initial prioritization of criminal justice responses: the US government often responds to human rights violations first by criminalizing behavior that is harmful. It also might be because other areas, such as prosecution, build on existing systems and institutions, making it easier for policymakers to envision and begin implementing anti-trafficking measures in those sectors. For prevention, it is less clear how best to proceed. With little evidence-based research in the early years of the Trafficking Victims Protection Act, it would have been difficult to identify at-risk youth consistently or to know how to prevent exploitation of those identified as being at heightened vulnerability. There is still much to learn, but there is growing recognition that more concerted efforts are needed to address prevention.

The federal government has supported selected efforts aimed at improving prevention, or at least early identification, of trafficking cases. The federal government supports training of key stakeholders. These training programs have the potential to increase awareness among individuals who might encounter trafficking victims and improve victim identification. There is limited evaluation of the effectiveness of these and other training programs. The US government also provides funding to support the National Human Trafficking Hotline, operated by Polaris Project, which has the potential to improve interventions and prevent trafficking cases.[58] These efforts might strengthen the capacity to identify victims of human trafficking.

Moving upstream, at the federal level few measures to address the root causes of trafficking of children—that is, programs aimed at reducing vulnerability of at-risk children or demand-reduction programs—have been promulgated. One example is the Street Outreach Program of the Department of Health and Human Services Youth Development Division, which aims "to prevent the sexual abuse or exploitation of young people living on the streets or in unstable housing."[59] Through the Street Outreach Program, the Family and Youth Services Bureau provides funding to support organizations that offer a range of services aimed at reducing vulnerability to exploitation, including street-based outreach to youth, trauma-informed counseling and treatment, emergency housing, prevention and education activities, crisis intervention, and follow-up support.[60] Additional focused programs are greatly needed to address the vulnerability of young people.

Beyond the limited number of targeted programs, the federal government does support broader awareness-raising efforts that arguably could contribute to prevention and early identification and intervention. The most well known initiative is the annual *Trafficking in Persons Report*, published by the US Department of State. The report, which ranks efforts by more than 170 countries to confront human trafficking, has been influential in pressing foreign governments to increase anti-trafficking efforts.[61] A secondary benefit of this annual report is that it draws significant media coverage, providing an opportunity to advance public awareness about the issue of human trafficking. In addition, in the United States, January is recognized by presidential proclamation as National Slavery and Human Trafficking Prevention Month.[62] The federal government has also supported state and local task forces that help raise awareness locally.[63] And it has developed educational materials, such as the Department of Education's publication *Human Trafficking of Children in the United States: A Fact Sheet for Schools*.[64] Through targeted training programs, educational materials, and broader public awareness campaigns, the US government seeks to raise awareness so that relevant individuals might facilitate earlier identification and intervention.

*Partnerships*  The federal government has undertaken a number of efforts to build partnerships in the fight against human trafficking. As discussed in the concluding chapter, partnerships are important to building a comprehensive, coordinated response to all forms of human trafficking. In 2002, Executive Order 13257 established a cabinet-level President's Interagency Trafficking Task Force, which is responsible for coordinating implementation of the TVPA and other anti-trafficking activities. Selected government agencies are also responsible for developing plans of action to set out a coordinated strategy for addressing child trafficking. For example, the PROTECT Our Children Act of 2008 requires the US attorney general to develop and implement a National Strategy for Child Exploitation Prevention and Interdiction. The first national strategy was produced in 2010, and a revised national strategy was published in 2016.[65] In 2013 the federal government promulgated the Federal Strategic Action Plan on Services for Victims of Human Trafficking in the United States 2013–2017.[66] Together, these activities both help secure high-level support for anti-trafficking activities and enhance agencies' work by seeking to ensure that it is well thought out, that it is embedded in a coordinated response, and that it can be evaluated so that responses can be improved. Finally, the federal government has also supported coordination and collaboration in more targeted ways. For example, the Internet Crimes Against Children Task Force Program facilitates information sharing among law enforcement agencies to help identify potential traffickers and possible victims.[67]

Across all four areas, the federal government is actively developing responses. However, further evaluation of specific laws and programs is needed to assess their effectiveness.

In 2003, Washington became the first state to pass an anti-trafficking law. Today, all fifty states have laws on human trafficking. These laws have important parallels with federal law; they typically emphasize criminalization and prosecution and have less well developed measures on assistance to survivors and prevention.[68] Also, as with federal law, there has been greater focus on sex trafficking than on labor trafficking in state law initiatives.

Many criminal provisions of state anti-trafficking law are modeled on the federal TVPA. State penalties for human trafficking crimes vary across states and in some instances are less than federal penalties.[69] In Massachusetts, for example, the sentence for both sex trafficking and labor trafficking of a minor ranges from a minimum of five years to a maximum of a life sentence.[70] In Colorado, sex trafficking and labor trafficking of a minor are subject to a sentence of eight to twenty-four years.[71] Like federal law, most state laws allow for seizure of assets of traffickers, and many states also include provisions on mandatory restitution and civil remedies.[72]

With respect to protection of and assistance to victims, there is an array of relevant state laws. State anti-trafficking laws have addressed aspects of victim assistance through support of task forces that aim to coordinate state-level responses and other measures designed to assess and meet victims' needs.[73] A significant state law development has been the adoption of "safe harbor" laws.

Safe harbor laws aim to shield child trafficking victims from prosecution for any crimes committed during their trafficking experience. For example, they can protect children from being charged with and convicted of prostitution when subjected to sex trafficking. Prior to the advent of safe harbor laws and even today, it is not uncommon for trafficking victims to suffer arrest and criminal prosecution. One study found that potential trafficking victims were arrested in "nearly one-third" of the cases analyzed for the study.[74] Where state laws depart from federal law on sex trafficking by requiring a showing of force, fraud, or coercion, a child can be recognized as a trafficking victim under federal law but be prosecuted for prostitution under state law. Safe harbor laws aim to address that disconnect and ensure that trafficked youth are treated as victims and receive assistance. In 2008, New York became the first state to adopt a safe harbor law. Today, at least thirty-four states claim to have some version of a safe harbor law. However, there are important differences among the various safe harbor laws; not all states fully protect exploited children from being charged with crimes (e.g., in some states it is an affirmative defense, which means that the burden remains on the child to raise this issue and prove that he or she was a victim).[75]

Selected states are also developing diversion programs that aim to ensure that trafficking victims are referred to needed services instead of facing criminal sanction. For example, New York State's Human Trafficking Intervention Courts aim to connect sex trafficking victims with counseling and social services instead of imposing jail time.[76] Similarly, the Succeeding Through Achievement and Resilience (STAR) Court of Los Angeles Superior Court seeks to divert child sex trafficking victims to specialized services.[77] Overall, the trend in safe harbor laws, the emergence of specialized courts in selected jurisdictions, and the development of other programs are encouraging steps. Much more is needed, not only to ensure appropriate assistance to young trafficking survivors but also to intervene earlier in the process.

On prevention, state legislatures are in the early stages of developing effective responses. As the National Academies of Sciences, Engineering, and Medicine study committee report described, "Prevention-oriented provisions that do exist relate to human trafficking task forces, training of various state law enforcement personnel and other state employees, and public awareness campaigns."[78] States are exploring various ways to address aspects of the problem. Two notable examples are requiring the posting of human trafficking awareness notices at certain businesses and expanding child abuse mandatory reporting laws to covering human trafficking. First, a number of states have opted to require specified businesses to post a notice in their places of employment with telephone numbers that employees or others can call if they or persons they know are victims of human trafficking (see box 3.1). The aim of the notices is to raise awareness among individuals who visit or work at locales where trafficking or

**Box 3.1. Notice Requirement**

A number of states require the posting of notices about human trafficking at various sites. Two critical variables in these state law provisions are the requirements related to where the notices must be posted and the content of the notices:

In New Mexico, employers subject to the Minimum Wage Act must post a sign that reads, in part:

> Obtaining forced labor or services is a crime under New Mexico and federal law. If you or someone you know is a victim of this crime, contact the following: . . .

California has a similar requirement, although its model notice uses less technical language:

> If you or someone you know is being forced to engage in any activity and cannot leave—whether it is commercial sex, housework, farm work, construction, factory, retail, or restaurant work, or any other activity—call. . . .

Although these signs do raise awareness, their efficacy has not been evaluated. Research shows that many human trafficking victims do not self-identify as being trafficked, suggesting that signs using technical language might be less helpful than signs that ask about particular behaviors or conditions of employment.

See N.M.S.A. 1978, § 30-52-2.1; and West's Ann.Cal.Civ.Code, § 52.6.

labor exploitation might occur. Second, in recent years, some states have expanded their child abuse mandatory reporting laws to cover sex trafficking, labor trafficking, or both.[79] The idea behind these measures is to task individuals who work with children with identifying children who might be at risk of trafficking or already exploited so that these children can be referred to the appropriate authorities and receive the services and support they need.[80]

It is important to note that state anti-trafficking laws do not exist in a vacuum. These more recent developments in anti-trafficking law add to an array of state and local laws that are relevant in the context of child trafficking, including both other criminal law and victim services. In terms of criminal law, state and local jurisdictions have well-developed laws on prostitution, pimping, and pandering, as well as criminal laws prohibiting sex with a minor (e.g., statutory rape laws).[81]

In terms of services for child trafficking victims, state laws and systems dealing with child welfare, health care, housing, education, and employment are all implicated by the needs of child trafficking survivors.[82] Many child trafficking survivors have prior involvement with the child welfare system or the juvenile justice system and thus are subject to the court's jurisdiction, which can shape how the young person accesses needed services.[83] Other child survivors must navigate an array of laws and systems. Many of these laws and systems are general in nature rather than specifically identified as programs for trafficking survivors. For example, eligibility for support for health care services is a function of both state regulations and federal law and programs, including Medicaid and the Children's Health Insurance Program (CHIP).[84] Access to educational support, job training, and housing are all critical to survivors' recovery, and for all of these programs, both federal and state laws in each of these areas help determine eligibility and access.[85] These services are potentially beneficial to child survivors of trafficking even though they are not specifically identified as programs for trafficking victims. However, the general nature of these programs creates two important challenges: first, it can make it harder for trafficking survivors and their advocates to identify and secure these services; and second, it might also mean that such services are not tailored to the unique circumstances and needs of trafficking survivors.[86]

Overall, state laws, like their federal counterparts, are still weighted toward criminal justice responses to human trafficking. Much more work is needed to develop effective prevention measures and to meet the needs of survivors.

### Beyond the Government

In addition to federal, state, and local government action, there are hundreds of nongovernmental organizations actively working to address various aspects of child trafficking. Nongovernmental organizations play a number of critical roles, from legislative advocacy to providing direct services for survivors.

Organizations like ECPAT-USA (Ending Child Prostitution and Trafficking), HEAL Trafficking, Polaris Project, Shared Hope International, and many others are actively involved in advocacy efforts at the federal and state levels, pressing legislators to strengthen the law and ensure that adequate resources are available for survivors, and spurring the development of initiatives in various sectors.[87] Nongovernmental organizations also play a major role as services providers, covering a range of issues, including emergency shelter, health care services, job training, and legal services.[88] Nongovernmental organizations and academic institutions also produce critical research that contributes to the evidence base from which more effective policies and programs can be developed. Overall, nongovernmental organizations have been critical to developing momentum to address child trafficking and to providing services to survivors.

## Assessing the Current State of Anti-Trafficking Responses

### Criminal Justice Frameworks

Most professionals working on child trafficking or human trafficking agree that criminal justice frameworks have been the primary driver of anti-trafficking law, policy, and programs.[89] Calls for victim-centered responses have increased in recent years and in many instances have helped shape policy and programs to be more attuned to the experiences and needs of survivors.[90] However, law enforcement-centered responses continue to predominate.

Apprehending traffickers is important. Moreover, law has an expressive function, and criminal law on human trafficking expresses a societal view that such acts are deplorable and unacceptable. Criminal law plays a key role in addressing harms such as human trafficking. That said, while law enforcement is necessary, it is not sufficient.

Law enforcement-centered responses to human trafficking have been the subject of increased criticism, including from victim advocates.[91] Not only does a law enforcement-centered approach risk overlooking victims' needs but criminal law on its own has limited capacity to achieve its own primary goals—holding perpetrators of crimes accountable and deterring those who might consider breaking the law.[92] There has been significant progress since the adoption of the TVPA. In fiscal year 2015 the Department of Justice opened 802 human trafficking investigations, initiated 257 federal human trafficking prosecutions, and secured convictions against 297 traffickers.[93] Given the wide-ranging estimates of prevalence, it is difficult to say with confidence what percentage of human trafficking crimes are identified and investigated by law enforcement. However, even assuming the low end of estimates, the number of convictions is only a small percentage of the total number of trafficking cases.[94] The gap between the prevalence of human trafficking and the number of convictions is not necessarily an indictment of law enforcement efforts (these cases can be complex and challenging).[95] Instead, it indicates that a law enforcement–centered approach by itself cannot eliminate human trafficking.

That a law enforcement–centered approach has limited success will not surprise most public health scholars and professionals. In the public health arena, criminal sanctions have had limited impact in terms of changing behaviors and reducing harm (e.g., in the war on drugs).[96] Beyond public health, other research demonstrates similar limitations of criminal justice responses: the existence of a criminal justice system has a deterrent effect, but enhancing criminal sanctions as a way to maximize deterrence tends to be less effective.[97] What we do see in successful public health campaigns is that when criminal sanctions are employed, they are used in conjunction with other strategies focused on prevention and harm reduction to produce a comprehensive response to a particular harm.[98]

The three-pronged approach to human trafficking—prosecution, protection/assistance, and prevention—makes clear that criminal law is only one component of a successful response.

### The Challenge of Adapting Current Responses

Not only are the prevailing responses limited in key aspects but they create path dependency. Consider the emphasis on criminal law in international law responses to child trafficking. By imposing stronger obligations in their criminal law provisions, the Trafficking Protocol and the Sale of Children Protocol create an "anchoring effect," making it more likely that subsequent efforts will be framed by a criminal law approach.[99] Research on anchoring in the field of negotiation demonstrates that an initial step (such as a first offer in negotiations), whatever it may be, significantly influences and shapes the subsequent course of action and final outcomes (e.g., the remainder of the negotiation and the settlement amount agreed to by the parties).[100] This research helps us understand how, in a similar manner, the initial framing of human trafficking as a criminal law issue has limited the range of responses contemplated when addressing human trafficking generally and child trafficking more specifically. More recently, anti-trafficking professionals have expressed support for more holistic responses to human trafficking. Indeed, there is growing recognition of the importance of engaging other sectors, not just law enforcement and social services but also health care, education, media, the private sector, and others.

Overcoming constraints embedded in current responses requires more than an awareness of current limitations and an interest in other frameworks, including public health frameworks. Research shows how agencies with multiple goals, some of which may conflict, will perform over time, finding that "agencies faced with conflicting tasks will systematically overperform on the tasks that are easier to measure and have higher incentives, and underperform on the tasks that are harder to measure and have lower incentives."[101] In responding to child trafficking, there have been calls in recent years for law enforcement to adopt a so-called victim-centered approach. Although some progress has been made, this research helps us understand that over time law enforcement and prosecutors are likely to prioritize arrests, prosecutions, and convictions of perpetrators over survivors' recovery-related considerations, given their own departmental expertise and the incentives and pressures they face.[102]

The early bias toward focusing on sex trafficking at the expense of labor trafficking provides an important lesson. The early focus on sex trafficking was reflected in the prosecutions and convictions of traffickers globally.

For example, in 2008 approximately 6 percent of prosecutions (312 of 5,212) and just over 3 percent of convictions (104 of 2,983) globally for human trafficking were for labor trafficking cases.[103] During the Obama administration, there was much greater attention to labor trafficking and a global push to address both labor and sex trafficking. Yet the on-the-ground impact has been limited. In 2015, while the number of prosecutions and convictions increased significantly, the percentages of labor trafficking cases remained very small: 4.5 percent of prosecutions (857 of 18,930) and 6.8 percent of convictions (456 of 6,609).[104]

All of this should not suggest that change is impossible. Rather, it indicates that adopting new frameworks and changing strategy will require nuanced attention to how law, policy, and programs reinforce existing priorities at the expense of improving responses. It will require attention also to institutional restrictions and incentives. Law and policy can play a critical role in advancing anti-trafficking responses, but they must be evidence-based and attuned to existing constraints.

## Conclusion

The early work in developing law and policy to respond to human trafficking was critical. An elaborate body of law now exists at the international, national, and local levels. Despite these developments, critical questions remain about the effectiveness of this law and policy. Subsequent chapters explore how public health thinking and methodologies might strengthen law and policy responses to child trafficking and spur the development of programs that not only effectively assist survivors but also prevent the harm from occurring in the first place.

PART II  **THE PUBLIC HEALTH APPROACH**

# Public Health Methods and Perspectives

ALTHOUGH CRIMINAL JUSTICE frameworks have driven much of the prevailing response to child trafficking and to human trafficking more broadly, the prior chapters reveal that health care and other sectors—from education to the private sector—have an important role to play. Securing the involvement of all sectors is important. However, optimizing responses to child trafficking is not merely about increasing the number of individuals engaged in anti-trafficking work. New strategies and frameworks are critical. Public health insights and strategies can significantly advance efforts to prevent, identify, and respond appropriately to child trafficking.[1]

Existing evidence supports understanding and treating the trafficking of human beings as a public health issue. Its health consequences are significant, and the scale of human trafficking, with perhaps millions of victims globally, suggests population-level implications. Moreover, given public health's decades of work on violence prevention,[2] applying that public health knowledge to child trafficking makes sense. Viewing child trafficking from a public health perspective offers important benefits. First, it enables anti-trafficking initiatives to draw upon public health methodologies that have been effective in addressing other complex social problems. Second, a public health perspective can advance understanding of the root and systemic causes of child trafficking, and we can use that knowledge to design more effective responses.

In this chapter, we discuss four important "tools" from public health that can advance efforts to prevent child trafficking. We then explore how public health perspectives and experience can improve our understanding of the underlying causes of these harms.

The public health approach discussed in this chapter provides the framework for the remaining chapters in part II. Chapter 5 investigates risk factors, which are relevant both to ensuring an in-depth understanding of child trafficking and its causes and to developing more effective responses across all sectors. Then, in chapters 6 and 7 we use the health care sector as a case study to explore how responses to child trafficking can be strengthened. We begin first by examining the value of a public health framework and what it offers for child trafficking.

## The Value of Public Health Methods

A public health approach would bolster efforts to combat child trafficking by its focus on and experience in four areas. First, a public health approach emphasizes the importance of relying on evidence-based research to develop and implement relevant law, policy, and programs.[3] Evidence-based research helps show us what interventions will work and which ones will not work or will even be harmful. Second, public health approaches center on prevention.[4] Thus, immunization programs aim to reach populations before they are struck by disease so that individuals do not suffer any harm, just as we should aim to reach vulnerable children before they are trafficked. Third, public health seeks to understand and confront the underlying causes of adverse health outcomes rather than settle for band-aid solutions.[5] A public health approach employs the socio-ecological model to identify and address individual, relationship, community, and societal factors that increase risk of or lead to adverse health consequences and, conversely, the factors or interventions at each level that can prevent or mitigate harm.[6] Among other things, as we highlight in this chapter, this can include exploring the individual, community, and societal attitudes and behaviors that increase the risk of harm.[7] Fourth, public health methodologies aim to engage all individuals and groups that can play a role in supporting an intervention to address a particular health issue, including the target population. Thus public health strategies can enhance efforts to build a comprehensive, integrated response to child trafficking.[8]

### Evidence-Based Responses

Public health demands, and relies upon, evidence-based research.[9] Adopting a public health approach to child trafficking would compel the development of evidence-based responses to child trafficking.

In developing a scientific approach to violence prevention, public health experts have identified four critical steps: (1) defining the problem, not merely by counting cases but also by collecting "information on the demographic characteristics of the persons involved, the temporal and geographic characteristics of the incident, the victim/perpetrator relationship, and the severity and cost of the injury"; (2) identifying risk factors; (3) developing interventions based on information collected and testing those interventions; and (4) implementing proven interventions and assessing cost-effectiveness.[10] All these steps are relevant to the child trafficking context.[11]

Yet this methodology for developing effective responses to health risks differs from many of the responses to human trafficking undertaken to date. Although many individuals in the field of human trafficking work tirelessly to apprehend perpetrators and aid survivors, most policies and programs have emerged from a sporadic trial-and-error approach rather than from systematic research and evaluation aimed at identifying and developing promising or best practices.[12] Today, a growing number of professionals working on human trafficking recognize the importance of program evaluation and evidence-based research.[13] And recent legislation is also starting to reflect that understanding of the importance of evidence-based research. For example, the Justice for Victims of Trafficking Act of 2015 included a mandate that the Department of Justice enter into a contract with a nongovernmental organization (which could be an academic institution) "to conduct periodic evaluations of grants made [pursuant to the act] to determine the impact and effectiveness of [funded] programs."[14] Although these are positive trends, we must acknowledge that research on human trafficking, and child trafficking more specifically, is still in its early stages. Accurate data are lacking on many aspects of human trafficking, making it difficult to get a true picture of the nature and scope of the problem or to develop a body of knowledge of which interventions work for which populations. Without an accurate understanding of the problem, survivor assistance programs and law enforcement initiatives might not be well targeted, and prevention efforts might have little or no impact.

In recent years, several studies have begun to address human trafficking more systematically. Their findings challenge some conventional wisdom on the issue and demonstrate the value of and need for further evidence-based research. For example, a persistent belief about human trafficking is that traffickers are men and the vast majority of victims are women and children.[15] However, it is not only men who are engaged in the business of trafficking. Women are also involved in trafficking operations, often as recruiters.[16] In research in Southeast Europe, the International Organization for Migration found that more than 40 percent of recruiters were women.[17] Thus, a law enforcement initiative or prevention strategy that presumes traffickers are all men will miss opportunities to identify and apprehend female perpetrators and uncover trafficking networks. Adding to the complexity of identifying human trafficking is the fact that the dichotomy between perpetrator and victim is overstated in some cases; some victims end up participating in the exploitation of others (e.g., when female victims are compelled or convinced to recruit or "manage" younger victims, or when youth serve as transporters of victims).[18] A more nuanced understanding of the complex dynamics of trafficking emerges from rigorous research on the topic.[19]

By relying on evidence-based research, police and immigration officers can better tailor their law enforcement strategies to account for the realities of the situation on the ground. In addition, drawing on this research, prevention programs can educate at-risk children about the realities of the risks of trafficking, including, for example, the fact that women, including women they know, might seek to recruit and exploit them.[20]

Similarly, the dominant narrative on trafficking continues to portray victims as women and girls who are victims of sex trafficking.[21] This construct of trafficking shapes the responses that are developed.[22] For example, shelters for trafficking survivors are a vital tertiary prevention program, as safe, secure housing can reduce vulnerability and the attendant risk of being retrafficked. Given popular narratives on trafficking victims, it is not surprising that a study of shelters for trafficking survivors, which identified 529 beds in the United States designated exclusively for human trafficking survivors, found that only two beds were reserved exclusively for men or boys and none were "exclusively designated for labor trafficking survivors."[23] Some beds were available to both males and females and survivors of labor or sex trafficking, but even if those beds are included in the results, still only a minority of the supply of shelter beds are available to males or labor trafficking survivors.[24] The point is not to suggest that beds should be taken away from girls and made available to boys. Girls are at risk, and services for girls need to be expanded considerably.[25] But boys are victimized too.[26] In some studies, nearly half the victims identified were boys.[27] And transgender as well as cisgender youth are at risk, so appropriately tailored services need to be available to all youth who are at risk or exploited.[28]

Evidence-based research helps us understand that although girls are at risk, they are not the only ones. A more nuanced understanding of the problem can help lead to improved prevention programs that reach cisgender and transgender boys and girls and to more effective assistance programs that are available to all youth who need them.

A better knowledge base on human trafficking and the unique characteristics of child trafficking can help ensure better-trained health care professionals, social workers, law enforcement officers, educators, and others so that communities do a better job of identifying and intervening earlier in the lives of at-risk and exploited youth. Related, evidence-based research can bolster our understanding of risk factors for all children so that more effective prevention strategies can be developed (see chapter 5).

The research discussed above demonstrates the importance of understanding the true nature of child trafficking. As research on trafficking develops, anti-trafficking law, policy, and programs must build on this research. As Robert Freeman-Longo writes about law-based interventions, "Passing legislation should follow a process by which legislators research the issue, have some supportive evidence that the law will work, and are willing to allocate funds at state and federal levels to ensure states will carry out and uphold the law."[29] The same holds true for anti-trafficking programs and services. They should be evidence-based and systematically evaluated so that we can learn from what we have tried, distinguish between successful and unsuccessful interventions (including disaggregating findings so we know what works well for which youth populations), and continually revise laws, policies, and programs until we have developed truly successful interventions. And even after we identify best practices, evaluation should continue to ensure that they are still successful.

As noted above, public health methodologies incorporate four processes that facilitate development of effective measures to address child trafficking: (1) public health surveillance, (2) risk group identification, (3) risk factor exploration, and (4) program implementation and evaluation.[30]

Surveillance is a key component of public health, providing the data needed to understand health risks, properly educate the public, and design appropriate interventions.[31] Dating back to the nineteenth century, state laws and regulations have required doctors to track and report on contagious diseases in order to prevent major outbreaks.[32] Public health surveillance constitutes "ongoing, systematic collection, analysis, and interpretation of health data essential to the planning, implementation, and evaluation of public health practice, closely integrated with the timely dissemination of these data to those who need to know."[33] Policymakers and other professionals can use these data to ensure that sufficient resources —human, financial, and informational—are directed to the areas where the needs are greatest.

Building a system of data collection, analysis, and dissemination can help facilitate the development of targeted prevention strategies that identify at-risk individuals before they are exploited. It can help direct relevant training to those professionals working in areas with a high prevalence of trafficking so that key personnel have the capacity to identify vulnerable or trafficked children and the skill set to intervene appropriately. Such a system could also help ensure that services are well tailored to meet the needs of survivors. Legislation plays a key role in all of this by creating the mandate for public health surveillance on this issue and authorizing the funding necessary to conduct the surveillance, provide training to key personnel, and develop tailored services for survivors. But legislation alone is not sufficient. There must be a commitment to implement and continually strengthen any laws, policies, and programs.

Applied to child trafficking, public health surveillance methods can provide important data that can form the basis of more effective anti-trafficking laws, policies, and programs. And we are beginning to see efforts on this front. The Administration for Children and Families of the Department of Health and Human Services has been developing a Human Trafficking Data Collection Project.[34] In June 2018 the Centers for Disease Control and Prevention (CDC) added new data collection fields to the ICD-10-CM List of Diseases and Injuries.[35] This step by the CDC will enable hospitals and health care providers to distinguish human trafficking victims from victims of other forms of abuse and violence, which will enable us to obtain a clearer picture of prevalence in particular locales and who is suffering harm. To develop surveillance of human trafficking, we can also build on existing systems. For example, at the international level, the International Labour Organization has extensive knowledge and experience with data collection on child labor,[36] which can be drawn upon to improve data collection on all forms of trafficking of children. All of these steps provide opportunities to improve our understanding of the problem of human trafficking.

Second is risk group identification. Progress on risk group identification in the area of human trafficking is greatly needed. As the 2013 Institute of Medicine and National Research Council report on sex trafficking of children confirmed, the disaggregated data on child sex trafficking are minimal.[37] And even less is known about child labor trafficking.[38] In public health, risk group identification includes identification not only of individual risk factors but also of relationship, community, and societal risk factors.[39] Risk group identification would provide opportunities for early intervention that could prevent exploitation of at-risk individuals. Illustrative risk factors for child trafficking are shown in figure 4.1 (see page 96), and they and other risk factors are discussed in detail in the next chapter.

Third, risk factor exploration includes "the analytic exploration of potentially causative risk factors for the [harm] as suggested by the nature of the high risk population and other research."[40] In the context of child trafficking, exploration of risk factors and causality is vital to going beyond laws, policies, and programs based on anecdotal evidence. Understanding better what makes a person vulnerable to being trafficked is essential to developing effective responses.[41] The research base is developing, as discussed in chapter 5, but there is still much more work to do.

Fourth and finally, evidence-based research requires monitoring and evaluation of laws, policies, and programs. Public health programs typically incorporate monitoring and evaluation.[42] Monitoring and evaluation components of public health programs enable policymakers and stakeholders to distinguish between *doing something* and *doing something effective*.

Research on child obesity highlights this important distinction. Child obesity has received increased attention in recent years and is recognized as a significant public health issue with both short- and long-term repercussions.[43] School-based measures are a key component of responses aimed at countering the problem, given the substantial amount of time most children spend in school.[44] However, public health research reveals that not all school nutrition programs are created equal. For example, one study compared students in three groups—those attending schools with no nutrition program, those at schools with a nutrition program, and those at schools with a nutrition program that is part of a coordinated program that incorporates the CDC recommendations for school-based healthy eating programs.[45] It will not be a surprise to learn that students in this last group exhibited significantly lower rates of overweight and obesity.[46] Perhaps surprisingly, however, students from schools that had another nutrition program did not have substantially healthier body weights than students from schools with no nutrition program.[47] In other words, simply having a school nutrition program might not be sufficient; such a program must be based on proven methods.[48]

Similarly, in the context of child trafficking, doing something (e.g., adopting new criminal laws or requiring signs about human trafficking to be posted in certain locales) may or may not produce any real benefit for children. In most cases, we do not know the answer because there has been little or no evaluation of the impact of new laws and programs on the prevalence of trafficking or on the well-being of survivors over time.[49] Recognition of the importance of evaluation is gaining traction. The 2008 and 2013 Trafficking Victims Protection Reauthorization Acts called for improved monitoring and evaluation of federal and state efforts.[50] The Justice for Victims of Trafficking Act of 2015 similarly acknowledges the need for evaluation of programs.[51] Since then, the federal government has emphasized evaluation more in its anti-trafficking work.[52] A public health approach helps ensure that monitoring and evaluation are built into all laws, policies, and programs so that rigorous research can inform the further development of anti-trafficking initiatives.

Rigorous research would also include monitoring and evaluation of law, policies, and programs for unintended consequences. For example, interventions that aim to address child exploitation by raising the minimum age for certain employment might protect some children from unhealthy or harmful workplaces, but it could also increase the risk of exploitation of other family members or push younger children into riskier informal sector work.[53] These examples do not mean that preventing children from working in certain settings is a bad idea; rather, addressing these issues requires accounting for potential unintended consequences so that the end result is not more harm. Too often, law prohibiting certain activities does not come along with resources to provide education and job training and other support to children and their families so that they can avoid worse outcomes.

With respect to all aspects of the problem of human trafficking, there is benefit to be gained from deepening our understanding of the problem, its root causes, how it impacts different populations, and the effectiveness of responses. Public health methodologies, with their emphasis on rigorous research and their experience evaluating responses to violence and other harms, provide a model for advancing our capacity to address child trafficking.

### Emphasis on Prevention

Public health places prevention at the forefront of its programming.[54] Whether confronting infectious diseases or violence, public health recognizes that prevention must be the goal. More than twenty-five years ago, a team of public health experts examined the US approach to violence prevention, finding that "America's predominant response to violence has been a reactive one—to pour resources into deterring and incapacitating violent offenders by apprehending, arresting, adjudicating, and incarcerating them through the criminal justice system."[55] Despite the passage of time, the prevailing approach to child trafficking reflects a similar mindset—largely reactive rather than proactive and emphasizing a criminal law framework.

Although a law enforcement–centric model is built on the assumption that criminal law sanctions deter crime and thus will prevent future exploitation of children, evidence-based research raises questions about criminal law's capacity to change behavior.[56] Evidence suggests that a law prohibiting specific conduct does have some deterrent effect but that increasing penalties (a strategy that has been employed at the federal and state levels in the human trafficking context over the past decade) has limited additional impact.[57] In other words, criminal justice methods cannot end trafficking on their own. In a best-case scenario, a criminal justice approach still deals with many cases of child trafficking only after some harm occurs.

A public health perspective sheds light on the limitations of current responses. In the public health arena, few would consider it good policy if the government's approach to infectious diseases was to wait for an outbreak and then investigate and hold responsible those individuals who caused the loss of life. No, success occurs when a vaccination program is fully implemented, communities are then protected from disease, and individuals do not suffer harm. Similarly, people would be troubled if in response to the threat of bioterrorism, the government did not focus on preparedness but instead told the public not to worry because following any bioterrorist attack, it would seek to hold perpetrators responsible and that would serve to deter future attacks. No, prevention and preparedness are what make sense in the bioterrorism context. That is the public health approach.

*Success* from a public health perspective results from fully immunizing a community so that no one gets ill, or from a well-prepared and coordinated response team acting quickly to minimize the impact of a bioterrorist attack or contain a contagious disease. As with other public health issues, with child trafficking prevention must be the goal. We should continue to pursue and apprehend traffickers, and we must expand services for survivors, but we also must do more to prevent these harms from occurring in the first place. Adopting a public health approach to child trafficking would help prioritize prevention.

Developing successful prevention initiatives would require an examination of the root and systemic causes of child trafficking. It would mean, in part, taking a scientific approach to identifying why certain individuals are more vulnerable to being trafficked and why there is such demand for the goods and services produced by trafficked persons. In short, a public health approach shifts away from "a focus limited to reacting to violence to a focus on changing the social, behavioral, and environmental factors that cause violence."[58]

As public health's ultimate goal is prevention, to ensure the best prevention model possible, public health methodologies require an evidence-based assessment of both the problem and any prevention strategies. The social-ecological model, which is employed, for example, by the CDC in its violence prevention work, contemplates the "complex interplay between individual, relationship, community, and societal factors" and offers one possible methodology for developing trafficking prevention measures.[59] Such a prevention program would look at (1) individual risk factors; (2) relationships that might increase the risk of being trafficked, including those with peer groups and partners; (3) the role of community settings, such as schools and neighborhoods; and (4) societal factors, including social and cultural norms.[60]

Employing the social-ecological model to address child trafficking would require the development of strategies that address each of the four levels—individual, relationship (including family members and peers), community, and societal factors. It would necessitate accounting for the ways the different levels of the socio-ecological model interact with one another, either to further heighten vulnerability or to strengthen resilience and protective factors. It would also require an understanding of the myriad types of child trafficking exploitation experiences and recognition that these various situations may demand different, tailored responses.

One example of an approach that would account for all four levels of the socio-ecological model might look as follows: At the individual level, child trafficking prevention strategies might include education and life skills training for youth.[61] It could draw upon research on individual risk factors to focus interventions in particular on those young people with heightened vulnerability. Individual-level interventions could include programs that help empower vulnerable individuals, build resilience, and reduce the risk of exploitation by providing vulnerable youth with needed information and tools and by addressing individual risk factors. For example, one study of trafficked children found that all the children interviewed felt that they did not have the information they needed to avoid being trafficked.[62] Schools might offer one venue for both educating vulnerable children about how to minimize risk and intervening early to assist and support at-risk youth. A school-based intervention could be an effective means of reaching some youth, but we need to keep in mind that those young people who are not in school may be among the most vulnerable. Thus, a school-based program by itself will not be sufficient. Partnerships between schools and health care professionals could develop educational programs and other interventions that provide youth with the information they need to reduce their vulnerability. Further, relationships with health care providers can help meet the needs of both young people in school and those no longer in school either because they left school early or graduated (see chapters 6 and 7).

At the relationship level, prevention might include mentoring and peer programs and other interventions that encourage the development of healthy, supportive relationships.[63] Research suggests that homeless youth —who are at heightened risk of trafficking (see chapter 5)—are less likely to be trafficked if they have a supportive adult in their life.[64] More generally, mentoring programs have shown positive benefits; they can help children stay in school, which can reduce the risk of exploitation.[65] Mentoring programs also encourage positive relationships and, correspondingly, positive outcomes. One study found that adolescents with a mentor are "fifty-three percent more likely to advance to the next level of education" than adolescents who do not have a mentor.[66] Simultaneously, mentoring potentially reduces the risk of exposure to negative relationships and unhealthy or high-risk behavior, including drug and alcohol use.[67] Mentoring is but one of many potential options for interventions that may address relationship dynamics that affect the risk of being trafficked.

Third, community-level prevention measures would look at vulnerabilities created or accentuated by schools, neighborhoods, and other settings in which youth spend their time. Creating safer neighborhoods where there are more positive opportunities for young people is a major task, one that can take significant time and resources. But there are other steps that can address community-level factors. Such measures can include programs "designed to impact the climate, processes, and policies in a given system. Social norm and social marketing campaigns are often used to foster community climates that promote healthy relationships."[68] Anti-trafficking initiatives could benefit from social marketing campaigns to raise awareness about the problem and counter views, behaviors, and practices that both heighten vulnerability and foster the demand for exploited persons. Addressing the latter, for example, might necessitate targeted messaging to populations that could play more constructive roles in this area. These interventions could both reduce demand and enhance community-based protective factors.

For example, both sex trafficking and labor trafficking often occur along major trucking routes.[69] Some truckers visit commercial sex workers while on the road.[70] One component of a public health strategy could be to develop a targeted campaign to help transform long-distance truckers from a population that at times contributes to the demand for sex trafficking to one that can help exploited, runaway, and homeless youth access safe havens and obtain the assistance and services they need. Truckers could be educated about the issue of child sex trafficking, their role in fostering demand, and the harm adolescent victims suffer. Such a public health campaign would inform truckers about what works to prevent the sex trafficking of minors, how they can contribute to prevention efforts, and appropriate steps to take if they believe they have identified an exploited youth at a truck stop or elsewhere. Similarly, truckers could be educated to spot labor trafficking in agricultural settings, the construction industry, and many other sectors that intersect with the long-distance trucking industry. Truckers should be made aware of entities to call and given phone numbers or information about places where young people can receive services and support. They also should be made to understand the consequences for themselves if they are involved in trafficking of minors either as a trafficker or as a purchaser of services. With appropriate training, a trucker might choose to help secure safe transport for a child to a local police station and/or social service agency where the child could receive assistance.[71] Such a program could be developed through a public-private partnership involving the relevant law enforcement, social services agencies, and private sector entities.

Further consideration is needed to develop effective, targeted messaging that reduces demand for exploitative services and reduces the vulnerability of at-risk individuals. And these activities must also be evaluated so that we can ensure that they are having a positive impact and avoiding adverse unintended consequences. However, these and other community-based interventions show the value of a public health approach. Rather than relying solely on an individual to avoid harm—which may be an unfair burden given the number of risk factors some youth experience—the socio-ecological model compels us to identify the opportunities at every level to confront the problem.

Finally, societal-level prevention measures include addressing discrimination, poverty, and other social ills that leave certain individuals vulnerable and devalued. Interventions at this level would include confronting "the health, economic, educational and social policies that help to maintain economic or social inequalities between groups in society."[72] With respect to child trafficking, addressing the root and systemic causes—including poverty, lack of economic and social rights, discrimination, structural violence, and other factors—is essential to making meaningful progress in preventing child trafficking. For example, marginalized individuals, including children, are often at heightened risk of exploitation, including trafficking.[73] Poor children whose health and education rights are impeded are more vulnerable to trafficking.[74] Without consistent access to health care, children's health needs are often unmet.[75] These unmet health needs may cause children to miss school and fall behind their peers, and they can increase the risk of dropping out of school.[76] Youth who do not finish school enter the workforce at a younger age with fewer skills, leaving them at heightened risk of a broad array of exploitative practices, including trafficking.[77] Similarly, discrimination, stigma, and biases all serve to create barriers to individuals' full realization of their rights and opportunities, pushing primarily minorities, women, and children to the margins and increasing their risk of exploitation.[78]

Tackling any one of these systemic issues is not easy, and tackling them in the aggregate is harder still. If, however, governments and communities want to reduce the prevalence of child trafficking, they must begin to confront these issues. It is important that policymakers recognize the significant cost of the failure to address root causes. Continuing along the path of dealing with child trafficking after the harm occurs will require significant expenditures on investigations and prosecutions of perpetrators, treatment for trafficking survivors, and long-term costs associated with correctional facilities (to house perpetrators) and/or social services programs that perpetrators and some victims might utilize for years to come.

Equally important, governments may begin to address root causes with a number of relatively low-cost interventions. For example, school lunch programs, which are relatively low-cost, have been found to foster better attendance in certain poorer communities and simultaneously reduce child malnutrition, enabling children to perform better, stay in school, and

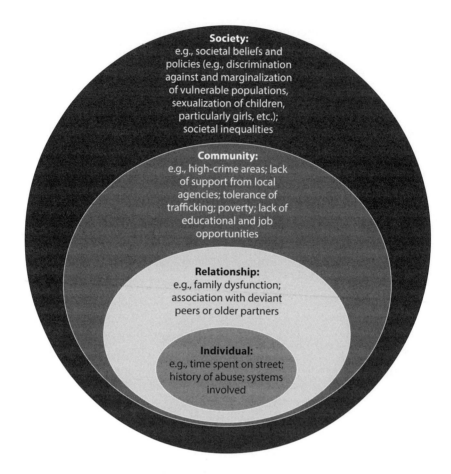

Figure 4.1. The socio-ecological model of risk factors for child trafficking. The diagram includes examples of risk factors at each level. It is not intended to be comprehensive. See chapter 5 for more detailed discussion of risk factors.

avoid harmful situations.[79] Further research is needed to determine what the most cost-effective interventions are in the area of child trafficking and which interventions work best for particular target groups. And as we discuss later, ultimately a comprehensive, integrated strategy will be needed. Paying attention to root and systemic causes in conjunction with shorter-term measures (such as the targeted campaign for truckers) and attempting to mitigate the impact of discrimination, marginalization, and the denial of economic and social rights increases the likelihood that measures developed to prevent child trafficking might actually make a difference in the lives of vulnerable populations.

### Addressing Underlying Causes: Case Study on Changing Harmful Attitudes and Behaviors

A third area of focus—and strength—of a public health approach is identifying and confronting the underlying causes of adverse health outcomes.[80] In a public health response, this occurs at all levels of the socio-ecological model—individual, relationship, community, and societal. In practice, this often means confronting attitudes and behaviors that underlie the adverse health outcome. While all root causes must be addressed, we focus here on underlying attitudes and behaviors as a case study to show how public health strategies can help policymakers and other professionals to understand and address the upstream causes of a public health issue.

A core component of a public health approach is first to understand individual, community, and societal attitudes that increase risk or spur unhealthy behavior and then to work to transform these attitudes with the end goal of fostering healthier behaviors.[81] To be clear, this does not mean blaming at-risk and exploited youth for their actions. Moreover, we recognize that if a public health intervention changes a risk group's views or behaviors but does not address why those individuals were vulnerable in the first place, it is likely to have little meaningful impact. Instead, we mean that such a campaign must target changes at the individual, institutional, community, and societal levels that will achieve healthier outcomes in target populations.[82] In the context of child trafficking, it means addressing institutional, community, and societal beliefs and behaviors that foster or tolerate the exploitation of young people. It means addressing demand. And it means working with at-risk youth in a supportive, culturally competent way both to reduce risky behavior and to provide necessary support —e.g., housing assistance, education, job training, counseling, and other needed services—to enhance resilience and protective factors.

One element of a public health response would be to incorporate public health focused social marketing campaigns aimed at raising awareness of risky behaviors and their potential health impacts, addressing community and environmental factors,[83] confronting societal attitudes that contribute to the problem, and ultimately fostering healthier choices at all levels by individuals and institutions whose actions implicate child trafficking.

Social marketing and advertising campaigns have had success in addressing a range of public health issues, including youth smoking, obesity/diet, and seatbelt use.[84] For example, targeted public health media campaigns aimed at preventing youth from taking up smoking have proven successful, with one study finding that "the percentage of youths who held anti-tobacco attitudes and beliefs increased by an amount that ranged from 6.6% to 26.4% during the first 10 months of the ['truth' anti-smoking] campaign."[85] Moreover, as public health media campaigns have employed these methods for many years now, there is a substantial body of research that indicates what makes for an effective campaign.[86] Public health experts have learned and identified key steps, including strategies for "formulat[ing] effective objectives, identify[ing] target audiences, [and] develop[ing] culturally competent messages."[87]

In the context of child trafficking, the public is inundated with messaging that both serves to counteract the deterrent effect of criminal sanctions and fosters tolerance for such exploitation. At a societal level, discrimination—whether based on race, ethnicity, religion, gender, sexual orientation, or other factors—operates to devalue certain individuals, leading governments and other stakeholders to minimize or ignore harms that certain people suffer.[88] This othering and its attendant devaluation of certain groups simultaneously serve to create a myopic view of the self (or dominant group in society) as virtuous and without fault.[89] Yet the reality is that we all contribute to human trafficking. Consumerism and materialism drive demand for low-cost goods, which in turn incentivizes employers to exploit labor forces in order to produce products cheaply and maximize profits.[90]

Societal attitudes also enable sex trafficking. Examining sexual abuse in the United States, Freeman-Longo writes that "most sexual abuse is illegal, but there are aspects of our culture, lifestyle, and sexual interests and behaviors that are abusive of sexuality, and yet they are legal."[91] Similarly, aspects of culture and lifestyle in the United States facilitate child trafficking. Sexualization and objectification of girls feed demand for the sex industry, the end destination for many trafficked women and children.[92] The lives of pimps and exploiters are frequently glorified; for example, in 2006 the song "It's Hard Out Here for a Pimp" was honored with the Academy Award for Best Original Song.

Discrimination, materialism, consumerism, sexualization of youth, and other significant issues are not just reflected in attitudes and behaviors; they are also embedded in societal structures. In short, these are challenging issues to confront. But we have to start. Creating awareness about these underlying, ingrained attitudes and how they manifest in behaviors is the first step. That greater awareness can lead to improved recognition of how societal institutions and structures preserve inequality and leave many youth and their communities vulnerable. Public health media campaigns are not a singular solution; indeed the socio-ecological model used in public health makes that clear. However, policymakers and anti-trafficking advocates can draw upon the experience of public health professionals in developing strategies to address these underlying beliefs and behaviors so that we can begin to move toward a more just society in which the exploitation of certain individuals is no longer tolerated.

Public health campaigns aimed at reducing violence have identified several essential component goals.[93] First, public health campaigns must help raise awareness of the nature and magnitude of the problem.[94] Today, there is increased attention to the problem of child trafficking, but still significant portions of the US population are either unaware of the problem or unaware that it is an issue in the United States.[95] Moreover, much of the popular narrative on human trafficking misrepresents the issue, creating a skewed understanding that can lead to overlooking victims or misunderstanding the nature of the crime and the factors that contribute to it.[96] In short, both broader awareness and a deeper understanding of human trafficking are needed.

Second, public health campaigns must convey to individuals and communities information about what works to prevent the harm and how they can contribute to prevention efforts.[97] Thus, policymakers and anti-trafficking advocates must identify steps that individuals and communities can take to reduce the prevalence of child trafficking. In turn, laws and policies can be adopted to provide the support communities need to take these steps or even incentives to do so. Public health campaigns can inform choices that are relevant to child trafficking, just as they have done successfully with other health issues.[98]

Equally important, research on public health media campaigns shows us what strategies are likely to be successful. For example, what the campaign seeks to do, that is, whether it seeks to prevent behavior, promote behavior, or cease behavior, makes a difference.[99] Meta-analyses of existing research suggest that "campaigns promoting the commencement of a new [desirable] behavior will have a greater average effect size than campaigns promoting prevention of an undesirable behavior, which, in turn, will have a greater average effect size than campaigns promoting the cessation of an existing undesirable behavior."[100] As commencement campaigns appear to have greater success in shaping behavior than cessation campaigns,[101] anti-trafficking programs might be more successful if they developed campaigns seeking to persuade the public to adopt a positive practice. For example, spurring the public to take small steps to inform themselves about prospective purchases (and whether trafficked labor was used to manufacture such products) could be successful if relevant information is made readily accessible (e.g., for internet purchases).

Some research has shown that public health campaigns aimed at behavior change produce only modest results.[102] Leslie Snyder and her co-authors reported that campaigns to change public behavior on average produced a change in behavior on the part of 8 percent of the population, although campaigns with enforcement messages changed behavior in 17 percent of the target population.[103] However, programs that produce even modest changes, when scaled up, can still result in thousands or possibly millions of people changing their behavior to avoid activities that foster exploitation of children.[104] The idea is not that one single intervention will "solve" the problem of child trafficking but that we must look for all the potential ways we can act to address trafficking.

Further, public health research reveals that regardless of the behavior change sought, targeted campaigns are more successful, as evidenced by the important role played by targeted public health campaigns aimed at preventing youth from taking up smoking.[105] Therefore, public health campaigns to address child trafficking must identify target populations on both the supply side and the demand side of the equation. Such an approach would include creating targeted campaigns that prioritize reaching the most vulnerable individuals to reduce vulnerability to trafficking and developing focal populations for campaigns aimed at reducing demand (e.g., individuals who seek out commercial sex or certain goods produced by exploited labor).

Third, public health campaigns must "mobilize individuals, entities, and communities" to take action.[106] To a limited extent, heightened awareness of human trafficking in the United States has already begun to mobilize organizations and communities. Federal and state legislators continue to add to a growing body of law aimed at addressing human trafficking, and nonprofit organizations continue to build out training programs and services for survivors. These efforts, however, must expand beyond the usual participants (e.g., social services agencies and organizations) and mobilize individuals and organizations across a much broader terrain. Child trafficking affects almost all sectors of society (see chapter 1). Anti-trafficking campaigns must provide individuals and entities in all sectors with clear steps that each can undertake to advance efforts to reduce the prevalence of human trafficking.

Fourth, public health media campaigns must inform individuals about the specific steps that must be taken to ensure positive outcomes and success in preventing harm.[107] To date, most of the focus in the context of child trafficking has been on law enforcement initiatives and programs to assist survivors, both of which are interventions that take place after the harm occurs. There is minimal empirical evidence on what works to prevent child trafficking.[108] The results from public health campaigns can shed light on what might work in the context of child trafficking. For example, research demonstrates that effective campaigns need to "ensure that a high-threat appeal is accompanied by an equally high-efficacy (or greater) message."[109] In other words, campaigns must be designed to create a fear or threat associated with the high-risk behavior and be accompanied by a message that provides a viable alternative practice that is constructive.[110] Developing such strategies for prevention of child trafficking will be challenging, but public health offers a roadmap for what types of interventions can work. In short, there is much to learn from public health strategies to reduce harm and promote health and well-being. Anti-smoking campaigns have had varying levels of success in advancing measures such as getting warning labels on tobacco products and ensuring equal space for anti-smoking advertisements.[111] The success of these programs depends on their design as well as on other factors,[112] but the field of public health has extensive experience grappling with prevention on a range of issues, from tobacco-related harms to intimate partner violence. And, to reiterate, a key lesson is that a threat or scare tactic alone may not be very effective; it must be accompanied by clear messaging on available options that would produce a better outcome.

Fifth, public health media campaigns must be designed and implemented so that researchers can assess their effectiveness and identify best practices.[113] As discussed earlier in this chapter, monitoring and evaluation are essential to developing reliable evidence upon which effective prevention strategies can be built, and they must be incorporated into anti-trafficking initiatives.

Sixth and finally, public health campaigns must comply with relevant ethical guidelines. As public health campaigns aim to change attitudes and behaviors, they may have a paternalistic component. Public health also depends heavily on the public's trust.[114] Public health campaigns to address child trafficking must be developed and implemented in a way that is ethical, maintains the public's trust, and ensures appropriate respect for individuals' privacy and autonomy.

Human trafficking is a harm entirely created by human beings and therefore is driven in part by societal attitudes and behaviors that tolerate or encourage such exploitation. At a very basic level, it occurs because certain individuals are devalued and harm to them is accepted in pursuit of greater profits or cheaper goods and services. Modifying harmful or risky beliefs and behaviors is crucial to fostering healthier outcomes.[115] Public health campaigns demonstrate that efforts to foster behavior change must utilize a multifaceted approach that addresses individual, relationship, community, and societal factors. Moreover, public awareness campaigns and education aimed at behavior change cannot operate in isolation. Campaigns aimed at changing individual behavior work better when coupled with strategies that address community and environmental factors.[116] Experience from past public health campaigns reveals that success is most likely to be achieved when public awareness and education initiatives are "coupled with other incentives—criminal liability, taxes, use restrictions—as they have been in campaigns against smoking, drunk driving, and non-use of seatbelts."[117] Policymakers, government agencies, and nongovernmental organizations must draw upon this extensive body of evidence and experience from the public health arena to develop effective strategies for addressing the underlying societal views and behaviors that facilitate human trafficking.

### Engaging All Essential Partners

Public health campaigns, with their focus on prevention, pay significant attention to identifying vital partners, engaging affected communities, and fostering community coordination and preparedness.

To begin, public health campaigns typically focus on identifying all essential partners. Public health's approach to violence has focused on "establishing links with each of the sectors that figures in violence prevention: education, labor, public housing, media, business, medicine, and criminal justice."[118] In the child trafficking context, many initiatives rely primarily upon law enforcement, immigration and customs officials, and social services organizations. Health care professionals have become increasingly engaged in anti-trafficking efforts, while other sectors, notably education, media, and the private sector, have joined selected initiatives.

Preventing child trafficking will require a comprehensive, integrated response. As earlier chapters detailed, health care facilities may offer one of the few windows of opportunity to identify trafficked children because traffickers will bring their victims to emergency rooms or other health clinics for necessary health care, not wanting to lose their investment.[119] And further upstream, teachers and other school personnel have opportunities to prevent child trafficking by identifying at-risk children before they are exploited.[120] In addition, many entities and sectors currently facilitate (often unknowingly) the trafficking of persons, including the tourism industry, the airline industry, the shipping industry, the transportation sector, the textiles industry, and others.[121] These partners must be engaged when developing prevention strategies so that they contribute to anti-trafficking efforts rather than facilitate child trafficking or simply stand by idly. In short, as one public health initiative explains, partnerships are "essential" for achieving program goals, and the prevention of threats to human health "will require improved communication, cooperation, and collaboration across disciplines, institutions, and countries. It will require valuing our existing partnerships while building new ones."[122] That mindset, common in public health, must be applied to initiatives aimed at preventing child trafficking.

Next, public health strategies recognize the need to engage the most affected communities and target interventions.[123] Participatory epidemiology ensures community participation and respect for local knowledge and concerns. Many public health initiatives emphasize that "community members should be involved in identifying any new health threats confronting the community."[124] As a threshold matter, engaging target communities helps foster greater community buy-in and support for such programs.[125] Engaging the community at the outset and throughout the process helps ensure that policies and programs are culturally appropriate and supported by the target populations.[126] Engaging local partners also enables programs to take advantage of potential synergies by "building upon existing social and community networks."[127] Equally important, it also helps facilitate consideration of a broader range of ideas and spurs innovation, increasing the likelihood that better ideas for prevention programs will be identified and pursued and less viable ideas will be discarded.[128]

Children and adolescents are a critical part of this effort. As UNICEF states, "Too often, prevention strategies do not take into account and incorporate the views of children, or fail to empower children to meaningfully engage in prevention activities and decision-making processes."[129] Involving children in discussion about issues that affect their lives can have many advantages, ranging from boosting self-esteem and empowering youth to ensuring better outcomes. In considerations about the design and implementation of programs that help prevent child trafficking, youth perspectives can provide insights that adults may not have. Mike Dottridge explains that children "are 'experts' on the factors that make children vulnerable, their reasons for leaving home, and their special needs regarding prevention, assistance[,] and protection. Children and young people have an important role to play in helping to identify areas for intervention, design relevant solutions[,] and act as strategic informants of research."[130]

In one study, child survivors of trafficking reported knowing little about trafficking or prevention measures prior to being trafficked.[131] "All children indicated that schools did little to provide relevant information to protect them from trafficking."[132] Listening to children and giving due weight to their insights can help us identify new or more effective ways to intervene before harm occurs. This study also reported that the main reason children left school was lack of finances, a finding that reveals additional information relevant to developing more targeted preventive interventions.[133] Finally, many children in this study identified a "changing point," a specific event or crisis that made them more vulnerable to exploitation.[134] "The types of changes that appear to have had the greatest impact include a change of residence or of family composition, or in the child's own interaction and relationship with friends and peers."[135] This final area of change—peer relationships—underlines the importance of ensuring that youth have a voice. Peer relationships have a significant impact on young people. Children can readily identify peer pressure and peer-on-peer violence, whereas many adults miss these signs, often because they occur when adults are not present.[136]

Engaging youth meaningfully is challenging.[137] The children selected to participate may not be representative of the entire population of children who are vulnerable to trafficking and related harms. Like adults, children are a heterogeneous group. Therefore, simply involving some youth in program development does not mean that all youth voices are represented. In some programs, adults tend to rely on the same children because those children are already familiar with the process, leading to a "professionalization" of selected youth. Another problem involves sustaining initiatives as children grow up; when they turn eighteen, they are no longer children. This consistent turnover in a youth group makes it more difficult to sustain youth-led and youth-informed initiatives. Finally, adults must guard against manipulating youth to serve adult agendas. Manipulation can occur even when adults are well intentioned and is a greater risk when younger children are involved.[138] Beyond these more general obstacles to meaningful youth participation, additional issues arise in the context of child trafficking, most importantly the risk of retraumatizing children.[139] Equally important, many children may be reluctant to participate because of concerns about being stigmatized and possibly ostracized.[140] These concerns must be dealt with thoughtfully and respectfully in ways that would enable participation by those young people who want a voice in the process.

Finally, public health programming recognizes the need to respond quickly and efficiently at times, such as when responding to a contagious disease outbreak. Thus, more than in many other disciplines, public health policies and programs typically incorporate a focus on ensuring effective coordination among government agencies at the various levels of government, between government and the public, and among key partners in each community.[141] Responses to human trafficking are in significant need of improved coordination. The 2009 UN Secretary-General report, which discusses coordination efforts in anti-trafficking initiatives, found that "coordination is often lacking among various law enforcement agencies, such as immigration, workplace inspectors and police authorities. This results in agencies working at cross-purposes. . . . Poor coordination between law enforcement and criminal justice service providers, on the one hand, and victim service providers, including NGOs, on the other, [is] a recurrent theme."[142]

A decade later, it appears that coordination is still an afterthought in many areas. Some cities have created task forces and other mechanisms to enhance interagency coordination,[143] but most locales have made limited progress in developing coordinated responses. Governments must take a lead role in improving coordination and community preparedness, and they must fully engage all community partners in this process. They also need to ensure that coordination efforts are not limited to or heavily weighted only toward law enforcement strategies.[144] Task forces and similar convening groups must have representation from all relevant sectors and be balanced and inclusive. And they must ensure that local community participation is meaningful, not just tokenistic, and that youth and survivor voices are included. Ultimately, a well-coordinated plan of action is needed at the national, regional, and local levels to ensure that all key partners understand their roles, are equipped with the necessary resources to carry out their responsibilities, and have an appreciation for how their activities dovetail with the actions of other partners working to combat child trafficking. In addition, all stakeholders should be cognizant of how at-risk and exploited youth might intersect with their services and the challenges that young people will face navigating and coordinating their own care. By placing ourselves in the shoes of those who might need assistance, we might be able to anticipate and address gaps in coverage and other barriers to accessing comprehensive, integrated services. And by ensuring that all relevant partners participate in the fight against child trafficking, we give ourselves the best chance of developing successful, sustainable initiatives that actually prevent the harm from occurring.

## The Value of Public Health Perspectives

The previous section detailed four key components of a public health framework that can strengthen current efforts to address child trafficking. They offer a set of tools and approaches that can help prevent child trafficking. But public health offers not only a significant set of tools and experience but also a lens through which we can understand more clearly the challenges we need to confront in order to combat child trafficking.

Assessing child trafficking through a public health lens helps improve our understanding of the problem and its root causes. In particular, public health perspectives help to identify two areas of potential challenges. First, there are ways in which public health methodologies themselves could present challenges (potential risks). Therefore, as we move forward with implementing a public health approach, it is critical that we account for these potential risks. Second, and perhaps more important, viewing the problem of child trafficking from a public health perspective helps uncover distinctive features of child trafficking that make it different from typical public health issues (potential constraints). Understanding how child trafficking differs from other issues is important to adapting public health strategies in ways that increase the likelihood of their success in confronting child trafficking.

### Learning from Other Public Health Initiatives

This section briefly identifies several potential risks that have arisen in other public health programming and discusses why in the context of preventing human trafficking these risks need not materialize and in some instances are easily avoided.

First, public health campaigns have confronted challenges related to stigma and discrimination associated with particular diseases, such as HIV/AIDS.[145] Child trafficking survivors frequently experience stigma and discrimination. Governments and anti-trafficking advocates must ensure that their efforts do not import additional stigma and prejudices that would further harm survivors. These risks arise potentially in all areas of anti-trafficking work, and public health measures are no exception. For example, public health programming that "focus[es] on HIV as the dominant issue in health and trafficking in women not so subtly implicates the women as 'vectors' of disease. . . . An HIV focus may unwittingly create prejudices and stigmatize women who are trafficked."[146] Policymakers and anti-trafficking advocates must carefully review anti-trafficking strategies and seek input from survivors to ensure that programs do not stigmatize the individuals they seek to support and assist.

Another potential challenge is that the needs and priorities of child trafficking survivors might differ from those of public health officials or anti-trafficking advocates.[147] For example, while some public health officials might want to focus on controlling the spread of HIV or other diseases, trafficked children might view other health issues, such as physical violence or mental health needs, as more pressing than testing for sexually transmitted infections (STIs).[148] This is one reason why it is essential to engage all key partners, including trafficking survivors, to avoid a top-down approach to the problem. This risk is present in any approach to child trafficking. For example, a law enforcement–centered model often produces these differences, as when prosecutors prioritize obtaining witness testimony from child trafficking survivors, who are focused on accessing services or who fear that cooperation will lead to retribution against them or their families.[149] It is important for policymakers and anti-trafficking advocates to be aware that the same risks arise with a public health approach and to ensure that when any action is taken the needs identified by survivors or other vulnerable persons are addressed.

Although the previous section focused on public health strategies that can help foster better outcomes vis-à-vis child trafficking, it would be misleading to suggest that a public health approach means simply working on population attitudes and behaviors and abandoning some of the strategies employed currently to combat child trafficking (e.g., law enforcement measures, health care and social services for victims). Road safety provides an illustrative example. A reduction in the number of traffic fatalities was achieved not merely by focusing on attitudes and changing individual behaviors (e.g., encouraging seatbelt use) but through the combination of a number of measures, including improved vehicle safety (through airbags and other safety features), improved roads, and drunk driving laws.[150] An integral part of these efforts was also changing public attitudes toward drunk driving (through campaigns by MADD and others).[151] As a result of all of these measures, between 1982 and 1999 deaths from alcohol-related accidents declined by 37 percent.[152] In other words, interventions must be multifaceted. And the public health approach points us in that direction by prompting us to use the socio-ecological model and consider not only individual factors but also relationship, community, and societal factors. A multipronged strategy has worked when addressing road safety, tobacco use, intimate partner violence, and other public health issues.[153] And that is what is needed to shift from dealing with trafficking after individuals have been exploited to preventing trafficking from occurring in the first place.

A separate challenge arises when campaigns seek to raise public awareness of criminal behavior, such as child trafficking. Some stakeholders might be resistant to such negative publicity about their communities.[154] Business owners might fear a decline in tourists or other visitors, and members of the public might become unduly alarmed (and possibly take matters into their own hands).[155] Programs developed to prevent child trafficking must engage the private sector and other key partners to address the problem. Engaging key stakeholders to strategize around this issue can help ensure that rather than being stigmatized through negative publicity, such partners can be seen as playing a valuable role in the solution and prevention. ECPAT-USA (End Child Prostitution and Trafficking) developed a code of conduct for businesses in the travel industry. That program offers important lessons, as while early on, businesses were reluctant to sign on to the code, now momentum has grown significantly, with companies like Delta Airlines, Hyatt, and Hilton now participating along with early supporters such as Carlson.[156]

Finally, a central issue in public health is the balance between the state's responsibility to protect the public's health and individual autonomy.[157] Public health aims to adopt the least restrictive option that will achieve the community's or the population's health goals.[158] This approach is driven in part by public health's reliance on maintaining the public's trust.[159] In order to continue to enjoy public support, public health must ensure that privacy and related issues remain a primary consideration. For example, public health surveillance programs must weigh the need to obtain important data against potential interference with individuals' privacy rights.[160] By their very nature, public health surveillance programs present "privacy risks as governments must collect sensitive medical information from patients, travelers, migrants, and other vulnerable populations."[161] In the context of child trafficking, careful consideration would need to be given to the data needed and any potential privacy implications. Policymakers would need to collaborate with attorneys, public health professionals, health care professionals, experts on child trafficking, and trafficking survivors to review relevant privacy laws and ensure that they enable collection of needed data while protecting individuals' privacy.[162]

The fact that child trafficking involves criminal behavior and thus law enforcement complicates the issues, as marginalized communities might be more wary of public health initiatives that are closely tied to policing. For example, public health strategies in immigrant communities where there are significant numbers of undocumented individuals or mixed-status households might be less effective if it is perceived that data collected is shared with law enforcement or immigration authorities.[163]

There are also concerns about the collection of particular types of data, such as race and ethnicity data.[164] Unlike other fields, public health is an area in which collecting data on race and ethnicity can be important, particularly given the pressing need to address health disparities.[165] Thus, in the context of child trafficking, where data suggest that marginalized populations are at heightened risk, collection of sensitive data, including race and ethnicity data, can help in addressing disparities in access to needed services. Policymakers, public health professionals, and anti-trafficking advocates must ensure an appropriate balance between accessing data needed for evidence-based research and the development of effective responses and respecting individuals' privacy, particularly when working with vulnerable populations.

Public health professionals have confronted all the above risks when addressing other issues that affect population health. Models from public health campaigns to address violence, road safety, youth smoking, and other issues need to be modified to fit the exigencies of child trafficking scenarios so that the benefits of public health methodologies can be reaped while the risks are minimized if not avoided altogether.

### Challenges Unveiled through a Public Health Lens

Viewing the problem of child trafficking through a public health lens sheds light on constraints embedded in the problem itself. In this respect, this subsection is less about "limitations" of a public health approach than it is about the importance of a public health perspective. For it is through a public health lens that we can see one of the most significant challenges to meaningful progress in preventing child trafficking.

This challenge relates to the concern expressed by some scholars that violence issues are an awkward fit for public health.[166] Their argument is that, unlike lung cancer or malaria, for which the pathogen is readily identifiable (nicotine and protozoan parasites, respectively), violence-based health issues have a less clear "pathogen."[167] If pathogens create the risk of harm in other areas of public health, what parallel agent creates the risk of harm in child trafficking settings? One might posit that the risk of harm is caused by the traffickers. Certainly, traffickers harm children they exploit. However, such a view too narrowly construes the cause of the harm. In the drug trafficking arena, kingpins might supply the drugs, but the end users are the ones who sustain the demand for the drug trade. Similarly, child trafficking—both labor trafficking and sex trafficking—thrives because of the demand for cheap goods and services. Public health initiatives in the child trafficking context, therefore, can help reorient anti-trafficking initiatives to focus on the underlying demand issues.

The demand for trafficked individuals' services differs, however, from demand for drugs in important ways. Most fundamentally, from a public health perspective, drug use harms the individual user. So in the case of drugs, or smoking for that matter, education about the dangers of cocaine or nicotine can raise public awareness about the harm individuals inflict upon themselves by using drugs or smoking tobacco (recognizing that addiction plays a key role in those contexts). In contrast, individuals who spur demand for services provided by trafficked people—whether labor that produces inexpensive food and clothing or provides commercial sex services—do not expose themselves to a "pathogen" that could harm them (except potentially, in the case of sex, with STIs). The harm instead is inflicted upon individuals who are trafficked. Indeed, those who purchase inexpensive food and clothing produced by trafficked labor potentially reap a benefit through cost savings.

Efforts to address other harms might offer closer analogies. Second-hand smoking presents an interesting comparison. It differs from trafficking in important respects; for example, on the "demand" side, a public health initiative aimed at reducing harm caused by secondhand smoking nevertheless also encourages smokers to take action (read: stop smoking) that will benefit themselves. Despite this and other differences, the secondhand smoking analogy has some fit with the "supply" side of human trafficking, as public awareness campaigns may seek to educate nonsmokers on how to reduce the risk of, or exposure to, secondhand smoking. Public health responses to intimate partner violence may be still a better analogy. There are numerous examples of public health models aimed at addressing intimate partner violence (IPV).[168] Such models offer important parallels, given that both involve violence against vulnerable individuals and the power dynamics that create barriers to victims reporting the harm. Also, both IPV and child trafficking operate on similar societal beliefs that devalue certain individuals, particularly women and girls. However, important differences remain. For example, while some of the reasons why men abuse their partners, such as gender-based discrimination, are applicable in the context of sex trafficking, the analogy may be less applicable to the demand for cheap food and clothing. The idea behind looking at other public health models is not that we should expect to discover an exact fit; rather, it is to see that public health has confronted a range of harms and that that experience could be brought to bear and adapted as needed to address child trafficking.

So, for example, as occurs with public health interventions on other issues, anti-trafficking programs could target those vulnerable to human trafficking and identify steps to reduce their vulnerability and their corresponding risk of being trafficked. Recall, however, that public health approaches, such as the socio-ecological model, emphasize the importance of addressing not only individual factors but also relationship, community, and societal factors. To reduce individuals' vulnerability to trafficking, governments and civil society must address structural disadvantages, such as abject poverty, gender-based violence and discrimination, and other forms of discrimination. Relying solely on vulnerable persons engaging in self-help will be ineffective and place an undue burden on vulnerable individuals.

Ultimately, the demand for trafficked persons, their bodies, and their labor is at the root of the harm. That demand comes from various segments of society, from individuals seeking cheap goods to businesses simply wanting to further maximize profits. Therefore, although public health methodologies are relevant, traditional public health models might need to be adapted to account for the ways in which the relational dynamics in the child trafficking context differ from those associated with more traditional public health issues.

Take, for example, public health media campaigns aimed at changing attitudes and behaviors that spur demand for trafficked persons. The different relational dynamics of child trafficking highlight the issue of effective messaging, a key component of strategies aimed at shaping societal behavior and promoting healthier outcomes. Anti-smoking messages, anti–drunk driving messages, and similar media campaigns rely on fear appeals (persuasive messages that arouse fear).[169] Research demonstrates that for campaigns to be effective they need to "ensure that a high-threat appeal is accompanied by an equally high-efficacy (or greater) message."[170] That is, persuasive messages that arouse fear must be accompanied by a recommended response that individuals believe will work to avert the threat.[171] The challenge then is to create anti-trafficking messaging (and related programs) that will persuade a potential customer in the sex industry that not going to a prostituted child will reduce child trafficking, or will persuade a shopper that not buying a particular brand of jeans or basketball shoes will reduce the exploitation of trafficked children in sweatshops, or will motivate a CEO to prioritize safe working conditions in supply chains over the additional profits that could be gained through exploitation. For those in the consumer's position, the current reality is that buying a more expensive brand does not guarantee that one is getting an item made by workers who were treated more humanely; in fact, it might just mean that the retailers or suppliers have higher profit margins. Thus, the research on public health campaigns suggests that new models or modified versions of existing public health strategies need to be developed in order to address the different relational dynamics inherent in child trafficking. Otherwise, efforts to change destructive behaviors will have limited impact.

Public health's road safety "success" story provides an interesting comparison. Some have posited that individuals do not drive more safely than drivers drove fifty years ago.[172] However, over the past fifty years the number of automobile fatalities per mile driven has declined by more than 80 percent.[173] An array of measures have fostered much greater safety, including significant improvements in safety features of automobiles and improved roads, as well as changes in attitudes about driving while intoxicated. Applied to child trafficking, we believe that the automobile safety movement suggests that an important component must be included: structural factors. The prevalence of fatalities on the road declined because pressure was brought to bear not just on drivers but also on automakers, which ultimately produced safer cars.[174] Similarly, in the labor trafficking context, interventions focused on individual purchasing choices will need to be accompanied by efforts that spur corporations to change their business model and produce their products without using exploited labor. The key lesson here is that by looking at child trafficking from a public health perspective, we are much closer to understanding some of the systemic issues and relational dynamics that have been largely ignored to date but must be accounted for to achieve success in preventing trafficking.

## Conclusion

The merits of a public health approach are considerable. Public health draws upon methodologies that have been underutilized in the area of human trafficking but offer significant benefits. Public health approaches also provide a roadmap for improving our responses to the problem of child trafficking. First, our actions must be driven by evidence-based research. The limited reliable data on human trafficking currently available leave policymakers and advocates uncertain whether their actions will make a difference. We need to know what works so that law, policies, and programs will produce the desired result, that is, a reduction in the prevalence of trafficking and better outcomes for those who are trafficked.

Second, public health's prevention focus would significantly advance anti-trafficking initiatives, which currently deal with the harm primarily after it occurs. We need to move upstream toward the root causes so that we can prevent harm to children before it happens.

Third, public health shows us the importance of addressing underlying issues. We focused in this chapter on changing attitudes and behaviors as a case study. Those steps are critical. Human trafficking is deeply ingrained in our society and around the globe; as noted in chapter 1, exploitation of human beings is not new. Discrimination and marginalization contribute to this exploitation. Poverty, denials of basic human rights, structural violence, and other root causes must also be addressed. For addressing the underlying causes of a problem, public health offers a critical framework, the socio-ecological model. Using the model to identify and address factors at the individual, relationship, community, and societal levels will help advance efforts to prevent trafficking of children.

Fourth, public health's traditional emphasis on engaging all community stakeholders will add value at all stages of anti-trafficking efforts. From the drafting of relevant laws and policies to the implementation of prevention programs, every step in the process will be enhanced if key partners, including youth and survivors, have the opportunity to participate fully. And ultimately that will lead to better outcomes.

In addition to providing these four critical tools, a public health approach can help enrich our understanding of the complex dynamics of child trafficking so that we can develop strategies that will effectively account for those dynamics.

In short, public health offers a valuable set of tools greatly needed in the fight against child trafficking. By drawing upon and utilizing public health methodologies, we can move from confronting harm only after children have suffered to a scenario in which individuals and communities have a significantly strengthened capacity to prevent child trafficking.

# Understanding Risk Factors

J ANET IS a twenty-two-year-old Latina who has been coming to Mount Sinai Adolescent Health Center (MSAHC) since she was a teenager. The first time she came to the center, she was brought by another sex trafficking survivor. Janet has a long history of childhood physical abuse and sexual abuse, including incest, and she has been a victim of intimate partner violence as she has been repeatedly physically abused by her boyfriend/trafficker. When the center social worker first met her, Janet was engaging in cutting and bulimic behaviors, and she regularly used alcohol and illicit substances.

Andrea, a seventeen-year-old African American female, came to MSAHC for services after she was attacked by peers. She reported a history of early childhood sexual abuse, neglect, exposure to domestic violence, and ongoing sexual exploitation (sex trafficking). She had symptoms consistent with complex PTSD, including avoidance of certain situations that reminded her of the abuse, nightmares, panic attacks, and intrusive thoughts. This trauma was likely linked both to her history of childhood sexual abuse, neglect, and exposure to domestic violence and to the ongoing sexual exploitation. Both she and Janet were identified as trafficking victims during their visits to MSAHC.

These cases highlight some of the risk factors for human trafficking. These risks include childhood maltreatment, including sexual abuse, exposure to domestic violence, and a history of trauma. Like many trafficking survivors, these two young women are from low socio-economic backgrounds and marginalized groups. Their cases involve a broad spectrum of risks interrelated and intertwined. Janet's and Andrea's histories of childhood physical and sexual abuse and intimate partner violence placed them at risk for further victimization. In their cases, that meant sex trafficking. For others, it ends in labor trafficking. And for still other vulnerable youth, it may end in exploitation in non-trafficking settings.

While histories like Janet's and Andrea's are not uncommon among sex trafficking survivors, no single profile captures the diversity of children at risk for both sex trafficking and labor trafficking. Human trafficking spans all demographics. Yet we know that certain circumstances or factors make children and adolescents more susceptible to trafficking and its attendant forms of exploitation. Individual, family, peer, community, and societal dynamics correspond to risk factors such as a history of childhood abuse, family dysfunction and peer pressure, unsafe neighborhoods, marginalization and the sexualization of children, and others.

Determining the risk factors for child trafficking is a vital step in preventing such exploitation. Key components of a public health approach are its focus on prevention and its emphasis on identifying risk and protective factors so that interventions can be designed to prevent harm from occurring. Similarly, the goal of the anti-trafficking movement is, or at least should be, to end human trafficking or prevent trafficking-related harms. Responses to human trafficking can be enhanced, therefore, by drawing upon public health expertise to help identify who is particularly vulnerable to exploitation. Many current responses to human trafficking focus on those already identified as trafficking victims or survivors. While meeting the needs of survivors is critical, we also need to direct resources to determining who is vulnerable. By improving our understanding of why a child is vulnerable and which children are most vulnerable, we can do a better job of identifying vulnerable and exploited children and adolescents before they are harmed.

In this chapter, we examine the risk factors for child trafficking. The evidence detailed in this chapter informs subsequent chapters' exploration of

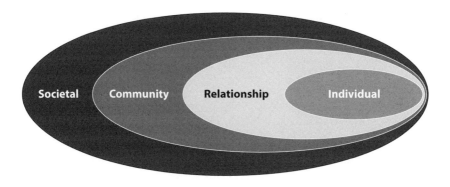

*Figure 5.1.* Overview of the socio-ecological model

health care responses to the problem. It is also relevant to other professionals who work with children and are concerned about children vulnerable to or harmed by human trafficking. Finally, as we discuss in the concluding chapter, ultimately we need to develop a comprehensive, integrated response to child trafficking, and to do so will require an in-depth understanding of the factors that increase vulnerability to trafficking-related harms.

## Risk Factor Levels: An Overview

The socio-ecological model (figure 5.1), often used in public health responses to violence, provides a useful framework for understanding the range of factors that shape children's vulnerability to trafficking. The socio-ecological model examines the individual, relationship, community, and societal factors that operate—and interact with one another—to leave children and adolescents vulnerable to harm.[1] This model can help enhance understanding of the complexity of factors that influences who is trafficked.

## Individual-Level Factors

A number of individual-level factors increase the vulnerability of youth. These include homelessness or unstable housing; childhood abuse, neglect, or other trauma, especially a history of sexual abuse; gender; LGBTQ status; disability; "systems" involvement (meaning previous involvement with the child welfare or juvenile justice system); substance use/dependence/addiction; and gang involvement.

## Homelessness

Homeless youth are at a heightened risk of exploitation for a variety of reasons, including a lack of shelter, food, financial resources, and support from family or other caregivers.[2] Some at-risk adolescents move in and out of homelessness and may sell or exchange sex in order to survive.[3] Running away from home can have a multiplier effect on a young adolescent's risk for trafficking.[4] It is critical to note that young people typically run away because they are trying to escape from harm at home or from living in a dysfunctional, unstable family. Other youth are on the street because they have been thrown out of their homes by their families for a variety of reasons, including a parent finding out that the young person was pregnant, LGBTQ, or using drugs.[5] In these instances, being on the street leaves these children particularly vulnerable to exploitation, especially if they have a prior history of abuse and other trauma.

A number of studies have shown that homeless youth are at much greater risk of exploitation than housed youth.[6] A 2016 study of ten cities in the United States and Canada found that nearly one in five homeless or runaway youth experiences some form of trafficking (14% reported sex trafficking; 8%, labor trafficking; and 3%, both).[7] In another study, using a nationally representative sample of homeless and sheltered youth, 27.5 percent of homeless youth and 9.5 percent of youth in shelters reported having engaged in survival sex.[8] A similar study conducted in Seattle found that 47 percent of females and 37 percent of males had been propositioned to exchange sex for money or items of value.[9] In short, homelessness and unstable housing significantly increase the vulnerability of youth to a variety of forms of exploitation, including human trafficking. Their lack of support and heightened needs make them an easy target for people who prey on vulnerable youth. Public health interventions need to focus not only on ensuring stable housing for youth but also on fostering safe and supportive home environments.

## Childhood Maltreatment

Childhood maltreatment is a major public health issue.[10] According to the National Child Abuse and Neglect Data System (NCANDS), child protective services agencies in the United States received about 4.1 million child abuse and neglect referrals involving 7.4 million children in fiscal year 2016.[11] Although not all referrals result in a finding of abuse or neglect, there are also many cases that go undetected and unreported. By all accounts of those working on child maltreatment, it is a significant problem. And the negative outcomes from child maltreatment are extensive. These adverse consequences include poor self-esteem, substance abuse, eating disorders, obesity, risky sexual behaviors, unintended pregnancy, depression, trauma, anxiety, suicidality, and other conditions.[12]

The trauma that children suffer from maltreatment leaves them at heightened risk of a range of subsequent harms, including exploitation in human trafficking. Sexual abuse, in particular, has been associated with subsequent sexual exploitation and sex trafficking.[13] Studies have found a significant association between sexual, physical, and emotional maltreatment experienced during childhood and later involvement in prostitution.[14] More generally, studies report that minors who are commercially sexually exploited and trafficked identify the sexual abuse they suffered as a child as a major factor for experiencing commercial sexual exploitation.[15]

Most of the research on the link between child maltreatment and subsequent involvement in sex trafficking involves retrospective studies. In other words, most who are exploited in sex trafficking have a history of sexual or other childhood abuse, but the fact that one is abused as a child does not necessarily mean that he or she is likely to be trafficked.[16] This prompts questions about other factors that might work in conjunction with a history of child sexual abuse or other forms of maltreatment to put a particular child at heightened risk of exploitation. As noted above, being on the street is one such factor, and notably abuse and maltreatment in the home can push young people to the street, but other factors also contribute. Finally, as noted above, much of the research focuses on sex trafficking of children. Even less is known about how child maltreatment interacts with subsequent exploitation in labor trafficking. However, given the strong association between a history of child maltreatment and later exploitation, early identification and response to child maltreatment should be a significant focus of public health interventions to prevent human trafficking.

### Gender

The stereotypical portrayal of human trafficking involves the trafficking of a young woman or girl for sex. However, the reality is that trafficking victimizes cisgender and transgender girls and boys, as well as gender-fluid youth. And youth are trafficked for exploitation in a wide range of labor settings, as well as in the commercial sex industry.

Girls are at heightened risk of exploitation in trafficking. Historical and ongoing gender-based discrimination and violence leave girls at heightened risk of harm and with more limited means of accessing help.[17] The sexualization of young girls and attendant devaluation of girls increases the risk of sex trafficking victimization. But girls can also be trafficked for labor in a variety of settings, including domestic service, agriculture, textile industries, and more.[18] The gendered nature of poverty, which typically has greater adverse consequences for women and children, as well as discrimination in education, employment, and access to financial resources, increases the vulnerability of girls to a variety of harms, including exploitation.[19]

While much of the focus on human trafficking has centered on sex trafficking of young women and girls,[20] there has been a general lack of awareness of the exploitation of boys and young men in human trafficking.[21] Boys are exploited in a variety of labor settings, and in some locales more boys are trafficked than girls.[22] And boys are also exploited in sex trafficking.[23] Among all populations, boys may be the most misidentified and underreported victims of domestic sex trafficking.[24] Some boys end up in sex trafficking because they are trying to escape an abusive or dysfunctional home situation and find themselves on the street forced to engage in survival sex (e.g., to exchange sex for food, shelter, money, or other necessities), while others have been victimized by early childhood sexual abuse conditions, heightening their risk of being pulled into sex trafficking.[25] Researchers have suggested additional reasons for boys' vulnerability and the limited attention to their involvement in sex trafficking, including societal constructs around masculinity.[26] Boys are expected to be strong and in control, to know about sex, and to be able to take care of themselves— all of which make it harder for them to disclose their exploitation, ask for help, or seek services.[27]

Transgender youth also are at particularly high risk for trafficking.[28] They may be condemned or rejected by their families or peers upon disclosure of their gender identity, which may be followed by mistreatment and violence, making them more vulnerable targets. Rejection by their family may lead to homelessness, which, as noted above, can increase vulnerability to exploitation in trafficking. In addition, "LGBTQ youth are overrepresented in the child welfare system where they are more likely to have negative experiences and less likely to achieve permanency than their heterosexual and cisgender peers."[29] Discrimination in employment can reduce options and push transgender youth into riskier workspaces.[30] All these experiences heighten the vulnerability of transgender youth to a range of harms, including trafficking.

In short, while trafficking victimizes youth of all profiles, gender plays an important role, heightening vulnerability of girls in some locales and sectors, boys in others, and transgender youth as well.

### Lesbian, Gay, Bisexual, Transgender, and Questioning Youth

Sexual and gender minority youth are at higher risk for trafficking. For example, research findings indicate that among self-identified homeless youth attending a free clinic in Los Angeles, youth in the sex trade were five times more likely to identify as LGBT than the self-identified homeless youth who were not prostituted.[31] One reason for the vulnerability of

LGBT adolescents is that they are at higher risk of being "thrown away" by their families and may suffer greater exposure to parental conflict than their heterosexual counterparts. Boys may experience vulnerability if they are rejected or alienated following disclosure to a parent that they are gay.[32] Also, as noted above, "LGBTQ youth are overrepresented in the child welfare system where they are more likely to have negative experiences and less likely to achieve permanency than their heterosexual and cisgender peers."[33] More broadly, emerging sexual identity for adolescents can occur at the same time as other risk factors, such as lack of acceptance from parents or peers, resulting in heightened vulnerability, in particular for LGBTQ youth.[34]

### Youth with Disabilities

Disability has also been recognized as a risk factor, as youth with disabilities have higher rates of exploitation, including in human trafficking.[35] This includes individuals who are deaf, have mental illness, or have developmental or learning disabilities, as well as others.[36] Persons with disabilities are targeted in both labor trafficking and sex trafficking operations. One of the earliest cases recognized as a human trafficking case in the United States involved fifty-five deaf Mexican nationals who were brought to New York City to beg or sell trinkets on the subway.[37] Sex trafficking cases involving victims with cognitive or mental health disabilities have been identified in numerous states, including Michigan, Ohio, Pennsylvania, and Virginia.[38]

Disability-based discrimination marginalizes these individuals and creates a variety of barriers, from lack of sign language interpreters to lack of wheelchair access to public buildings, that can impede access to assistance and remedies when persons with disabilities do encounter threats of violence and exploitation.[39] Moreover, the barriers and rights violations that youth with disabilities experience in other arenas can increase their vulnerability. For example, many schools provide insufficient accommodation to youth with disabilities, leading these children to fall behind their peers and in some cases drop out early.[40] Often young people with disabilities have fewer employment opportunities.[41] In other cases, children with disabilities might be abandoned by their families, leaving them on the streets, where they are vulnerable to a range of harms.[42]

Finally, it should be noted that the trauma inflicted by the trafficking experience can leave survivors with disabilities.[43] These can include disability as a result of permanent physical injury, as well as mental or developmental disabilities caused by extensive trauma. Thus, disability is relevant not only in identifying risk factors but also when screening and treating youth who may have been trafficked or exploited in other ways. This demonstrates the bidirectionality of the relationship between disability and human trafficking, a feature of many risk factors of human trafficking.

### Systems-Involved Youth

#### Foster Care System

Children and adolescents are placed in foster care usually because of a history of child maltreatment. They may also have grown up in poverty and experienced other family challenges, including limited parental supervision.[44] These background characteristics are among the risk factors for child trafficking. Moreover, children in foster care can experience continued family instability, as they may be moved multiple times, from one foster family to another. As a result, children in foster care are at heightened risk for sex trafficking.[45] In addition, particular foster care placements, notably group homes, can put young people at risk.[46] Traffickers often target youth in foster care, who are easy targets because their history of maltreatment likely has disrupted their healthy development and left them lacking, and often searching for, a sense of security and safety.[47] Because of the difficulty of establishing kinship care arrangements or permanency for teenagers, these youth are often placed together in group homes or residential units, where they are vulnerable to being targeted by exploiters.[48] In addition, young people may recruit other young people in this and other settings.[49]

Similar to youth in the foster care system, children in the juvenile justice system often have a prior history of maltreatment and other traumas.[50] Youth swept up in trafficking situations may get involved in criminal activities such as petty theft, survival theft, or theft related to drug misuse, or they may become involved with illicit drugs themselves.[51] Exposure to the criminal justice system also puts them at risk of being recruited into trafficking situations. Involvement with the criminal justice system can marginalize youth and make them less trusting of traditional authority figures, increasing their vulnerability to being taken advantage of by traffickers and other exploiters.[52]

In addition, we know that trafficking victims, particularly sex trafficking victims, can end up arrested or detained as a result of their trafficking experience. (As discussed in chapter 3, some states have attempted to address this through "safe harbor" laws.) Being arrested and charged with prostitution or other offenses can leave these at-risk and exploited youth with a criminal record, making it more likely that subsequent encounters with law enforcement will lead to arrest, conviction, and incarceration rather than assistance. It also makes it easier for traffickers to manipulate and persuade these young persons that going to the police will work against them.

In short, while systems like child welfare can offer support to some youth, being "systems involved" can also have negative consequences that leave youth at greater risk of harm.

### Substance Use and Abuse

Substance use and abuse play an important role as a risk factor for trafficking of minors.[53] There is evidence of high rates of drug use among youth in sex trafficking.[54] Traffickers use drugs on vulnerable young people to make them dependent and as a way of coercing and controlling their victims.[55] Some trafficking victims turn to drugs in order to cope with their trafficking experience or their earlier childhood abuse.[56] Drug dependency has also been identified as a major obstacle to permanently leaving the sex trade.[57]

## Gang Involvement

A variety of levels of organized criminal groups are involved in human trafficking because of its profitable nature. Many youth are recruited from among street youth and other maltreated adolescents whose physiological or safety needs have not been met.[58] Often because they grew up in an unstable home environment, these children want and need to develop a sense of belonging outside the home. This desire for a sense of belonging may lead some youth to join a gang to re-create a sense of family. These children are prime candidates for grooming by sex traffickers, who offer a false sense of belonging. When youth are recruited, often by peers, they may be promised protection from the violence often encountered when living on the street. Some of these gangs are engaged in sex trafficking. Targeted youth may become involved in sex trafficking as part of the initiation into a gang or to accumulate power and wealth.

Advances in technology have made it easier for street gangs to operate sex trafficking rings. Gangs commonly use social media websites to lure young girls into sex trafficking.[59] In a 2011 study analyzing federal court cases, researchers identified more than two hundred federal cases of "street gangs, motorcycle gangs, and prison gangs in which commercial sex acts, prostitution, or human trafficking are mentioned."[60] Such exploitation occurs, at least in part, because human exploitation is seen by perpetrators as a relatively low-risk, high-reward endeavor, since the selling of sex has moved from the streets to the internet, with mobile brothels advertising via social media and text-based exchanges.[61]

## Individual Factors Interact with One Another

Each of the factors discussed above heightens the vulnerability of children and adolescents to exploitation. Equally important, many of these risk factors do not operate in isolation. Frequently, the most vulnerable children and adolescents are confronting and struggling to cope with multiple risks, the abovementioned ones as well as community or societal factors that disproportionately affect them or their families, such as poverty and discrimination. Intersectionality theory helps explain how these different risk factors create heightened risk for these children and adolescents. As Kimberlé Crenshaw explains, "Intersectionality simply came from the idea that if you're standing in the path of multiple forms of exclusion, you're likely to get hit by [all of them]."[62] And it also means that in advocacy efforts to address one form of discrimination or another, individuals with intersectional identities "are marginalized in both."[63] The multiple risks that certain children experience heighten their risk of exploitation and marginalize them further, making it difficult to avail themselves of the help they need to prevent or recover from the harm of trafficking.

For example, studies have identified links between child abuse and becoming homeless.[64] Being homeless in turn presents significant challenges to children's educational progress, and disruptions in schooling can further heightened vulnerability.[65] Systems-involved youth often enter foster care or the juvenile justice system having experienced multiple risks, and their experience in these systems frequently adds to their vulnerability. Youth who have been in foster care are at a particularly high risk of becoming homeless.[66] Homeless youth are also at high risk for substance abuse.[67] And LGBTQ youth experience higher rates of homelessness and sexual violence, as well as widespread stigma and discrimination.[68]

In short, individual risk factors are deeply interlaced, leaving certain children and adolescents at heightened risk of falling prey to trafficking and other harms. Children's vulnerability resulting from individual risk factors is further exacerbated by risks created by relationship, community, and societal factors. These risk factors often co-occur and accumulate in vulnerable youth, resulting in adverse consequences for their development and well-being. The impact of multiple risk factors operating simultaneously also creates an interdependent system of inequity, vulnerability, and disadvantage that presents barriers to affected youth who seek to extricate themselves from a trafficking situation and rebuild their lives.[69]

It is important to recognize and understand these intersections when considering policy and programmatic responses to child trafficking.

## Relationship Factors

### Family Factors

A healthy, safe, and consistent family environment is vital to children's development and well-being. When the family environment is toxic, as is the case with abusive families, children are at heightened risk. Unhealthy family environments include ones in which children experience—directly or indirectly—neglect, abuse, and domestic violence.[70] Families with high levels of conflict, dysfunction, or disruptions similarly hurt children's development and increase children's vulnerability to trafficking. Research has found that those youth who were sexually exploited experienced higher levels of family dysfunction.[71] Incest and rape have been identified as underlying factors in the risk for sex trafficking.[72] In some cases, children and youth living in toxic family environments may be trafficked by family members or acquaintances.

As to the impact of family economic status on the risk of trafficking, research findings vary. In one study, the researchers did not find that family socio-economic background was a significant factor.[73] However, other researchers have found that low-income children are at risk because they are more vulnerable owing to financial strains and the appeal of earning money to extricate themselves from poverty.[74] While poverty is often a risk factor for exploitation,[75] it is not exclusively poor children who are trafficked.[76] This suggests that the most vulnerable children are the ones who experience multiple risks simultaneously.

### Peer and Extrafamilial Factors

Peers play a critical role in the lives of young people. Peer pressure influences group members to conform to particular norms.[77] If an adolescent's peer group engages in deviant behaviors, the young person is more likely to be influenced in that direction, especially if no other relationships offer a counter to such influence. Conversely, if friends engage in prosocial behaviors, the adolescent is likely to be influenced in that direction. Youth may model peer behaviors, especially when they observe peers being positively reinforced for those behaviors.

Similar influences can play out in the context of commercial sexual exploitation, as youth may be lured by what they perceive in peers as evidence of a desirable lifestyle, such as the display of money and new clothes. Some peers also actively recruit their contemporaries into commercial sexual exploitation in their neighborhood, schools, foster care settings, and the criminal justice system. Homeless youth are not only victims of commercial sexual exploitation: studies have shown that some may recruit their peers.[78] In one study involving six-to-fourteen-year-old boys and girls, peer pressure was determined to be a factor associated with initiation into a child sex trafficking ring.[79] Other research has also identified peer pressure as a risk factor for prostitution.[80] Finally, peer pressure can adversely influence whether a young person leaves a trafficking situation.[81]

Other critical relationships for young persons are the ones they have with romantic partners (e.g., boyfriends or girlfriends). In some cases, young people are introduced into human trafficking by romantic partners, who use psychological manipulation to control them and to persuade them that they must engage in commercial sex or other exploitation for the relationship.[82] In published studies, male partners are more frequently discussed than female partners. In the sex trafficking context, many traffickers groom their victims so that, for example, the adolescent believes that the trafficker is a boyfriend who loves him or her.[83] In one study, 64 percent of participants described their trafficker as their boyfriend.[84] In other studies, 16–27 percent of sex trafficking victims reported being recruited into trafficking by a boyfriend.[85] In many of these cases, "boyfriends" become increasingly violent over time as a way of maintaining control over their trafficking victims, leading to other trauma and injuries.[86] Youth who have grown up experiencing high levels of domestic violence are often at risk of becoming involved in intimate partner relationships that are violent and include sexual exploitation.[87]

In addition to influencing entry into sex trafficking directly, peer relationships can also shape decisions that affect other risk factors, such as the decision to run away from home.[88] In this way, relationship-level factors interact with and increase individual-level factors, heightening the overall risk of exploitation.

## Community Factors

The community plays an important role in the lives of its residents, including the children and adolescents. What happens in the neighborhood partly depends on community norms, how connected and accountable its residents are to one another, and how the residents value and protect the community's children and youth.

Poverty, residential instability, high crimes rates, gang presence, and other factors all weaken community supports and structures.[89] As the Institute of Medicine and National Research Council study on sex trafficking of minors found, "When neighborhood control mechanisms are lacking, residents may be more tolerant and accepting of delinquency and criminal behavior among youth, including greater tolerance of violence in general, male violence against females in particular, as well as of sexual exploitation."[90] More cohesive communities may provide greater support for their youth in schools and also provide after-school extracurricular opportunities that keep youth engaged in well-supervised positive development activities.[91] In contrast, in neighborhoods where human trafficking flourishes, there may be few, if any, alternatives for youth beyond recruitment into illicit or exploitative activities.

In addition, neighborhood norms and expectations can influence the trajectory of the community's youth. The availability of opportunities for young people depends in part on a community's characteristics (level of crime, air quality, availability of jobs, quality of schools, etc.). In neighborhoods where there are few role models employing legitimate means of earning money, criminal behavior may be seen as more acceptable.[92] Local factors, such as the presence of businesses associated with trafficking (e.g., commercial sex establishments), can further shape the risk profile of young people living in these communities.[93]

The community-based factors described above do not necessarily mean that all adolescents living in high-risk neighborhoods will end up pursuing or involved in harmful behaviors. However, fractured neighborhoods and communities undermine social supports that can protect children, leaving them more vulnerable. In contrast, cohesive neighborhoods with good schools, resources for after-school programs, and employment opportunities can offer protective factors and help youth develop resilience. Thus community makeup is an important factor in assessing risk.

## Societal Factors

Societal factors also influence vulnerability to trafficking among children and adolescents. Systemic issues—poverty; lack of access to health care, education, and economic opportunities; discrimination; and other factors—contribute to increasing vulnerability to exploitation.[94]

Poverty can be a significant factor for children and their families. Poverty may force adults to take great risks seeking employment, leading to involvement in—and exploitation through—labor trafficking or sex trafficking. And youth may feel compelled to pursue risky opportunities in hopes of making enough money to improve, or merely maintain, their family's or their own socio-economic status. Poverty can affect access to needed health care and to safe, quality schools. In short, research shows clearly that the social determinants of health and well-being significantly shape outcomes.[95]

Research shows that young people who do not have regular access to health care have a greater number of health issues.[96] Poor health status then interferes with education, as children who are ill more often have higher absenteeism rates and are at risk of falling behind their peers in school. In turn, children who fall behind in school and have high absenteeism are at risk of dropping out (or being expelled). Once out of school, these young persons, with limited education and skills, face challenges in securing employment that is safe and well paid. All these factors push children and adolescents into riskier employment spaces, increasing their vulnerability to various forms of exploitation, including through trafficking.

Stigma and discrimination are also risk factors for sex trafficking and labor trafficking victimization. Individuals are more likely to feel disconnected from society and its institutions if they perceive being stigmatized and discriminated against because of their social status or membership in a historically marginalized group (whether based, for example, on race, ethnicity, sex, gender identity, sexual orientation, or disability).[97] Discrimination goes well beyond just spurring a sense of disconnect. For individuals who are stigmatized and experience discrimination, it can be more difficult to secure employment, affordable housing, and quality health care, among other social goods.[98] This marginalization can make individuals more vulnerable to exploitation.[99] And once any exploitation occurs, discrimination and marginalization make it more difficult for youth who are trafficked or exploited in other ways to avail themselves of assistance and other resources needed to extricate themselves from harm.

Take the case of homeless youth. Homeless youth face intense social stigma, which can have an adverse impact on mental health.[100] In one study of youth homelessness and social stigma, researchers found that ethnicity, sexual orientation, job, and total time spent on the streets predicted self-reported feelings of experiencing stigma.[101] Furthermore, reported experience of stigma was found to be related to "low self-esteem, suicidal ideation, loneliness, and feeling trapped."[102] This isolation resulting from stigma and discrimination can further heighten the vulnerability of children and adolescents to being preyed upon by those who seek to exploit young people.[103]

And homelessness is only one factor. Young people are stigmatized and discriminated against based on their race, ethnicity, religion, LGBTQ status, immigration status, disability, socio-economic status, and other factors. Societal and individual bias, both explicit and implicit, operate to harm youth both through discrimination against them and also by exposing them to greater risk that results from being marginalized and devalued.

Finally, cultural and societal norms can play a role in shaping actions and attitudes of the government as well as private individuals. Cultural norms often spur support for, or at least tolerance of, the exploitation of certain individuals. Sex trafficking thrives in part because our culture increasingly sexualizes younger children, fostering tolerance of the objectification of children, especially girls.[104] And labor trafficking benefits from the demand for cheap goods and services by consumers and the demand for greater profits and lower production costs by corporations and their leaders.[105] All these elements of our culture feed the demand for goods and services provided by exploited labor, including trafficked children.

## Putting It All Together

Risk factors interact both within levels (e.g., homelessness, child maltreatment, and LGBTQ status combine to heighten risk) and between levels (e.g., individual risk factors combine with unsafe neighborhoods and other community-based factors). Because of the multiple forces involved, prevention and intervention efforts targeting only single risk factors or only a single level of factors may have limited impact.

A study comparing children aged ten to eighteen involved in sex trafficking with other children found that those who were subjected to commercial sexual exploitation "were more likely to be runaways and homeless, and reported lower family cohesion, greater parental alcohol abuse, and more interparental conflict."[106] Responding appropriately and effectively requires addressing individual risk factors, family/relationship issues, community-based challenges, and societal factors that further marginalize vulnerable individuals.

A child subjected to abuse might feel compelled to run away from the violence. Research has found that youth unable to tolerate their family environment because of child maltreatment, unresolved family conflict, or family disruption are more likely to run away, leading to unstable housing or homelessness.[107] Once on the street, if a child lives in an unsafe community, he or she might be targeted for further abuse and exploitation. Some youth in those circumstances may end up exchanging sex for food and other basic necessities, often as a means of survival.[108] Or the child might pursue risky employment opportunities and end up in a labor trafficking situation. In addition to these individual-level factors, peer groups can play a role in influencing whether a runaway child ends up trafficked. Furthermore, there are more risks for youth if there are few resources in the community, high levels of community disorganization, and limited social supports. The cumulative impact of risks at different levels or within levels can lead to trafficking of some youth, particularly in a society where children and youth are sexualized or demand for ever-increasing profits pushes business to ignore exploitation in supply chains.

We must remember that risk factors are just that. Not every child with one or more risk factors will be trafficked, and some children who have no risk factors can end up being exploited. However, the socio-ecological model and its framing of risk factors helps us identify who is at heightened risk of harm. With that knowledge and an understanding of how the various risk factors interact with one another and exacerbate vulnerability, we can begin to develop more effective responses—including ones that use a public health framework—and ultimately prevent human trafficking.

## Conclusion

There are many risk factors that make young people vulnerable to trafficking. These risk factors occur at the individual, relationship, community, and societal levels. Further research is needed to better understand the various risk factors and how they interact with one another. In addition, much more work is needed on identifying protective factors and developing policies and programs that foster resilience. As Rachel Lloyd, founder and CEO of Girls Educational and Mentoring Services (GEMS) explains, "Rescue can't be a plan for anyone's life. . . . That's not a long term plan. [Our response] has to be about empowerment, about opportunity, about building on the inherent strengths that someone has."[109] Although we need a deeper, more nuanced understanding of risk and protective factors, what we do know now can provide a basis for developing early public health interventions and for improving identification of and responses to at-risk and exploited children.

# Improving Identification

## A Case Study of Health Care Settings

ANDREA, A seventeen-year-old African American female, came to the Mount Sinai Adolescent Health Center Primary Care Clinic for services after she was attacked by peers. The doctor helped make Andrea feel comfortable by engaging her in a welcoming manner and discussing the clinic's policies on privacy and confidentiality. Next, the doctor asked questions to understand Andrea's health history. The doctor explained that the same questions are asked of every patient. At MSAHC, providers typically start a visit by focusing on strengths—attributes a patient likes about herself or himself, such as "I have a nice personality" or "I'm good at drawing"—and take time to establish rapport with the patient in order to build trust before shifting the conversation to more difficult issues that some adolescents confront. During this time, the provider may ask questions such as "Has anyone ever touched your body when you did not want them to?," "If so, where were you touched?," "Was it your father, mother, sibling, grandparent, stranger, friend, or another person?," and "Have you ever been expected to have sex in exchange for food, shelter, money, or anything else you received?" During the initial conversation with the provider, Andrea—who visited the clinic that day because she had just been "jumped" by a group of female peers—disclosed that she had been sexually exploited beginning when she was eleven years old and had been in "the life" since that time.

In the months since that initial meeting, Andrea has been engaged in comprehensive and integrated services at MSAHC and has extricated herself from her trafficking situation. None of this was easy, of course, and Andrea deserves the lion's share of the credit for putting in the work to heal and improve her life. However, the treatment she has received (see chapter 7 for a discussion of treatment) and the progress she has made were possible in part because the clinic's providers were able to successfully identify her as a trafficking survivor and connect her with appropriate services.

As Andrea's case demonstrates, health care providers can play a critical role in identifying at-risk and exploited young persons. When Andrea first came to MSAHC, her health care provider did not deem her a "bad kid" or treat her dismissively. The provider also did not simply treat her physical symptoms without further inquiry into her life. Instead, having been trained to look for and identify risk factors (see chapter 5), the provider recognized her as an adolescent in need of assistance on multiple fronts. That triggered a more holistic engagement that ultimately led Andrea to disclose that she was a victim of sex trafficking.

Identification of trafficking survivors and other vulnerable youth in health care settings is critical. In many cases, health care professionals may represent one of the few opportunities available to reach vulnerable and exploited youth who otherwise might be missed by other members of society and left to suffer further trauma. Identifying at-risk and exploited children is challenging, but we cannot overlook such opportunities to assist young people in need.

At-risk and exploited children and adolescents visit a variety of health care settings, including emergency departments, physicians' offices, hospital outpatient clinics, teen clinics, school-based clinics, community health centers, health department clinics, obstetrics/gynecology clinics, family planning clinics, specialty clinics, mental health clinics, and dental clinics. In this chapter, we use the health care sector as a case study to explore ways to identify at-risk and exploited youth, detailing strategies for facilitating identification and challenges encountered when trying to identify these children and adolescents. The health care sector's role in assisting vulnerable and exploited youth is a critical component of a comprehensive public health response to child trafficking.

## Trafficking Victims in Health Care Settings

Children are, by their nature, more vulnerable to exploitation than adults. They may be more limited in terms of their physical and emotional maturity, leaving them vulnerable to adult abusers. Furthermore, they may lack the language skills needed to call attention to themselves when their rights are violated.[1] This puts young people at a disadvantage. Moreover, the hidden nature of child trafficking makes it challenging to identify victims.

Many young people who are victims of child trafficking live at the margins of society, disconnected from traditional structures and institutions. These youth rarely self-identify as trafficking victims. Their failure to self-identify in many cases may be a result of their limited development or of the exploitation and trauma they have suffered at the hands of traffickers, exploiters, purchasers, and others. In addition, other prior negative experiences—with law enforcement, health care providers, or others—may make them reluctant to trust adults and to disclose their situation to an unfamiliar individual. They may be aware of the stigma associated with human trafficking and anticipate negative responses if they disclose what is happening. In some cases, they are afraid of their trafficker, who may have threatened to harm them or their families. These young individuals may feel that there is no other option but to cooperate with their trafficker.

In other cases, trafficked children may have been groomed or primed by a trafficker.[2] The trafficker might persuade the child that he or she is the child's "boyfriend or "girlfriend." In such cases, trafficked children may think or insist that they are choosing to help their boyfriend or girlfriend and are not being exploited.

Though trafficked youth are often isolated, they live among us, in urban, suburban, and rural areas. They reflect all walks of life: male and female cisgender, transgender, and gender-fluid youth; all racial and ethnic backgrounds; and every socio-economic class and religious group. Traffickers and those individuals who spur demand for exploited children also include people of all backgrounds and socio-economic class. Those who exploit these children include, in various cases, family members, acquaintances, community members, people from outside the community, gang members, and strangers.

Health care providers are well situated to identify child and adolescent survivors of trafficking. In some clinical settings, such as MSAHC in New York City and the Pediatric Clinic at the University of San Francisco, patients are routinely screened and assessed in a culturally competent and trauma-informed manner for sex trafficking risk.[3] Such recognition of the problem of trafficking is spreading (though responses frequently focus primarily or even exclusively on sex trafficking), and training programs are developing in a number of health care settings.[4] A limited number of "screening tools" have been developed, though they need further evaluation.[5] While this progress in selected locations is encouraging, it is still the case that built-in screening and assessment protocols for trafficking-related harms are the exception rather than the rule in the health care sector.[6] Moreover, most medical and other health professional schools do not include adequate information about human trafficking, its various forms, and related types of exploitation in their curricula, nor do they provide trainees with the skills, training, and experience they will need in clinical settings where they would encounter youth at heightened risk for trafficking. Traditionally these programs do not teach students how to identify and serve trafficked populations. In sum, although awareness of the problem of human trafficking has increased to some extent in general and in particular in the health care sector, many still believe that trafficking is not prevalent in their community. Therefore, universal screening is not routinely built into clinical training and practice.

The absence of training on human trafficking in medical and other professional schools or in clinical settings is a complex issue. There are multiple reasons for this gap, including the fact that curricula are already overcrowded; many important issues that should be included in curricula are not, especially in the didactic portion of training. But additional reasons specific to human trafficking include a lack of awareness of both the problem and the ways in which it implicates the health care sector. Some people do not believe that trafficking victims seek health care services during their trafficking experience.[7] Therefore, even when there is awareness of the problem of human trafficking in a general sense, many health care professionals may believe that they are not in a position to address the problem even though recent research suggests otherwise.[8] As discussed in the introduction, children who are vulnerable to and exploited through human trafficking often seek out health care services, but few providers identify them as victims.[9]

Research on why some physicians do not ask about childhood abuse is informative in this context. It reveals that some physicians feel that there is insufficient time to probe sensitive issues, are uncomfortable asking or do not know how to ask, are concerned that asking might lead to responses that the health care provider is not equipped to handle, and are uncertain about their competence to assess for child abuse.[10] This is likely also the case in the context of human trafficking and child trafficking. Providers may not know what to ask or what to do with a positive "screen," and they may feel uncomfortable asking questions regarding sensitive and private issues. In addition, cultural biases and public misperceptions about trafficking may lead some providers to believe that boys cannot be victims, youth on the street are "bad" kids, or other misconceptions that result in providers overlooking opportunities to identify trafficked youth.

One study on survivors of international sex trafficking found that 50 percent of survivors had encountered a health care professional during their trafficking experience.[11] In another study, which interviewed survivors of domestic sex trafficking, researchers found that 87.8 percent of survivors had encountered one or more health care professionals sometime during the period in which they were trafficked. It appears that none of the survivors in either study had been identified as trafficking victims as a result of their encounters with the health care sector.[12] More recent research shows that the vast majority of adolescents identified as potential sex trafficking survivors access care at a health care facility.[13]

Not only do trafficking victims and survivors access the health care sector but they interact with a variety of health care professionals. A national anonymous survey of 173 adults who were sex trafficking or labor trafficking victims and had received health care found that the health care professionals most commonly encountered were those working within an emergency department/urgent care facility (55.6%), followed by primary care physicians (44.4%), dentists (26.5%), OB/GYNs (25.6%), traditional/alternative medicine providers (8.5%), and pediatricians (3.4%).[14] A number of trafficking survivors reported receiving services from more than one category of providers (which also explains why the total of percentages for the study exceed 100).[15] Despite seeing a range of providers and in many cases more than one provider, many of these individuals were not identified as trafficking victims during these interactions.[16] Only thirty-six individuals (of 173) reported having spoken to a health care provider about their situation. Of those thirty-six, 72 percent stated that they had been "offered information on how to escape."[17] These findings indicate that the vast majority of victims went unidentified.

Although research shows that trafficking victims access the health care system, studies highlight gaps in knowledge and training on the part of medical professionals.[18] Among health care professionals, emergency room personnel are particularly likely to encounter an individual being trafficked. Yet in a study examining emergency room personnel's understanding of human trafficking, findings indicated that only 29 percent of the personnel understood human trafficking to be an issue in their communities, only 13 percent felt confident or very confident that they could identify a trafficking victim, and fewer than 3 percent had received training in victim identification.[19] A lack of training increases the chances that a person being trafficked will be missed entirely or misidentified as a runaway, a rape victim, a domestic violence victim, or an undocumented immigrant.[20] Individuals may indeed be all these things (and may receive some services), but they may also be victims of human trafficking in need of specialized services tailored to meet the unique circumstances of exploitation through human trafficking.

Given that trafficking victims interact with the health care system, opportunities exist for early intervention if health care professionals and staff are equipped to identify at-risk and exploited children. Providers need to know what to look for and how to navigate potentially suspicious circumstances. Youth who show up at an emergency department, a hospital, a clinic, or a practice may be under the control of a trafficker. The control may be physical, such as when the trafficker accompanies the victim and speaks for the victim as a "buddy," "boyfriend," "girlfriend," "relative," or "associate." Such situations restrict communication between patient and provider, making it hard for the patient to communicate directly with or be alone with the staff. Alternatively, the control may be psychological and displayed through frequent texting or phone calls during the health care visit. In some cases, prior threats or violence might leave the young person so fearful that texts or calls are not needed to intimidate and ensure the silence of the victim. Young patients in this category may appear unusually anxious or in a hurry. Thus, even if not physically present with the victim during the health care visit, a trafficker can continue to exert control over the victim during the clinical encounter. At times, traffickers send someone else with the victim to exert control. Providers need to observe their patients' behavior very closely. But identification is about more than simply observing patient behavior; it is about every stage in the process, from creating an environment that facilitates identification to developing the skills of all professionals involved in patient care.

### Creating an Environment Conducive to Identification

In order for minors who are human trafficking victims to be identified in health care settings, those settings should be designed in a way that allows young people to utilize them easily and comfortably. The program design needs to be youth friendly, including services that are developmentally appropriate, confidential, and, when needed, free to the recipient. Research shows that services that are youth friendly lead to increased utilization by young people.[21] According to the World Health Organization, providing "adolescent-friendly services" means ensuring that the services are

Accessible. Adolescents *are able to* obtain the health services that are available.

Acceptable. Adolescents *are willing to* obtain the health services that are available.

Equitable. *All adolescents*, not just select groups, are able to obtain the health services that are available.

Appropriate. The *right health services* (i.e., the ones they need) are provided to them.

Effective. *The right services are provided in the right way*, and make a positive contribution to their health.[22]

The design of youth services at MSAHC is shaped and guided by a set of service and operational principles: "Service principles guide why types of programs and services are provided," while "operational principles are the foundation for how care is provided to young people."[23] They are discussed below as illustrative of the components of a health care practice that can facilitate identification of human trafficking survivors.

*Service principles* include providing a safe space; services that are accessible, both financially and geographically; care that is comprehensive, integrated, and easy to navigate; care that is equally accessible regardless of gender, ethnicity, religion, disability, social status, or other characteristics or conditions; care that is high quality; and transition services to adult health care facilities as youth age out of the adolescent care center.[24] Having a comprehensive, integrated care model is vital to ensuring that youth "receive a continuum of preventive and curative services according to their needs over time and across different levels of the health system."[25] The services need to be easy to navigate and flexible, including, for example, allowing youth to walk in for services when they feel they need care. These service principles are particularly important for young people who are trafficked.

*Operational principles* drive how services are delivered to young people in every aspect. This includes ensuring that services are

1. informed and driven by young people;
2. engaging to young people;
3. developmentally appropriate and tailored;
4. nonjudgmental and without stigma;
5. trauma informed;

6. relationship based; and

7. supportive of one-on-one adolescent-provider interactions.[26]

Detailed discussion of these principles follows.

## Informed and Driven by Young People

Mainstreaming—which has been applied in the context of both gender issues and children's rights—involves incorporating missing or marginalized perspectives into the design, implementation, monitoring, and evaluation of law, policies, and programs affecting a target population.[27] Mainstreaming has value in the health care context, particularly when serving vulnerable, marginalized populations such as trafficked youth. It is important to incorporate, or mainstream, the voices and perspectives of young people, in particular at-risk and exploited youth, in all aspects of developing and maintaining a program serving trafficked youth. That means including youth in the design, development, delivery, and monitoring and evaluation. This inclusion and involvement will help empower young people and help them become educated health care consumers. It will also help ensure that services are designed and provided in a way that maximizes their utility to youth.

Establishing youth-friendly channels for children and adolescents to contribute to the development of new programs and provide feedback on existing programs is critical. For example, at MSAHC, staff were told by youth trafficking survivors that it was virtually impossible for them to come to weekly psychotherapy sessions on a specific day at a specific time. When asked what would enable them to attend psychotherapy sessions, they reported that they needed to be whenever they were able to show up, most typically when they came in for a medical issue. MSAHC then adapted its approach in response to youth input, providing psychotherapy services for youth when they came in for a medical visit.

## Engaging to Young People

At both the initial meeting and during every subsequent visit, the young person should feel welcome and comfortable. Engaging youth is key to connecting with them and retaining them in health services. Aspects of engagement include greeting them with a smile, welcoming them, and explaining how care will be provided. Further, youth should be encouraged to ask questions or to ask for clarifications, and providers should build in time to allow for questions. Providers should also validate the young person's feelings to help them feel supported, and they should be nonjudgmental about how the young person presents, their situation, and their experiences. The health care provider needs to let a young person know that doctors and other clinical staff will ask a lot of questions, that every young person is asked these questions to provide an opportunity to share what is happening in their life, and that they should share what they are comfortable sharing.[28]

At MSAHC, engagement is critical. We see a first visit as an opportunity to get a second visit, the second visit as an opportunity to get a third visit, and so on. It is always important to address the issue that brought the young person in for that visit, while at the same time engaging them in more holistic services.

### Developmentally Appropriate and Tailored

Providers need to take into account the developmental stage of the young person. That is, clinicians and staff need training on and understanding of the range of maturity, education, health literacy, and communication skills of youth.[29] Interacting with youth in ways that are understandable to them without being condescending is essential. Providers need to use direct and simple language but not "talk down" to youth. Finally, it is essential to frame health issues in ways that matter to the young person now rather than relying on statistics about long-term impacts.[30]

### Nonjudgmental and without Stigma

Research shows that young people prefer a provider who is nonjudgmental and direct but expresses genuine concern, empathy, and respect for them.[31] Adolescents are particularly sensitive to adult behaviors that are impolite, judgmental, or overbearing. In fact, such attitudes and behaviors may cause adolescents to leave the clinic before they obtain needed care, not to comply with treatment plans, or to refuse or ignore follow-up care.[32] Health care providers should serve young people without judgment, regardless of their behavior. For example, the provider should never react with shock if young people share that they have a history of incest, have had sex with dozens of partners, or are being trafficked. One of the provider's goals is to ensure that the young person feels comfortable enough to share what is really happening in their life and to be inclined to return for additional care or follow-up visits as needed. Adolescents do not respond well to criticism or judgment and are not likely to return to a place where they sense disapproval.

At MSAHC, we believe that a "one service, one clinic" model helps foster a stigma-free environment. Thus, youth come to "an adolescent health center" rather than a family planning clinic, HIV clinic, substance abuse clinic, mental health clinic, or other type of clinics that might expose them to stigma and discrimination.[33] All patients use the same entrance to the clinic and sit in the same waiting room, no matter why they are there. This reduces stigma and helps protect patient privacy. To further avoid stigma, no patient is separated out or isolated unless there is a medical reason (e.g., a patient is clinically unstable or has a condition that could be infectious or contagious). As young people register for their appointments and are called by the provider, the reason for their visit remains private. Along with creating a stigma-free environment, it is critical to hire staff who enjoy working with young people, want to listen to youth, and will not be judgmental.

### Trauma Informed

Because adversity and trauma are so common in the lives of at-risk and trafficked youth, it is important to use a trauma lens in this work. The DSM-5, the diagnostic manual used by mental health professionals, defines trauma as "Exposure to actual or threatened death, serious injury, or sexual violence in one (or more) of the following ways: directly experiencing the traumatic event(s); witnessing, in person, the traumatic event(s) as it occurred to others; learning that the traumatic event(s) occurred to a close family member or close friend; or experiencing repeated or extreme exposure to aversive details of the traumatic event."[34] A trauma-informed approach, therefore, is aware of and responsive to this experience. Employing a trauma-informed approach includes "establishing safety in the physical location of the program; providing clear and consistent messages about what will happen during each visit; ensuring that all staff maintain appropriate interpersonal boundaries; and maximizing the young person's choice and control in terms of which services are received, when they are received, and the characteristics (e.g., gender, culture) of the provider(s) with whom they interact."[35]

MSAHC has adopted a number of trauma-informed practices. These include the following:

- Security staff members have the competence to interact with young people and relay a nonthreatening sense of safety.
- The registration process and steps that follow (triage, having vital signs taken, seeing the provider) are organized in ways that are easy for the young person to use, and the young person is informed about what will happen at each stage of the visit.
- All staff take the time to greet the young person, answer questions, and interact in a warm and professional manner so as to relay a sense of welcome and safety.
- Staff are trained to build trust over time so that they can engage the young person and ask direct questions to identify and explore traumatic experiences and their impact on the young person's health and well-being.
- Options to address trauma are available onsite and immediately as needed, including crisis intervention, one-on-one psychotherapy, group therapy, family therapy, and legal services.

## Relationship Based

Relationships are essential to any successful patient-provider interaction. An adolescent-focused health center can serve as a source of support even if a young person does not have a health care need. At MSAHC, everything, from policies to procedures to practices, is relationship based. An underlying goal is for the young people who visit the center to develop strong relationships with the center itself and with staff members so that they feel a sense of connection.[36] The emphasis on relationship building has resulted in youth coming to the center at times simply to say hello, to show their report card, or to share other news even when they are not in need of health care services. Providing this level of caring is a way to help youth feel connected and to engage them in long-term interventions that reduce the ongoing harm of experiencing or witnessing traumatic events.[37] At MSAHC, the relationship and connection are seen as part of the healing process. When youth are treated as partners in their health care, they are empowered, not just served.

### Supportive of One-on-One Adolescent-Provider Interactions

Supporting one-on-one interactions between adolescent and provider helps foster positive relationships and, ultimately, positive outcomes. One-on-one interactions can create a space in which young people can share sensitive issues. Policies and procedures should be in place at the facility to support the confidential nature of clinic visits while acknowledging and conveying the limits of that confidentiality (e.g., if a young person's life or someone else's life is in danger, that cannot be kept confidential). The provider should always spend time alone with the patient regardless of who accompanies the young person to the visit. Although it is important to involve parents, guardians, or other adults who may have brought the patient to the facility, part of the visit should be "patient only" unless the doctor needs a staff member or a translator in the room during the patient's visit. This time will give the patient the opportunity to share privately, without the presence of the individual(s) who brought him or her to the clinic.

All these service and operating principles are intended to help make young people feel safe, comfortable, and supported. In short, they are aimed at creating an environment conducive to identifying trafficking survivors or any other youth in need of assistance.

## Identifying Cases of Child Trafficking

Building and strengthening capacity to identify trafficking victims and survivors requires attention to every stage of an individual's visit to a health care facility (or other entity). From setting the initial tone of the interaction with a young person, through taking a history, to the physical exam, health care entities and organizations can develop procedures and protocols that facilitate successful interventions in the lives of at-risk and exploited youth.

### Setting a Tone That Empowers the Youth

Health care providers should start all visits by personally acknowledging the young person, addressing him or her directly by name, and offering a handshake (when culturally appropriate) as an introduction. Evidence indicates that a strong, personal introduction is a key factor in ensuring that young people have positive perceptions about their health care, and it can influence whether they will return.[38]

Creating a positive health care experience is important. Asking youth about their interests, acknowledging their uniqueness, and displaying an interest in them as persons are all constructive steps that can foster trust and help youth feel comfortable. This means not merely focusing on the risks and problems of young people but also seeing them in their totality and inquiring about their strengths and assets. Because of training and time pressures, health care providers are often focused on diagnosis and treatment. That narrow focus may not be as effective with young people, who will not necessarily volunteer important information about what is happening in their lives if they perceive that the provider is not genuinely interested in them.[39] However, if they are asked directly in the context of a supportive health visit, young people are more likely to share what is really going on. Many youth say that when they seek health care, they are asked infrequently about sensitive issues.[40] Youth can have better outcomes if providers take the time to identify what is happening in their lives and provide them with skills and tools to make appropriate and informed decisions. At MSAHC, providers ask direct questions of every young person, with as many follow-up questions as necessary to identify thoughts, feelings, motivations, and behaviors.

## Creating Time Alone with the Patient

When a trafficking victim has health problems, the trafficker or a designee may accompany the young person to the health visit and may be reluctant to leave the trafficked child alone with the staff. This makes it difficult for a provider to open a conversation that would encourage the young person to talk about the exploitation. In these cases, health care entities and providers can take steps to overcome these barriers. It is good practice to always spend time alone with young people, outside the presence of any person who comes with them, regardless of who accompanies them or the reason for the visit, or whether or not they are suspected victims of human trafficking.

If a young person is accompanied to a health care visit by others, it is important to welcome them all and bring them into the office/examination room and discuss the confidential nature of the visit with everyone present. This initial discussion can include an overview of the policies and procedures of the particular facility that require youth to be seen alone for part of the visit. Once the more general conversation has taken place, everyone who came with the patient should be asked to wait in the waiting room. During that time, the provider can take the patient's additional medical history, including broaching sensitive issues to find out what else might really be happening. This time also ensures that the patient has space to ask questions.

Even if the person accompanying the child is a parent, maintaining a practice of having some time alone with the patient is important for all adolescents because they may not disclose important information about their lives when others are in the room. Spending time without other people known to the patient is particularly important for youth with a possible history of exploitation, including human trafficking. In some instances, parents are involved in the trafficking of their children.[41] One study in New York found that 36 percent of children in the study had been trafficked by their parents or immediate family members, 27 percent had been trafficked by their boyfriends, 14 percent by employers, 14 percent by friends of family, and 9 percent by strangers.[42] A provider can rely on a variety of reasons for time alone with patients, such as hospital or clinic protocol or the need for an exam. It is highly unlikely that a patient will disclose any relevant information if the trafficker or associate is with or near the victim.

In some cases, even when patients are seen alone and the provider has worked to make them feel comfortable, the extensive nature of their past trauma may cause them to distrust the provider (or they may still fear their trafficker). Or they might not be ready to disclose information. In those cases, providers must refrain from judging or becoming frustrated. Providers should keep in mind the adolescents' perspective; they might have a long history of being treated poorly and judged harshly by adults (e.g., maltreated in the home and in foster care settings, arrested by law enforcement, punished by teachers, judged by prior providers, abused by traffickers and purchasers, etc.).[43] Patience and understanding of their prior experiences and current situation are critical. The goal is to make sure the young person feels good enough about this health care experience to return, so that the patient-provider relationship continues to grow and the youth becomes more comfortable. Providers should continue to ask questions, as that signals to the youth that these issues are important. Equally important, providers must continue to ask questions in a manner that is nonjudgmental. By showing consistent interest, providers can foster a relationship in which adolescents eventually feel comfortable disclosing sensitive information.

Even if youth disclose little during the first or second interaction, it is critical that they have time alone with the provider so that the provider can ask direct questions and provide them opportunities to share anything they want to share (and might not share in the presence of family members, friends, or other individuals). Bear in mind that if a vulnerable or exploited youth has returned for follow-up visits, that is a positive step. Continuing to create opportunities for relationship building and information exchange is vital. The provider is more likely to get an accurate history of sensitive issues and behaviors by having time alone with the adolescent and asking direct questions in a sensitive, empathetic, and caring way.

More broadly, time alone with patients should be part of a holistic strategy for increasing their comfort level and emotional safety. This holistic strategy includes having a youth-friendly environment that is comfortable, is welcoming, and conveys supportive messages that help young people feel acknowledged and accepted. It can also mean allowing young people to use their cell phones and other electronic devices. It also includes giving young people a sense of privacy. As part of this strategy, it is important for the providers and other staff to ask whether patients are warm enough or need something to drink, when they last ate, and so on. In other words, tending to young persons' basic physical needs can help them feel safe, supported, and taken care of, and it can also help build trust between the patient and provider.

### Making the Patient Comfortable While Taking a History

When taking a history from a suspected or confirmed trafficking victim or survivor, the clinician should show warmth and be patient, open minded, accepting, respectful, and nonjudgmental.[44] Being nonjudgmental means that the provider is there to find out how to best help, empower, and serve the young person regardless of the patient's lifestyle or behavior. For example, if an adolescent is having unprotected sex, the provider should aim to help the youth understand why it matters for the youth to use protection and make sure that the youth has the necessary skills to navigate situations in which protection is needed. The provider should not make the adolescent feel "bad" about having unprotected sex. In other words, it is critical to distinguish between the behavior and the person. Discussing the former is essential, but it must be done without condemning the individual. The goal is to work with young people so that they start adopting healthier practices. However, even if they do not, the goal should be to ensure they leave the office or clinic feeling that they can still return for help.

Health care professionals—or any others who work with youth—should never give up on a young person but instead should continue to educate them on the benefits of adopting healthier practices. Staff should also acknowledge young people's strengths and provide positive feedback on what they are doing well. It might take multiple visits for a patient to develop trust in a provider given the difficult life experiences many of these young people have had. In addition, young people may feel that other needs, such as food, safety, shelter, and money, are more pressing. Assisting youth with these basic needs can help build a trusting relationship between them and their health care provider.

Keeping in mind how often at-risk and exploited youth are mistreated or judged negatively, it is essential to model and normalize healthy interactions. When beginning to take a history, the provider should ask what brought the young person in for services and what they need. Then, the provider can begin to focus on general health and ask general questions about the young person's life or daily activities in order to establish a rapport before addressing the more sensitive topics. When the provider is alone with the patient and progresses to more sensitive issues, the provider should not react with shock or disapproval if the patient discloses having had "hundreds of sexual partners" or "too many to count." Instead, it is critical to explore the circumstances and the possibility of sexual exploitation. As providers do this, they need to be attuned to how the adolescent reacts and responds. Some trafficking survivors prefer that providers not ask about the number of sexual partners they have had, and thus providers need to be capable of using alternative lines of questioning to explore these topics. Once a young person discloses any potential issue, the conversation must probe further in a nonthreatening manner. The young person needs to perceive this history taking as evidence of a genuine interest in their well-being by an individual who wants to help, and not merely an exercise in getting information for the staff's use.

Overall, the history taking should operate like a conversation. The health provider should use straightforward language that recognizes and addresses the young person's strengths and assets, as well as their vulnerabilities. Because providers may not know ahead of time who is at risk or who is a victim or survivor of labor trafficking or sex trafficking, they need to take a thorough history that will help reveal how this particular young

Table 6.1. *Taking a history: A closer look*

In general, it is better to start with more general or basic background questions before moving on to more sensitive and probing ones. These questions may cover different areas, including demographics, living situations, relationships, general health/functioning, and sensitive issues, including potential abuse or exploitation. All these categories, including the more introductory ones, can help reveal risk factors and potentially reveal circumstances suggesting that the young person is a victim of human trafficking. It is important to note that every patient is unique, so every conversation will be as well. The questions below are suggested starting points, rather than a comprehensive list. And not every question needs to be asked of each child. Taking a history is a dynamic process, and providers should balance letting the conversation evolve organically with needing to ask essential questions. Finally, the history should end on a positive note.

| Part of History | Relevance | Sample Questions |
| --- | --- | --- |
| Background demographic and developmental data | Can provide insights into developmental stage; family composition; living arrangements, including homelessness; and school attendance and performance.<br><br>Can give the patient time to get comfortable and can help show genuine interest and build trust. | How old are you? Where do you live? Who do you live with? Are you in school? How are you doing in school? Has your school performance changed in any way? If not in school, why are you not attending school? Are you working? What do you like about yourself? What are you interested in? |
| Relationships and functioning | Can reveal the types of relationships the young person has with family members, friends, and romantic partners. | How do you get along with your parents? How do you communicate with your parents? Do you share everything with them? Do you feel loved and supported by your mom/dad/guardian? Do you have siblings? How do you get along with them? Do you have friends? Do you have a best friend? What are their names? Do you feel included in the activities of your peers? Are you in a relationship? With whom? How old is the person? How do you two get along? How does this person treat you? Do you feel loved and supported? |

| | | |
|---|---|---|
| | Can reveal potential for pregnancy, risk of sexually transmitted infections, HIV. | For females: Have you ever had your period? When was your last menstrual period? For all patients: Have you ever had vaginal intercourse? Anal intercourse? Oral sex? How old were you the first time you had any or each of these? Have you ever been pregnant or fathered a child? When? What was the outcome of each pregnancy? Have you been tested for sexually transmitted infections, including HIV? Have you been told that you had any of these infections? |
| Mental health and drug use | Can reveal whether the person is depressed or suicidal. | How do you feel? Are you feeling sad? Have you thought of killing yourself? Do you have a plan? Have you tried to kill yourself? |
| Substance use and abuse | Can reveal whether the person uses cigarettes, alcohol, or drugs. | Do you smoke cigarettes? Do you drink alcohol? Do you use marijuana? cocaine? heroin? anything else? How often do you use any of these? Do you use them with others? if so, with whom? Or do you use them alone? Note: There are also validated screening tools that providers can use to address these issues. |
| Childhood abuse | Will reveal possibility of physical or sexual abuse or other unwelcome sexual exposures. | How do your parents show you they think you've done something well? How do your parents reward you for what they consider good behaviors? How do your parents discipline or punish you? Do they ever hit you? Has anyone ever touched your body when you did not want them to? Where did they touch you? Has anyone made you touch, kiss, masturbate, or perform oral sex on them? Has anyone made you have oral, vaginal, or anal sex when you did not want to? Was it a boyfriend/girlfriend/family member/relative/stranger? How old were you? |

*continued*

Table 6.1. (continued)

| Part of History | Relevance | Sample Questions |
|---|---|---|
| Human trafficking | Can help identify possibility of risk for or actual sex trafficking. | Have you ever been pressured to have sex from someone who gave you food, a place to sleep, money, or drugs? Have you ever had to exchange sex for food, shelter, drugs, or money? Have you ever been in "the life"? |
| | Can help identify exploitative employment practices including labor trafficking. | Are you working? What type of work do you do? Where? How many hours do you work? What is your salary? Are you free to leave the job whenever you would like? Are you working for these people or this company to pay a debt to them? to pay a debt to someone else? for what? Are you in control of all your documents? Are you in control of your salary? |

person is doing, what they are involved with, and what is really going on in their life.

Table 6.1 provides a breakdown of the components of a sample history, the relevance of each line of questioning, and illustrative questions. Additional resources may be found in the appendix.

*A Note on Interpreters* The ideal communication setting would allow for direct dialogue between the health care professional and the young person who presents for care. However, because of language and cultural barriers that is not always possible. Although it is essential that all staff be trained to have cultural humility, that may not be sufficient. Language differences will create the need for interpreters in selected cases (including sign language interpreters). When an interpreter is needed, it is best to use a professional interpreter service. Moreover, interpreters should be screened to ensure that they understand the health care context and medical language and have experience translating highly personal, sensitive information, such as a young person's history of sexual abuse. In some instances, staff who speak the relevant language may be used, but this should be done only when staff have sufficient language skills or if there are genuine time or resource constraints, and not merely for staff convenience or as a cost-saving measure.[45] In all cases, but particularly if a provider suspects trafficking or related exploitation or abuse, it is important not to use people known to the young person. Even if the patient does not know the interpreter, health care providers should screen the interpreter to ensure that they do not know the victim or the traffickers and do not have any other conflict of interest.[46]

## Beyond a Standard History

In addition to the above, there are areas of further inquiry that can help identify labor trafficking or sex trafficking.

The possibility of labor trafficking should be explored by finding out if the young person is working and the circumstances under which he or she is employed. This includes the young person's relationship to their employer, supervisor, or others in charge; the environment and circumstances in which they work; salary arrangements, including whether the young person is paid directly; who holds their identity documents and work permits (if applicable); and whether they can leave whenever they would like. To the extent that any of these questions implicate immigration or citizenship status, providers need to be careful how they probe these issues and only ask about immigration status if it is relevant to care.

The possibility of sex trafficking should be explored by probing any relationships with older or controlling men. Sex trafficking survivors sometimes refer to their boyfriends as "daddy." It is not uncommon for a thirteen- or fourteen-year-old girl to refer to a man in his twenties or thirties as her "boyfriend." Recalling that women can be traffickers as well, it is also appropriate to explore relevant relationships with women.[47] By exploring relationships, a provider can assess whether there are additional relationship-level risk factors (see chapter 5).

During the initial interactions with a young person, providers should look out for a range of possible signs of human trafficking, including being tired from working long hours, reverse sleeping patterns (sleeping during the day and up at night), always hurrying because they have to be at work, having little or no money because they are not being paid directly or paid appropriate wages, submissiveness, lack of a clear home address, a history of homelessness, no identification, giving a false age, truancy or inconsistent school attendance, or recent changes in school performance.[48] In addition, young people seeking care may have any of a number of psychological issues, including anxiety symptoms or post-traumatic stress disorder (PTSD), including complex PTSD, or substance abuse issues.[49] They may also show symptoms of emotional blunting, sleep problems, somatization, depression, hostility, low self-esteem, suicidal ideation, dissociation, fear, excessive guilt or shame, or poor interpersonal relationships.[50] Additional warning signs include multiple health issues, seeking care late for a condition, and evidence of lack of preventive health care and dental care.[51] Moreover, in the sex trafficking context, red flags can also include having multiple hotel keys or carrying large amounts of cash.[52] If a provider identifies any of these issues or other risk factors (see chapter 5), especially if multiple factors are present, further inquiry is warranted.

As noted above, some questions might implicate immigration status. Immigration status can be relevant in both sex trafficking and labor trafficking cases. Questions related to or implicating immigration status should be probed carefully and sensitively and only when necessary. It is best to approach this topic after the provider has established a strong relationship with the young person. Moreover, any decision to probe such areas should be contemplated in advance at an institutional level with an understanding of the political climate and any potential legal implications with regard to reporting undocumented immigrants. From a clinical perspective, immigration status can be relevant because undocumented individuals may have experienced additional trauma as a result of their vulnerable status. Immigrants, especially undocumented immigrants, may have been exploited and traumatized prior to or during their journey to the United States and are also at higher risk of labor trafficking and sex trafficking once in the United States.[53] Undocumented immigrants may be reluctant to come forward because they fear being arrested or deported. This fear of deportation makes them less likely to report abuses and thus more vulnerable to exploitation.[54] In contrast, some asylum seekers may be more willing to come forward because they seek help with the logistics of the asylum process and want to connect with an agency that can assist them. Many asylum seekers are likely to have trauma and financial pressures that increase their vulnerability to human trafficking.[55] In addition, many children in the United States now live in mixed-status homes.[56] As a result, sometimes even young people who are US citizens may avoid seeking help or discussing their personal or family information when seeking help because of concerns that the authorities will learn that one or both of their parents are undocumented. Not only is immigration status relevant to uncovering exploitation, but it is also relevant to health care and other services. Immigration status can affect a young person's eligibility for a variety of services.[57]

Finally, the health history or interview should end on a positive note. Providers can encourage a more positive end by asking the young person questions such as, What would you change in your life if you could? What do you like about yourself? What are your aspirations, hopes, and dreams? How would you like for me to be helpful to you?

The physical exam can also facilitate identification. During the physical exam, health care providers should be aware that a range of signs and symptoms might suggest human trafficking. For sex trafficking cases, potential signs include wearing clothing inconsistent with the weather; unusual tattoos on the neck, chest, arms, or other parts of the body that could be branding of the trafficker's name or some other marker that identifies the victim as the trafficker's possession; or a tattoo the young person does not know how to explain or is reluctant to explain.[58] For labor trafficking cases, reporting of work-related physical injuries or environmental health issues might suggest possible exploitation. Some of the environmental issues may include exposure to chemicals, weather-related exposures from working outside all day, burns, or other harms resulting from harsh environmental conditions.[59] A person who reports feeling tired and not eating well or being undernourished may have been exploited. A person who reports being or appears to be always in a hurry to get back to work or calls work often during the medical visit may be someone who is being exploited or harmed in some way.

In terms of physical injuries, trafficking victims might exhibit or report musculoskeletal stress and strain from arduous labor; chronic pain and fatigue from extended working hours; hearing loss or broken teeth due to injury; malnourishment, dehydration, and diarrheal and/or respiratory diseases due to poor sanitation; scars from cigarette burns; and other unexplained bruises and/or other signs of abuse. As to environmental health issues, trafficking victims are subject to a variety of industry-specific occupational hazards, including biological pathogens from livestock farms; pesticide chemicals from commercial agriculture; and other toxic materials, such as ammonia and asbestos.[60]

In addition to being treated for the acute problem that brought the young person in for services that day, they also need to receive a comprehensive history and physical exam, including being checked for any sign of physical trauma. If warning signs of trafficking are present, a complete genital and rectal examination should be considered; if it is appropriate to proceed, it should be done with care to reduce as much as possible any pain, trauma, and discomfort for the young patient. Testing for sexually transmitted diseases should be done, and an HIV pre-test/test should be considered. Females should have a pregnancy test. All these steps should be undertaken in partnership with the young patient.

Providers should be sure that they communicate with the young person at every stage of the physical exam. Trafficked youth typically have experienced violations of bodily integrity (in both sex trafficking and labor trafficking) and are sensitive to any additional unwelcomed contact. It is critical for providers to explain each step of a physical exam and get the young person's permission before taking the action and to share any findings with the patient. This can help build trust that might lead a young person to disclose critical information late in the visit.

Other aspects of the physical exam—including discussion of findings and treatment options, if relevant—are discussed in the next chapter. For additional information on symptoms and other potential signs of human trafficking or related exploitation, see the resources listed in the appendix.

## Follow-Up

As noted earlier, a key goal of an initial visit (and each subsequent visit) is to continue to build the relationship between staff and the youth so that the young person will return for subsequent visits. A valuable resource has been the development of better tools that children and adolescents can use to communicate with their providers and ask questions remotely. This way, patients can feel connected between visits, ask questions of their provider, and receive information and assistance without always having to return to the office or clinic. It also helps them feel more connected and supported.

MSAHC, partnering with young people, developed a health app called "Health Squad." Young people chose both the name and the logo design. Via this app, young people can set up reminders for when they need to take medication. They can receive messages about healthy lifestyles. And they can request clinic appointments. This way of working with young people helps them become more informed about their well-being and their health care and provides them with a greater sense of control over their bodies and their lives. They can submit questions about health issues at any time, and a provider will respond within one business day. Overall, these interactions via the app complement the in-person visits and help young people become better health care consumers.

Putting the Pieces Together

A word of caution is warranted. Many of the symptoms and behaviors described as possible evidence of human trafficking are also present in children and adolescents who have experienced other forms of trauma. Depression, drug use, and a reluctance to trust authority figures and open up to a healthcare provider do not mean that a particular child is definitely a trafficking victim. Three points are worth keeping in mind: First, the traits and experiences described here are common to many young people. If a young person presents at a health care facility with multiple risk factors, there is no guarantee that the youth is a trafficking victim. Rather, these risk factors should prompt further investigation by health care providers to identify what is going on and encourage the provision of services to address any concerns. Second, if an adolescent presents with several of these risk factors, but the provider determines that the child is not a trafficking victim, the risk factors still suggest that the child is in need of help. As discussed in earlier chapters, trafficking falls on a spectrum. Even if a child's experience falls short of the legal definition of trafficking, it might still be the case that the child has suffered some type of trauma and needs assistance. By looking for trafficking, providers can identify other youth in need. Third, all of this reinforces the importance of ensuring that health care professionals and staff are adequately trained to identify and respond to child trafficking. We need to ensure that providers accurately assess and diagnose issues that children and adolescents are experiencing.

In summary, health care providers need to take a holistic approach to identifying victims of trafficking. At the outset, policies and procedures must create an environment conducive to disclosure to build a patient-provider partnership. The youth might disclose information, but as noted earlier, most trafficked youth do not self-identify. Thus, it is important for the provider to ask the right questions in a direct, sensitive, and culturally competent manner and to be able to identify critical details shared by the youth. The provider should combine this information with the findings from a physical exam and use informed judgment to assess whether a child is at risk of or has been exploited by human trafficking.

### Barriers to Identification

The barriers to identification are many. These barriers can relate to the provider, the institution, or the patient.

Health Care Provider or Institutional Barriers

Barriers to identification of human trafficking include lack of awareness, lack of understanding, stereotypes and misperceptions, and lack of training. Many health care providers remain unaware of the prevalence of child trafficking or unaware that it happens in their community. The result is that trafficked youth may come to emergency rooms or other health care settings and receive treatment for specific conditions but not be identified as trafficked victims. Stereotypes and misperceptions also present a barrier. These young people are often misclassified based on cultural assumptions or as a result of being judged delinquent youth. These misperceptions and misclassifications are all related to a lack of training of health care professionals. Without adequate and ongoing training, many providers are unsure how to identify trafficking victims or where to refer them if they suspect that trafficking has occurred or if they actually find out a young person has been trafficked.

Institutional barriers relate to and can compound provider ones. Many health care institutions are similarly unaware that human trafficking is a problem in their community. As a result, they may not see it as a priority issue and might not allocate sufficient resources to ensure that staff are trained to identify, treat, or refer trafficking survivors. They also may not invest the resources needed to create an environment in which trafficking survivors can access the comprehensive range of services they need. Failure to develop trauma-informed systems can result in exploited youth encountering numerous potential obstacles to needed services.

In recent years, some state legislatures have imposed a mandate on health care professionals that might spur the development of training programs and other measures to address child trafficking. Specifically, some states have amended their mandatory reporting laws for child abuse to include sex trafficking, labor trafficking, or both.[61] Although only a minority of states has done this, all fifty states and the District of Columbia include sexual abuse or sexual exploitation in their mandatory reporting laws.[62] This coverage arguably should prompt the reporting of sex trafficking, given that its symptoms often parallel those of sexual abuse or sexual exploitation.[63] In other words, when a provider sees evidence of sexual assault or sexual abuse, it should prompt further inquiry and lead to identifying sex trafficking, if present.[64] On the other hand, there is arguably a greater need to include labor trafficking in mandatory reporting laws, as such laws as currently constituted may not cover all the harms experienced by labor trafficking victims.[65] Regardless, this attention to mandatory reporting laws should encourage health care institutions to review their policies and procedures and ensure that their practices support the identification of all forms of harm against children, including human trafficking.

Even assuming that other states follow this emerging trend of including child trafficking in their mandatory reporting child abuse laws, such a mandate might not be sufficient on its own. Despite the legal and professional imperatives for health care providers to identify and report child abuse, many providers are reluctant to do so, and thus much abuse remains unidentified, underreported, and untreated in clinical settings, including pediatric practices.[66]

The reasons why some health care providers do not screen for child abuse in clinical settings is poorly understood. Only a few studies have examined why a history of abuse is not always taken from children and adolescents by most physicians who provide health services to them,[67] as well as from adults.[68] In one study, research showed that primary care physicians failed to evaluate adult patients' history of childhood abuse because they lacked the techniques to do so.[69] Another study reported that among the reasons offered by physicians for not asking about childhood abuse are uncertainty about their own competence to assess for abuse (when there are no physical signs and symptoms) and discomfort asking about it.[70] Additional research found that many physicians feel less confident assessing sexual abuse than they do assessing physical abuse and more anxious about rendering an opinion about sexual abuse or testifying about it in court.[71] Other providers have expressed concerns that reporting cases of abuse might put the child in a worse situation.[72] This concern reflects the reality that many locales lack sufficient services to meet the needs of trafficking survivors and other exploited individuals. Ultimately, that concern should be addressed by investing in and developing the infrastructure and resources needed to assist trafficking survivors rather than refraining from reporting suspected cases, which inevitably leaves child trafficking victims to endure further trauma.[73]

More generally, it is important that health care institutions not put the burden of identification solely on individual health care professionals. Health care institutions can create and support a practice culture that aims to engage youth holistically, identify and respond to both apparent and hidden harms, and provide comprehensive, integrated services to all youth who need them.

### Patient-Related Barriers

Barriers can also be patient related. Trafficking survivors may not perceive themselves as victims, or if they do, they may be reluctant to share this information with a provider. As previously discussed, most trafficking survivors do not readily self-identify. However, it is our experience that if asked appropriate questions about their circumstances in a nonjudgmental way by caring health care providers, those who have experienced harm likely will describe behaviors consistent with victimization.

In other cases, survivors may lack knowledge of US laws and thus may feel that they have contractual obligations to their trafficker or believe they will be arrested for trafficking-related crimes. Other survivors may have language barriers or be illiterate or simply are so afraid or ashamed that it may be hard for them to reveal what is occurring. Given the various barriers, health care providers concerned about human trafficking need to appreciate that identification might take more than one interaction with a young patient.

Finally, it is critical that patient-related barriers be handled in culturally sensitive, understanding, and nonjudgmental ways. The patient should never be blamed or be made to feel that he or she did wrong or failed by not disclosing information. The focus should be on building trust, explaining why disclosure is important and beneficial to the young person, and supporting a young person who does share information about exploitation and other harms.

## At-Risk Youth

In addition to the many trafficking victims and survivors who appear at various health care facilities, an even greater number of youth are at risk of being trafficked or exploited in other ways. In this context, health care professionals can play a role in preventing exploitation before it happens. Providers need to be familiar with what puts young people at risk, and they must work with young people determined to be at risk in order to prevent the progression toward exploitation.

For example, research shows that homelessness is a proximal risk for sex trafficking.[74] Therefore, homeless youth should be connected with services that can help them address housing-related issues as well as any other issues that increase their risk of maltreatment or exploitation. Because most sex trafficking victims and survivors have a history of childhood sexual abuse, when a provider learns that a young person has a history of sexual abuse, he or she needs to connect the young person with services specializing in treating youth survivors of sexual abuse to help the young person process the trauma and start the healing process. The same holds true for adolescents who have substance abuse issues. They need to be connected with appropriate services, both to treat the issues they are struggling with and to prevent further harm. Equally important, when these risk factors are identified, the provider needs to probe further to see what other risk factors are present and whether the child has suffered through trafficking or in another exploitative situation. This includes exploring risk factors at all levels of the socio-ecological model—individual, relationship, community, and societal (see chapter 5).

Health care professionals know that there are other populations of youth who are at heightened vulnerability, such as youth in the child welfare system.[75] This does not mean that it should be assumed that all foster children are trafficking victims; rather, awareness of the risk factors enables health care professionals and other partners to educate at-risk youth about trafficking-related harms and to partner with other adults in these children's lives to enhance resilience and strengthen protections for at-risk youth so that young people can avoid the traumatic experience of exploitation.

## Conclusion

In this chapter, we discussed operating principles and screening and assessment techniques that health care institutions and professionals can employ to build their capacity to identify at-risk youth and exploited youth. We also outlined opportunities for identification during the taking of a patient's history and the physical examination. These are important opportunities for health care providers to assist children and youth at risk of or exploited by human trafficking. In many ways, given the nature of the patient-provider relationship in health care, providers are in a unique position to identify and intervene, not only when individuals are trapped in trafficking situations but also earlier, when they are at risk. Ongoing, specific training is needed to ensure that health care providers feel confident in their ability to screen, assess, and evaluate cases. Developing and implementing policies and procedures that enhance providers' ability to identify trafficking victims is critical. Ensuring institutional support for providers on the front line is essential. Once trafficked youth are identified, health care professionals and institutions must be positioned to ensure that these children and adolescents receive the treatment and services they need in a sensitive and culturally competent manner. Finally, the health care setting can serve as a platform for prevention by educating young people about the issues of exploitation, including human trafficking, before it occurs.

# Assisting Vulnerable and Exploited Youth

## Health Care Responses

Andrea, whose story was introduced in prior chapters, was successfully identified as a trafficking victim when she came to the Mount Sinai Adolescent Health Center Primary Care Clinic. As a result, the center was able to connect her with a range of services that she needed. In her first appointment with a psychologist, Andrea reported symptoms consistent with complex post-traumatic stress disorder that may have been a result of early childhood sexual abuse, neglect, exposure to domestic violence, and ongoing sexual exploitation (sex trafficking).

In the months since that initial appointment, Andrea has engaged in comprehensive, integrated services at MSAHC and has extricated herself from her trafficking situation. This represents a major achievement, and Andrea deserves a tremendous amount of credit for putting in the work to get out of a terrible situation and begin the healing process. Andrea is now connected to multiple providers at MSAHC and appears to be benefiting from these services. In addition, the center's patient advocate/lawyer assisted Andrea in applying for and securing government benefits, so that she has financial support for her recovery-related services.

MSAHC serves as a home base for Andrea, who both comes for regular appointments and reaches out during periods of crisis or uncertainty to obtain guidance, advice, and care. For example, in the aftermath of a recent sexual assault, Andrea called her MSAHC therapist for immediate emotional support and guidance and quickly followed up with integrated medical, sexual and reproductive health, and mental health services. Andrea also gave permission for the MSAHC therapist to speak with her mother about the impact of this sexual assault. On another occasion, Andrea reached out to her MSAHC therapist after an incident of dating violence. The therapist helped her find a safe shelter and since then has engaged Andrea and her current partner in couples' therapy aimed at reducing the risk of continued violence. Andrea reports that she feels "safe" and "special" at MSAHC and that these feelings of safety and security lead her to continue to reach out for guidance and support.

Ultimately, in collaboration with Andrea, her doctor was able to develop a treatment plan that secured the delivery of comprehensive, integrated services in a sensitive and culturally informed manner. The comprehensive care embodied some of the service and operational principles of the MSAHC model; it was youth friendly, developmentally tailored and appropriate, relationship based, and youth driven.

Trafficking victims come to MSAHC for a variety of reasons. Often young people come with specific concerns, as did Joseph, a young man who came to MSAHC because of potential exposure to HIV. He identified himself as having sexual relationships with other men, and over time he disclosed to staff that he was involved in sex trafficking. After addressing his initial concerns by providing HIV testing, staff provided him with additional health education, skill building, informational materials, condoms, and HIV pre-exposure prophylaxis medications to help him maintain an uninfected status. Joseph continues to return for services, adheres to his medication as prescribed, and continues to test negative for HIV. His doctor, who gained his trust, was also able to connect Joseph with a mental health professional at the center, who provided psychotherapy and helped connect Joseph to some of the center's other services (e.g., educational and legal services). All these steps, including addressing the sex trafficking activity, supported Joseph in addressing his trauma, beginning to heal, and developing a positive sense of self and well-being. With ongoing medical care, psychotherapy, and other services, there is a strong likelihood that Joseph will continue to reach encouraging milestones.

As these cases demonstrate, health care professionals can play a vital role in both addressing the health needs of trafficked youth and connecting them with a wide range of other professionals—educators, lawyers, social workers, and others—who can support their healing. In this chapter, we continue our case study on the health care sector response, examining possible interventions and treatments for young people who are victims of trafficking. The health care response to trafficking victims needs to be comprehensive and integrated.

## From Identification to Treatment

A critical first step to treating children and youth who are trafficking survivors or who are at risk of exploitation is to ensure that these young people are identified as at risk for human trafficking or trafficked so that providers can offer relevant services. As described in chapter 6, health care professionals, including physicians, advanced practice nurses, physician assistants, nurses, health educators, mental health providers, dentists, and others, are well positioned to identify victims of human trafficking.[1] Once survivors are identified, the next step is to offer appropriate care and support and the opportunity to connect to needed services. Health care services are an essential component of this response.

## Treatment Framework

There are several important guiding principles and core components of a treatment plan for young people who are at risk of or exploited by human trafficking. These include

1. a case management system to help children and adolescents navigate available systems and access care and assistance;
2. survivor-led or survivor-informed programming;
3. youth-friendly services;

4. trauma-informed and trauma-focused clinical responses; and
5. comprehensive services encompassing multiple systems to address all needs of these children and adolescents.

It is critical that health care entities and professionals tailor their services to address the unique needs of child and adolescent survivors of trafficking. In addition to health care, at-risk and exploited youth often have pressing needs for a range of other services. Communities need to develop comprehensive, integrated services that span multiple systems and include "shelter, physical and mental health services, street outreach, transportation assistance, legal advocacy, educational and employment resources, and referrals for other services (e.g., substance abuse treatment)."[2] A challenge for health care providers is to provide trauma-informed care to address the issues within their respective expertise while also facilitating adolescents' access to all other services needed. This section focuses on developing responsive health care services. We believe that in addition to providing a starting point for health care providers, this discussion can help inform thinking in other sectors, as other professionals develop their own responses to child trafficking and as professionals in all sectors—including health care—begin to think about how to connect and integrate all these services.

### Case Management

Case management is a key component of caring for trafficking survivors because of their numerous and complex needs. Child trafficking survivors often interact with multiple systems, including the health care system; education; child protective services, including foster care; and the juvenile justice system. A case manager can assess a young person's needs and help identify and coordinate services for him or her. Through case management, an individual in need of assistance receives support throughout the recovery process, rather than being left alone to figure out the often complicated systems of benefits programs and services. Research has shown that case management helps international victims of human trafficking navigate complex systems and achieve self-sufficiency and that case management would likely be beneficial to victims and survivors who are US citizens and permanent residents.[3] The role of case management in taking care of these victims has been examined,[4] but this research is in its early stages. However, case management is a common component of a multidisciplinary team approach to assisting other types of victims and has produced positive outcomes.[5]

Shelter and housing needs, which are often pressing among survivors of human trafficking, offer one example of the potential benefits of employing a case management system. Many children vulnerable to trafficking are homeless as a result of running from abusive situations or being kicked out of their homes or for other reasons.[6] A 2012 Polaris Project survey of organizations that provide shelter services in the United States and its territories found that only 1,644 beds were available to human trafficking victims for overnight stays.[7] Of those, 529 were designated exclusively for human trafficking survivors, with 348 of these restricted to sex trafficking survivors and the other 181 beds available for survivors of either labor trafficking or sex trafficking. The remaining 1,115 shelter beds are situated in facilities run by organizations that serve both human trafficking survivors and other populations in need. These shelter beds are available to human trafficking survivors but are not reserved for trafficking cases.

Of the 1,644 beds, only 517 were reserved for minors (with an additional 519 available to adults or children).[8] Because of the limited number of beds nationwide for human trafficking victims, many survivors are placed in domestic violence and sexual assault shelters. Shelter stays can be time limited, and housing for male victims of sex trafficking is often lacking.[9] A 2013 study of residential centers for human trafficking survivors found that twenty-eight states had no shelters reserved exclusively for human trafficking victims.[10] With limited housing options (which may vary in the services they provide), it is critical that trafficking survivors have the support of individuals who both are knowledgeable about available housing options and their programs and can navigate benefits programs to secure financial access to safe housing. Expecting child trafficking survivors to assess and obtain housing options on their own is a recipe for disaster. In short, as housing and shelter issues demonstrate, case managers are essential to helping young trafficking survivors meet all of their needs.

### The Integral Role of Survivors, including Youth

Survivor-led and survivor-informed approaches are very important for trafficking survivors.[11] There are positive models of survivor-led programs in the United States, including Courtney's House in Washington, DC, GEMS in New York City, and MISSEY in Oakland, California.[12] Rachel Lloyd, founder and CEO of GEMS, found that youth leadership development was important to the personal growth and development of survivors of commercial sexual exploitation and sex trafficking.[13] Yet survivor-led and survivor-informed programs are still the exception rather than the rule. As UNICEF explains, "Too often, prevention strategies do not take into account and incorporate the views of children, or fail to empower children to meaningfully engage in prevention activities and decision-making processes."[14]

The value of survivor-led and survivor-informed processes extends beyond the children themselves. It leads to better outcomes. Children and adolescents have insights that adults may not perceive. As Mike Dottridge explains, "[Children] are 'experts' on the factors that make children vulnerable . . . and their special needs regarding prevention, assistance and protection. Children and young people have an important role to play in helping to identify areas for intervention, design relevant solutions and act as strategic informants of research."[15]

For example, trafficked children interviewed in one study "reported that most had received little information about trafficking and ways to avoid being trafficked before they were trafficked."[16] By listening to children, we can identify opportunities for effective intervention, including before children are trafficked. In the same study, most children reported that they had left school because they thought their families could not afford it.[17] This finding can help inform policy decisions that might produce more effective, targeted interventions prior to exploitation. As stated in chapter 4, the study also found that many youth could identify a "changing point," an event or crisis that left them more vulnerable. Disruptions that appear to have had the greatest impact include changes in residence, in family composition, or in peer relationships.[18] Providing survivors and vulnerable youth a voice in the development and implementation of relevant policies and programs can help ensure that insights such as these are not overlooked.[19] In other words, including survivors and youth in the design, implementation, and evaluation of policies and programs can help produce better outcomes.[20]

### Health Care Services: Youth Friendly and Trauma Informed

The physical and mental health needs of trafficking survivors are multifaceted and include medical care, sexual and reproductive health care, sexual assault response and care, dental care, and behavioral and mental health care. Some of these complex needs may require specialized services such as substance abuse treatment and management of chronic illness, including HIV or other sexually transmitted infections.[21] However, for health care providers who identify victims, it is essential that they recognize and treat all the needs of survivors either directly or via referrals.

There have been a limited number of studies on the physical and mental health needs of adult sex trafficking victims and the health care services they received during their trafficking experience. A study of international victims receiving services found that 63 percent of the women reported at least ten concurrent physical health problems.[22] Commonly reported symptoms included "headaches (82%), feeling easily tired (81%), dizzy spells (70%), back pain (69%), memory difficulty (62%), stomach pain (61%), pelvic pain (59%), and gynecological infections (58%)."[23] Survivors also reported high rates of depression, and 39 percent admitted that they had had suicidal thoughts within the prior week.[24] In an international study focused on prostituted children, researchers found high rates of sexually transmitted infections, pregnancy-related complications, substance abuse, PTSD, and suicide attempts.[25] Furthermore, they found a high prevalence of physical and sexual violence.[26]

In a study of trafficking victims in the United States (domestic and international victims), victims reported high rates of physical health symptoms; mental health issues, including suicidal ideation; and other, co-occurring illnesses such as sexually transmitted infections.[27] Other studies report similarly high rates of a range of other health problems.[28] Trauma is likewise common, both as a result of the trafficking experience and from an earlier history of abuse, causing adverse impacts on health and behavior that can persist over the lifespan.[29] The negative impacts of trauma include depression, anxiety, anger, dissociation, fearfulness, hopelessness, poor self-image, distrust of the environment, and difficulty maintaining healthy interpersonal relationships.[30] Researchers have found an association between sexual trauma and risky sexual behavior and substance use.[31] Researchers have likewise found an association between sexual trauma and aggressive behavior, depression, and low self-worth.[32]

Although the research on sex trafficking is relatively limited, even less is known about the physical and mental health needs of labor trafficking victims. However, studies have found that labor trafficking victims similarly suffer a range of physical and mental health consequences.[33] Adverse consequences include work-related injuries (frequently the result of performing hazardous work for long hours with limited, if any, breaks), physical and emotional abuse, exposure to environmental hazards (which may cause respiratory or dermatological issues), poor nutrition, diseases from overcrowding and poor sanitation, and a variety of mental health issues, including anxiety and PTSD.[34] Labor trafficking victims experience trauma and physical, sexual, and emotional abuse.[35] Finally, more recent research has identified that labor trafficking victims frequently have a history of polyvictimization, further highlighting their vulnerability.[36]

Responding to a population that is confronting multiple health issues simultaneously is challenging. As discussed in chapter 6, Mount Sinai Adolescent Health Center has adopted the following core operational principles, which guide how services are delivered to all youth. This includes ensuring that all services are

- informed and driven by young people;
- engaging to young people;

- developmentally appropriate and tailored;
- nonjudgmental and without stigma;
- trauma informed;
- relationship based; and
- supportive of one-on-one adolescent-provider interactions.[37]

Although in chapter 6 these practices are detailed in the context of initial screenings and identification of at-risk and trafficked youth, they are relevant at all stages of treatment of child trafficking survivors. In the following discussion of treatment, we highlight two critical components of treatment: youth-friendly services and trauma-informed care. We then build on those in the subsequent section, on the importance of comprehensive, integrated services.

## Youth-friendly Services

When serving any child or adolescent, youth-friendly services are critical to meeting their developmental needs effectively. Services must also be tailored to address the unique needs and circumstances of youth who are human trafficking victims, including by using a victim/survivor-centered approach. This means being attuned to common presentations and barriers to treatment, such as cost, ability to return for follow-up care, and lack of transportation. Because trafficked youth often have no health insurance and traffickers often control their finances and their time, facilities and providers need to address cost issues in advance and offer flexible scheduling. Providers need to figure out how to deliver these services, and they need to be able to assure youth that they can receive services whenever they are able to show up and without having to worry about cost. Also, trafficking survivors frequently need services to be confidential. Moreover, it is important to treat survivors with injections or pills that can be taken on site whenever possible rather than treating with take-home prescriptions. Take-home prescriptions increase the likelihood that a trafficker or others will discover that the young person sought health care or was treated for a particular condition. If a young person needs transportation or money for transportation, it is important to facilitate that. At

In developing capacity to treat child and adolescent survivors of human trafficking, health care institutions should consider a range of skill sets that would benefit their staff. For example, in addition to training staff on working with youth and trauma-informed care, Mount Sinai Adolescent Health Center also provides staff with training in motivational interviewing.

Motivational interviewing is a positive way of engaging at-risk and exploited young people. It is a goal-oriented, client-centered counseling style focused on exploring the pros and cons of changing or maintaining behavior. The goal of motivational interviewing is to resolve ambivalence through increasing clients' awareness of how their behavior may cause problems for them, the consequences they experience, and the risks they face because of the behavior. MSAHC staff have found that youth respond positively to open-ended questions, affirmations, reflective listening, and the provision of summary statements.

Staff use motivational interviewing with youth for a variety of purposes, including to look back on prior experiences, to explore a typical day, to discuss the importance of change, and to look forward and develop confidence about change.

See Levensky et al., "Motivational Interviewing."

MSAHC, youth are given Metrocards so that they can take the subway or a bus.

All staff should be trained and involved in creating a youth-friendly, trauma-informed environment that engages and supports young people (see box 7.1). This includes staff who answer the phones, security personnel, and staff who first encounter, welcome, and register young people. It also includes coordinators of health care insurance or benefits eligibility and medical technicians who perform initial screenings. These individuals set the tone for a young person's visit, as the adolescent may well see several of these staff members before meeting the health care provider. Each of these staff members must be trained to work with youth who have experienced trauma. At MSAHC, at times we have had individuals—

"lifelines"—guide the young persons through the different steps of the clinic visit. Regardless, every staff person is trained to make sure that there is a "warm" handoff from staff to staff (e.g., from medical provider to mental health provider). Owing to the confidential nature of many of the services provided at MSAHC, many young people are using health services on their own for the first time. The staff provide support to the young person, ensure that all of the young person's questions are answered, and act as a reassuring presence during the visit.

Staff are also trained to help youth understand "next steps" in their care and to empower them to become effective health care consumers. MSAHC's physical environment is designed to make it easy for youth to navigate; sections are color coded so that young people can easily find the designated "red," "blue," "yellow," or "green" clinical areas when directed. Additional information is provided on flat screens in the waiting rooms, and a free app allows young people to learn more about their health and how to be agents of their care.

Once identified, trafficking survivors need providers to acknowledge the abuse and trauma they have suffered. The physical health needs of trafficking survivors must be addressed. As highlighted above, trafficking survivors frequently report multiple health concerns. Survivors may show signs of acute or chronic conditions as other patients do, but they also tend to show signs of other issues, including dermatological diseases and infections, dental neglect, injury, weight loss, inadequate nourishment, gastrointestinal problems, pregnancy-related issues, STIs, HIV, and hepatitis.[38] Because survivors frequently lack preventive health care, many of them have conditions that could have been easily prevented or treated but have become worse, critical, even life threatening.

In addition to the physical health needs that must be addressed, trafficking survivors may have mental health and other needs resulting from their history of trauma. Being attuned to the trauma of the trafficking experience as well as both earlier trauma and any ongoing trauma is critical to providing effective care. A number of ways to address people with a history of trauma have evolved, and the nomenclature used to define these approaches is not always clear or consistent. Here, we provide an overview of the importance of interacting with and caring for individuals with a history of trauma, focusing on trauma-informed practices and trauma-focused interventions.

## Trauma-Informed Practices

Trauma-informed practices reflect an overarching approach in child welfare, health care, and other systems that seeks to educate all stakeholders engaged with survivors and their families about trauma and the impact of trauma.[39] It includes systematically screening individuals and providing resources on trauma-specific interventions. In health care, staff using a trauma-informed approach will understand the impact of trauma, use trauma-assessment tools,[40] and provide trauma-informed services in a place where people feel safe.[41] Trauma-informed practices have been shown to help facilitate the healing process.[42]

Trauma-informed care is "a strengths-based framework that is grounded in an understanding of and responsiveness to the impact of trauma, that emphasizes physical, psychological, and emotional safety for both providers and survivors, and that creates opportunities for survivors to rebuild a sense of control and empowerment."[43] Providers of trauma-informed care adopt a survivor-centered treatment approach, empower the trafficking survivor, avoid judgment, provide a supportive and holistic response, and respect "the patient's rights to information, privacy, bodily integrity and participation in decision making."[44]

When interviewing a potential survivor of trauma, such as a human trafficking victim, it is critical to use a trauma-informed approach. Trauma-informed practices recognize the impact of traumatic experiences and the connections between past abuses and current trauma symptoms. Trauma-informed practices seek to encourage an understanding among health care professionals of how traumatic experiences may affect their patients' behaviors and bodies (e.g., substance abuse, eating disorders, depression, anxiety, perception of body image, etc.).[45] The approach requires knowledge of trauma and its impact, as well as an understanding of trauma triggers (the victim's and the provider's), in order to minimize re-traumatization.[46] It also means providing information to victims about trauma, to help victims manage feelings and develop a healthy internal locus of control. And it incorporates opportunities for victims to give input on programs and services and on supportive activities that fosters the emotional safety of victims and staff.[47]

Trust is key to successful treatment of survivors with a history of trauma.[48] Health care professionals need to take time to build rapport with patients who are survivors of human trafficking and gain their trust, recognizing that trust building can be a slow and difficult process. In some cases, trust can be built by meeting the individual's immediate needs (physical or emotional). An example of this may be as basic as providing them with food or snacks. Other opportunities to build trusting relationships occur throughout the care continuum by, for example, ensuring that care is easy to access and health services are welcoming; taking time to discuss and ensure privacy and confidentiality; and providing a safe space in which patients can have time alone with staff during each visit. Because victims typically will not disclose information about sensitive issues, including human trafficking, without prompting, it is important to create an opportunity for the provider to raise those topics.

There is growing recognition of the importance of trauma-informed practices. For example, a Department of Justice report on children exposed to violence urges that "service and treatment providers who help children and their families exposed to violence and psychological trauma *must* provide trauma-informed care, trauma-specific treatment, or trauma-focused services."[49]

Trauma-Focused Interventions

Trauma-focused psychotherapies are specific mental health interventions with survivors and their families. The American Academy of Child and Adolescent Psychiatry recommends trauma-focused therapies (instead of nonspecific or nondirective therapies) as the first-line treatment for all patients with a history of trauma.[50] Trauma-focused therapy addresses traumatic experiences and helps survivors overcome avoidance of trauma-related memories, beliefs, and feelings through the use of gradual exposure, a therapy technique in which mental health professionals create

## Box 7.2. Reflection: A "Radar" for Trauma

It is important to have a "radar" for trauma. You develop a radar for trauma by reading about it, through training on trauma and its impact, and by asking patients about all types of traumas, including childhood neglect, physical abuse, sexual abuse, rape, trafficking (for labor or sex), survival sex, teen dating violence, domestic violence, and so on. As you work with more patients—both those who have experienced trauma and those who have not—you start to learn how trauma affects people and to observe characteristics that many victims have in common. When I was in training, I did not understand trauma. Acquiring an understanding of trauma is a first step in developing a radar for trauma. I realized decades ago that while we were providing great health care to our patients, we were not aware of the childhood trauma they had suffered or were suffering. Upon grasping this, I sought to increase my understanding of trauma's prevalence, impact, presentation, and so on. I realized that one of the reasons I was missing the history of trauma was that I was not asking the right questions, and patients were not coming to me saying they had a history of childhood abuse or other types of trauma. To learn about any trauma in the patient's life, I had to ask my patients directly either while taking their medical history or via questionnaires. I started to ask every patient, and I realized that a very large number of patients had a history of trauma. By having these conversations, I learned from patients the types of traumas they had experienced, the evolution of the traumas, how they had been affected, and how they were trying to cope. Moreover, I learned that individuals use different techniques to cope; some may be perceived as adaptive and others as maladaptive. But the truth of the matter is that they do what they need to do to survive. Over the years, I have become very comfortable talking with my patients about trauma and have developed a "radar" for trauma.

During this time, I also learned about the process of building trust. Working with young people with a history of trauma includes carrying out risk assessments to identify and meet their immediate and longer-term needs, including physical, emotional, mental health, social, economic, and educational needs. It is important to allow the youth to come to the health facility whenever they feel the need even if they don't require services. This will help them feel connected and engaged in their care. I say to my patients:

> We are always here for you. If you have questions about anything, you can send them to our texting service, use our app, use our medical record portal, call us, or just walk in and ask for me; if I am not available, ask to speak to one of our staff. Even if you do not have a medical problem but have something you want to share with us, you can use any of these ways to communicate with us. We also have a call-in service, which you can use any time the clinic is closed—during the night, Sundays, and holidays. We always have a doctor on call to address your questions and health needs.

We see all young people with or without appointments (walk-ins). When working with young people, it is important for the facility to allow for walk-in services in addition to appointments. Young people need this flexibility, especially if they are seeking confidential services or are victims of any type of trauma. Investing in training and developing a "radar" for trauma will enhance your capacity to serve at-risk and exploited youth.

—Dr. Angela Diaz

a safe environment to "expose" individuals gradually to the things they fear and avoid.[51] It helps victims regain a degree of control over the trauma. Furthermore, it helps them understand their symptoms and behaviors as common and reasonable responses to the trauma they have experienced. This type of therapy addresses patients' sense of shame and helps them think or talk about their trauma without becoming overwhelmed by it.[52] Trauma-focused interventions can be a valuable tool in providing care for and assisting trafficking survivors.[53]

One form of trauma-focused therapy is trauma-focused cognitive behavioral therapy (TF-CBT).[54] Evidence indicates the effectiveness of TF-CBT in reducing trauma symptoms in children who have experienced sexual abuse and in youth who have experienced complex trauma.[55] TF-CBT reduces depression, anxiety, self-esteem issues, sexual risk be-

haviors, and unhealthy beliefs about sexuality.[56] Trauma-focused therapies have been found to be effective with various populations, including:
adjudicated and at-risk youth in residential treatment;[57] women experiencing co-occurring disorders, including substance abuse and depression;[58]
and women with criminal justice system involvement.[59] But the effectiveness of trauma-focused therapies for victims and survivors of commercial
sexual exploitation and sex trafficking of minors has yet to be evaluated.
The US Department of Health and Human Services' report *Evidence-Based
Mental Health Treatment for Victims of Human Trafficking* recognizes the
limitations of attempting to address the specific needs of child victims
of sex trafficking given the lack of available evidence.[60] Still, the report
emphasizes the need to provide trauma-focused therapies to victims of
human trafficking, including children, because of the high levels of trauma
these survivors experience.[61] Trauma-focused therapies need to address
"posttraumatic stress disorder, anxiety disorder, panic disorder, obsessive-
compulsive disorder, dissociative disorder, major depressive disorder, and
substance abuse disorder."[62] Others emphasize the need for long-term
mental health services for trafficking survivors to support those individuals who are rebuilding their lives and, in some cases, to help those who
return to trafficking situations.[63] In addition, the inclusion of parents and
caregivers in the treatment can be important.[64]

Trauma-informed practices and trauma-focused interventions have
the potential to be important tools in responding to and supporting trafficking survivors. Trauma is an important component of their exploitation
experience. And many trafficking survivors have experienced trauma
prior to their trafficking situation. More generally, youth-friendly services
and trauma-informed practices and interventions must be situated within
a broader framework that ensures trafficking survivors access to comprehensive, integrated services.

### Comprehensive Services

Ensuring that victims and survivors receive all the services they need requires the involvement of a wide range of agencies and professionals. And

it requires effective communication and coordination among all involved. Health care facilities should aim to provide as many services in one place as possible so that survivors can avail themselves of the different services they need during a single visit. MSAHC has worked to develop comprehensive, integrated services, including medical, sexual and reproductive health, dental, optical, health education, behavioral health, mental health, substance abuse, HIV treatment and counseling, health insurance enrollment, legal, and other services. For needed services that are not available at MSAHC, staff facilitate connections with services such as housing, schooling, and benefits.

While having all services under one roof is ideal, we recognize that this is not possible for all health care facilities or practices. That said, entities that are not able to have comprehensive services on site can develop linkages with other programs to connect their young patients with needed services such as ongoing counseling, substance abuse treatment, and legal assistance. For services not on site, it is essential to have seamless referral systems to facilitate young people's access to needed services. The key point is that limitations on resources or services available at a particular site should not be seen as an insurmountable barrier to engaging human trafficking survivors. What is critical is that relevant facilities work to partner with other service providers to ensure that together they can provide comprehensive, integrated services.

Comprehensive, integrated services should encompass wellness, education, prevention, identification, intervention, and anticipatory guidance. These services should be provided in a way that makes young people feel safe, with an understanding of youth culture and with overall cultural humility. And services may well go beyond what a health care provider typically considers (which presents challenges in terms of skillset, capacity, and resources). For example, while many health care providers recognize the importance of connecting victimized youth with physical, sexual and reproductive, and mental health services, they might not necessarily think to connect a young person to dental services. Yet trafficked youth are often in need of dental services. Similarly, optical services may be needed, as a young person may have vision problems that have not been identified, need eyeglasses, and not have insurance or financial resources to pay for eye exams or glasses.

Working with and across multiple systems means that service providers must communicate regularly to better serve these young people. This must be done while respecting adolescents' privacy and confidentially. To achieve this, it is important for all these agencies to receive training on an ongoing basis and to establish effective plans for communicating with one another in support of the youth they serve.

As health care providers and others start to look for, identify, and respond to child trafficking victims and survivors, providers will end up working with young people who are actively in a trafficking situation. It is critical in these situations to work with such youth on an effective exit strategy. This includes creating a safety plan and considering whether and how to reconnect with the young person's community and social infrastructures such as family, friends, schools, and religious and other community institutions.

If a young person is able to connect providers with family members who are willing to participate, family therapy can help with the reintegration of the survivor back into family life. Many of these young people have been separated from their families, and there tend to be other family issues that preceded the trafficking, so the transition back to one's family often requires support. Offering consistent attention and support will help build trust and will support these young people to heal and reconnect.

Other critical needs must be addressed as well. These include access to services and benefits that can help provide basic necessities such as food, clothing, transportation, and housing. Further, helping young people reconnect to their education, develop skills, secure employment, and develop leadership skills can facilitate their exit from exploitation and help them stay out of such harmful situations.

Health care facilities and providers do not necessarily have to provide all of these services. Rather, the health care provider should work with youth to identify their needs and then continue to work with them to help ensure that they are connected to other service providers who can address needs beyond health care. These young people need support and an advocate and/or case manager who will help ensure that they can access the resources and services they need in order to succeed.

Providers must also be aware that helping youth leave their trafficking situations and successfully rebuild their lives takes time and persistence. Our clinical practice at Mount Sinai Adolescent Health Center has shown us that preparing trafficking victims to get out of their situation of exploitation is an important component of any intervention. However, as we and others have observed, it can take multiple attempts, in some cases six or more, before a young person is able to extricate himself or herself from the exploitation and remain out. Providers should not give up on any child or adolescent because the young person does not leave a situation of exploitation the first (or second or third) time the provider advises them to do so or because the adolescent returns to their trafficking situation. All this needs to be understood as part of some young people's journey.

What providers can do is offer necessary treatment and services that can help young people prepare to leave—and ultimately leave—their situation of exploitation. In this regard, providers should recognize opportunities to address both short- and long-term needs. Trafficked youth often need crisis services (food, crisis safety plans, crisis shelter services, emergency medical care, crisis legal advocacy). They also need a range of trauma-informed health care services (physical health care, sexual and reproductive health care, sexual assault response and care, mental health care, substance abuse care, dental services, and plastic surgery to remove tattoos that the trafficker branded them with if the patient would like them removed). They also need medium- to longer-term services, including ongoing basic necessities, transitional housing, education, job training, long-term housing, life skills training, leadership training, and more.

Providing all these resources is challenging, but the alternative is giving up on young people and allowing them to suffer further exploitation and harm. We must build on existing capacities, strengthen cooperation among agencies, forge new partnerships, and develop a comprehensive set of integrated services. Such services can be provided to those youth who need them when they are ready for them. Recalling the importance of survivor-led processes, it is critical that child and adolescent survivors of trafficking be allowed to direct their own recovery process so that they feel empowered and so that we avoid further traumatizing or re-victimizing them.

## Developing an Effective Treatment Framework: Training—A First Step

Health care professionals are highly trained so that they can provide the best possible care for their patients, including diagnosing and treating a variety of health conditions to improve their patients' health and well-being. Every time a new disease appears or health conditions evolve, they need additional training in order to be able to continue to meet patients' needs. This was the case when practicing physicians started to see and recognize signs of child abuse in young patients. It was true again when physicians saw patients with HIV/AIDS for the first time. And it should be the case now in response to the new awareness of human trafficking. With the proper training, health professionals who encounter an individual who is a survivor of trafficking should be able to identify them as trafficking survivors and intervene in ways that are effective. Health care professionals can help survivors in many different ways, including providing the best possible health care and providing support and assistance as needed. Training in how to work with trafficking survivors is very important, as identifying and helping survivors is complicated and requires specialized training.

The training of health professionals needs to start at the university or graduate school level. A 2011 study of 262 Canadian medical students demonstrates both the lack of knowledge about human trafficking and a growing recognition that the issue is important to learn about.[65] Most participants in the study reported that they were not knowledgeable (48.5%) or only somewhat knowledgeable (45.4%) about human trafficking. Nearly 90 percent of participants (88.9%) were not familiar with the symptoms or warning signs of human trafficking. However, 76 percent of the participants believed that it was important to learn about human trafficking, identification of cases, and the health needs of trafficking survivors. Despite the medical students' recognition that knowledge of human trafficking was relevant to their future practice, none reported learning about human trafficking as part of their medical school curriculum—although a majority had heard about the issue before entering school.[66]

Although growing recognition of the importance of the issue is positive, training of providers has lagged. A study of health care providers who work in emergency departments—where health care often intersects with the lives of trafficking survivors—shows both that training is greatly needed and its positive effects.[67] The study found that while nearly 80 percent of emergency department providers reported knowing what human trafficking was, only 2.2 percent had received any formal training in identifying victims.[68] Only 4.8 percent of health care providers felt confident that they could identify trafficking victims in a clinical setting, and only 7.7 percent felt confident that they could treat them effectively.[69] An intervention was then designed and developed to train providers in the emergency department to identify and treat victims. Immediately following the educational intervention, 90 percent of the participants reported feeling very confident that they could identify and treat victims of trafficking.[70]

Another study, using an online survey of physicians in Kansas, explored doctors' knowledge of, attitudes toward, and training related to domestic sex trafficking of minors.[71] Even though the response rate was very low and thus findings are not generalizable, the results were similar to those of other studies: while 86 percent of respondents identified domestic sex trafficking of children as a problem in the United States, only 12 percent felt confident that they could identify victims who might come to their office, clinic, or hospital for care.[72] Only 11 percent reported screening patients for domestic sex trafficking of minors.[73] Physicians identified a number of barriers to reporting, including uncertainty about whether patients were victims (73.9%), lack of familiarity with how to report such cases (30.4%), encountering victims who did not act as if they needed help (4.3%), and insufficient time to report (2.9%).[74] Even though the majority (66.7%) reported wanting to receive training on sex trafficking of minors, very few had received such training: 5.8 percent had received general training on child sex trafficking, 10.1 percent had received training in victim identification, and 13 percent had received training in reporting.[75]

This research reveals that many health care professionals lack training and confidence in their ability to identify and assist victims. Research also highlights that with the appropriate training, health care professionals' ability to work with this population improves.[76] As the above study on emergency department providers demonstrated, training and education can improve providers' knowledge about identifying and treating human trafficking victims and their confidence in their ability to do so.[77] There is a clear need for educating health care professionals on human trafficking, victim identification, and appropriate assistance to victims, including treatment as well as reporting and referrals to other agencies. Additional specific training is needed in addressing confidentiality concerns, gaining survivors' trust, collaboration, outreach methods, managing medical and mental health issues, cross-cultural issues, and staffing challenges, among other issues.[78]

The Institute of Medicine and National Research Council report *Confronting Commercial Sexual Exploitation and Sex Trafficking of Minors in the United States* identified a number of barriers to the training of health care professionals, including misperceptions and stereotypes about sex trafficking of minors; limited availability of evidence-based training and educational programs; limited resources, including funding; and competing demands for health professionals' time.[79] Among the misperceptions and stereotypes, some health care providers assume that victims of sex trafficking are all young, foreign girls brought to the United States for forced prostitution.[80] Such assumptions can result in health care providers' overlooking other potential victims who do not fit the stereotype, such as US citizens, cis male or transgender victims, or labor trafficking victims. Another mischaracterization is labeling victims as "child prostitutes" or assuming that they are voluntarily engaged in the sex industry.[81]

While training health care professionals is an appropriate way to address misconceptions about trafficking, there is limited "appropriate, well-designed training/education offered by individuals qualified to facilitate or provide it," and a lack of data prohibits effectively measuring the current training efforts used to improve identification of and assistance to victims by health care providers.[82] There are also limited resources available to create, administer, and evaluate training programs.[83] In states that have recently added trafficking to child abuse mandatory reporting requirements, such changes have come with limited, if any, resources to ensure adequate training of health care professionals or others now tasked with identifying and reporting trafficking.[84] Thus, although such laws require that health care professionals be on the lookout for human trafficking, they provide no resources to ensure that providers are equipped to recognize the signs. In addition, there are often competing priorities for health care entities and professionals, who are already overburdened with various required trainings and continuing education requirements.[85] At times, it is hard for the health professional to balance the time allocated to seeing each patient with the tremendous needs of some individuals. It takes time to screen effectively for a condition or behavior, and when patients have multiple conditions and behaviors that need to be addressed, time pressures can be exacerbated.

In addition, in the past, most professional schools did not incorporate training on human trafficking in their curriculum for health care professionals.[86] As training programs and clinical practices develop—and a small number of medical and other professional schools are adding training on human trafficking[87]—they need to be evidence based.[88] Given the limited evidence-based research to date on human trafficking, health care entities and providers should support the development of such research and systematically evaluate their own policies and practices.

## Practice Note: The Impact on Professionals Who Work with Trafficking Survivors

As discussed in this chapter and in chapter 6, numerous challenges confront trafficking survivors as they seek to access needed services. They have multiple health needs, often lack health insurance, have a history of trauma, and may feel unable to share what has happened to them because they are accompanied by the trafficker or an associate or because of the impact of the trauma they have experienced.[89] In short, the full range of challenges in serving this population creates pressure on health care providers and institutions.

Although we urge health care organizations and providers to play a more active role in preventing, identifying, and responding to child trafficking, we recognize that there are risks associated with doing so. In addition to genuine concerns about how to ensure that interventions actually help survivors and do not discourage others from seeking health care, attention must be paid to the impact of such work on health care professionals (or other professionals and staff) working to address human trafficking. One of the challenges of working with vulnerable patients—and this is true for health care providers, mental health personnel, health educators, and others—is that such work can take a toll on the clinicians and staff. Empathy is a major part of working with trauma victims and their families. When doing this work, some professionals take on some of the physiological, psychological, and emotional consequences of the abuse.[90] Vicarious trauma can develop over an extended period of engagement in this type of work or after only one case.[91] Health care professionals working with vulnerable and traumatized populations may experience burnout or compassion fatigue.[92] In one UK study of health care and support service providers, researchers found that working with sex trafficking survivors had a significant impact on the physical and psychological health of providers.[93] Study participants reported experiencing burnout and feeling undersupported and insufficiently trained.[94] In such instances, the adverse consequences not only affect individual providers but can affect care and lead to high turnover rates, with further implications for service delivery to trafficking survivors.

Health care entities and providers must be attuned to the collateral impact on providers and other staff and offer or seek out appropriate support services. To mitigate the impact of vicarious trauma, the National Society for the Prevention of Cruelty to Children highlights the importance of developing a culture that recognizes the gravity of the issue, having peer support mechanisms, ensuring appropriate managerial and clinical supervision of work, and providing structured and intensive debriefing processes.[95] Any potential negative consequences experienced through working with traumatized children and families needs to be offset by appropriate support, time to recover after particularly difficult cases, and recognition of good work.[96] As Margaret Pack recommends, a multilayered approach to intervention is needed in order to address vicarious trauma and develop resilience on the part of providers who work with survivors of sexual violence.[97]

In short, all professionals who work to address child trafficking—including both labor trafficking and sex trafficking—need to be attuned to the impact of the experience on their own well-being and professional performance. Entities and individuals need to work to ensure that the appropriate supports are in place.

## Conclusion

Overall, by making care accessible through meeting children and adolescents where they are and by using trauma-informed care and trauma-focused interventions, health care providers can respond more effectively to youth survivors of human trafficking. The care provided by physicians and other health care professionals is critical to addressing the needs of trafficking survivors. But that is not all they need. Ultimately, health care must be situated in a broader response, as these children and adolescents need comprehensive, integrated services.

It is important for health care professionals, as well as service providers in other sectors, to facilitate children's access to other needed services, including housing, legal assistance, and education and job training programs. Currently, too few health care systems are set up to ensure the full range of services that trafficking victims and survivors need. Training in trauma-informed practices and trauma-focused interventions, effective case management systems, and input from survivors are all vital to developing a strong health care system response. The needs of this population are broad and diverse, and it is unlikely that a single sector can meet all their needs. Health care providers who identify victims will likely need to provide some vital services and refer and connect patients to other services, including dental, mental health, substance abuse, and legal services. Ultimately, the health care response needs to be integrated into a robust public health framework that advances a multisector strategy that ensures comprehensive services for any child or adolescent at risk of or a victim or survivor of human trafficking.

# Building an Effective Response to Child Trafficking

C ONFRONTING CHILD TRAFFICKING is an enormous task. As we have seen, trafficking survivors have multiple needs, requiring coordinated multisector responses. In addition, many young people who have been trafficked have a history of victimization and trauma that predates their trafficking experience, which adds to the complexity of developing appropriate systems and services for at-risk and exploited children. That said, it is important to recognize that there have been significant efforts over the past two decades. We identify more victims and apprehend more perpetrators than we did twenty years ago, or even a decade ago. And there is greater public awareness of the problem and support for anti-trafficking initiatives. But no matter how adept we become at identifying and assisting trafficking survivors or rooting out and arresting perpetrators, each of those "successes" signals a failure: a failure to reach that young person earlier and prevent the harm from occuring in the first place.

A public health approach challenges us to rethink how we address child trafficking and what we consider to be success. Success in the world of public health is preventing an outbreak, reducing prevalence of a disease, or otherwise reducing harm to individuals and the broader population. Put another way, public health aims to "move upstream" in order to prevent harmful outcomes.

The idea of moving upstream is pertinent to child trafficking. A simple story, variants of which are told in the world of public health, illustrates the point:

> While walking along the banks of a river, a passerby notices that someone in the water is drowning. After pulling the person ashore, the rescuer notices another person in the river in need of help. Before long, the river is filled with drowning people, and more rescuers are required to assist the initial rescuer. Unfortunately, some people are not saved, and some victims fall back into the river after they have been pulled ashore. At this time, one of the rescuers starts walking upstream. "Where are you going?" the other rescuers ask, disconcerted. The upstream rescuer replies, "I'm going upstream to see why so many people keep falling into the river."[1]

Prevention is and must always be the end goal. We must move upstream; that is, we must figure out why certain young people end up trafficked and address those issues. We must intervene before vulnerable youth are harmed. And for those who have been victimized, we must seize earlier opportunities for intervention so that the harm is minimized and recovery and healing can begin.

This chapter aims to provide guidance on how individuals, organizations, and communities might move forward using a public health approach to child trafficking. It outlines key questions and steps that should be addressed, using a public health lens. At its core, in the context of addressing child trafficking, the public health approach brings two critical points to the forefront: (1) the goal must be prevention; and (2) a comprehensive, integrated approach is needed to achieve this goal.

Public health tools and methods can help prioritize prevention and identify steps necessary to develop a comprehensive, integrated response. Moreover, the public health lens can enhance our understanding of child trafficking and its root causes, enabling us to build more effective responses to the problem.

## A Public Health Approach to Criminal Activity

Trafficking of human beings is a complex problem. Given the illicit nature of the activity, it is understandable that law enforcement action and criminal justice frameworks have dominated responses over the past two decades. Human trafficking is a grave violation of human rights; we should seek to hold all perpetrators accountable. However, by viewing child trafficking or human trafficking through a public health lens, we can see the limitations of current strategies. Simply put, we cannot prosecute our way out of this problem. While pursuing perpetrators of human trafficking is important, expecting criminal sanctions to single-handedly eliminate human trafficking is shortsighted. Public health responses to other issues —e.g., violence, road safety, and youth smoking—recognize that criminal sanctions can play a role, but they do not over-rely on the criminal justice system to solve the issue.

The public health approach also reminds us that there are other uses of law beyond criminal sanction. Public health utilizes law and policy to address all aspects of a problem, from individual factors to structural issues. In other words, law and policy still play critical roles,[2] but their value is not limited to serving as a vehicle for punishment; and criminal law, while still relevant, is no longer the primary tool for preventing harm.[3]

A public health approach can foster meaningful progress on trafficking because it seeks to identify and address the underlying causes of the issue with the goal of harm prevention or, at a minimum, harm reduction. For example, public health's focus on identifying risk factors—at the individual, relationship, community, and societal levels—can help identify the reasons why certain individuals are more vulnerable and facilitate earlier interventions that reach at-risk individuals before they are trafficked. In addition, a public health approach also goes beyond the criminal law's narrow focus on the state-perpetrator dynamic to address community- and population-based impacts.[4] In short, a public health perspective reveals that there are other strategies that might be more effective in reducing the prevalence of child trafficking.

## The Public Health Toolkit

Since the publication of "Moving Upstream" in 2011 on the benefits of a public health approach to human trafficking,[5] a growing number of entities have endorsed responding to human trafficking through a public health lens.[6] Educating policymakers, anti-trafficking professionals, and the general public on the value of a public health approach is important. We need to continue to do that while also mapping out how to implement such an approach. The following discussion highlights steps that are necessary to advance efforts to address trafficking. The questions we raise below (which emerge, in part, from the discussion in chapter 4) are intended as a starting point so that we can begin to develop more effective responses that reduce the prevalence of child trafficking.

The toolkit, which has seven components, starts with prevention, as that goal must be at the forefront of all that we do. Second is to utilize the socio-ecological model, a core model of public health approaches, as it provides the foundation for developing a deeper understanding of the problem of human trafficking and its causes and for structuring interventions. Third is to address the underlying causes of child trafficking, because the public health model presses us to move upstream to identify and address the root causes of social harms. Following these three core components are three tools, or means, by which public health advances the goal of prevention: relying on evidence-based research in developing responses; engaging community partners and target populations; and ensuring coordination among stakeholders. Last is the need to pay greater attention to unintended consequences. Good intentions do not guarantee good outcomes. We have seen well-intentioned policies produce harmful outcomes, and thus we believe it is important to consider this issue separately.

### Emphasizing Prevention

- For every law, policy, and program, whether already in place or proposed, we need to ask, Does this step help *prevent* young people from being trafficked? If so, how does it do that? If not, can it be modified to add a prevention component? If it cannot, what else can be done to address prevention?

Anti-trafficking efforts must confront the prevention challenge in a meaningful way. Prevention is the ultimate goal. If we are to take prevention seriously, it needs to be part of every conversation. That does not mean that action can be taken only if it prevents trafficking. Some measures aimed at providing assistance to survivors do not address prevention but are critical (and may help prevent re-trafficking of survivors). The point is that each time we contemplate or take a step, we should understand whether it actually might prevent harm from occurring. And if, on evaluation, we see that very little of what we are doing actually addresses prevention, then we need to explore what else can be done. And public health's expertise in prevention, including, notably, violence prevention, can help inform the development of more effective policies and programs for preventing child trafficking.

### Utilizing the Socio-ecological Model

- We need to be cognizant of the different levels of the socio-ecological model. For each proposed or existing law, policy, or program, we need to ask what level the intervention is targeting—individual, relationship, community, or societal. Does it adequately account for all levels and the ways different levels and different risk factors interact with and affect one another? And with respect to the level of risk factor it does address, will it reach all individuals, or does it target only certain populations?

As we saw in chapter 5, the socio-ecological model can help us understand the complexity of vulnerability and how our interventions may or may not be successful in reducing harm. A school-based intervention might help reach some children, but it will fail to reach out-of-school children and may not be successful in helping those children who are in school but are confronting multiple risks simultaneously. The socio-ecological model can help us see how certain interventions—for example, an individual-level intervention that does not account for community-level risk factors—miss critical elements of the problem, limiting the effectiveness of that policy or program.

Both public and private agencies and organizations should use the socio-ecological model to better understand the problem of child trafficking and how their mandate or work intersects with the different levels of the model. They should also use the model when designing, implementing, and evaluating measures aimed at responding to child trafficking.

### Addressing the Underlying Causes of Child Trafficking

- We need to focus more on the root causes of the problem of child trafficking and ask, What are the relevant individual, community, or societal attitudes, behaviors, or conditions underlying the harm that we need to address? Does a proposed step—e.g., law, policy, or program—address the root causes of vulnerability or the underlying demand for exploited individuals that allows this exploitation to persist? Does it address the relevant structural issues?

The root causes of human trafficking, and child trafficking in particular, are complex. Discriminatory attitudes and actions devalue and marginalize certain individuals, increasing their vulnerability to exploitation. Poverty also plays a role, pressing young people into risky work settings. The risk factors described in chapter 5 are also among the underlying issues that foster conditions in which trafficking can thrive. And demand for cheap goods and services also drives the problem. These are all big issues to address. However, ignoring them guarantees that the measures we implement will be band-aids at best. They won't actually reduce the prevalence of harm.

Public health has a wealth of experience confronting the root causes of problems. That includes determining how we change harmful behaviors. How do we get individuals to stop smoking or never start? How do we get drivers to wear seatbelts and take other safety precautions? How do we break the cycle of violence in families where child abuse has occurred? All these issues compel us to address attitudes and behaviors that communities and society tolerate. Progress on these and other public health issues occurred in part because interventions helped change community and societal perceptions of what is acceptable. Progress was possible also by confronting structural issues and conditions, as opposed to focusing only on individual behavior.

Child trafficking requires similar attention to root causes. Trafficking thrives because of both conditions that create vulnerability (e.g., poverty, marginalization, etc.) and community and societal attitudes that tolerate the devaluation of certain populations.[7] In short, to make meaningful progress, we have to confront these underlying harmful societal beliefs, behaviors, and conditions.

As discussed in chapter 4, compared with certain other public health issues, child trafficking presents unique challenges. However, pulling together teams of public health experts (who know what can work to address underlying issues), child trafficking experts (who understand the complexity of this form of exploitation), trafficking survivors, and other relevant experts can be a starting point for developing a more sophisticated strategy of fostering healthier attitudes and behaviors that can reduce the prevalence of child trafficking. These partnerships can also work to address the equally difficult challenge of addressing societal conditions, including the social determinants of health.

### Relying on Evidence-Based Research

- With every law, policy, and program, we need to ask whether the action contemplated or undertaken is based on evidence-based research? If not, what does evidence-based research say would work in this instance?

As Margaret Malloch and Paul Rigby write, "Human trafficking occurs in a highly politicised arena with a flimsy evidence base on which to institute good practice and fragmented responses to this complex issue."[8] We can do better. We must do better. Public health emphasizes evidence-based responses. The field of public health has a wealth of expertise not only in conducting evidence-based research and evaluating programs but also in developing programs based on evidence-based research. Policymakers and anti-trafficking advocates need to ensure that their programs are based on rigorous research. That means starting by insisting on systematic evaluation of existing laws, policies, and programs aimed at addressing human trafficking, and child trafficking in particular. Are they making a difference? If not, what changes are needed? The need for evidence-based research highlights another partnership opportunity: those working in the field can and should partner with experienced academic partners and other researchers who can ensure proper evaluation of the work being done. And after evidence-based research has been completed, it needs to feed back into new law, policies, and programs. That means that policymakers and professionals working on child trafficking need to be receptive to the evidence and willing to adapt what they are doing to ensure the steps taken to address trafficking will actually make a difference.

### Engaging Community Partners

- With every law, policy, and program, we need to ask whether the initiative was designed in partnership with survivors, young people, their families, and other relevant community members.

It is a basic principle of public health work—as well as international development work—that it is essential to work with target populations if an intervention is to be successful. Too often, survivors are not consulted in the development of anti-trafficking measures. Youth are also ignored in the design and development of policies and programs that ultimately will affect their lives. And young people who are survivors are even more likely to have their voices marginalized. As UNICEF has written, "Children's experiences, recommendations and actions to prevent trafficking are often overlooked when developing programmes and initiatives designed to combat trafficking and to assist those children who have been trafficked."[9]

These are missed opportunities to improve our responses. Survivors and children must be engaged in a meaningful way. That doesn't mean asking them to testify for the sake of engendering sympathy or garnering support for others' initiatives. We must see them as experts. Survivors and young people must be incorporated into the design, implementation, and evaluation phases of all anti-trafficking efforts. We must see them as partners and approach them in a way that recognizes and respects their agency and insights. By partnering with survivors, young people, and others in affected communities, we can develop more effective responses to child trafficking.

### Ensuring Coordination among Relevant Stakeholders

- As discussed throughout this book, a comprehensive, integrated response is needed, so we should always ask whether an initiative identifies and maps out a strategy for successful collaboration among relevant stakeholders. Are all stakeholders at the table and contributing to the development and implementation of responses? In addition, stakeholders should ask how their work fits with all the other work being done to address child trafficking.

Public health responses rely on public trust; they are inherently a partnership with the community. And with regard to child trafficking, the community involves everyone. The old saying that "it takes a village to raise a child" is relevant here. It takes a village to prevent child trafficking and related forms of exploitation. At a macro level, that means ensuring that every sector is involved, not only law enforcement and social services but also education, health care, transportation, media, the private sector, and more. And within each sector, it means going beyond the "usual suspects" to advance a more comprehensive response that will address all needs of at-risk and exploited children. So law enforcement initiatives cannot involve only special task forces on human trafficking but must include all law enforcement personnel (often the neighborhood, or "beat," cop is the first to encounter a trafficking victim or situation). In health care, we have seen the relevance of emergency department professionals and also pediatricians. But trafficking also implicates dentists (victims often experience dental issues), plastic surgeons (traffickers often brand their victims, and thus plastic surgery expertise is needed for tattoo removal and similar services), and mental health professionals (to help children address the trauma they have suffered). In the education sector, teachers are at the front line, but they already face multiple competing demands for their attention. Teachers can be more engaged, but they need help. Guidance counselors, coaches, school health and mental health staff, administrators, and other personnel need to be involved as well. And that is what is needed for those children who are in school. To reach out-of-school children, we need to identify and incorporate community leaders in places where out-of-school youth spend their time, whether that is at a youth center, a group home, or somewhere else. We know that many at-risk children are systems-involved youth; that is, they have had prior involvement with the child welfare system or the juvenile justice system. Both of these systems need to be active partners in any coordinated effort to address child trafficking. In short, we need to effectively incorporate and coordinate all relevant stakeholders.

### Anticipating and Accounting for Unintended Consequences

- When contemplating, developing, or implementing a new law, policy, or program, we should always ask the "then what" question.[10] That means anticipating not only what barriers might impede implementation of the new policy or program but also what might occur if the law, policy, or program does exactly what it is intended to do, as even well-intended efforts can produce unintended consequences that are harmful. Evaluation must also look for and assess unintended consequences.

This component of the toolkit may well be thought of as a word of caution. The trafficking of children is a horrific abuse and violation of children's rights. It is no surprise, therefore, that it sparks outrage and a determina-

## Box C.1. If We Don't Coordinate . . .

For a number of years, when giving public lectures in different cities, I would ask the audience the following question: Do you have a database for the city that simply lists all organizations working on human trafficking, what they do, and the population(s) they serve? The answer was almost always no. In some cities, advocates would reply that they had one but that it had not been completed or was out of date.

The database should be simple, a spreadsheet with four columns: names of organizations; contact information; the organization's work (health care, victim assistance, etc.); and the population served (children, girls, boys, immigrants, etc.). Yet even those working on human trafficking in the same city or town aren't always aware of who else is doing the same work (risking duplication) or complementary work (risking gaps or disruptions in services). If those of us working on human trafficking do not know the lay of the land, how can we expect trafficking survivors, who have experienced and are trying to cope with significant trauma, to navigate available services effectively? And by not coordinating effectively, what opportunities are we missing? And how many children are we missing? In short, how far short are we falling of what our collective efforts could do if they were well coordinated? Coordination matters—to survivors and to the overall effort to end human trafficking. We need to take the time and invest the resources necessary to ensure effective coordination of work.

Quite obviously, effective coordination and collaboration require much more than a database. Beyond memoranda of understanding, data-sharing agreements, and other steps, it requires a genuine commitment on the part of institutions, their leadership, and their rank and file to work together and create integrated systems that truly serve at-risk children and trafficking survivors. The "database" question asks about the most basic step. It is necessary but by no means sufficient. Yet, many communities do not even have that. Ultimately, coordination must be integrated both across and within relevant sectors so that responses can be timely for and accessible to at-risk and exploited youth.

—Jonathan Todres

tion to act quickly. Too often, either in a rush to act or because there are misconceptions about the true nature and causes of child trafficking, responses end up failing to help or, in some cases, even cause more harm.[11]

For example, when well-intentioned policymakers and anti-trafficking advocates conceive of their goal as "rescuing" victims, not only do they fail to recognize the agency of survivors but they may also fail to address the circumstances that left a particular individual vulnerable. Thus, a so-called rescue followed by return of a survivor to his or her community without proper support—e.g., safe housing, educational and employment opportunities, etc.—might result in that child being re-trafficked soon thereafter. Similarly, raising the minimum age in certain labor sectors or shutting down exploitative venues without providing proper support for the children affected may actually increase their risk of exploitation. For example, in 2005 the Indian province of Maharashtra passed a new law banning dance performances in certain venues.[12] Various rationales were offered for the law, including the need to protect women from the risk of trafficking.[13] Although the law may have been well intentioned, "forcing the women out of the bars would make them more vulnerable to being forced into sex work and subject to highly exploitative working conditions and violence."[14] Although the measure was eventually struck down by the courts, this example shows what happens when steps are taken without asking "then what?" and accounting for potential unintended consequences. This particular regulation failed to account for what had made these women vulnerable in the first place or to provide for assistance programs that would empower them and enable them to choose better employment options. The point is not that certain actions, like shutting exploitative establishments, should not be taken but rather that they should only be taken in conjunction with other actions that would help ensure positive outcomes for the young people the initiative aims to assist.

Building in a process of anticipating unintended consequences is critical. Including youth, survivors, and more diverse participation in the development of initiatives would help avoid unintended consequences. In the Indian example, such a process would have prompted questions, prior to the adoption of the law, about what these women would do when they lost their jobs. What risks would they face? Similarly, in situations in which law enforcement or others have "rescued" a young trafficking victim, the "then what" question would prompt them to think about and address the risks a survivor would confront when returning to their home community.

For each of the above seven components of the toolkit, from prevention to coordination to unintended consequences, the questions listed above should be asked regardless of the action being considered. Legislators should ask these questions when considering a new anti-trafficking bill. Hospital administrators should ask these questions when considering how to respond to trafficking in their community. School administrators and teachers should ask these questions when contemplating how to prevent trafficking of children in their schools. Businesses should ask these questions when reviewing their supply chains. And so on. Every individual and organization in every sector should consider these questions.

## Toward a Comprehensive, Integrated Approach

### Involving All Sectors

When terrorism shook the United States on September 11, 2001, the US government responded in part by creating the "If You See Something, Say Something" campaign.[15] Of course, such campaigns can involve risks. Is the public trained to spot red flags correctly? How often will implicit (or even explicit) bias lead to false accusations? These are legitimate concerns. The broader point, however, is that everyone has the potential to contribute to the solution. This is also true as we seek to confront and ultimately eliminate the trafficking of children (and adults).

Everyone can play a role. We do not need to reinvent the wheel.[16] Nor do we necessarily need to have everyone develop a new skillset. To the contrary, we believe that people need to develop an understanding of human trafficking, its causes, and its impact and then explore how their existing skillset might be utilized or fine-tuned to contribute to the fight against human trafficking. Law enforcement, health care professionals, educators, and social workers each have a skillset that is relevant and needed. But so too are the skillsets of the media, technology companies, financial institutions, retailers and manufacturers, transportation companies, and numerous others. The goal should be to help individuals and organizations understand the problem and its root causes, their role in contributing to the problem or fostering conditions under which it can flourish (if relevant), and the ways their skillsets can be used to address trafficking.

One example of using one's skills comes from the United Arab Emirates, where camel racing is popular. Thousands of young boys, some as young as four years old, had been trafficked from Bangladesh, Pakistan, Sudan, and Mauritania to the United Arab Emirates and other countries to be used as camel jockeys.[17] These boys often suffered significant injuries during races and were underfed and housed in unsanitary conditions.[18] After human rights groups drew attention to this form of trafficking and pressed the government to respond, the UAE government took two steps: it banned the practice in 2005, and it partnered with the private sector to help address the problem, resulting in a Swiss company developing a robot jockey that eliminated the need to exploit children in this setting.[19] Of course, the Swiss company did not solve the problem of child trafficking. The UAE government still must enforce the law. And even if the UAE government does this, children in Bangladesh or Sudan who no longer face the risk of trafficking for exploitation in camel racing are still vulnerable. But the point is not that one entity has to solve the entire problem. The partnership between the UAE and the Swiss company helped reduce one form of demand. Other individuals, entities, and sectors can bring their expertise and skills to bear to reduce the vulnerability of children and support sustainable development in communities vulnerable to trafficking so that those children and communities have less risky options to pursue.

Like the robot jockey example, there are numerous other opportunities for private sector entities. Retailers and manufacturers can ensure that no trafficking or child labor occurs in their supply chains.[20] Financial institutions can help assist law enforcement in investigating human trafficking by using a "financial footprint" to vet millions of credit card transactions in a fraction of the time it would otherwise take law enforcement.[21] Tech companies can create cell phone apps for a variety of purposes, ranging from ensuring that youth have access to information that can help protect them to giving consumers readily accessible, real-time information on products they might purchase, including whether trafficked or forced labor was used to make those products.[22] In the private sector alone there are countless opportunities. And these private sector initiatives must be integrated with the work done by health care professionals, educators, social workers, law enforcement professionals, and others to build a comprehensive multisector response.

### Ensuring an Integrated Approach

Building a successful response is not only about securing the participation of entities across all relevant sectors. It is equally about ensuring that all the work is well coordinated and integrated. Too often the various sectors implicated by child trafficking operate in silos. Achieving effective cooperation and collaboration requires addressing long-standing barriers. Information sharing is often restricted, in many cases for good reason, as children's privacy rights must be respected. But relevant entities must figure out ways to share critical information to advance protection for children while maintaining privacy rights. Entities must also confront different work cultures. For example, while public health relies on public trust and pushes for transparency, law enforcement often needs to keep certain information confidential. These and other challenges must be confronted, and there are existing examples of how to do so; for example, law enforcement and public health have collaborated on bioterrorism preparedness since 9/11. The critical question is whether steps taken (or not taken) enhance protections for children or increase their vulnerability and make it harder for them to access needed services and assistance.

Part of the task of building integrated responses is to consider current systems from the perspective of the young people who intersect with them. Are the various service agencies and organizations set up to serve youth in a comprehensive, seamless way? Is it easy for an adolescent to access needed services and address his or her multiple needs simultaneously? Or do barriers remain? If we evaluate policies, programs, and services from the perspective of children and adolescents, those insights can drive the development of more effective collaboration and ultimately more integrated systems.

### Education for a Comprehensive, Integrated Response

To build a comprehensive, integrated response to trafficking requires a more widespread and deeper understanding of the problem, its causes, and appropriate responses. Some of the public are still largely unaware of the problem or unaware that it occurs in their communities. For this portion of the population, there is a pressing need for general education on human trafficking and child trafficking. Others are aware of the problem but have misconceptions about the issue (e.g., assuming that only women and girls are victims). There is a lot of misinformation about human trafficking, and more targeted education campaigns are necessary to overcome common misrepresentations of the issue.[23] Beyond this education for the broader public, there is an urgent need for effective, more specialized training that can position those trained to identify and respond appropriately in trafficking situations.

Along with other individuals and entities, we have called for relevant training for all individuals who work with children in a professional or volunteer capacity.[24] This would include not only health care providers, teachers, social workers, and law enforcement personnel but also coaches, bus drivers, and many others. Not only must training reach all relevant individuals but its content is critical. Training programs need to cover all types of trafficking—including both labor trafficking and sex trafficking—and be "victim-centered, culturally-relevant, evidence-based, gender-sensitive, and trauma-informed."[25]

There is growing attention to training.[26] But reports suggest that the training offered is often general in nature (so-called Human Trafficking 101), does not detail specific risks for children, and does not adequately teach individuals how to recognize, identify, and respond appropriately to child trafficking.

Take, for example, the US Department of Transportation numbers on training of relevant personnel. First, it bears noting that it is positive that the Department of Transportation recognizes that it has a role and has mobilized to train its personnel. In fact, the Department of Transportation has made a significant commitment to addressing human trafficking. It reports, "In 2012, DOT mandated that all 55,000 employees take human trafficking awareness training. By the end of calendar year 2012, nearly all DOT employees completed the training."[27] This sounds very positive and determined, but what does it mean? First, there is the question why the agency's webpage, "Human Trafficking and the Department of Transportation," although last updated in June 2018 still has only 2012 data. Are the numbers they report still a reflection of what is current practice? Are there no more recent evaluation data? Even assuming the above statement is true as of 2018, it still tells us very little. For example, it does not tell us whether the training was Human Trafficking 101 or provided more in-depth, specialized skills to identify potential cases. We also do not know why some employees had not done the training. And for the majority who did, we do not know about job turnover. Are the fifty thousand or so who received training still with the department? How many have left? Have their replacements been trained? And with respect to those who completed the training, we do not know what they learned, whether they retained what they learned, or how it affected their actions, if at all. Although training is critical, without repeat training and assessment we do not know what, if any, impact it has had on individuals, their responses, and anti-trafficking efforts more broadly.

In many fields, training on human trafficking, where it exists, has focused primarily on general awareness about trafficking as opposed to specialized skill development.[28] We now need to move to the next phase. We need to develop evidence-based, tailored training programs that empower professionals to act effectively to intervene appropriately to address instances of suspected human trafficking.[29] And we are starting to see those programs emerge.[30] They must be evaluated and, if demonstrated effective, disseminated broadly.

Finally, it is important to emphasize the need for ongoing training, in part because it may take time to overcome inaccurate popular portrayals of the issue or deep-seated beliefs about trafficking. In one federal human trafficking case involving two defendants who, among other things, threatened to kill their victims, brandished weapons, and pinned their victims against a wall until they passed out, the judge declined to order restitution (even though restitution is required by law in these cases). The judge explained the reason in a single sentence: "Restitution is not ordered because there is no victim other than society at large."[31] This single instance shows the need for ongoing training in all sectors. After all, if judges are unaware of the law and dismissive of the harms of human trafficking, then that limits both the effectiveness of anti-trafficking laws and the availability of remedies through the justice system. And it would be naive to think that these misconceptions and lack of genuine understanding of the experience of survivors exist only in certain professions. Indeed, because they confront identified human trafficking cases, one might expect that judges would be more aware than other professionals. The point is that if there is a lack of awareness in a sector that is tasked explicitly with addressing trafficking, then surely knowledge about the true nature of human trafficking, including the trafficking of children, is lacking in other sectors. Education is critical. It must extend to every sector implicated by human trafficking. And we need to ensure that education and training programs are effective.

### In It for the Long Haul

Building a comprehensive, integrated response will take time and resources. It also will require a sustained commitment. Long-term commitments do not always sell well with politicians, who need to show immediate results prior to the next election. But from public health to international development to human rights, evidence is clear that success requires a sustained commitment. We have witnessed what short-term, piecemeal thinking looks like in a human trafficking response.

Take, for example, services for survivors. Although we have seen growth in the number of shelters for trafficking survivors, there are still too few. Equally important, many of these programs have not been adequately evaluated for effectiveness, and they are not integrated with continuing support for trafficking survivors after they leave their shelter experience. A UK study found that many trafficking survivors are at risk of revictimization after short-term shelter and related services end.[32] A similar report by the International Organization for Migration found that of trafficking survivors who received services, including vocational training, none were able to secure regular employment; the result was that "the employment situation of many of the trafficking persons at the end of the reintegration assistance was therefore similar to their situation immediately prior to first recruitment by their traffickers."[33] In other words, the quick fix did not work, or it left survivors at heightened risk of subsequent harm. Assisting survivors is not as simple as securing short-term services (and even achieving that for all survivors would require a great effort). We need to provide sustained services to ensure that survivors receive the support they need to recover and succeed.[34] This example of the survivor experience is illustrative of the broader point: we need to commit to addressing human trafficking for the long haul. That means developing responses, evaluating them, improving our interventions based on that evidence, and sustaining best practices over the long term. And it means emphasizing prevention so that we can reduce the number of individuals harmed and in need of assistance.

As noted above, a sustained commitment will require resources, both financial and human. This means that policymakers have to allocate sufficient resources in the short and the long term. Given the importance of national standards, and given that trafficking cases have been identified across the United States, the federal government has an important role to play. Among other things, federal funding will be needed to ensure robust program evaluation. But all levels of government are implicated, so state and local governments must also allocate sufficient resources. Beyond the government, we also need to be more innovative in securing private sector and foundation support for anti-trafficking programs.

Some have questioned whether we should be expending significant resources on addressing human trafficking.[35] Our response is twofold. First, the simple answer, as noted in chapter 1, is that we should be motivated to act so long as children continue to be exploited. Nelson Mandela said that "there can be no keener revelation of a society's soul than the way in which it treats its children."[36] What would it say about us if we chose not to spend more money to prevent children from being brutally traumatized?

Second, although we believe that people should be motivated to act if any children are at risk, we also know that resources are finite. Public health grapples with this concept frequently, as it has to decide priorities given limited health budgets and numerous public health threats. Beyond the moral justification for addressing trafficking, there are two additional reasons for a long-term commitment to addressing child trafficking: (1) the best available information is that the scale of the problem is significant, and so it *is* a pressing public health issue; and (2) figuring out how to address trafficking will enhance our capacity to address other harms. Although the needs of trafficking survivors are unique in many respects, they also have experienced many harms that other vulnerable youth have experienced. If we are able to develop strong systems that can effectively respond to trafficking-related harms and reduce vulnerability, we might be able to adapt those systems to respond to other harms or draw important lessons that can guide our responses to other issues affecting children.

We spoke earlier in this book about understanding trafficking on a spectrum: at one end of the spectrum there are safe, secure employment opportunities for individuals that provide a living wage or better, while the other end of the spectrum is populated with trafficking, forced labor, and other exploitative labor settings, in which rights of workers are blatantly violated and workers are at risk of significant harm (see chapter 1). Children and adolescents who are trafficked are at risk of a variety of forms of exploitation. Not every vulnerable child ends up trafficked, but many vulnerable children end up harmed. Building a better capacity to identify at-risk and exploited youth will help us identify children in need regardless of the nature of the threat. This will enable us to assist and support more children. Empowering young people, strengthening communities, and bolstering protective factors at all levels of the socio-ecological model will help us prevent all forms of exploitation, including but not limited to human trafficking.

In short, if we seize upon this opportunity when there is interest in and momentum to address human trafficking, we have the potential to build systems that can be applied to address a range of potential harms to children and adolescents.

## Ethical Considerations

Public health methods, with their prevention focus, are valuable tools. It must also be recognized that as with any other strategy, there are ethical considerations to attend to. Well intentioned does not necessarily mean well planned. And while public health has a long history of successful interventions, there also have been policies and programs implemented that we now recognize as having been unethical, at least.[37]

- Changing attitudes and behaviors. We live in a world where freedom of thought is a treasured value. Rightly so. Of course, while every individual is free to believe whatever he or she wants, we have never held that individuals are free to act on their beliefs without any regard to consequences. Some actions are harmful to others and should be addressed. Still, as we identify harmful practices that encourage trafficking, we need to be careful to avoid stigmatizing individuals. Stigma can be a valuable vehicle for fostering behavioral changes. The stigma associated with tobacco use played a role in reducing the prevalence of smoking.[38] But we want to be careful to focus on the unhealthy behavior and not stigmatize the individual. We do not want interventions to impose stigma and further marginalize already vulnerable individuals.
- Research. Evidence-based research is critical to public health. There is a dearth of research on human trafficking. As we move forward seeking to develop a more robust base of evidence and to evaluate current policies and programs, we need to be sure that any research comports with legal and ethical obligations for conducting research involving human subjects.[39]
- Survivors. Assisting survivors is essential. But we need to be sure that our efforts to assist and support do not subject survivors to

further trauma. We need to partner, not preach; collaborate, not condescend. Rachel Lloyd, founder and CEO of GEMS, a survivor-led organization, eloquently describes the harm that well-intentioned "good guys" can inflict. She writes:

> Today I was humiliated. Publicly. It happened at an anti-trafficking event where I was presenting to over 100 law enforcement and I'd just finished a solid, engaging presentation that acknowledged the fact that I was a survivor but that didn't go into details about my "story," concentrating instead on the issue itself, how far we've come and how far we still need to go. Grasping me by my hand and framing it with, "what Rachel didn't tell you was" the host inexplicably felt the need to fairly graphically describe my past including my "multiple rapes by multiple men." I focused on a spot on the floor and didn't look up until he was finished. I'd spent two hours talking about my 16 years in the movement, the thousands of girls and young women I'd served and the organization GEMS that I'd built from scratch into the largest service provider to commercially sexually exploited and domestically trafficked girls in the country. I'd spent two hours as a professional, as the Chief Executive Officer of GEMS, as an expert, and within a couple of minutes he reduced me to a rape victim. Some of the women who worked there came up to me afterwards with tears in their eyes, apologizing profusely. As survivors of sexual assault themselves, they were both mortified and incredibly triggered by their colleague's behavior. His closing remarks had taken what had been a successful event, and at least for me, and likely other survivors of sexual violence in the room, completely tainted the experience.[40]

Individuals who are not survivors—from policymakers to advocates—need to spend more time listening to survivors and to make sure that they understand what survivors know, want, and need.

Human trafficking is an urgent problem. Each case in which a child is victimized heightens the urgency to act. But we should not sacrifice ethical obligations in the name of expedience. We should not further traumatize survivors to advance our agenda. We can be deliberate, act on evidence-based research, follow ethical and moral guidelines, and still make progress.

## A Special Note on Health Care Professionals

As we have emphasized throughout, health care professionals are uniquely situated to facilitate prevention, identification, and early intervention, thereby reducing harm that children suffer. We have focused primarily on the fact that trafficking victims frequently access health care services, so health care providers see trafficking victims (even if they do not recognize them). However, there is a related reason why it is so important for health care providers to be engaged. The patient-provider relationship is based on care. Many other relationships in the lives of children are not, and so the health care provider relationship is unique. People expect care from doctors and other health care professionals. And they are willing to share private information with them that they might not share with others. Furthermore, physicians and other health care providers who work with children and adolescents have an expertise, an understanding of how to work sensitively with young people. It is for this reason that we also urge anti-trafficking initiatives to ensure that their multidisciplinary teams include health care providers. Health care providers can offer important insights on interacting with and caring for young people that will be relevant to other professionals engaging in anti-trafficking initiatives, from law enforcement to social workers, educators, media professionals, and others.

## Conclusion

The task of ending child trafficking, and human trafficking more broadly, is enormous. But it is possible. The problem of human trafficking is one that is within our control. Human beings created the problem, and we believe human beings can end it. A public health approach brings us closer to the prevention of trafficking of children and young adults. That is the ultimate goal.

Below is a list of selected resources on child trafficking and, more broadly, human trafficking. The list is not intended to be comprehensive but rather to provide a starting point for those interested in obtaining more specific information on human trafficking (such as lists of indicators of human trafficking that can facilitate identification), reading more about human trafficking generally, or learning about selected federal government initiatives and resources.

Futures without Violence. *Anti-Human Trafficking Resources*. https://www.futureswithoutviolence.org/wp-content/uploads/Resource-List-on-HT-Trafficking.pdf.

HEAL Trafficking. www.healtrafficking.org.

Institute on Healthcare and Human Trafficking, Children's Healthcare of Atlanta. www.vIHHT.org.

National Human Trafficking Resources Center. *Identifying Victims of Human Trafficking: What to Look for in a Healthcare Setting*. https://humantrafficking hotline.org/resources/what-look-healthcare-setting.

Office on Trafficking in Persons, Office of the Administration for Children and Families. https://www.acf.hhs.gov/otip.

Polaris Project. https://polarisproject.org/.

US Department of Health and Human Services.
  *Federal Strategic Action Plan on Services for Victims of Human Trafficking in the United States 2013–2017*. https://www.ovc.gov/pubs/FederalHuman TraffickingStrategicPlan.pdf.
  *Services Available to Victims of Human Trafficking: A Resource Guide for Social Service Providers*. https://www.acf.hhs.gov/sites/default/files/orr /traffickingservices_0.pdf.

US Department of Justice (DOJ). "Human Trafficking." https://www.justice.gov /humantrafficking.

US Department of Justice, Office for Victims of Crime (OVC). "Human Trafficking." https://ovc.ncjrs.gov/humantrafficking/index.html.

US Department of Justice, Office of Juvenile Justice and Delinquency Prevention (OJJDP). "Commercial Sexual Exploitation of Children." https://www.ojjdp .gov/programs/csec_program.html.

*Introduction.* Child Trafficking in Our Communities

1. Lederer and Wetzel, "Health Consequences," 77.

2. Chisolm-Straker et al., "Health Care and Human Trafficking," 1228-29.

3. Chisolm-Straker and Richardson, "Assessment."

4. Chisolm-Straker and Richardson, "Assessment."

5. In reality, each of these other categories should also spur health care providers to provide needed assistance and services.

6. Obama, Presidential Proclamation.

7. Protocol to Prevent, Suppress and Punish Trafficking in Persons (hereinafter cited as Trafficking Protocol), art. 3(a).

8. International law and the law of many jurisdictions treat sex trafficking and labor trafficking in the same way: when a minor is the victim, the means are irrelevant. However, under US federal law, when a minor is the victim, the means are deemed irrelevant only for sex trafficking. See chapter 3 for a detailed discussion of the law.

9. See, e.g., UN Global Initiative to Fight Human Trafficking, *Human Trafficking and Business*, 17-18; and Oram and Zimmerman, "Health of Persons Trafficked."

10. Zimmerman et al., *Health Risks and Consequences*, 45.

11. US Department of State, *Trafficking in Persons Report 2017*, 18; Bales, Fletcher, and Stover, *Hidden Slaves*, 35-41; Oram and Zimmerman, "Health of Persons Trafficked"; Barrick, "Human Trafficking," 149.

12. Baldwin et al., "Identification of Human Trafficking Victims," 36, 40.

13. Bales, Fletcher, and Stover, *Hidden Slaves*.

14. Bales, Fletcher, and Stover, *Hidden Slaves*; Institute of Medicine and National Research Council, *Confronting Commercial Sexual Exploitation*.

15. World Health Organization, *World Health Statistics*, 30.

16. Centers for Disease Control and Prevention, "Tuberculosis (TB)."

17. See Centers for Disease Control and Prevention, "Timeline of Violence" (describing how in 1983 the CDC established a Violence Epidemiology Branch to address violence as a public health issue); World Health Assembly, *Prevention of Violence* (declaring in 1996 that "violence is a leading worldwide public health problem"); and Rosenberg and Fenley, *Violence in America*, 11-12.

18. Todres, "Widening Our Lens," 56-57, 63-66.

19. Office on Trafficking in Persons, "Power of Framing"; Chisolm-Straker and

Stoklosa, *Human Trafficking*; Todres, "Moving Upstream"; University of Kansas Anti-Slavery and Human Trafficking Initiative, "Research: The ASHTI Prevention Strategies Model."

20. Todres, "Moving Upstream," 452.

21. Hartman et al., "National Health Spending," 150.

22. Chisolm-Straker and Richardson, "Assessment."

*Chapter 1.* Understanding Child Trafficking

1. UN Office on Drugs and Crime, *Global Report 2014*, 7.

2. See Smith et al., "Mankiller Lurking."

3. US Department of State, *Trafficking in Persons Report 2017*.

4. US Department of State, *Trafficking in Persons Report 2017*.

5. US Department of Education, *Human Trafficking of Children*, 1.

6. International Labour Office, *ILO Global Estimate*, 13.

7. International Labour Office, *ILO Global Estimate*, 14.

8. International Labour Office, *ILO Global Estimate*, 15.

9. International Labour Office and Walk Free Foundation, *Global Estimates*, 9.

10. International Labour Office and Walk Free Foundation, *Global Estimates*, 9–10.

11. Bruner, *Inaccurate Numbers*, 11–18.

12. International Labour Office and Walk Free Foundation, *Global Estimates*, 11.

13. See, e.g., Gallagher, "Unravelling the 2016 Global Slavery Index"; Guth et al., "Proper Methodology"; Stransky and Finkelhor, *How Many Juveniles*; and Weitzer, "New Directions."

14. Bruner, *Inaccurate Numbers*, vi.

15. Stransky and Finkelhor, *How Many Juveniles*, 1 (capitalization in original).

16. Stransky and Finkelhor, *How Many Juveniles*, 1.

17. Kempe et al., "Battered Child Syndrome."

18. Institute of Medicine and National Research Council, *Confronting Commercial Sexual Exploitation*, xii.

19. Children's Bureau, *Childhood Maltreatment 2016*.

20. Gilbert et al., "Burden and Consequences," 68–69.

21. US Department of State, "Global Law Enforcement Data."

22. Guth et al., "Proper Methodology," 16.

23. Compare 18 U.S.C. § 1589 (2016) (providing no separate language for labor trafficking cases involving child victims) with 18 U.S.C. § 1591 (2016) (establishing that prosecution does not require proof of force, fraud, or coercion for sex trafficking cases involving a child). See also Trafficking Protocol, art. 3(c) (no proof of means required for cases involving a child victim of either labor trafficking or sex trafficking).

24. Chuang, "Exploitation Creep," 619.

25. Kessler, "Why You Should Be Wary of Statistics."

26. Guth et al., "Proper Methodology," 14. See also Surtees and Craggs, *Beneath the Surface*, 13.

27. Guth et al., "Proper Methodology," 14–15.

28. Chuang, "Exploitation Creep," 618.

29. Chuang, "Exploitation Creep," 619.

30. Chuang, "Exploitation Creep," 619.

31. Guth et al., "Proper Methodology," 20.

32. See Zhang et al., "Estimating Labor Trafficking," 65, 66.

33. Chuang, "Exploitation Creep," 610.

34. Trafficking Protocol, art. 3(a).

35. Trafficking Protocol, art. 3(a).

36. Trafficking Protocol, art. 3(c). As detailed in chapter 3, the US definition of labor trafficking does not follow this aspect of international law, requiring proof of force, fraud, or coercion in labor trafficking cases even when the victim is a minor. See 18 U.S.C. § 1589.

37. UN Office on Drugs and Crime, *Toolkit*, 4.

38. UN Office on Drugs and Crime, *Toolkit*, 4-5.

39. UN Office on Drugs and Crime, *Toolkit*, 4-5.

40. Tripp and McMahon-Howard, "Perception vs. Reality," 747.

41. UN Office on Drugs and Crime, *Toolkit*, 4-5.

42. Logan, Walker, and Hunt, "Understanding Human Trafficking"; Bravo, "Exploring the Analogy."

43. Elbagir et al., "People for Sale."

44. Kara, *Sex Trafficking*, 23.

45. Nagle, "Selling Souls," 131; Encinas, "Correlation between Globalization and Human Trafficking."

46. Engle, "Corporate Social Responsibility," 105; Nagle, "Selling Souls," 139; Bravo, "Exploring the Analogy," 241-42.

47. Bennet et al., *Global Report on Internal Displacement*; UN Office for the Coordination of Humanitarian Affairs, "Case Studies."

48. Todres, "Human Rights, Labor," 145-46.

49. Aronowitz, Theuermann, and Tyurykanova, *Analysing the Business Model*, 22-23.

50. Aronowitz, Theuermann, and Tyurykanova, *Analysing the Business Model*, 22-23.

51. Aronowitz, Theuermann, and Tyurykanova, *Analysing the Business Model*, 23.

52. Verité, *Tool 2*, 2.

53. Verité, *Tool 2*, 2.

54. Miko, "Trafficking in Women and Children," 5.

55. Laczko and Gramegna, "Developing Better Indicators," 188.

56. Greenbaum, "Commercial Sexual Exploitation," 249.

57. See, e.g., Lillie, "How Street Traffickers Recruit"; and Office of Juvenile Justice and Delinquency Prevention, "Commercial Sexual Exploitation of Children," 5.

58. Shen, "Female Perpetrators"; Gotch, "Preliminary Data"; Durchslag and Goswami, *Deconstructing the Demand for Prostitution*, 2; US Department of State, *Trafficking in Persons Report 2011*, 7.

59. Choi-Fitzpatrick, "The Good, the Bad, the Ugly"; Gotch, "Preliminary Data"; Surtees, "Traffickers"; UN Office on Drugs and Crime, *Role of Recruitment*; Raphael et al., *What We Know about Sex Trafficking*, 3-4.

60. US Department of State, *Trafficking in Persons Report 2017*.

61. Smith and Vardaman, "Legislative Framework," 279–82.

62. Todres, "Widening Our Lens," 61–63; Nagle, "Selling Souls," 150–51.

63. Aronowitz, Theuermann, and Tyurykanova, *Analysing the Business Model*, 9–10.

64. US Department of State, *Trafficking in Persons Report 2017*, 9.

65. US Department of State, *Trafficking in Persons Report 2017*, 9.

66. US Department of State, *Trafficking in Persons Report 2017*, 9.

67. US Department of State, *Trafficking in Persons Report 2017*, 9.

68. Gleave, Miller, and Sellers, "Transportation Officials."

69. Lampert, "U.N. Agency Urges Mandatory Training."

70. ECPAT-USA, *No Vacancy*, 7; TheCode.Org, "Members of the Code."

71. Gabers, "Nail Bars Are Havens." See also Nir, "Price of Nice Nails."

72. See Pierce, "Turning a Blind Eye," 594–96; and Verité, *Why Modern Slavery Persists*.

73. UN Global Initiative to Fight Human Trafficking, *Human Trafficking and Business*, 17–18.

74. US Department of State, *Trafficking in Persons Report 2016*, 30–31.

75. Weitzer, "New Directions," 7.

76. National Human Trafficking Resource Center, *Labor Trafficking Cases*, 2–6. See also Finnemore, "Human Tender," 19.

77. Spires, *Preventing Human Trafficking*, 23; Black, *Politics of Human Rights Protection*, 127; Todres, "Private Sector's Pivotal Role," 85.

78. Petriliggieri, "Poverty," 24–25.

79. Petriliggieri, "Poverty," 24–25.

80. Todres, "Law, Otherness," 607–8.

81. Centers for Disease Control and Prevention, "Social-Ecological Model."

Chapter 2. The Consequences of Child Trafficking

1. Institute of Medicine and National Research Council, *Confronting Commercial Sexual Exploitation*, 19, 372.

2. Todres, "Moving Upstream," 463.

3. Byrne, Parsh, and Ghilain, "Victims of Human Trafficking," 50–51.

4. Richards, "Health Implications," 159; Raghavan and Doychak, "Trauma-coerced Bonding," 583–84.

5. Reid, "Human Trafficking of Minors," 309–10.

6. Todres and Wolf, "Complexities of Conducting Research."

7. Geynisman-Tan, "All the Darkness," 136–37.

8. Human Rights Watch, *"I Wanted to Lie Down and Die,"* 26, 33–34.

9. Oram et al., "Prevalence and Risk."

10. Zimmerman et al., *Stolen Smiles*, 10.

11. Zimmerman et al., *Stolen Smiles*, 11–12, 14.

12. Zimmerman et al., *Stolen Smiles*, 14, 20.

13. Zimmerman et al., *Health Risks and Consequences*, 4.

14. Bales, Fletcher, and Stover, *Hidden Slaves*, 35.

15. Bales, Fletcher, and Stover, *Hidden Slaves*, 35.

16. Bales, Fletcher, and Stover, *Hidden Slaves*, 35.

17. Oram and Zimmerman, "Health of Persons Trafficked."

18. Oram and Zimmerman, "Health of Persons Trafficked."

19. Oram and Zimmerman, "Health of Persons Trafficked."

20. US Department of State, *Trafficking in Persons Report 2017*, 18; Bales, Fletcher, and Stover, *Hidden Slaves*, 35–41. See also World Health Organization, "What Are the Health Risks."

21. Link and Phelan, "Fundamental Sources of Health Inequalities," 71.

22. Oram and Zimmerman, "Health of Persons Trafficked."

23. Bales, Fletcher, and Stover, *Hidden Slaves*, 38.

24. US Department of Health and Human Services, *Fact Sheet: Labor Trafficking*.

25. Bales, Fletcher, and Stover, *Hidden Slaves*, 37–39.

26. Oram and Zimmerman, "Health of Persons Trafficked."

27. Barrick, "Human Trafficking," 149.

28. Byrne, Parsh, and Ghilain, "Victims of Human Trafficking," 50; Sidner, "Old Mark of Slavery."

29. Hammond and McGlone, "Entry, Progression, Exit," 166.

30. Normandin, "Child Human Trafficking," 589; Sabella, "Role of the Nurse," 34.

31. Sabella, "Role of the Nurse," 32.

32. Geynisman-Tan, "All the Darkness," 136; Crane and Moreno, "Human Trafficking," 13.

33. Bales, Fletcher, and Stover, *Hidden Slaves*, 38.

34. Crane and Moreno, "Human Trafficking," 13–14; Zimmerman et al., *Health Risks and Consequences*, 4.

35. Toney-Butler and Mittel, *Human Trafficking*.

36. Zimmerman et al., *Stolen Smiles*, 13, 21.

37. Lederer and Wetzel, "Health Consequences," 81.

38. Goldberg et al., "Domestic Minor Sex Trafficking Patients," 114.

39. Oram et al., "Prevalence and Risk," 9; National Sexual Violence Resource Center, *Assisting Trafficking Victims*, 10.

40. Global Freedom Center, *Overlooked*, 1; Pocock et al., "Labour Trafficking among Men," 9.

41. Pocock et al., "Labour Trafficking among Men and Boys," 9; ECPAT-USA, *And Boys Too*, 5–7.

42. See, generally, Polaris Project, *Sex Trafficking and LGBTQ Youth*; and Rothman, Exner, and Baughman, "Prevalence of Sexual Assault."

43. Zimmerman et al., *Health Risks and Consequences*, 4; Normandin, "Child Human Trafficking," 589.

44. Zimmerman et al., *Health Risks and Consequences*, 4.

45. Bales, Fletcher, and Stover, *Hidden Slaves*, 38.

46. Lederer and Wetzel, "Health Consequences," 66.

47. Lederer and Wetzel, "Health Consequences," 72.

48. Lederer and Wetzel, "Health Consequences," 73.

49. Lederer and Wetzel, "Health Consequences," 73.

50. Lederer and Wetzel, "Health Consequences," 73.

51. Baldwin et al., "Identification of Human Trafficking Victims," 36, 40.

52. McClain and Garrity, "Sex Trafficking," 246; Gupta et al., "HIV Vulner-abilities," 33.

53. Lederer and Wetzel, "Health Consequences," 71–72.

54. Lederer and Wetzel, "Health Consequences," 72.

55. Bulletti et al., "Endometriosis and Infertility," 441.

56. Bulletti et al., "Endometriosis and Infertility," 442.

57. Silverman et al., "HIV Prevalence," 538.

58. Silverman et al., "Syphilis and Hepatitis B," 932–33.

59. Dennis, "Women Are Victims," 12.

60. ECPAT-USA, *And Boys Too*, 5–7.

61. Global Freedom Center, *Overlooked*, 1.

62. Cornell, "Interaction of Drug Smuggling."

63. Pinto et al., "Radiological and Practical Aspects," 5–6.

64. Crane and Moreno, "Human Trafficking," 15; Zimmerman et al., *Health Risks and Consequences*, 4; Gibbons and Stoklosa, "Identification and Treatment," 717–18.

65. Gerassi, "From Exploitation to Industry," 596.

66. Clawson et al., *Human Trafficking*, 7.

67. Clawson et al., *Human Trafficking*, 12.

68. Gerassi, "From Exploitation to Industry," 597; US Department of Health and Human Services, *Fact Sheet: Labor Trafficking*.

69. Clawson et al., *Human Trafficking*, 12.

70. Gerassi, "From Exploitation to Industry," 599.

71. Anda et al., "Enduring Effects," 180.

72. Gerassi, "From Exploitation to Industry," 595–96.

73. Clawson et al., *Human Trafficking*, 13.

74. Valera, Sawyer, and Schiraldi, "Perceived Health Needs," 58.

75. Abas et al., "Risk Factors," 5.

76. Hopper, "Trauma-Informed Psychological Assessment," 13.

77. Task Force on Trafficking of Women and Girls, *Report of the Task Force*, 42; Cloitre et al., "Treatment of Complex PTSD"; Sar, "Developmental Trauma."

78. Sadruddin, Walter, and Hidalgo, "Human Trafficking," 399.

79. Reid, "Human Trafficking of Minors," 309–10.

80. Felitti et al., "Childhood Abuse and Household Dysfunction."

81. Morisano, Babor, and Robaina, "Co-Occurrence," 10.

82. Hollen and Ortiz, "Mental Health and Substance Use Comorbidity," 103, 105.

83. Eisen et al., "Alcohol, Drugs, and Psychiatric Disorder," 259. See also Grella et al., "Drug Treatment Outcomes."

84. Hammond and McGlone, "Entry, Progression, Exit," 161–62.

85. Clawson et al., *Human Trafficking*, 8.

86. Hammond and McGlone, "Entry, Progression, Exit," 165.

87. Raphael, Reichert, and Powers, "Pimp Control and Violence," 95.

88. Raphael, Reichert, and Powers, "Pimp Control and Violence," 89, 101.

89. Farley et al., "Prostitution and Trafficking," 34.

90. Institute of Medicine and National Research Council, *Confronting Commercial Sexual Exploitation*, 84–85.

91. Institute of Medicine and National Research Council, *Confronting Commercial Sexual Exploitation*, 84.

92. Wickrama, Wickrama, and Baltimore, "Adolescent Precocious Development," 121–22. See also Wickrama et al., "Linking Early Risks," 63.

93. Wickrama, Wickrama, and Baltimore, "Adolescent Precocious Development," 122. See also Institute of Medicine and National Research Council, *Confronting Commercial Sexual Exploitation*, 85.

94. Institute of Medicine and National Research Council, *Confronting Commercial Sexual Exploitation*, 85.

95. Briain, van den Borne, and Noten, *Combating the Trafficking*, 20, 35.

96. National Center for Homeless Education, *Sex Trafficking of Minors*, 4.

97. National Center for Homeless Education, *Sex Trafficking of Minors*, 5; Todres, "Taking Prevention Seriously," 49–50.

98. Rafferty, "Impact of Trafficking on Children," 14.

99. Institute of Medicine and National Research Council, *Confronting Commercial Sexual Exploitation*, 85.

100. Task Force on Trafficking of Women and Girls, *Report of the Task Force*, 45.

101. Rafferty, "Impact of Trafficking on Children," 14.

102. Briain, van den Borne, and Noten, *Combating the Trafficking*, 21; Todres, "Taking Prevention Seriously," 49.

103. UN Office on Drugs and Crime, *Human Trafficking Indicators*.

104. Zimmerman, Hossain, and Watts, "Human Trafficking and Health," 331.

105. International Labour Office, *Profits and Poverty*, 13.

106. Southern Poverty Law Center, "$20 Million Settlement Agreement Reached."

107. United States v. Webster, No. 3:06-cr-0096-HRH (D. Alaska April 1, 2009) (Order of Restitution).

108. Levy, *United States Federal Courts' Continuing Failure*, 1.

109. Levy and Vandenberg, "Breaking the Law," 53 (emphasis in original).

110. Institute of Medicine and National Research Council, *Confronting Commercial Sexual Exploitation*, 87.

111. Clawson and Dutch, *Addressing the Needs*, 1.

112. Polaris Project, *Shelter Beds*, 1.

113. Nack, "Next Step," 839; Maney et al., *Meeting the Service Needs*, 14.

114. Maney et al., *Meeting the Service Needs*, 14.

115. Mehlman-Orozco, "What Happens"; Mehlman-Orozco, "Plight of Sex-Trafficking Survivors," 1.

116. Bean, *LGBTQ Youth at High Risk*.

117. Polaris Project, *Shelter Beds*, 6–7.

118. Raney, "Unseen Victims of Sex Trafficking."

119. Maney et al., *Meeting the Service Needs*, 4.

120. Maney et al., *Meeting the Service Needs*, 18.

121. Reichert and Sylwestrzak, *National Survey*, 14.

122. Maney et al., *Meeting the Service Needs*, 19.

123. Maney et al., *Meeting the Service Needs*, 20.

124. Maney et al., *Meeting the Service Needs*, 24.

125. US Department of Health and Human Services, *Coordination, Collaboration, Capacity*, 38.

126. Goździak and Lowell, *After Rescue*, 5; Hammond and McGlone, "Entry, Progression, Exit," 166; Macy and Johns, "Aftercare Services," 93.

127. Soohoo, *Criminalization of Trafficking Victims*, 2–3.

128. In re B.W., 313 S.W.3d 818, 824–25 (Tex. 2010).

129. ECPAT-USA, *Alternative Report: An NGO Response*, 7.

130. Soohoo, *Criminalization of Trafficking Victims*, 2.

131. Soohoo, *Criminalization of Trafficking Victims*, 3.

132. Soohoo, *Criminalization of Trafficking Victims*, 3.

133. Rhodan, "Deportation Fears."

134. Soohoo, *Criminalization of Trafficking Victims*, 6. See also Corbett, "Voices of Survivors," 97.

135. Office of Justice Programs, *Victim as a Witness*.

136. 22 U.S.C. § 7105(b)(l)(C) (2018). For certain foreign adults, cooperation with law enforcement may be required in order to stay in the United States. See 22 U.S.C. § 7105(b)(l)(E)(i) (2018).

137. Vacatur laws can be an important tool in helping trafficking survivors move on from their trafficking experience and rebuild their lives. See Castillo, "Vacatur Laws."

138. Ijadi-Maghsoodi et al., "Commercially Sexually Exploited Youths' Health Care Experiences," 339.

*Chapter 3.* Current Responses to Child Trafficking

1. Obama, Remarks.

2. Dottridge, introduction, 1.

3. Dottridge, introduction, 1; Todres, "Human Rights, Labor," 151; Chuang, "Redirecting the Debate," 106.

4. Institute of Medicine and National Research Council, *Confronting Commercial Sexual Exploitation*, 373, 383–84; Todres, "Moving Upstream," 493–97.

5. Trafficking Protocol.

6. Optional Protocol on the Sale of Children (hereinafter cited as Sale of Children Protocol).

7. See, e.g., Trafficking Protocol, arts. 5–6, 9; and Sale of Children Protocol, arts. 3, 8–9.

8. Clinton, Memorandum on Steps to Combat Violence.

9. Clinton, Memorandum on Steps to Combat Violence.

10. See US Department of State, *Trafficking in Persons Report 2016*, 55–56. The *TIP Report*, as it is known, assesses countries' efforts to combat human trafficking using the three-pronged approach championed by the United States. Countries that fall short of minimum requirements as set forth in the TVPA risk being subjected to US sanctions. This report and its attendant threat of sanctions have proven highly influential in anti-trafficking efforts.

11. UN Treaty Collection, "Status of Ratifications: Protocol to Prevent."

12. UN Treaty Collection, "Status of Ratifications: Optional Protocol."

13. Trafficking Protocol, art. 5; Sale of Children Protocol, art. 3.

14. Trafficking Protocol, art 5 (emphasis added).

15. Sale of Children Protocol, art. 3(1) (emphasis added).

16. Sale of Children Protocol, art. 5.

17. Trafficking Protocol, arts. 10-11.

18. Trafficking Protocol, art. 6(3).

19. Trafficking Protocol, art. 6(3).

20. Sale of Children Protocol, art. 9(3).

21. Sale of Children Protocol, art. 8.

22. Trafficking Protocol, art. 9(1)-(2).

23. Sale of Children Protocol, art. 9.

24. Trafficking Protocol, art. 4.

25. Sale of Children Protocol, art. 3(1).

26. Trafficking Protocol, art. 5.

27. US Department of State, *Trafficking in Persons Report 2010*, 1 (introductory letter from Secretary Hillary Clinton).

28. 18 U.S.C. § 1591.

29. 18 U.S.C. § 1591.

30. 18 U.S.C. §§ 1589 and 1590.

31. International Labour Office, *Unbearable to the Human Heart*, 7.

32. 18 U.S.C. § 1591(b).

33. 18 U.S.C. §§ 1589 and 1590.

34. US Department of State, *Trafficking in Persons Report 2016*, 389.

35. US Department of State, *Trafficking in Persons Report 2016*, 389.

36. Justice for Victims of Trafficking Act of 2015, Public Law No. 114-22, 129 Stat. 227, § 108(a)(1) (2015) (codified as amended at 18 U.S.C. § 1591).

37. 18 U.S.C. § 1592.

38. 18 U.S.C. § 1594.

39. White Slave Traffic (Mann) Act, ch. 395, 36 Stat. 826 (1910), (codified as amended at 18 U.S.C. §§ 2421-24 (2016)).

40. 18 U.S.C. §§ 2421-23.

41. See, e.g., Langum, Crossing over the Line.

42. 18 U.S.C. § 2423(a).

43. 18 U.S.C. § 2422.

44. 18 U.S.C. § 2423(b). Unlike federal anti-trafficking law, the Mann Act includes an affirmative defense for individuals charged with traveling in interstate or foreign commerce to engage in illicit sexual conduct with a minor: "the defendant must establish by a preponderance of the evidence, that the defendant reasonably believed that the person with whom the defendant engaged in the commercial sex act had attained the age of 18 years." 18 U.S.C. § 2423(g).

45. 18 U.S.C. § 2423(d).

46. 18 U.S.C. § 1594(a); 18 U.S.C. § 2428(d).

47. US Department of State, *Trafficking in Persons Report 2016*, 390.

48. Institute of Medicine and National Research Council, *Confronting Commercial Sexual Exploitation*, 149-50.

49. Preventing Sex Trafficking and Strengthening Families Act, Public Law No. 113-183, 128 Stat. 1919, § 101 (codified as amended at 42 U.S.C. § 671(a)(9)).

50. Justice for Victims of Trafficking Act of 2015, § 802 (codified as amended at 42 U.S.C. § 5101 et seq.).

51. Justice for Victims of Trafficking Act of 2015, §§ 103 (codified as amended at 34 U.S.C. § 20703) and 702.

52. Justice for Victims of Trafficking Act of 2015, § 601 (codified as amended at 34 U.S.C. § 10381 et seq.).

53. 18 U.S.C. § 1593. The "full amount of the victim's losses" includes (1) medical services relating to physical, psychiatric, or psychological care; (2) physical and occupational therapy or rehabilitation; (3) necessary transportation, temporary housing, and child care expenses; (4) lost income; (5) attorneys' fees, as well as other costs incurred; and (6) any other losses suffered by the victim as a proximate result of the offense. Losses shall in addition include the greater of the gross income or value to the defendant of the victim's services or labor and the value of the victim's labor as guaranteed under the minimum wage and overtime guarantees of the Fair Labor Standards Act. 18 U.S.C. §§ 1593(a)(3) and 2259(b)(3).

54. Levy, *United States Federal Courts' Continuing Failure*, 1.

55. United States v. Webster, Order of Restitution, 14-15.

56. 18 U.S.C. § 1595.

57. Nam, "Case of the Missing Case," 1684-85.

58. National Human Trafficking Hotline, "Mission."

59. Family and Youth Services Bureau, *Street Outreach Program*, 1.

60. Family and Youth Services Bureau, *Street Outreach Program*, 1.

61. US Department of State, *Trafficking in Persons Report 2017*.

62. See, e.g., Obama, Presidential Proclamation.

63. Administration for Children and Families, "Grants"; US Department of State, *U.S. Government Entities Combating Human Trafficking*.

64. US Department of Education, *Human Trafficking of Children*.

65. US Department of Justice, *National Strategy for Child Exploitation Prevention*.

66. US Department of Health and Human Services, *Coordination, Collaboration, Capacity*, 90.

67. US Department of Justice. *OJJDP FY 2017*, 4.

68. Polaris Project, *How Does Your State Rate*, 2-3.

69. Polaris Project, *Analysis of State Human Trafficking Laws*, 7.

70. Mass. Gen. Laws Ann., ch. 265, §§ 50-51 (West 2012).

71. Colo. Rev. Stat. Ann. §§ 18-3-503, 18-3-504, and 18-1.3-401 (West 2016).

72. Polaris Project, *Analysis of State Human Trafficking Laws*, 15-16; Shared Hope International, *National State Survey Law*, 1-4.

73. Polaris Project, *Analysis of State Human Trafficking Laws*, 27.

74. Farrell et al., "Prosecution of State-Level Human Trafficking Cases," 57.

75. US Department of State, *Trafficking in Persons Report 2016*, 389; ECPAT-USA, *Steps to Safety*, 5, 15-16.

76. Center for Court Innovation, *State Court Snapshot*, 1-2.

77. California Courts, *Handbook for STAR Court*.

78. Institute of Medicine and National Research Council, *Confronting Commercial Sexual Exploitation*, 157.

79. Todres, "Can Mandatory Reporting Laws Help," 69–70.

80. Todres, "Can Mandatory Reporting Laws Help," 70.

81. Institute of Medicine and National Research Council, *Confronting Commercial Sexual Exploitation*, 144–46.

82. Institute of Medicine and National Research Council, *Confronting Commercial Sexual Exploitation*, 167–70.

83. Institute of Medicine and National Research Council, *Confronting Commercial Sexual Exploitation*, 168–69.

84. Institute of Medicine and National Research Council, *Confronting Commercial Sexual Exploitation*, 167.

85. Institute of Medicine and National Research Council, *Confronting Commercial Sexual Exploitation*, 170.

86. Some state social service entities, whose mandate traditionally covers child maltreatment in the home, have expressed uncertainty about whether they have jurisdiction over child trafficking victims, especially if there is no evidence of abuse in the home environment. To address this issue, in 2014 California amended its law to clarify that Child Protective Services (CPS) has jurisdiction over children who are sex trafficking victims, enabling CPS to help facilitate safe placement and/or housing for these children, as well as other services. See California Welf. & Inst. Code § 300(b)(2) (2018).

87. Shared Hope International, ECPAT-USA, and Protection Project of the Johns Hopkins University School of Advanced International Studies, *U.S. Mid-Term Review*, 9, 34.

88. US Department of Health and Human Services, *Services Available to Victims*, 2–3.

89. See, e.g., Chacón, "Tensions and Trade-Offs"; Chuang, "Rescuing Trafficking"; Dottridge, introduction; and Haynes, "(Not) Found Chained." See also Gallagher, *International Law*, 68 (explaining how the 1990s marked "an important shift in the international legal framework around trafficking" away from human rights approaches and toward a transnational organized crime model).

90. Todres, "Child Rights Framework," 570–72.

91. Haynes, "(Not) Found Chained," 345–52; Todres, "Moving Upstream," 456–63; Chuang, "Redirecting the Debate," 106.

92. Haynes, "(Not) Found Chained," 347–49.

93. US Department of State, *Trafficking in Persons Report 2016*, 389.

94. Haynes, "(Not) Found Chained," 347–48.

95. US Department of Justice, *Facts about the Department of Justice's Anti-Trafficking Efforts*, 4 ("Child sex tourism cases are very resource-intensive, requiring gathering evidence abroad, bringing victims to the United States to testify, and coordination with foreign law enforcement agencies"); Clawson et al., *Prosecuting Human Trafficking Cases*, 20 ("[Most of the respondents [of a survey of prosecutor's in ten federal jurisdictions] indicated that TVPA cases are more resource intensive, time consuming, emotionally draining, reactive, and victim-oriented and victim-focused"); US

Government Accountability Office, *Human Trafficking*, 20 ("Trafficking in persons cases are difficult to pursue because they are multifaceted, complex, and resource intensive").

96. See, e.g., Burris et al., "Do Criminal Laws Influence HIV Risk Behavior?," 468; and Welsh, "Public Health," 23.

97. Robinson and Darley, "Does Criminal Law Deter?"; Robinson and Darley, "Role of Deterrence," 977. See also Mercy et al., "Public Health Policy," 11 ("Although the average prison time served for a violent crime in the United States tripled between 1975 and 1989, there was no concomitant decrease in the level of violent crimes").

98. See, e.g., National Conference of State Legislatures, "Issue in Focus"; National Conference of State Legislatures, "Shaken Baby Syndrome"; and Gever, "Legislators Hope."

99. See, e.g., Galinsky, "Should You Make the First Offer?," 3; and Adler, "Flawed Thinking," 711.

100. Adler, "Flawed Thinking," 711–12; Galinsky, "Should You Make the First Offer?," 3.

101. Biber, "Too Many Things to Do," 9.

102. See Biber, "Too Many Things to Do," 11 ("Tasks that are more easily measured are more likely to be performed at a higher level by an agent as compared to tasks that are harder to measure"). This makes it likely that law enforcement will continue to focus on arrests, prosecutions, and convictions—readily measurable criteria—rather than on the emotional well-being of victims. See also Goodmark, "Autonomy Feminism," 5–6 (highlighting how mandatory arrests and no-drop prosecution rules in domestic violence cases often conflict with the goals of women who are victims); and Lawson, "A Shift toward Gender Equality," 188–89 (noting that prosecutorial decisions "attempt to accomplish multiple goals, such as: punishing the individual criminal actor, vindicating the injury of the victim, and alerting the public in an effort to deter future crime" and that they "have historically neglected the special needs of victimized women and failed to give their cases adequate attention").

103. US Department of State, *Trafficking in Persons Report 2016*, 40.

104. US Department of State, *Trafficking in Persons Report 2016*, 40.

*Chapter 4.* Public Health Methods and Perspectives

1. Todres, "Moving Upstream," 447; Zimmerman and Kiss, "Human Trafficking and Exploitation," 1; Chisolm-Straker and Stoklosa, *Human Trafficking*, 1–3.

2. See Centers for Disease Control and Prevention, "Timeline of Violence"; World Health Assembly, *Prevention of Violence*; and Rosenberg and Fenley, *Violence in America*, 11–12.

3. Garrison, "Reforming Child Protection," 600; American Public Health Association, "Supporting Research."

4. Garrison, "Reforming Child Protection," 600.

5. Braveman and Gottlieb, "Social Determinants of Health"; Orgera and Artiga, *Disparities in Health and Health Care*.

6. Centers for Disease Control and Prevention, "Social-Ecological Model." See

also Gómez et al., *Community-Based Approaches to Intimate Partner Violence*, for an example of the socio-ecological model applied to violence.

7. The socio-ecological model can help identity harmful attitudes and behaviors at different levels, ranging from individual risk behaviors (e.g., visiting commercial sex workers) to societal attitudes (e.g., beliefs that foster the sexualization of girls and the marginalization of minority communities).

8. Mercy et al., "Public Health Policy," 8.

9. See, e.g., Brownson et al., *Evidence-Based Public Health*, 1–18.

10. Mercy et al., "Public Health Policy," 14–15. See also World Health Organization, "Public Health Approach."

11. Todres, "Moving Upstream," 470–71. See also Rothman et al., "Public Health Research Priorities," 1045–46.

12. Twis and Shelton, "Systematic Review of Empiricism," 432; Goździak and Bump, *Data and Research*, 9.

13. Davy, "Understanding the Support Needs," 318; Zimmerman et al., "Rigged or Rigorous?," 95; Todres, "Assessing Public Health Strategies," 97; Rothman et al., "Public Health Research Priorities," 1046; Okech et al., "Seventeen Years of Human Trafficking Research," 117–18; Hemmings et al., "Responding to the Health Needs," 2; Greenfield, Paoli, and Zoutendijk, "Harms of Human Trafficking," 152.

14. Justice for Victims of Trafficking Act of 2015, § 203(e).

15. UN Office on Drugs and Crime, "UNODC Launches Global Initiative"; Goździak and Bump, *Data and Research*, 7; Todres, "Human Trafficking and Film," 11–13.

16. Kangaspunta, *Social Etiology of Human Trafficking*, 3; Guilbert, "Number of Women Convicted."

17. Laczko and Gramegna, "Developing Better Indicators," 188–89.

18. Viuhko, "Hardened Professional Criminals," 186. See also Palmer and Missbach, "Trafficking within Migrant Smuggling Operations."

19. Viuhko, "Hardened Professional Criminals," 182–83; Moore and Goldberg, "Victims, Perpetrators," 16. See also Palmer and Missbach, "Trafficking within Migrant Smuggling Operations."

20. See Laczko and Gramegna, "Developing Better Indicators," 189. See also Scullion, "Gender Perspectives on Child Trafficking," 55–54.

21. See Todres, "Human Trafficking and Film," 9–13; Haynes, "(Not) Found Chained," 342; and Feingold, "Think Again," 26.

22. Todres, "Human Trafficking and Film," 20–22.

23. See Polaris Project, *Shelter Beds*, 5.

24. Polaris Project, *Shelter Beds*, 5.

25. See Fong and Cardoso, "Child Human Trafficking Victims," 315.

26. Institute of Medicine and National Research Council, *Confronting Commercial Sexual Exploitation*, 13.

27. Curtis et al., *Commercial Sexual Exploitation of Children*, 34.

28. Curtis et al., *Commercial Sexual Exploitation of Children*, 34; Institute of Medicine and National Research Council, *Confronting Commercial Sexual Exploitation*, 245–46; Martinez and Kelle, "Sex Trafficking of LGBT Individuals," 1.

29. Freeman-Longo, "Reducing Sexual Abuse in America," 316.

30. See, e.g., Ruttenberg, "Limited Promise," 1889–90.

31. Gostin and Berkman, "Pandemic Influenza," 133, 151–52, 161–62.

32. Mariner, "Mission Creep," 349.

33. Stoto, "Public Health Surveillance," 703 (quoting a long-standing CDC definition).

34. Office on Trafficking in Persons, Administration for Children and Families, "Human Trafficking Data Collection Project." See also Office on Trafficking in Persons and Office on Women's Health, *Human Trafficking Data Element Worksheet*.

35. Office on Trafficking in Persons, Administration for Children and Families, "CDC Adds New Human Trafficking Data Collection Fields."

36. International Labour Organization, "Child Labour Statistics."

37. Institute of Medicine and National Research Council, *Confronting Commercial Sexual Exploitation*, 42.

38. Gibbs et al., *Evaluation of Services*, ES-3.

39. Centers for Disease Control and Prevention, "Social-Ecological Model."

40. Ruttenberg, "Limited Promise," 1890.

41. See UN Inter-Agency Project on Human Trafficking, *Targeting Endemic Vulnerability Factors*, 1.

42. INFO Project and Johns Hopkins Bloomberg School of Public Health, "What Is Monitoring and Evaluation?"; Centers for Disease Control and Prevention, *Program Evaluation*, 2–3.

43. Güngör, "Overweight and Obesity," 136–37.

44. See US Department of Health and Human Services, *School-Based Obesity Prevention Strategies*, 1.

45. Veugelers and Fitzgerald, "Effectiveness of School Programs," 432.

46. Veugelers and Fitzgerald, "Effectiveness of School Programs," 434 (4.1% were obese in the schools with a CDC-structured nutrition program, compared with 10.4% in schools with another nutrition program, and 9.9% in schools with no program).

47. Veugelers and Fitzgerald, "Effectiveness of School Programs," 434.

48. See, e.g., DuBois et al., "Effectiveness of Mentoring Programs," 157, 180.

49. Williamson, Clawson, and Chen, *Where Is the Research on Human Trafficking*, 1, 3–5.

50. William Wilberforce Trafficking Victims Protection Reauthorization Act of 2008, Public Law No. 110-457, 122 Stat. 5044 (2008); Violence Against Women Reauthorization Act of 2013, Public Law No. 113-4, sec. 2, title XII, § 1203, 127 Stat. 54, 138–39 (including the 2013 TVPRA).

51. Justice for Victims of Trafficking Act of 2015, § 203(e).

52. See, e.g., Walters et al., *Evaluation of Domestic Victims of Human Trafficking Demonstration Projects*, iii; and Office of Planning, Research & Evaluation, "Evaluation of Domestic Victims of Human Trafficking Program."

53. Stoklosa, *Background Paper*, 4–6. But see Marlegna et al., "Changing the Child Labor Laws for Agriculture," 276.

54. Mercy et al., "Public Health Policy," 11.

55. Mercy et al., "Public Health Policy," 11.

56. See, e.g., Evans, Neville, and Graham, "General Deterrence of Drunk Driving," 279; and Robinson and Darley, "Role of Deterrence," 1001.

57. See, generally, Robinson and Darley, "Does Criminal Law Deter?"

58. Mercy et al., "Public Health Policy," 8.

59. Centers for Disease Control and Prevention, "Social-Ecological Model."

60. Centers for Disease Control and Prevention, "Social-Ecological Model."

61. Centers for Disease Control and Prevention, "Social-Ecological Model."

62. Dottridge, "Young People's Voices," v.

63. Centers for Disease Control and Prevention, "Social-Ecological Model."

64. Chisolm-Straker et al., "Supportive Adult," 119.

65. See Smink, "Mentoring," 140; Tierney, Grossman, and Resch, *Making a Difference*, 29; McLearn, Colasanto, and Schoen, *Mentoring Makes a Difference*, 4; and Dottridge, *Kids as Commodities*, 29.

66. Erickson, McDonald, and Elder, "Informal Mentors and Education," 354.

67. Tierney, Grossman, and Resch, *Making a Difference*, ii.

68. Choose Peace Stop Violence, "Model Approach."

69. Lederer, "Ending Demand," 135-36, 144-45; Polaris Project, "On-Ramps, Intersections, and Exit Routes," 33; Truckers Against Trafficking, "Labor Trafficking."

70. Stratford et al., "Highway Cowboys," 743; Nag, "Sexual Behaviour in India," 297.

71. Truckers Against Trafficking, "Labor Trafficking."

72. Centers for Disease Control and Prevention, "Social-Ecological Model."

73. Dottridge, *Kids as Commodities*, 28.

74. Dottridge, *Kids as Commodities*, 69; Todres, "Child Rights Framework," 586-89.

75. Kogan et al., "Underinsurance," 842; Newacheck et al., "Health Insurance," 514-16.

76. Jukes, Drake, and Bundy, *School Health, Nutrition and Education*, 41; Del Rosso, Miller, and Marek, *Class Action*, 11; Crooks, "American Children at Risk," 78.

77. See Dottridge, *Kids as Commodities*, 69.

78. Todres, "Importance of Realizing 'Other' Rights," 891; Bond, "International Intersectionality," 112; Coomaraswamy, *Fifteen Years*, 13-14.

79. See Del Rosso, Miller, and Marek, *Class Action*, 11, 27; Crooks, "American Children at Risk," 57, 78; and Ames et al., "Food Insecurity and Educational Achievement," 21.

80. Braveman and Gottlieb, "Social Determinants of Health"; Orgera and Artiga, *Disparities in Health and Health Care*.

81. Wolf, "Is Breast Really Best?," 595. But see Hemenway, "Reducing Firearm Injury and Violence," 644.

82. Larkin and McGowan, "Introduction: Strengthening Public Health," 4; Siegel and Lotenberg, *Marketing Public Health*, 5.

83. Hemenway, "Reducing Firearm Injury and Violence," 649.

84. See, e.g., Farrelly et al., "Evidence of a Dose-Response Relationship," 425; Holtgrave et al., "Cost-Utility Analysis," 385; Maddock, Maglione, and Barnett, "Statewide Implementation," 953; and Vasudevan et al., "Effectiveness of Media and Enforcement Campaigns," 330. But see also Garrison, "Reviving Marriage," 324.

85. Farrelly et al., "Getting to the Truth," 905.

86. Mercy et al., "Public Health Policy," 23.

87. Mercy et al., "Public Health Policy," 23.

88. Todres, "Law, Otherness," 621–22.

89. Todres, "Law, Otherness," 654.

90. See Engle, "Corporate Social Responsibility," 105.

91. Freeman-Longo, "Reducing Sexual Abuse in America," 305.

92. Task Force on Trafficking of Women and Girls, *Report of the Task Force*, 22–23.

93. Mercy et al., "Public Health Policy," 23.

94. Mercy et al., "Public Health Policy," 23.

95. Greenbaum, "Child Sex Trafficking."

96. Todres, "Human Trafficking and Film," 9–19.

97. Mercy et al., "Public Health Policy," 23.

98. Gómez et al., *Community-Based Approaches to Intimate Partner Violence*, 15–16.

99. Snyder et al., "Meta-Analysis," 72.

100. Snyder et al., "Meta-Analysis," 73.

101. Snyder et al., "Meta-Analysis," 86.

102. Snyder et al., "Meta-Analysis," 89.

103. Snyder et al., "Meta-Analysis," 89.

104. Snyder et al., "Meta-Analysis," 89.

105. See, e.g., Farrelly et al., "Getting to the Truth," 905.

106. Mercy et al., "Public Health Policy," 23.

107. Mercy et al., "Public Health Policy," 23.

108. See Goździak and Bump, *Data and Research*, 9; and Twis and Shelton, "Systematic Review of Empiricism," 10.

109. Witte and Allen, "Meta-Analysis of Fear Appeals," 606.

110. Witte and Allen, "Meta-Analysis of Fear Appeals," 606–7.

111. Leichtman, "Top Ten Ways," 733.

112. Romer et al., "Desire versus Efficacy in Smokers' Paradoxical Reactions"; Knox, *Big Surprise*, 3.

113. Mercy et al., "Public Health Policy," 23.

114. Burke and Friedman, *Management and Leadership*, 93.

115. Gómez et al., *Community-Based Approaches to Intimate Partner Violence*, 15–19.

116. Garrison, "Reviving Marriage," 323–24; Gómez et al., *Community-Based Approaches to Intimate Partner Violence*, 15–20.

117. Garrison, "Reviving Marriage," 324.

118. Mercy et al., "Public Health Policy," 16.

119. Miller et al., "Migration, Sexual Exploitation, and Women's Health," 490.

120. See Institute of Medicine and National Research Council, *Confronting Commercial Sexual Exploitation*, 6–7; and ECPAT-USA, *Alternative Report to the Initial Report*, 2.

121. See, e.g., Lim, *Sex Sector*, 1–7, 185.

122. National Center for Zoonotic, Vector-Borne, and Enteric Diseases, *Confronting Infectious Diseases*, i.

123. See Food and Agricultural Organization et al., *Contributing to One World, One Health*, 32.

124. Food and Agricultural Organization et al., *Contributing to One World, One Health*, 32.

125. See Bessette, *Involving the Community*, 141; and Jennings, *Participatory Development as New Paradigm*, 1-2.

126. See Bessette, *Involving the Community*, 16. On the challenges of engaging historically marginalized communities, see, e.g., Todres, "Taking Prevention Seriously," 23-24.

127. Food and Agricultural Organization et al., *Contributing to One World, One Health*, 32.

128. See Jennings, *Participatory Development as New Paradigm*, 1-2; and Wagle, "Policy Science of Democracy," 220. See also Orentlicher, "Diversity," 780.

129. UNICEF, *Reversing the Trend*, 59.

130. Dottridge, "Young People's Voices," vi.

131. Dottridge, "Young People's Voices," 13.

132. Dottridge, "Young People's Voices," 13.

133. Dottridge, "Young People's Voices," 13, 48.

134. Dottridge, "Young People's Voices," 16-17.

135. Dottridge, "Young People's Voices," 16.

136. See Pinheiro, *World Report*, 11, 19-20.

137. Lansdown, *Promoting Children's Participation*, 34.

138. Todres, "Taking Prevention Seriously," 10.

139. Dottridge, "Young People's Voices," 52.

140. Dottridge, "Young People's Voices," 41-42, 44.

141. See, e.g., World Health Organization, *Report of the International Consultation*, 12.

142. United Nations, "Background Paper," 12. See also American Public Health Association, "Expanding and Coordinating"; and US Department of Justice, *National Strategy to Combat Human Trafficking*, 1-2. There is significant difficulty with coordination among entities working within the United States on these issues. See, e.g., California Alliance to Combat Trafficking and Slavery Task Force, *Human Trafficking in California*, 8.

143. See, e.g., Institute of Medicine and National Research Council, *Confronting Commercial Sexual Exploitation*, 223; and Tourtchaninova and Kandel, *Mayor's Task Force*, 13.

144. See PROTECT Our Children Act of 2008, S. Res. 1738, 110th Cong. (2008).

145. See, generally, Brown, Trujillo, and Macintyre, *Interventions to Reduce HIV/AIDS Stigma*, 1, 9; and Bayer, "Stigma and the Ethics," 464.

146. Zimmerman and Watts, "Documenting the Effects," 167.

147. See Zimmerman et al., "Health of Trafficked Women," 58.

148. Zimmerman and Watts, "Documenting the Effects," 167.

149. See Cianciarulo, "Trafficking and Exploitation Victims Assistance Program," 407.

150. Isaacs, "Where the Public Good Prevailed."

151. DeJong and Hingson, "Strategies," 359-60.

152. Isaacs, "Where the Public Good Prevailed."

153. See Hemenway, "Motor Vehicles, Tobacco, and Alcohol"; Gómez et al.,

*Community-Based Approaches to Intimate Partner Violence*; and Walden and Wall, *Reflecting on the Primary Prevention*.

154. Barthe, *Crime Prevention Publicity Campaigns*, 15–16.

155. Barthe, *Crime Prevention Publicity Campaigns*, 15.

156. TheCode.Org, "Members of the Code." Carlson's hotel subsidiaries were sold to the HNA Tourism Group in 2016.

157. See, e.g., Puzio, "Overview of Public Health," 179.

158. Stoto, "Public Health Surveillance," 717.

159. See Annas, "Blinded by Bioterrorism," 56; and Puzio, "Overview of Public Health," 198.

160. Stoto, "Public Health Surveillance," 717; Mariner, "Mission Creep," 395.

161. Gostin and Berkman, "Pandemic Influenza," 156.

162. See Gostin and Berkman, "Pandemic Influenza," 156–57.

163. Sadruddin, Walter, and Hidalgo, "Human Trafficking," 384.

164. See Ogolla, "Racial Statistics," 3.

165. Ogolla, "Racial Statistics," 3.

166. See, e.g., Ruttenberg, "Limited Promise," 1887.

167. Ruttenberg, "Limited Promise," 1887–88.

168. See, e.g., Gómez et al., *Community-Based Approaches to Intimate Partner Violence*; Walden and Wall, *Reflecting on the Primary Prevention*; and Kirk et al., "Effectiveness of Secondary and Tertiary Prevention."

169. Witte and Allen, "Meta-Analysis of Fear Appeals," 592.

170. Witte and Allen, "Meta-Analysis of Fear Appeals," 606.

171. Witte and Allen, "Meta-Analysis of Fear Appeals," 592.

172. Hemenway, "Reducing Firearm Injury and Violence," 648.

173. Hemenway, "Reducing Firearm Injury and Violence," 648.

174. Hemenway, "Motor Vehicles, Tobacco, and Alcohol," 382–86.


*Chapter 5.* Understanding Risk Factors

1. Centers for Disease Control and Prevention, "Social-Ecological Model."

2. Institute of Medicine and National Research Council, *Confronting Commercial Sexual Exploitation*, 86.

3. Miller et al., "Individual and Structural Vulnerability," 37; Greene, Ennett, and Ringwalt, "Prevalence and Correlates," 1406–8.

4. Connecticut Alliance to End Sexual Violence, *Homelessness and Sexual Violence*; Institute of Medicine and National Research Council, *Confronting Commercial Sexual Exploitation*, 86; National Network for Youth, *Human Trafficking*, 1.

5. Institute of Medicine and National Research Council, *Confronting Commercial Sexual Exploitation*, 88–89.

6. Estes and Weiner, *Commercial Sexual Exploitation of Children*, 10–14; National Alliance to End Homelessness, *Homeless Youth and Sexual Exploitation*, 2–3; Connecticut Alliance to End Sexual Violence, *Homelessness and Sexual Violence*.

7. Murphy, *Labor and Sex Trafficking*, 4.

8. Greene, Ennett, and Ringwalt, "Prevalence and Correlates," 1408.

9. Wagner et al., "Snapshot of Homeless Youth," 223.

10. World Health Organization, "Childhood Maltreatment"; Tonmyr and Hovdestad, "Public Health Approach to Child Maltreatment."

11. Children's Bureau, *Childhood Maltreatment 2016*, xii.

12. Trickett, Putnam, and Noll, *Longitudinal Study*, 3; Diaz, Simantov, and Rickert, "Effect of Abuse on Health," 811.

13. Lalor and McElvaney, "Child Sexual Abuse," 159; Lamont, *Effects of Child Abuse and Neglect*, 7; Dalla, Xia, and Kennedy, "You Just Give Them What They Want," 1369-70; Silbert and Pines, "Sexual Child Abuse," 407-8.

14. Stoltz et al., "Associations between Childhood Maltreatment and Sex Work," 1215, 1219; Silbert and Pines, "Victimization of Street Prostitutes," 407; Institute of Medicine and National Research Council, *Confronting Commercial Sexual Exploitation*, 80.

15. Hopper, "Polyvictimization and Developmental Trauma," 164; Silbert and Pines, "Sexual Child Abuse," 407.

16. Lalor and McElvaney, "Child Sexual Abuse," 164; Institute of Medicine and National Research Council, *Confronting Commercial Sexual Exploitation*, 83.

17. Limoncelli, "Trouble with Trafficking," 262.

18. Zimmerman and Kiss, "Human Trafficking and Exploitation," 2; International Labour Organization, "Gender and Child Labour in Agriculture"; Verité, *Help Wanted*, 5, 10.

19. Inter-Agency Coordination Group against Trafficking in Persons, *Gender Dimensions of Human Trafficking*, 1.

20. Todres, "Human Trafficking and Film," 11-12.

21. Pocock et al., "Labour Trafficking among Men and Boys," 1-2; Goździak and Walter, "Misconceptions about Human Trafficking," 59; Upadhyay, "Human Trafficking," 48-49; ECPAT-USA, *And Boys Too*, 5.

22. UN Office on Drugs and Crime, *Global Report*, 54, 89, 95, 96, 102, 106, 159, 202, 217, 220; Pocock et al., "Labour Trafficking among Men and Boys," 1; Wulfhorst, "Human Traffickers Preying More on Children, Men, Laborers"; International Labour Organization, "Fishing and Aquaculture"; US Department of State, *Assisting Male Survivors of Human Trafficking*.

23. ECPAT-USA, *And Boys Too*, 5.

24. ECPAT-USA, *And Boys Too*, 5; Institute of Medicine and National Research Council, *Confronting Commercial Sexual Exploitation*, 92-93.

25. National Alliance to End Homelessness, *Homeless Youth and Sexual Exploitation*, 2.

26. ECPAT-USA, *And Boys Too*, 11; Jones, "Invisible Man," 1145, 1175.

27. Lillywhite and Skidmore, "Boys Are Not Sexually Exploited?," 355; ECPAT-USA, *And Boys Too*, 11.

28. Hampton and Lieggi, "Commercial Sexual Exploitation of Youth," 1; Tomasiewicz, *Sex Trafficking of Transgender and Gender Nonconforming Youth*, 3; Office of Juvenile Justice and Delinquency Prevention, "Child Labor Trafficking," 3.

29. Tomasiewicz, *Sex Trafficking of Transgender and Gender Nonconforming Youth*, 6.

30. Hampton and Lieggi, "Commercial Sexual Exploitation of Youth," 6.

31. Yates et al., "Risk Profile Comparison," 547.

32. Polaris Project, *Sex Trafficking and LGBTQ Youth*.

33. Tomasiewicz, *Sex Trafficking of Transgender and Gender Nonconforming Youth*, 6.

34. Polaris Project, *Sex Trafficking and LGBTQ Youth*.

35. US Department of State, *Trafficking in Persons Report 2012*, 39.

36. Human Trafficking Pro Bono Legal Center and National Disability Rights Network, *Trafficking of Persons with Disabilities*.

37. United States v. Paoletti-Lemus, et al., No. 1:97-cr-00768 (E.D.N.Y. 1998), cited in Human Trafficking Pro Bono Legal Center and National Disability Rights Network, *Trafficking of Persons with Disabilities*.

38. Human Trafficking Pro Bono Legal Center and National Disability Rights Network, *Trafficking of Persons with Disabilities*. See also Reid, "Sex Trafficking of Girls," 114–15.

39. US Department of State, *Trafficking in Persons Report 2012*, 39.

40. Zablocki and Krezmien, "Drop-Out Predictors among Students," 59–61.

41. Kruse and Schur, "Employment of People with Disabilities," 33.

42. UNICEF, "Children with Disabilities."

43. Office of Justice Programs, *Victims with Physical, Cognitive, or Emotional Disabilities*.

44. Institute of Medicine and National Research Council, *Confronting Commercial Sexual Exploitation*, 87–88.

45. Hannan et al., "Children at Risk," 110–13.

46. Shaw et al., "Adolescent Victims of Commercial Sexual Exploitation," 328; Institute of Medicine and National Research Council, *Confronting Commercial Sexual Exploitation*, 88.

47. Maslow, "Theory of Human Motivation," 376.

48. Shaw et al., "Adolescent Victims of Commercial Sexual Exploitation," 328–29.

49. Greenbaum, "Commercial Sexual Exploitation," 249–50; Lillie, *Unholy Alliance*.

50. Reavis et al., "Adverse Childhood Experiences," 47; Fox et al., "Trauma Changes Everything," 164.

51. Center for Public Policy Studies, *Human Trafficking Victims*.

52. Ijadi-Maghsoodi et al., "Understanding and Responding to the Needs of Commercially Sexually Exploited Youth," 110, 113.

53. Office of Justice Programs, *Substance Abuse Needs*.

54. Cusick, Martin, and May, *Vulnerability and Involvement*, 5–6; Miller et al., "Individual and Structural Vulnerability," 39.

55. Institute of Medicine and National Research Council, *Confronting Commercial Sexual Exploitation*, 89.

56. Cusick, Martin, and May, *Vulnerability and Involvement*, 5. See also Ravi et al., "Trafficking and Trauma Insight and Advice," 1019.

57. Cusick, Martin, and May, *Vulnerability and Involvement*, 37.

58. Maslow, "Theory of Human Motivation," 376; Stoltz et al., "Associations between Childhood Maltreatment and Sex Work," 1215, 1217.

59. Lillie, "Gang Involvement with Human Trafficking."

60. Lederer, "Sold for Sex," 8.

61. Carpenter and Gates, *Nature and Extent of Gang Involvement*, 15.

62. Crenshaw, "Interview of Professor Kimberlé Crenshaw," 455.

63. Crenshaw, "Mapping the Margins," 1244.

64. Gwadz et al., "Initiation of Homeless Youth into the Street Economy," 358; National Alliance to End Homelessness, *Homeless Youth and Sexual Exploitation*, 1–2.

65. Cobb-Clark and Zhu, "Childhood Homelessness and Adult Employment," 896.

66. National Alliance to End Homelessness, *Homeless Youth and Sexual Exploitation*, 2.

67. Gleghorn et al., "Drug Use Patterns and HIV Risks," 219.

68. National Alliance to End Homelessness, *Homeless Youth and Sexual Exploitation*, 7–8; Rew et al., "Sexual Health Risks," 11.

69. Layne, Briggs, and Courtois, "Introduction to the Special Section," S3.

70. Anda et al., "Enduring Effects." See also Klatt, Cavner, and Egan, "Rationalising Predictors," 253.

71. Nadon, Koverola, and Schludermann, "Antecedents to Prostitution," 208.

72. Institute of Medicine and National Research Council, *Confronting Commercial Sexual Exploitation*, 85.

73. Nadon, Koverola, and Schludermann, "Antecedents to Prostitution," 214.

74. McClain and Garrity, "Sex Trafficking," 245.

75. McClain and Garrity, "Sex Trafficking," 244.

76. UN Office of Drugs and Crime, *Toolkit*, 454–55.

77. Institute of Medicine and National Research Council, *Confronting Commercial Sexual Exploitation*, 95.

78. Rotherham-Borus et al., "Lifetime Sexual Behaviors," 16.

79. Burgess, Groth, and McCausland, "Child Sex Initiation Rings," 113.

80. Bao, Whitbeck, and Hoyt, "Abuse, Support, and Depression," 409; Ennett, Bailey, and Federman, "Social Network Characteristics," 66.

81. Institute of Medicine and National Research Council, *Confronting Commercial Sexual Exploitation*, 95.

82. Raphael, Reichert, and Powers, "Pimp Control and Violence," 91–92.

83. Raphael, Reichert, and Powers, "Pimp Control and Violence," 91–92.

84. Raphael, Reichert, and Powers, "Pimp Control and Violence," 95.

85. Raphael, Reichert, and Powers, "Pimp Control and Violence," 91–92; Bigelsen and Vuotto, *Homelessness, Survival Sex, and Human Trafficking*, 10.

86. Raphael, Reichert, and Powers, "Pimp Control and Violence," 91; UN Office on Drugs and Crime, *Anti-Human Trafficking Manual*, 9–10; Leidholdt, "Human Trafficking and Domestic Violence," 18.

87. Papalia et al., "Further Victimization of Child Sexual Abuse Victims," 122–23; Finkelhor, Ormrod, and Turner, "Re-Victimization Patterns."

88. Flowers, *Runaway Kids and Teenage Prostitution*, 41–42.

89. Hayes-Smith and Whaley, "Community Characteristics and Methamphetamine Use," 549.

90. Institute of Medicine and National Research Council, *Confronting Commercial Sexual Exploitation*, 96. See also Popkin, Leventhal, and Weismann, "Girls in the 'Hood," 720.

91. Eccles and Templeton, "Extracurricular and Other After-School Activities," 127.

92. Akers, Muhammad, and Corbie-Smith, ""When You Got Nothing to Do,"" 92, 94.

93. Estes and Weiner, *Commercial Sexual Exploitation of Children*, 6.

94. Todres, "Importance of Realizing 'Other' Rights," 888.

95. Braveman and Gottlieb, "Social Determinants of Health," 19-21.

96. Prentice and Pizer, "Delayed Access to Health Care," 654-55.

97. Kidd, "Youth Homelessness and Social Stigma," 291.

98. Hahna, Truman, and Williams, "Civil Rights," 17.

99. Cusick, Martin, and May, *Vulnerability and Involvement*, 4-5.

100. Kidd, "Need for Improved Operational Definition of Suicide Attempts," 450-52; Kidd and Scrimenti, "Evaluating Child and Youth Homelessness," 326.

101. Kidd, "Youth Homelessness and Social Stigma," 296.

102. Kidd, "Youth Homelessness and Social Stigma," 297.

103. Poucki and Bryan, "Vulnerability to Human Trafficking," 151.

104. Task Force on Trafficking of Women and Girls, *Report of the Task Force*, 23.

105. Todres, "Moving Upstream," 489.

106. Institute of Medicine and National Research Council, *Confronting Commercial Sexual Exploitation*, 93; Nadon, Koverola, and Schludermann, "Antecedents to Prostitution," 207-9.

107. Flowers, *Runaway Kids and Teenage Prostitution*, 146.

108. Nadon, Koverola, and Schludermann, "Antecedents to Prostitution," 218; Estes and Weiner, *Commercial Sexual Exploitation of Children*, 35.

109. GEMS, *Our Story*.

*Chapter 6.* Improving Identification

1. Van Bueren, *International Law*, xx; Todres, "Child Rights Framework," 586.

2. Reid, "Doors Wide Shut," 158.

3. Institute of Medicine and National Research Council, *Confronting Commercial Sexual Exploitation*.

4. Powell, Dickins, and Stoklosa, "Training US Health Care Professionals," 1-2. See also Ahn et al., "Human Trafficking."

5. Powell, Dickins, and Stoklosa, "Training US Health Care Professionals," 7-8.

6. Tracy and Macias-Konstantopoulos, "Identifying and Assisting," 446.

7. Edinburgh et al., "Assessing Exploitation Experiences," 52; Littrell, *Human Trafficking in America's Schools*, 4.

8. Lederer and Wetzel, "Health Consequences," 63-64, 78. See also Baldwin et al., "Identification of Human Trafficking Victims," 36.

9. Lederer and Wetzel, "Health Consequences," 78; Chisolm-Straker et al., "Health Care and Human Trafficking," 1221.

10. Leder et al., "Addressing Sexual Abuse," 273-74.

11. Baldwin et al., "Identification of Human Trafficking Victims," 40, 44.

12. Baldwin et al., "Identification of Human Trafficking Victims," 40 (none of the participants had been identified as trafficking victims through their health care sector experiences); Lederer and Wetzel, "Health Consequences," 78 ("Almost half of sur-

vivors (43.1%) (N=58) said the doctor asked them something about their lives, but only 19.5% of those who answered (N=41) reported that the doctor knew they had a pimp." The study does not indicate whether even in those cases the participants were identified as trafficking victims).

13. Hornor and Sherfield, "Commercial Sexual Exploitation of Children," 253.

14. Chisolm-Straker et al., "Health Care and Human Trafficking," 1227.

15. Chisolm-Straker et al., "Health Care and Human Trafficking," 1227.

16. Chisolm-Straker et al., "Health Care and Human Trafficking," 1227.

17. Chisolm-Straker et al., "Health Care and Human Trafficking," 1228.

18. Ijadi-Maghsoodi et al., "Commercially Sexually Exploited Youths' Health Care Experiences," 335.

19. Grace et al., "Educating Health Care Professionals on Human Trafficking," 858.

20. Chisolm-Straker and Richardson, "Assessment."

21. World Health Organization, *Making Health Services Adolescent Friendly*, 6.

22. World Health Organization, *Making Health Services Adolescent Friendly*, 7–8.

23. Mount Sinai Adolescent Health Center, *Blueprint*, 11.

24. Mount Sinai Adolescent Health Center, *Blueprint*, 14.

25. World Health Organization, *Integrated Health Services*, 3.

26. Mount Sinai Adolescent Health Center, *Blueprint*, 14.

27. Todres, "Mainstreaming Children's Rights in Post-Disaster Settings," 1251–52; UN General Assembly, "Report of the Economic & Social Council," 27.

28. Mount Sinai Adolescent Health Center, *Blueprint*, 14.

29. Mount Sinai Adolescent Health Center, *Blueprint*, 14.

30. Mount Sinai Adolescent Health Center, *Blueprint*, 14.

31. Wright and Ord, "Youth Work," 70.

32. Advocates for Youth, "Best Practices for Clinical Services," 4.

33. Mount Sinai Adolescent Health Center, *Blueprint*, 20.

34. American Psychiatric Association, *Diagnostic and Statistical Manual*, 308.3(F43.0).

35. Mount Sinai Adolescent Health Center, *Blueprint*, 24. See also Alameda County Behavioral Health Care Services, "Developing a Trauma Informed Agency."

36. Mount Sinai Adolescent Health Center, *Blueprint*, 25.

37. Sale et al., "Quality of Provider-Participant Relationships," 275; Taddeo, Egedy, and Frappier, "Adherence to Treatment in Adolescents," 21.

38. Makoul, Zick, and Green, "Evidence-Based Perspective," 1172–73.

39. Brown and Wissow, "Discussion of Sensitive Health Topics."

40. Surko et al., "Multiple Risks, Multiple Worries," 262; Schoen et al., *Commonwealth Fund Survey*, 5–6.

41. Bigelsen and Vuotto, *Homelessness, Survival Sex, and Human Trafficking*, 11; Murphy, *Labor and Sex Trafficking*, 19.

42. Bigelsen and Vuotto, *Homelessness, Survival Sex, and Human Trafficking*, 10.

43. See, generally, Wisdom, Clarke, and Green, "What Teens Want," 142.

44. Tervalon and Murray-Garcia, "Cultural Humility versus Cultural Competence," 120–21; Clawson and Dutch, *Identifying Victims of Human Trafficking*, 5.

45. There are entities that now offer free language interpreter services to providers who work with human trafficking victims and survivors. See, e.g., the Language Interpreter Services program of the Canadian Ministry of Citizenship and Immigration, http://languageinterpreters.on.ca/.

46. UN Office of Drugs and Crime, *Toolkit*, 285.

47. Roe-Sepowitz et al., "Sexual Exploitation of Girls," 2817-19.

48. Texas Human Trafficking Prevention Task Force, *Introduction to Human Trafficking*, 17, 21; Bayless, *How to Talk to Your Kids*, 7; US Department of State, "Identify and Assist."

49. Dovydaitis, "Human Trafficking," 463-64; Isaac, Solak, and Giardino, "Health Care Providers' Training Needs," 9.

50. Brick, "How Childhood Sexual Abuse Affects Interpersonal Relationships"; Breger, "Healing Sex-Trafficked Children," 1163-66; US Department of Health and Human Services, *Guidance to States*, 4-6.

51. US Department of Health and Human Services, *Resources: Health Care Provider Brochure*; Sabella, "Role of the Nurse," 32.

52. Texas Human Trafficking Prevention Task Force, *Introduction to Human Trafficking*, 21.

53. Bales, Fletcher, and Stover, *Hidden Slaves*, 9, 15.

54. Logan, Walker, and Hunt, "Understanding Human Trafficking," 13.

55. Harper and Scott, *Meeting the Needs*, 18.

56. Zong, Batalova, and Hallock, "Frequently Requested Statistics," 10.

57. Chen and Vargas-Bustamente, "Estimating the Effects," 671; Zong, Batalova, and Hallock, "Frequently Requested Statistics," 5.

58. Greenbaum, "Commercial Sexual Exploitation," 255, 261; Texas Human Trafficking Prevention Task Force, *Introduction to Human Trafficking*, 21, 27.

59. Pocock et al., "Labour Trafficking among Men and Boys," 4-6.

60. Macias-Konstantopoulos and Ma, "Physical Health," 195-97.

61. Todres, "Can Mandatory Reporting Laws Help," 70.

62. Todres, "Can Mandatory Reporting Laws Help," 71.

63. Todres, "Can Mandatory Reporting Laws Help," 70-71.

64. Todres, "Can Mandatory Reporting Laws Help," 72.

65. Todres, "Can Mandatory Reporting Laws Help," 74.

66. Leder et al., "Addressing Sexual Abuse," 270; Flaherty et al., "From Suspicion," 615-17; Jones et al., "Clinicians' Description of Factors," 259.

67. Leder et al., "Addressing Sexual Abuse," 270, 273-74.

68. Weinred et al., "Physicians' Perceptions," 417.

69. Weinred et al., "Physicians' Perceptions," 417-18.

70. Leder et al., "Addressing Sexual Abuse," 273.

71. Lane and Dubowitz, "Primary Care Pediatricians' Experience," 76, 80.

72. Flaherty et al., "From Suspicion," 615-17; Jones et al., "Clinicians' Description of Factors," 659.

73. Todres, "Can Mandatory Reporting Laws Help," 77.

74. Bigelsen and Vuotto, *Homelessness, Survival Sex, and Human Trafficking*, 14.

75. Napolitano, "At Greater Risk"; Children's Bureau, *Human Trafficking and Child Welfare*.

*Chapter 7.* Assisting Vulnerable and Exploited Youth

1. Macy and Graham, "Identifying Domestic and International Sex-Trafficking Victims," 61–63; Clawson and Dutch, *Case Management*, 2; Irazola et al., *Trafficking of US Citizens and Legal Permanent Residents*, 3.

2. Institute of Medicine and National Research Council, *Confronting Commercial Sexual Exploitation*, 263.

3. Clawson and Dutch, *Case Management*, 1, 4–5. See also Zimmerman and Borland, *Caring for Trafficked Persons*, 72.

4. Macy and Johns, "Aftercare Services," 89, 91.

5. Wolfteich and Loggins, "Evaluation," 340; Dell, "Long-Term Care and Beyond."

6. Schmitt, "How Your Community Can Stop the Trafficking," 1; Institute of Medicine and National Research Council, *Confronting Commercial Sexual Exploitation*, 20.

7. Polaris Project, *Shelter Beds*, 1, 5.

8. Polaris Project, *Shelter Beds*, 7.

9. Clawson et al., *Human Trafficking*, 14, 21, 33–34; Raney, "Unseen Victims of Sex Trafficking."

10. Reichert and Sylwestrzak, *National Survey*, 25.

11. Office for Victims of Crimes, "Victim-Centered Approach"; Institute of Medicine and National Research Council, *Confronting Commercial Sexual Exploitation*, 254–55.

12. These are illustrative examples but by no means the only survivor-led organizations working to address human trafficking.

13. Lloyd, *From Victim to Survivor*, 5.

14. UNICEF, *Reversing the Trend*, 58.

15. Dottridge, "Young People's Voices," vi. See also Phillips, "Black Girls," 1673.

16. Dottridge, "Young People's Voices," 13.

17. Dottridge, "Young People's Voices," 13.

18. Dottridge, "Young People's Voices," 16–17.

19. Todres, "Taking Prevention Seriously," 26.

20. International Youth Foundation et al., *Children & Young People*, 4.

21. Sabella, "Role of the Nurse," 32–33; Dovydaitis, "Human Trafficking," 464.

22. Zimmerman et al., "Health of Trafficked Women," 56.

23. Zimmerman et al., "Health of Trafficked Women," 56.

24. Zimmerman et al., "Health of Trafficked Women," 57.

25. Willis and Levy, "Child Prostitution," 1418.

26. Willis and Levy, "Child Prostitution," 1418.

27. Muftic and Finn, "Health Outcomes," 1859, 1878.

28. Oram et al., "Prevalence and Risk."

29. Hopper, Bassuk, and Olivet, "Shelter from the Storm," 80–81.

30. Fortier et al., "Severity of Child Sexual Abuse," 310–12.

31. Johnson and Johnson, "Factors Influencing the Relationship," 2324–28.

32. Zerk, Mertin, and Proeve, "Domestic Violence," 423, 429.

33. Bales, Fletcher, and Stover, *Hidden Slaves*, 35.

34. Bales, Fletcher, and Stover, *Hidden Slaves*, 35–41; Oram and Zimmerman,

"Health of Persons Trafficked"; Turner-Moss et al., "Labour Exploitation and Health," 477–78; US Department of State, *Trafficking in Persons Report 2017*, 18.

35. De Vries and Farrell, "Labor Trafficking Victimizations," 2.

36. De Vries and Farrell, "Labor Trafficking Victimizations," 2–3.

37. Mount Sinai Adolescent Health Center, *Blueprint*, 20.

38. Crane and Moreno, "Human Trafficking," 12–14; Dovydaitis, "Human Trafficking," 464; Zimmerman et al., *Health Risks and Consequences*, 4, 24–25.

39. US Department of Health and Human Services, "Trauma-Informed Practice."

40. Strand, Sarmiento, and Pasquale, "Assessment and Screening Tools."

41. Zimmerman and Borland, *Caring for Trafficked Persons*, 33–37. See also Guarino et al., *Trauma-Informed Organizational Toolkit*.

42. Covington et al., "Evaluation," 387, 396; Muraya and Fry, "Aftercare Services," 207–8.

43. Hopper, Bassuk, and Olivet, "Shelter from the Storm," 82 (quoting consensus-based definition).

44. Zimmerman and Borland, *Caring for Trafficked Persons*, 34–35.

45. Zimmerman and Borland, *Caring for Trafficked Persons*, 34.

46. Substance Abuse and Mental Health Service Administration, "Trauma-Informed Approach"; Zimmerman and Borland, *Caring for Trafficked Persons*, 33–34.

47. Substance Abuse and Mental Health Service Administration, "Trauma-Informed Approach"; Zimmerman and Borland, *Caring for Trafficked Persons*, 34–35.

48. Mount Sinai Adolescent Health Center, *Blueprint*, 23.

49. US Department of Justice, *Report of the Attorney General's National Task Force*, 13 (emphasis in original).

50. Cohen et al., "Practice Parameter," 421.

51. Cohen et al., "Practice Parameter," 421–22.

52. Cohen et al., "Practice Parameter," 421–22.

53. Clawson, Salomon, and Grace, *Treating the Hidden Wounds*, 4–7.

54. Schneider, Grilli, and Schneider, "Evidence-Based Treatments," 333.

55. Schneider, Grilli, and Schneider, "Evidence-Based Treatments," 334; Cohen et al., "Trauma-Focused CBT," 528.

56. Olafson, "Child Sexual Abuse," 17.

57. Raider et al., "Structured Sensory Therapy."

58. Conradi and Wilson, "Managing Traumatized Children," 622.

59. Covington et al., "Evaluation," 394–96.

60. Williamson, Dutch, and Clawson, *Evidence-Based Mental Health Treatment*, 4.

61. Williamson, Dutch, and Clawson, *Evidence-Based Mental Health Treatment*, 5–9.

62. Institute of Medicine and National Research Council, *Confronting Commercial Sexual Exploitation*, 289; Williamson, Dutch, and Clawson, *Evidence-Based Mental Health Treatment*, 2, 5.

63. Institute of Medicine and National Research Council, *Confronting Commercial Sexual Exploitation*, 290.

64. Cohen et al., "Practice Parameter," 418.

65. Wong, Hong, and Yin, "Human Trafficking."

66. Wong, Hong, and Yin, "Human Trafficking," 2062–63.

67. Chisolm-Straker, Richardson, and Cossio, "Combating Slavery," 982.

68. Chisolm-Straker, Richardson, and Cossio, "Combating Slavery," 983.

69. Chisolm-Straker, Richardson, and Cossio, "Combating Slavery," 983.

70. Chisolm-Straker, Richardson, and Cossio, "Combating Slavery," 982.

71. Reinhard et al., "Knowledge and Attitudes of Physicians," 144.

72. Reinhard et al., "Knowledge and Attitudes of Physicians," 147.

73. Reinhard et al., "Knowledge and Attitudes of Physicians," 151.

74. Reinhard et al., "Knowledge and Attitudes of Physicians," 149.

75. Reinhard et al., "Knowledge and Attitudes of Physicians," 147.

76. Chisolm-Straker, Richardson, and Cossio, "Combating Slavery," 983.

77. Chisolm-Straker, Richardson, and Cossio, "Combating Slavery," 983.

78. Clawson et al., *Needs Assessment*, 25.

79. Institute of Medicine and National Research Council, *Confronting Commercial Sexual Exploitation*, 275.

80. Todres, "Law, Otherness"; Clawson and Dutch, *Identifying Victims of Human Trafficking*; Institute of Medicine and National Research Council, *Confronting Commercial Sexual Exploitation*.

81. Institute of Medicine and National Research Council, *Confronting Commercial Sexual Exploitation*, 275–76.

82. Institute of Medicine and National Research Council, *Confronting Commercial Sexual Exploitation*, 276. See also Powell, Dickins, and Stoklosa, "Training US Health Care Professionals," 2–3.

83. Institute of Medicine and National Research Council, *Confronting Commercial Sexual Exploitation*, 276–77.

84. Todres, "Can Mandatory Reporting Laws Help," 74–76.

85. Institute of Medicine and National Research Council, *Confronting Commercial Sexual Exploitation*, 276–77.

86. Stoklosa, Grace, and Littenberg, "Medical Education on Human Trafficking," 917.

87. Powell, Dickins, and Stoklosa, "Training US Health Care Professionals," 1–3.

88. Stoklosa, Grace, and Littenberg, "Medical Education on Human Trafficking," 917; Todres, "Moving Upstream,"

89. Zimmerman and Borland, *Caring for Trafficked Persons*, 80–81. See also Crane and Moreno, "Human Trafficking," 9.

90. Salston and Figley, "Secondary Traumatic Stress Effects," 167–70.

91. National Society for the Prevention of Cruelty to Children, *Vicarious Trauma*, 1.

92. Salston and Figley, "Secondary Traumatic Stress Effects," 169–70.

93. Kliner and Stroud, "Psychological and Health Impact," 9, 13–14.

94. Kliner and Stroud, "Psychological and Health Impact," 9, 13–14.

95. National Society for the Prevention of Cruelty to Children, *Vicarious Trauma*, 1, 4, 5.

96. Pack, "Discovering an Integrated Framework," 82–83.

97. Pack, "Vicarious Traumatization and Resilience."

*Conclusion.* Building an Effective Response to Child Trafficking

1. Cohen and Chehimi, "Beyond Brochures," 4–5.

2. See, e.g., Coker and Martin, "Introduction," 3 (noting that law has been recognized as an important tool in public health for centuries).

3. See, e.g., Duffey, "Public Health and Law Enforcement" (identifying examples of criminal law being introduced in campaigns to combat bioterrorism, gun violence, and other issues).

4. Some criminal justice frameworks, notably restorative justice, have also departed from the traditional retributive justice model, which defines crime primarily as "an act against the state." Eisnaugle, "International 'Truth Commission,'" 213. See also Buel, "Effective Assistance of Counsel," 233 (criticizing criminal law's "myopic focus" on individual incidents in the area of domestic violence).

5. Todres, "Moving Upstream."

6. Office on Trafficking in Persons, "Power of Framing"; Chisolm-Straker and Stoklosa, *Human Trafficking*; University of Kansas Anti-Slavery and Human Trafficking Initiative, "Research: The ASHTI Prevention Strategies Model."

7. Todres, "Law, Otherness."

8. Malloch and Rigby, "Contexts and Complexities," 7.

9. UNICEF Innocenti Research Centre, *Child Trafficking in Europe*, v.

10. Todres, "Law, Otherness," 669–71.

11. This is not unique to the world of human trafficking. See Iyengar, "I'd Rather be Hanged for a Sheep than a Lamb" (discussing how "three strikes" laws, which were aimed at protecting society from repeat offenders, have been shown to increase the likelihood that repeat offenders will commit more violent crime when they already have two strikes).

12. The Bombay Police (Amendment) Act, 2005 (Maharashtra Act No. XXXV), § 33A(1)(a) (2005). The Bombay High Court struck down the law in 2006. Kapur, "Citizen and the Migrant," 551.

13. Kapur, "Citizen and the Migrant," 549.

14. Kapur, "Citizen and the Migrant," 551.

15. O'Haver, "How 'If You See Something, Say Something' Became."

16. Indeed, we can build on existing initiatives. For example, the Sustainable Development Goals have widespread support, and Target 8.7 addresses human trafficking ("Take immediate and effective measures to eradicate forced labour, end modern slavery and human trafficking and secure the prohibition and elimination of the worst forms of child labour, including recruitment and use of child soldiers, and by 2025 end child labour in all its forms").

17. Anti-Slavery International, "Ten Year Olds Forced to Risk Lives."

18. Asghar, Farhat, and Niaz, *Camel Jockeys of Rahimyar Khan*.

19. Knight, "Robot Camel-Jockeys."

20. Todres, "Private Sector's Pivotal Role," 85–89.

21. Institute of Medicine and National Research Council, *Confronting Commercial Sexual Exploitation*, 327.

22. Some smart phone apps have been created, but it is unclear whether they have been evaluated for effectiveness. See, e.g., US Department of Labor, "New Research."

23. Todres, "Human Trafficking and Film," 9–19.

24. ECPAT-USA, *Alternative Report to the Initial Report*, 2; Institute of Medicine and National Research Council, *Confronting Commercial Sexual Exploitation*, 6–7; Todres, "Child Rights Framework," 582–83.

25. Powell, Dickins, and Stoklosa, "Training US Health Care Professionals," 7–8.

26. Powell, Dickins, and Stoklosa, "Training US Health Care Professionals," 7–8; Greenbaum et al., "Multi-Level Prevention," 165.

27. US Department of Transportation, *DOT Trains Employees on Human Trafficking Awareness*.

28. Further, there is relatively little evaluation of existing training modules. Powell, Dickins, and Stoklosa, "Training US Health Care Professionals," 2–3.

29. For relevant materials, see, e.g., Institute on Healthcare and Human Trafficking, Children's Healthcare of Atlanta, www.vIHHT.org; and HEAL Trafficking, www.healtrafficking.org.

30. See Powell, Dickins, and Stoklosa, "Training US Health Care Professionals," 1–3. See also Institute on Healthcare and Human Trafficking, Children's Healthcare of Atlanta, www.vIHHT.org; and HEAL Trafficking, www.healtrafficking.org.

31. U.S. v. Gadley (N.D. Tex. 2011), quoted in Levy and Vandenberg, "Breaking the Law," 44.

32. Beddoe, Bundock, and Jardan, *Life beyond the Safe House for Survivors*. For more discussion of challenges confronted in post-trafficking contexts, see Lutnick, *Domestic Minor Sex Trafficking*, 97–106.

33. Jobe, *Causes and Consequences of Re-trafficking*, 49.

34. Okech et al., "Social Support," 215–16.

35. See, e.g., Mariano, "Despite Millions Spent."

36. Mandela, *In His Own Words*, 421.

37. For a discussion of public health ethics, see, e.g., Centers for Disease Control and Prevention, *Good Decision Making in Real Time*.

38. Stuber, Galea, and Link, "Smoking and the Emergence of a Stigmatized Social Status," 2.

39. Todres and Wolf, "Complexities of Conducting Research."

40. Lloyd, "At What Cost."

Abas, Melanie, Nicolae V. Ostrovschi, Martin Prince, Viorel I. Gorceag, Carolina Trigub, and Siân Oram. "Risk Factors for Mental Disorders in Women Survivors of Human Trafficking: A Historical Cohort Study." *BMC Psychiatry* 13, no. 204 (2013). http://www.biomedcentral.com/1471-244X/13/204.

Adler, Robert S. "Flawed Thinking: Addressing Decision Biases in Negotiation." *Ohio State Journal on Dispute Resolution* 20, no. 3 (2005): 683–774.

Administration for Children and Families. "Grants." Office on Trafficking in Persons. Accessed 6 November 2017. https://www.acf.hhs.gov/otip/grants.

Advocates for Youth. "Best Practices for Clinical Services." Accessed 26 October 2016. http://advocatesforyouth.org/resources/-best-practices-for-youth-friendly -clinical-services.

Ahn, Roy, Elaine J. Alpert, Genevieve Purcell, Wendy Macias-Konstantopoulos, Anita McGahan, Elizabeth Cafferty, Melody Eckardt, Kathryn L. Conn, Kate Cappetta, and Thomas F. Burke. "Human Trafficking: A Review of Educational Resources for Health Professionals." *American Journal of Preventive Medicine* 44, no. 3 (2013): 233–89. https://doi.org/10.1016/j.amepre.2012.10.025.

Akers, Aletha Y., Melvin R. Muhammad, and Giselle Corbie-Smith. "When You Got Nothing to Do, You Do Somebody: A Community's Perceptions of Neighborhood Effects on Adolescent Sexual Behaviors." *Social Science and Medicine* 72, no. 1 (2011): 91–99.

Alameda County Behavioral Health Care Services. "Developing a Trauma Informed Agency." Last modified 2013. http://alamedacountytraumainformedcare.org /trauma-informed-agencies/developing-a-trauma-informed-agency/.

American Psychiatric Association. *Diagnostic and Statistical Manual of Mental Disorders*. 5th ed. Washington, DC: American Psychiatric Association, 2013.

American Public Health Association. "Expanding and Coordinating Human Trafficking–Related Public Health Research, Evaluation, Education, and Prevention." APHA Policy Statement. 3 November 2015. https://www.apha.org /policies-and-advocacy/public-health-policy-statements/policy-database/2016 /01/26/14/28/expanding-and-coordinating-human-trafficking-related-public -health-activities.

———. "Supporting Research and Evidence-Based Public Health Practice in State and Local Health Agencies." APHA Policy Statement. 7 November 2017. https:// www.apha.org/policies-and-advocacy/public-health-policy-statements/policy

-database/2018/01/18/supporting-research-and-evidence-based-public-health
-practice.

Ames, Allison J., Glenn C. W. Ames, Jack E. Houston, and Simone Angioloni. "Food
Insecurity and Educational Achievement: A Multi-Level Generalization of Poisson
Regression." *International Journal of Food and Agricultural Economics* 4, no. 1
(2016): 21–34.

Anda, Robert F., Vincent J. Felitti, J. Douglas Bremner, John D. Walker, Charles Whit-
field, Bruce Perry, Shanta R. Dube, and Wayne H. Giles. "The Enduring Effects
of Abuse and Related Adverse Experiences in Childhood: A Convergence of Evidence from Neurobiology and Epidemiology." *European Archives of Psychiatry and
Clinical Neuroscience* 256, no. 3 (2006): 174–86. https://doi.org/10.1007/s00406
-005-0624-4.

Annas, George J. "Blinded by Bioterrorism: Public Health and Liberty in the 21st
Century." *Health Matrix* 13, no. 1 (2003): 33–70.

Anti-Slavery International. "Ten Year Olds Forced to Risk Lives Racing Camels in
UAE." 2 March 2010. https://www.antislavery.org/ten-year-olds-forced-risk-lives
-racing-camels-uae/.

Aronowitz, Alexis, Gerda Theuermann, and Elena Tyurykanova. *Analysing the
Business Model of Trafficking in Human Beings to Better Prevent the Crime.* Vienna:
Office of the Special Representative and Co-ordinator for Combating Trafficking
in Human Beings, May 2010. http://www.osce.org/cthb/69028?download=true.

Asghar, Syed Mehmood, Sabir Farhat, and Shereen Niaz. *Camel Jockeys of Rahimyar
Khan: Findings of a Participatory Research on the Life and Situation of Child Camel
Jockeys.* Peshawar, Pakistan: Save the Children Sweden, 2005. http://lastradainter
national.org/lsidocs/351%20Camel-jockeys_of_rahimyar_khan.pdf.

Baldwin, Susie B., David P. Eisenman, Jennifer N. Sayles, Gery Ryan, and Kenneth S.
Chuang. "Identification of Human Trafficking Victims in Health Care Settings."
*Health and Human Rights* 13, no. 1 (2011): 36–49. https:// cdn2.sph.harvard.edu
/wp-content/uploads/sites/125/2013/06/Baldwin-FINAL2.pdf.

Bales, Kevin, Laurel Fletcher, and Eric Stover. *Hidden Slaves: Forced Labor in the United
States.* Washington, DC: Free the Slaves & Human Rights Center, 2004. https://
www.freetheslaves.net/wp-content/uploads/2015/03/Hidden-Slaves.pdf.

Bao, Wan-Ning, Les B. Whitbeck, and Dan R. Hoyt. "Abuse, Support, and Depression
among Homeless and Runaway Adolescents." *Journal of Health and Social Behavior*
41, no. 4 (2000): 408–20.

Barrick, Kelle. "Human Trafficking, Labor Exploitation, and Exposure to Environ-
mental Hazards: The Abuse of Farmworkers in the U.S." In *The International
Handbook of Rural Criminology*, edited by Joseph F. Donnermeyer, 147–56. New
York: Routledge International Handbooks, 2016.

Barthe, Emmanuel. *Crime Prevention Publicity Campaigns.* Problem-Oriented Guides
for Police Response Guides Series No. 5. June 2006. https://ric-zai-inc.com
/Publications/cops-p099-pub.pdf.

Bayer, Ronald. "Stigma and the Ethics of Public Health: Not Can We but Should We."
*Social Science and Medicine* 67, no. 3 (2008): 463–72. https://doi.org/10.1016/j
.socscimed.2008.03.017.

Bayless, Angelyn. *How to Talk to Your Kids about Human Trafficking.* Arizona: TRUST.

Accessed 24 August 2018. endsextrafficking.az.gov/sites/default/files/aw-trust
-how-to-talk-to-your-children.pdf.

Bean, Lonnie James. "LGBTQ Youth at High Risk of Becoming Human Trafficking
Victims." 26 June 2013. US Department of Health and Human Services, Administration for Child & Families. https://www.acf.hhs.gov/archive/blog/2013/06
/lgbtq-youth-at-high-risk-of-becoming-human-trafficking-victims.

Beddoe, Christine, Lara Bundock, and Tatiana Jardan. *Life beyond the Safe House for
Survivors of Modern Slavery in London: Gaps and Options Review.* London: Human
Trafficking Foundation, 2015. https://static1.squarespace.com/static/599abfb4e
6f2e19ff048494f/t/599eeb28914e6b9ddcceace2/1503587117886/Web_Life
+Beyond+the+Safe+House.pdf.

Bennet, Kimberly, Alexandra Bilak, Noah Bullock, Ledio Cakaj, Margarite Clarey,
Bina Desai, Justin Ginnetti, Capucine Maus de Rolley, Padraic McClusky, Lisa
Monaghan, Sorcha O'Callaghan, Catherine Osborn, Andrés Lizcano Rodriguez,
Elizabeth J. Rushing, Dan Tyler, and Michelle Yonetani. *Global Report on Internal
Displacement.* Internal Displacement Monitoring Centre and Norwegian Refugee
Council, May 2017. http://www.internal-displacement.org/global-report/grid2017/.

Bessette, Guy. *Involving the Community: A Guide to Participatory Development Communication.* Ottawa: International Development Research Centre, 2004. https://
www.idrc.ca/en/book/involving-community-guide-participatory-development
-communication.

Biber, Eric. "Too Many Things to Do: How to Deal with the Dysfunctions of Multiple-
Goal Agencies." *Harvard Environmental Law Review* 33 (2009): 1–63.

Bigelsen, Jayne, and Stefanie Vuotto. *Homelessness, Survival Sex, and Human Trafficking: As Experienced by the Youth of Covenant House New York.* New York: Covenant
House, May 2013. http://humantraffickingsearch.org/wp-content/uploads/2017
/06/Covenant-House-trafficking-study.pdf.

Black, Jan K. *The Politics of Human Rights Protection.* Lanham, MD: Rowman &
Littlefield, 2009.

Bloom, Sandra. "The Sanctuary Model: Trauma-Informed, Trauma-Responsive
Culture." Accessed 23 October 2017. http://sanctuaryweb.com/PublicHealth
/Trauma-ResponsivePrograms/TheSanctuaryModelTrauma-Informed,Trauma
-ResponsiveCulture.aspx.

Bond, Johanna. "International Intersectionality: A Theoretical and Pragmatic
Exploration of Women's International Human Rights Violations." *Emory Law
Journal* 52 (2003): 71–186.

Braveman, Paula, and Laura Gottlieb. "The Social Determinants of Health: It's Time
to Consider the Causes of the Causes." *Public Health Reports* 129, no. 2 (2014):
19–31.

Bravo, Karen E. "Exploring the Analogy between Modern Trafficking in Humans and
the Trans-Atlantic Slave Trade." *Boston University International Law Journal* 25,
no. 2 (2007): 207–95.

Breger, Melissa L. "Healing Sex-Trafficked Children: A Domestic Family Law
Approach to an International Epidemic." *West Virginia Law Review* 118 (2016):
1131–80.

Briain, Muireann O., Anke van den Borne, and Theo Noten. *Combating the Trafficking in Children for Sexual Purposes: Questions and Answers.* Amsterdam: ECPAT, 2006. http://www.ecpat.org/wp-content/uploads/legacy/trafficking_faq_eng.pdf.

Brick, Neil D. "How Childhood Sexual Abuse Affects Interpersonal Relationships." S.M.A.R.T. 2005. https://ritualabuse.us/research/sexual-abuse/how-childhood -sexual-abuse-affects-interpersonal-relationships/.

Brown, Jonathan D., and Lawrence S. Wissow. "Discussion of Sensitive Health Topics with Youth during Primary Care Visits: Relationship with Youth Perceptions of Care." *Journal of Adolescent Health* 44, no. 1 (2009): 48–54. https://doi.org/10.1016 /j.jadohealth.2008.06.018.

Brown, Lisanne, Lea Trujillo, and Kate Macintyre. *Interventions to Reduce HIV/AIDS Stigma: What Have We Learned?* New York: Population Council, 2001. http://www .popcouncil.org/pdfs/horizons/litrvwstigdisc.pdf.

Brownson, Ross C., Elizabeth A. Baker, Terry L. Fleet, and Kathleen N. Gillespie. *Evidence-Based Public Health.* Oxford: Oxford University Press, 2003.

Bruner, Jessie. *Inaccurate Numbers, Inadequate Policies: Enhancing Data to Evaluate the Prevalence of Human Trafficking in ASEAN.* Honolulu: East-West Center, 2015.

Buel, Sarah M. "Effective Assistance of Counsel for Battered Women Defendants: A Normative Construct." *Harvard Women's Law Journal* 26 (2003): 217–350.

Bulletti, Carlo, Maria E. Coccia, Silvia Battistoni, and Andrea Borini. "Endometriosis and Infertility." *Journal of Assisted Reproduction and Genetics* 27, no. 8 (2010): 441–47. https://doi.org/10.1007/s10815-010-9436-1.

Burgess, Ann W., A. Nicholas Groth, and Maureen P. McCausland. "Child Sex Initiation Rings." *American Journal of Orthopsychiatry* 51, no. 1 (1981): 110–19.

Burke, Robert E., and Leonard H. Friedman, eds. *Essentials of Management and Leadership in Public Health.* Sudbury, MA: Jones & Barlett Learning, LLC, 2011.

Burris, Scott, Leo Beletsky, Joseph A. Burleson, Patricia Case, and Zita Lazzarini. "Do Criminal Laws Influence HIV Risk Behavior? An Empirical Trial." *Arizona State Law Journal* 39, no. 3 (2007): 467–520.

Byrne, Melissa, Bridget Parsh, and Courtney Ghilain. "Victims of Human Trafficking: Hiding in Plain Sight." *Nursing* 47, no. 3 (2017): 48–52. https://doi.org/10.1097/01 .NURSE.0000512876. 06634.c4.

California Alliance to Combat Trafficking and Slavery Task Force. *Human Trafficking in California: Final Report of the California Alliance to Combat Trafficking and Slavery Task Force.* Sacramento: California Attorney General's Office, October 2007. http://ag.ca.gov/publications/Human_Trafficking_Final_Report.pdf.

California Courts. *Handbook for STAR ("Succeed Through Achievement and Resilience") Court.* January 2014. http://www.courts.ca.gov/documents/LosAngeles-STAR Court-ProgramOutline_ikc.pdf.

Carpenter, Ami C., and Jamie Gates. *The Nature and Extent of Gang Involvement in Sex Trafficking in San Diego County.* San Diego, CA: University of San Diego and Point Loma Nazarene University, 2016. https://www.ncjrs.gov/pdffiles1/nij/grants /249857.pdf.

Castillo, Rudy. "Vacatur Laws: Decriminalizing Sex Trafficking Survivors." *Journal of Gender, Social Policy & the Law* (blog). *American University College of Law*, 24 May 2016. http://www.jgspl.org/vacatur-laws-decriminalizing-sex-trafficking -survivors/.

Center for Court Innovation. *State Court Snapshot: New York State's Human Traf-ficking Intervention Courts*. New York: Center for Court Innovation, 2016. http://cjinvolvedwomen.org/wp-content/uploads/2016/12/HTIC-1pager.pdf.

Center for Public Policy Studies. *Human Trafficking Victims as Criminal Defendants*. Human Trafficking and the State Courts Collaborative & State Justice Institute. November 2013. http://www.htcourts.org/wp-content/uploads/HT_Victims_asCriminalDefendants v01.pdf?InformationCard=HT-Victims-as-Criminal-Defendants.

Centers for Disease Control and Prevention. "Child Overweight and Obesity." Last modified 13 June 2018. http://www.cdc.gov/obesity/childhood/index.html.

———. *Good Decision Making in Real Time: Public Health Ethics Training for Local Health Departments; Facilitator's Manual*. Atlanta: US Department of Health and Human Services, 2012.

———. *Introduction to Program Evaluation for Public Health Programs: A Self-Study Guide*. Atlanta: US Department of Health and Human Services, October 2005. https://www.cdc.gov/eval/guide/cdcevalmanual.pdf.

———. "The Social-Ecological Model: A Framework for Prevention." Violence Prevention. Accessed 5 February 2018. http://www.cdc.gov/violenceprevention/overview/social-ecologicalmodel.html.

———. "A Timeline of Violence as a Public Health Issue." Violence Prevention. Accessed 5 February 2018. https://www.cdc.gov/violenceprevention/overview/timeline.html.

———. "Tuberculosis (TB): Data and Statistics." Last modified 5 June 2018. https://www.cdc.gov/tb/statistics/default.htm.

Chacón, Jennifer M. "Tensions and Trade-Offs: Protecting Trafficking Victims in the Era of Immigration Enforcement." *University of Pennsylvania Law Review* 158, no. 6 (2010): 1609–53.

Chen, Jie, and Arturo Vargas-Bustamente. "Estimating the Effects of Immigration Status on Mental Health Care Utilizations in the United States." *Journal of Immigrant Minority Health* 13, no. 4 (2011): 671–80. https://doi.org/10.1007/s10903-011-9445-x.

Children's Bureau. *Childhood Maltreatment 2016*. Washington, DC: US Department of Health and Human Services, 2018. https://www.acf.hhs.gov/sites/default/files/cb/cm2016.pdf.

———. *Human Trafficking and Child Welfare: A Guide for Caseworkers*. Washington, DC: Child Welfare Information Gateway, July 2017. https://www.childwelfare.gov/pubPDFs/trafficking_caseworkers.pdf.

Chisolm-Straker, Makini, Susie Baldwin, Bertille Gaïgbé-Togbé, Nneka Ndukwe, Pauline N. Johnson, and Lynne D. Richardson. "Health Care and Human Trafficking: We Are Seeing the Unseen." *Journal of Health Care for the Poor and Underserved* 27, no. 3 (2016): 1220–33. https://doi.org/10.1353/hpu.2016.0131.

Chisolm-Straker, Makini, and Lynne Richardson. "Assessment of Emergency Department (ED) Provider Knowledge about Human Trafficking Victims in the ED." *Academic Emergency Medicine* 14, no. 5, S1 (2008): S134. https://doi.org/10.1197/j.aem.2007.03.704/pdf.

Chisolm-Straker, Makini, Lynne D. Richardson, and Tania Cossio. "Combating

Slavery in the 21st Century: The Role of Emergency Medicine." *Journal of Health Care for the Poor and Underserved* 23, no. 3 (2012): 980–87. https://doi.org/10.1353 /hpu.2012.0091.

Chisolm-Straker, Makini, and Hanni Stoklosa, eds. *Human Trafficking Is a Public Health Issue: A Paradigm Expansion in the United States*. Cham, Switzerland: Springer, 2017.

Chisolm-Straker, Makini, Jeremy Sze, Julia Einbond, James White, and Hanni Stoklosa. "A Supportive Adult May Be the Difference in Homeless Youth Not Being Trafficked." *Children and Youth Services Review* 91 (2018): 115–20. https:// doi.org/10.1016/j.childyouth.2018.06.003.

Choi-Fitzpatrick, Austin. "The Good, the Bad, the Ugly: Human Rights Violators in Comparative Perspective." *Journal of Human Trafficking* 2, no. 1 (2016): 1–14. https://doi.org/10.1080/23322705.2016.1136166.

Choose Peace Stop Violence. "Model Approach." Understand Violence. Accessed 8 August 2018. https://www.choosepeacestopviolence.org/social-ecological-model.

Chuang, Janie A. "Exploitation Creep and the Unmaking of Human Trafficking Law." *American Journal of International Law* 108, no. 4 (2014): 609–49.

———. "Redirecting the Debate over Trafficking in Women: Definitions, Paradigms, and Contexts." *Harvard Human Rights Journal* 11 (1998): 65–106.

———. "Rescuing Trafficking from Ideological Capture: Prostitution Reform and Anti-trafficking Law and Policy." *University of Pennsylvania Law Review* 158, no. 6 (2010): 1655–1728.

Cianciarulo, Marisa Silenzi. "The Trafficking and Exploitation Victims Assistance Program: A Proposed Early Response Plan for Victims of International Human Trafficking in the United States." *New Mexico Law Review* 38, no. 2 (2008): 373–408.

Clawson, Heather, and Nicole Dutch. *Addressing the Needs of Victims of Human Trafficking: Challenges, Barriers, and Promising Practices*. Washington, DC: US Department of Health and Human Services, Office of the Assistant Secretary for Planning and Evaluation, 2008. https://aspe.hhs.gov/system/files/pdf/75471 /ib.pdf.

———. *Case Management and the Victim of Human Trafficking: A Critical Service for Client Success*. Washington, DC: US Department of Health and Human Services, Office of the Assistant Secretary for Planning and Evaluation, 2008. https://aspe .hhs.gov/basic-report/case-management-and-victim-human-trafficking-critical -service-client-success.

———. *Identifying Victims of Human Trafficking: Inherent Challenges and Promising Strategies from the Field*. Washington, DC: US Department of Health and Human Services, 2008. http://aspe.hhs.gov/hsp/07/HumanTrafficking/IdentVict/ib.pdf.

Clawson, Heather, Nicole Dutch, Susan Lopez, and Suzanna Tiapula. *Prosecuting Human Trafficking Cases: Lessons Learned and Promising Practices*. Fairfax, VA: ICF International, 30 June 2008. http://www.ncjrs.gov/pdffiles1/nij/grants/223972.pdf.

Clawson, Heather, Nicole Dutch, Amy Solomon, and Lisa Goldblatt Grace. *Human Trafficking into and within the United States: A Review of the Literature*. Washington, DC: US Department of Health and Human Services, 2009. http://aspe.hhs.gov /hsp/07/humantrafficking/litrev/.

Clawson, Heather, Amy Salomon, and Lisa Goldblatt Grace. *Treating the Hidden*

*Wounds: Trauma Treatment and Mental Health Recovery for Victims of Human Trafficking*. Washington, DC: US Department of Health and Human Services, Office of the Assistant Secretary for Planning and Evaluation. Accessed 24 August 2018. https://aspe.hhs.gov/system/files/pdf/75356/ib.pdf.

Clawson, Heather, Kevonne M. Small, Ellen S. Go, and Bradley W. Myles. *Needs Assessment for Service Providers and Trafficking Victims*. Fairfax, VA: Caliber Associates and US Department of Justice, 2013. https://www.ncjrs.gov/pdffiles1/nij /grants/202469.pdf.

Clinton, William J. Memorandum on Steps to Combat Violence Against Women and Trafficking in Women and Girls. 1998. Pub. Papers 358, 359 (11 March 1998).

Cloitre, Marylene, Christine A. Courtois, Anthony Charuvastra, Richard Carapezza, Bradley C. Stolbach, and Bonnie L. Green. "Treatment of Complex PTSD: Results of the ISTSS Expert Clinician Survey on Best Practices." *Journal of Traumatic Stress* 24, no. 6 (2011): 615-27. https://doi.org/10.1002/jts.20697.

Cobb-Clark, Deborah, and Anna Zhu. "Childhood Homelessness and Adult Employment: The Role of Education, Incarceration, and Welfare Receipt." *Journal of Population Economics* 30 (2017): 893-924.

Cohen, Judith A., Anthony P. Mannarino, Matthee Kliethermes, and Laura A. Murray. "Trauma-Focused CBT for Youth with Complex Trauma." *Child Abuse & Neglect* 36, no. 6 (2012): 528-41. https://doi.org/10.1016/j.chiabu.2012.03.007.

Cohen, Judith A., and Work Group on Quality Issues. "Practice Parameter for the Assessment and Treatment of Children and Adolescents with Posttraumatic Stress Disorder." *Journal of American Academy of Child and Adolescent Psychiatry* 49, no. 4 (2010): 414-30. https://www.jaacap.org/article/S0890-8567(10)00082-1/pdf.

Cohen, Larry, and Sana Chehimi. "Beyond Brochures: The Imperative for Primary Prevention." In *Prevention Is Primary: Strategies for Community*, edited by Larry Cohen, Vivian Chavez, and Sana Chehimi. San Francisco: Jossey-Bass, 2007.

Coker, Richard, and Robyn Martin. "Introduction: The Importance of Law for Public Health Policy and Practice." *Public Health* 120 (2006): 2-7.

Connecticut Alliance to End Sexual Violence. *Homelessness and Sexual Violence*. Hartford, CT: National Coalition for The Homelessness, 2018. https://endsexual violencect.org/resources/get-the-facts/homelessness/.

Conradi, Lisa, and Charles Wilson. "Managing Traumatized Children: A Trauma Systems Perspective." *Current Opinion in Pediatrics* 22, no. 5 (2010): 621-25. https:// doi.org/10.1097/MOP.0b013e32833e0766.

Coomaraswamy, Radhika. *Fifteen Years of the United Nations Special Rapporteur on Violence against Women, Its Causes and Consequences*. UN Human Rights Office of the High Commissioner, 2009. http://www.ohchr.org/Documents/Issues /Women/15YearReviewofVAWMandate.pdf.

Corbett, Annie. "The Voices of Survivors: An Exploration of the Contributing Factors That Assisted with Exiting from Commercial Sexual Exploitation in Childhood." *Children and Youth Services Review* 85 (2018): 91-98.

Cornell, Svante E. 2009. "The Interaction of Drug Smuggling, Human Trafficking and Terrorism." In *Human Trafficking and Human Security*, edited by Anna Jonsson, 48-66. New York: Routledge, 2009.

Covington, Stephanie S., Cynthia Burke, Sandy Keaton, and Candice Norcott.

"Evaluation of a Trauma-Informed and Gender-Responsive Intervention for Women in Drug Treatment." *Journal of Psychoactive Drugs*, no. S5 (2008): 387–98.

Crane, Patricia, and Melissa Moreno. "Human Trafficking: What Is the Role of the Health Care Provider?" *Journal of Applied Research on Children: Informing Policy for Children at Risk* 2, no. 1 (2011): 1–27.

Crenshaw, Kimberlé. "Interview of Professor Kimberlé Crenshaw." By Shelia Thomas. In *The Law of Sex Discrimination*, by J. Ralph Lingdren, Nadine Taub, Beth Ann Wolfson, and Carla M. Palumbo. Boston: Cengage Learning, 2011.

———. "Mapping the Margins: Intersectionality, Identity Politics, and Violence against Women of Color." *Stanford Law Review* 43 (1991): 1241–99.

Crooks, Deborah L. "American Children at Risk: Poverty and Its Consequences for Children's Health, Growth, and School Achievement." *American Journal of Physical Anthropology* 38, no. S2 (1995): 57–86.

Curtis, Ric, Karen Terry, Meredith Dank, Kirk Dombrowski, and Bilal Khan. *Commercial Sexual Exploitation of Children in New York City, Volume One: The CSEC Population in New York City; Size, Characteristics, and Needs.* New York: Center for Court Innovation, September 2008. https://www.ncjrs.gov/pdffiles1/nij/grants /225083.pdf.

Cusick, Linda, Anthea Martin, and Tiggey May. *Vulnerability and Involvement in Drug Use and Sex Work.* London: Home Office Research, Development and Statistics Directorate, 2003.

Dalla, Rochelle L., Yan Xia, and Heather Kennedy. "You Just Give Them What They Want and Pray They Don't Kill You: Street-Level Sex Workers' Reports of Victimization, Personal Resources and Coping Strategies." *Violence Against Women* 9 (2003): 1367–94. https://doi.org/10.1177/1077801203255679.

Davy, Deanna. "Understanding the Support Needs of Human Trafficking Victims: A Review of Three Human-Trafficking Program Evaluations." *Journal of Human Trafficking* 1, no. 4 (2015): 318–37. https://doi.org/10.1080/23322705.2015.1090865.

DeJong, William, and Ralph Hingson. "Strategies to Reduce Driving under the Influence of Alcohol." *Annual Review of Public Health* 19 (1998): 359–78. https:// doi.org/10.1146/annurev.publhealth.19.1.359.

Dell, Charlotte. "Long-Term Care and Beyond: Responding to Elder Abuse." *Care Management Journals* 10, no. 2 (2009): 64–68.

Del Rosso, Joy Miller, and Tonia Marek. *Class Action: Improving School Performance in the Developing World through Better Health and Nutrition.* Washington, DC: World Bank, 1996.

Dennis, Jeffery P. "Women Are Victims, Men Make Choices: The Invisibility of Men and Boys in the Global Sex Trade." *Gender Issues* 25, no. 1 (2008): 11–25. https://doi .org/10.1007/s12147-008-9051-y.

De Vries, Ieke, and Amy Farrell. "Labor Trafficking Victimizations: Repeat Victimization and Polyvictimization." *Psychology of Violence* (advanced online publication 2017). https://doi.org/10.1037/vio0000149.

Diaz, Angela, Elizabeth Simantov, and Vaughn I. Rickert. "Effect of Abuse on Health: Results of a National Survey." *Archives of Pediatrics and Adolescent Medicine* 156, no. 8 (2002): 811–17.

Dottridge, Mike. Introduction to *Collateral Damage: The Impact of Anti-Trafficking*

*Measures on Human Rights around the World*, edited by Global Alliance Against Traffic in Women, 1–24. Bangkok: Amarin, 2007.

————. *Kids as Commodities: Child Trafficking and What to Do about It*. Lausanne, Switzerland: International Federation Terre des Hommes, May 2004. http://www.terredeshommes.org/wp-content/uploads/2013/06/commodities.pdf.

————. "Young People's Voices on Child Trafficking: Experiences from South Eastern Europe." UNICEF Innocenti Working Papers No. IWP-2008-05. Florence: UNICEF, 2008.

Dovydaitis, Tiffany. "Human Trafficking: The Role of the Health Care Provider." *Journal of Midwifery & Women's Health* 55, no. 5 (2010): 462–67. https://doi.org/10.1016/j.jmwh.2009.12.017.

Dubois, David L., Bruce E. Holloway, Jeffrey C. Valentine, and Harris Cooper. "Effectiveness of Mentoring Programs for Youth: A Meta-Analytic Review." *American Journal of Community Psychology* 30, no. 2 (2002): 157–97. https://doi.org/10.1023/A:1014628810714.

Duffey, William S. "Public Health and Law Enforcement: Intersecting Interests, Collegiality and Cooperation." *Journal of Law, Medicine & Ethics* 32 (2004): 19–22.

Durchslag, Rachel, and Samir Goswami. *Deconstructing the Demand for Prostitution: Preliminary Insights from Interviews with Chicago Men Who Purchase Sex*. Chicago Alliance Against Sexual Exploitation. 2008. http://media.virbcdn.com/files/40/FileItem-149406-DeconstructingtheDemandForProstitution.pdf.

Eccles, Jacquelynne S., and Janice Templeton. "Extracurricular and Other After-School Activities for Youth." *Review of Research in Education* 26 (2002): 113–80. https://doi.org/10.3102/0091732X026001113.

ECPAT-USA. *Alternative Report: An NGO Response to the Periodic Report of the United States of America to the UN Committee on the Rights of the Child concerning the Optional Protocol to the Convention on the Rights of the Child on the Sale of Children, Child Prostitution, and Child Pornography*. Brooklyn: ECPAT-USA, 2016. https://static1.squarespace.com/static/594970e91b631b3571be12e2/t/5977cb0a725e25b1ccd42756/1501022994290/2016+ALTERNATIVE+REPORT+FINAL+June+27+2016.pdf.

————. *Alternative Report to the Initial Report of the United States of America to the UN Committee on the Rights of the Child concerning the Optional Protocol to the Convention on the Rights of the Child on the Sale of Children, Child Prostitution, and Child Pornography*. Brooklyn: ECPAT-USA, 2007.

————. *And Boys Too*. Brooklyn: ECPAT-USA, 2013. https://static1.squarespace.com/static/594970e91b631b3571be12e2/t/5977b2dacd0f688b2b89e6f0/1501016795183/ECPAT-USA_AndBoysToo.pdf.

————. *No Vacancy for Child Sex Traffickers Impact Report: The Efficacy of ECPAT-USA's Work to Prevent and Disrupt the Commercial Sexual Exploitation of Children in Hotels*. Brooklyn: EPCAT-USA, 2017. https://static1.squarespace.com/static/594970e91b631b3571be12e2/t/59c9b6bfb07869cc5d792b8c/1506391761747/NoVacany_Report.pdf.

————. *Steps to Safety: A Guide to Drafting Safe Harbor Legislation to Protect Sex-Trafficked Children*. Brooklyn: ECPAT-USA, 2015. https://www.ecpatusa.org/s/ECPAT-USA_StepsToSafety.pdf.

Edinburgh, Laurel, Julie Pape-Blabolil, Scott B. Harpin, and Elizabeth Saewyc. "Assessing Exploitation Experiences of Girls and Boys Seen at a Child Advocacy Center." *Child Abuse & Neglect* 46 (2015): 47-59. https://doi.org/10.1016/j.chiabu.2015.04.016.

Eisen, Susan, Deborah J. Youngman, Mollie C. Grob, and Diana L. Dill. "Alcohol, Drugs, and Psychiatric Disorder: A Current View of Hospitalized Adolescents." *Journal of Adolescent Research* 7, no. 2 (1992): 250-65. https://doi.org/10.1080/19371918.2013.774673.

Eisnaugle, Carrie J. Niebur. "An International 'Truth Commission': Utilizing Restorative Justice as an Alternative to Retribution." *Vanderbilt Journal of Transnational Law* 36 (2003): 209-41.

Elbagir, Nima, Raja Razek, Alex Platt, and Bryony Jones. "People for Sale: Where Lives Are Auctioned for $400." CNN, 14 November 2017. http://www.cnn.com/2017/11/14/africa/libya-migrant-auctions/index.html.

Encinas, Pamela. "The Correlation between Globalization and Human Trafficking." *Human Trafficking Center*, 28 March 2018. http://humantraffickingcenter.org/the-correlation-between-globalization-and-human-trafficking/.

Engle, Eric. "Corporate Social Responsibility (CSR): Market-Based Remedies for International Human Rights Violations?" *Willamette Law Review* 40 (Winter 2004): 103-21.

Ennett, Susan T., Susan L. Bailey, and E. Belle Federman. "Social Network Characteristics Associated with Risky Behaviors among Runaway and Homeless Youth." *Journal of Health and Social Behavior* 40, no. 1 (1999): 63-78.

Erickson, Lanice D., Steve McDonald, and Glen H. Elder Jr. "Informal Mentors and Education: Complementary or Compensatory Resources?" *Sociology of Education* 82, no. 4 (2009): 344-67. https://doi.org/10.1177/003804070908200403.

Estes, Richard J., and Neil A. Weiner. *The Commercial Sexual Exploitation of Children in the U.S., Canada, and Mexico.* Philadelphia: Center for the Study of Youth Policy, 2001.

Evans, William, Doreen Neville, and John D. Graham. "General Deterrence of Drunk Driving: Evaluation of Recent American Policies." *Risk Analysis* 11, no. 2 (1990): 279-89.

Fallot, Roger D., and Maxine Harris. "Trauma-Informed Approaches to Systems of Care." *Trauma Psychology* 3, no. 1 (Winter 2008): 6-7. http://traumapsychnews.com/wp-content/uploads/2016/01/newsletter_2008_winter.pdf#page=6.

Family and Youth Services Bureau. *Street Outreach Program: Fact Sheet.* Accessed 15 May 2017. https://www.acf.hhs.gov/sites/default/files/fysb/sop_facts_20170207.pdf.

Farley, Melissa, Ann Cotton, Jacqueline Lynne, Sybille Zumbeck, Frida Spiwak, Maria E. Reyes, Dinorah Alvarez, and Ufuk Sezgin. "Prostitution and Trafficking in Nine Countries: An Update on Violence and Posttraumatic Stress Disorder." *Journal of Trauma Practice* 2, no. 3-4 (2004): 33-74. https://doi.org/10.1300/J189v02n03_03.

Farrell, Amy, Monica J. DeLateur, Colleen Owens, and Stephanie Fahy. "The Prosecution of State-Level Human Trafficking Cases in the United States." *Anti-Trafficking Review* 6 (2016): 48-70. www.antitraffickingreview.org/index.php/atrjournal/article/download/169/157/.

Farrelly, Matthew, Kevin C. Davis, M. Lyndon Haviland, Peter Messeri, and Cheryl G. Healton. "Evidence of a Dose-Response Relationship between 'Truth' Antismoking Ads and Youth Smoking Prevalence." *American Journal of Public Health* 95, no. 3 (2005): 425–31. https://doi.org/10.2105/AJPH.2004.049692.

Farrelly, Matthew, Cheryl G. Healton, Kevin C. Davis, Peter Messeri, James C. Hersey, and M. Lyndon Haviland. "Getting to the Truth: Evaluating National Tobacco Countermarketing Campaigns." *American Journal of Public Health* 92, no. 6 (2002): 901–7.

Feingold, David A. "Think Again: Human Trafficking." *Foreign Policy* 150 (2005): 26–32. https://foreignpolicy.com/2009/10/20/think-again-human-trafficking/.

Felitti, Vincent J., Robert F. Anda, Dale Nordenberg, David F. Williamson, Alison M. Spitz, Valerie Edwards, Mary P. Koss, and James S. Marks. "Relationship of Childhood Abuse and Household Dysfunction to Many of the Leading Causes of Death in Adults: The Adverse Childhood Experiences (ACE) Study." *American Journal of Preventive Medicine* 14, no. 4 (1998): 245–58.

Finkelhor, David, Richard K. Ormrod, and Heather A. Turner. "Re-Victimization Patterns in a National Longitudinal Sample of Children and Youth." *Child Abuse & Neglect* 31, no. 5 (2007): 479–502.

Finnemore, Melody. "Human Tender: Oregon Attorneys, Law Enforcement Forge Collaborative Strategy to Combat Growing Trade in Human Trafficking." *Oregon State Bar Bulletin* 70 (December 2009): 19–23. http://www.osbar.org/publications/bulletin/09dec/humantender.html.

Flaherty, Emalee G., Robert D. Sege, John Griffith, Lori Lyn Price, Richard Wasserman, Eric Slora, and Niramol Dhepyasuwan. "From Suspicion of Physical Child Abuse to Reporting: Primary Care Clinician Decision-Making." *Pediatrics* 122, no. 3 (2008): 611–17.

Flowers, Ronald B. *Runaway Kids and Teenage Prostitution: America's Lost, Abandoned, and Sexually Exploited Children*. Westport, CT: Greenwood, 2001.

Food and Agricultural Organization, World Organisation for Animal Health (OIE), World Health Organization, UN Influenza Coordination, UNICEF, and World Bank. *Contributing to One World, One Health: A Strategic Framework for Reducing Risks of Infectious Diseases at the Animal-Human-Ecosystems Interface*. Rome: FAO et al., 14 October 2008. https://www.preventionweb.net/files/8627_OWOH14Oct08.pdf.

Fong, Rowena, and Jodi Berger Cardoso. "Child Human Trafficking Victims: Challenges for the Child Welfare System, Evaluation & Program Plan." *Evaluation and Program Planning* 33, no. 3 (2010): 311–16.

Fortier, Michelle. A, David DiLillo, Terri L. Messman-Moore, James Peugh, and Kathleen A. DeNard. "Severity of Child Sexual Abuse and Revictimization: The Mediating Role of Coping and Trauma Symptoms." *Psychology of Women Quarterly* 33, no. 3 (2009): 308–20. http://digitalcommons.unl.edu/psychfacpub/400.

Fox, Bryanna H., Nicholas Perez, Elizabeth Cass, Michael T. Baglivio, and Nathan Epps. "Trauma Changes Everything: Examining the Relationship between Adverse Childhood Experiences and Serious, Violent and Chronic Juvenile Offenders." *Child Abuse & Neglect* 46 (2015): 163–73.

Freeman-Longo, Robert E. "Reducing Sexual Abuse in America: Legislating Tougher

Laws or Public Education and Prevention." *New England Journal on Criminal and Civil Confinement* 23, no. 2 (1997): 303–31.

Gabers, Kate. "Nail Bars Are Havens for Modern Slavery: Here's How You Can Help." *Guardian*, 5 January 2018. https://www.theguardian.com/commentisfree/2018/jan/05/nail-bars-modern-slavery-discount-salons-booming-exploitation.

Galavotti, Christine, Katina A. Pappas-DeLuca, and Amy Lansky. "Modeling and Reinforcement to Combat HIV: The MARCH Approach to Behavior Change." *American Journal of Public Health* 91, no. 10 (2001): 1602–7.

Galinsky, Adam D. "Should You Make the First Offer?" *Negotiation*. Cambridge, MA: Harvard Law School, July 2004.

Gallagher, Anne T. *The International Law of Human Trafficking*. New York: Cambridge University Press, 2010.

———. "Unravelling the 2016 Global Slavery Index." *50.50*, 28 June 2016. https://www.opendemocracy.net/anne-gallagher/unravelling-2016-global-slavery-index.

Garrison, Marsha. "Reforming Child Protection: A Public Health Perspective." *Virginia Journal of Social Policy & Law* 12, no. 3 (2005): 590–637.

———. "Reviving Marriage: Could We? Should We?" *Journal of Law and Family Studies* 10 (2008): 279–335.

Gerassi, Lara. "From Exploitation to Industry: Definitions, Risks, and Consequences of Domestic Sexual Exploitation and Sex Work among Women and Girls." *Journal of Human Behavior in the Social Environment* 25, no. 6 (2015): 591–605. https://doi.org/10.1080/10911359.2014.991055.

Gever, Matthew. "Legislators Hope to Put Drowsy Drivers to Rest." *State Health Notes* 29, no. 511 (March 2008). http://www.ncsl.org/print/health/shn/shn511.pdf.

Geynisman-Tan, Julia M. "All the Darkness We Don't See." *American Journal of Obstetrics & Gynecology* 216, no. 2 (2017): 135–39. https://doi.org/10.1016/j.ajog.2016.09.088.

Gibbons, Patric, and Hanni Stoklosa. "Identification and Treatment of Human Trafficking Victims in the Emergency Department: A Case Report." *Journal of Emergency Medicine* 50, no. 5 (2016): 715–19. https://doi.org/10.1016/j.jemermed.2016.01.004.

Gibbs, Deborah, Jennifer L. Hardison Walters, Alexandra Lutnick, Shari Miller, and Marianne Kluckman. *Evaluation of Services for Domestic Minor Victims of Human Trafficking*. Washington, DC: National Institute of Justice, 2014. https://www.ncjrs.gov/pdffiles1/nij/grants/248578.pdf.

Gilbert, Ruth, Cathy Spatz Widom, Kevin Browne, David Fergusson, Elspeth Webb, and Staffan Janson. "Burden and Consequences of Child Maltreatment in High-Income Countries." *Lancet* 373 (2009): 68–81. https://doi.org/10.1016/S0140-6736(08)61706-7.

Girls Educational & Mentoring Services (GEMS). *Our Story*. Accessed 15 January 2019. https://www.gems-girls.org/our-story/.

Gleave, Madeleine, Alexandra Miller, and Caitlin Sellers. "Transportation Officials Have a Role in Human Trafficking Battle." *Baltimore Sun*, 7 June 2017. http://www.baltimoresun.com/news/opinion/oped/bs-ed-sex-trafficking-transportation-20170607-story.html.

Gleghorn, Alice, Rani Marx, Eric Vittinghoff, and Mitchell Katz. "Association between Drug Use Patterns and HIV Risks among Homeless, Runaway, and Street Youth in Northern California." *Drug and Alcohol Dependence* 51, no. 3 (1998): 219–27.

Global Freedom Center. *Overlooked: Sexual Violence in Labor Trafficking.* Accessed 24 August 2018. http://www.ncdsv.org/images/GFC_OverlookedSexualViolenceIn LaborTrafficking.pdf.

Goldberg, Amy P., Jessica L. Moore, Christopher Houck, Dana M. Kaplan, and Christine E. Barron. "Domestic Minor Sex Trafficking Patients: A Retrospective Analysis of Medical Presentation." *Journal of Pediatric and Adolescent Gynecology* 30 (2017): 109–15. https://doi.org/10.1016/j.jpag.2016.08.010.

Gómez, Margarita Puerto, Manuel Contreras-Urbina, Brian Heilman, Amber Hill, Anne von Au, Jennifer Zelaya, and Diana J. Arango. *Community-Based Approaches to Intimate Partner Violence.* Washington, DC: Global Women's Initiative and World Bank Group, May 2016. http://documents.worldbank.org/curated/en /907511467996712161 /AUS16688-REVISED-Community-Programs-Single Pages.pdf.

Goodmark, Leigh. "Autonomy Feminism: An Anti-Essentialist Critique of Mandatory Interventions in Domestic Violence Cases." *Florida State University Law Review* 37, no. 1 (2009): 1–48.

Gostin, Lawrence O., and Benjamin E. Berkman. "Pandemic Influenza: Ethics, Law, and the Public's Health." *Administrative Law Review* 59, no. 1 (2007): 121–75.

Gotch, Katherine. "Preliminary Data on a Sample of Perpetrators of Domestic Trafficking for Sexual Exploitation: Suggestions for Research and Practice." *Journal of Human Trafficking* 2, no. 1 (2016): 99–109. https://doi.org/10.1080/23322705.2016 .1136539.

Goździak, Elżbieta M., and Micah N. Bump. *Data and Research on Human Trafficking: Bibliography of Research-Based Literature.* Washington, DC: Institute for the Study of International Migration at Georgetown University, 2008. https://www.ncjrs .gov/pdffiles1/nij/grants/224392.pdf.

Goździak, Elżbieta M., and Lindsay B. Lowell. *After Rescue: Evaluation of Strategies to Stabilize and Integrate Adult Survivors of Human Trafficking to the United States.* Washington, DC: Institute for the Study of International Migration at Georgetown University, 2016. https://www.ncjrs.gov/pdffiles1/nij/grants/249672.pdf.

Goździak, Elżbieta, and Alissa Walter. "Misconceptions about Human Trafficking in a Time of Crisis." *Forced Migration Review* 45 (February 2014): 58–59.

Grace, Aimee M., Suzanne Lippert, Kristin Collins, Noelle Pineda, Alisha Tolani, Rebecca Walker, and Monica Jeong. "Educating Health Care Professionals on Human Trafficking." *Pediatric Emergency Care* 30 no. 12 (2014): 856–61. https:// doi.org/10.1097/PEC.0000000000000287.

Greenbaum, V. Jordan. "Child Sex Trafficking in the United States: Challenges for the Healthcare Provider." *PLOS Medicine* 14, no. 11 (2017). https://doi.org/10.1371 /journal.pmed.1002439.

———. "Commercial Sexual Exploitation and Sex Trafficking in the United States." *Current Problems in Pediatric Adolescent Health Care* 44, no. 9 (2014): 245–69. https://doi.org/10.1016/j.cppeds.2014.07.001.

Greenbaum, V. Jordan, Kanani Titchen, Ingrid Walker-Descartes, Anastasia Feifer, Corey J. Rood, and Hiu-fai Fong. "Multi-Level Prevention of Human Trafficking: The Role of Health Care Professionals." *Preventive Medicine* 114 (2018): 164–67.

Greene, Jody M., Susan T. Ennett, and Christopher L. Ringwalt. "Prevalence and Correlates of Survival Sex among Runaway and Homeless Youth." *American Journal of Public Health* 89, no. 9 (1999): 1406–9.

Greenfield, Victoria A., Letizia Paoli, and Andries Zoutendijk. "The Harms of Human Trafficking: Demonstrating the Applicability and Value of a New Framework for Systematic, Empirical Analysis." *Global Crime* 17, no. 2 (2016): 152–80. https://doi .org/10.1080/17440572.2016.1161037.

Grella, Christine E., Yih-Ing Hser, Vandana Joshi, and Jennifer Rounds-Bryant. "Drug Treatment Outcomes for Adolescents with Comorbid Mental and Substance Use Disorders." *Journal of Nervous and Mental Diseases* 189, no. 6 (2001): 384–92.

Guarino, Kathleen, Phoebe Soares, Kristina Konnath, Rose Clervil, and Ellen Bassuk. *Trauma-Informed Organizational Toolkit.* Rockville, MD: Center for Mental Health Services, Substance Abuse and Mental Health Services Administration, and the Daniels Fund, the National Child Traumatic Stress Network, and the W. K. Kellogg Foundation, 2009. https://www.air.org/sites/default/files/downloads/report /Trauma-Informed_Organizational_Toolkit_0.pdf.

Guilbert, Kieranl. "Number of Women Convicted for Human Trafficking 'Exception-ally High'—UN." Thomson Reuters Foundation News. 24 November 2014. http:// news.trust.org//item/20141124163933-6vy1j/.

Güngör, Neslihan Koyuncuoğlu. "Overweight and Obesity in Children and Adoles-cents." *Journal of Clinical Research in Pediatric Endocrinology* 6, no. 3 (2014): 129–43. https://doi.org/10.4274/jcrpe.1471.

Gupta, Jhumka, Anita Raj, Michele R. Decker, Elizabeth Reed, and Jay G. Silverman. "HIV Vulnerabilities of Sex-Trafficked Indian Women and Girls." *International Journal of Gynecology & Obstetrics* 107, no. 1 (2009): 30–34. https://doi.org/10.1016 /j.ijgo.2009.06.009.

Guth, Andrew, Robyn Anderson, Kasey Kinnard, and Hang Tran. "Proper Methodol-ogy and Methods of Collecting and Analyzing Slavery Data: An Examination of the Global Slavery Index." *Social Inclusion* 2, no. 4 (2014): 14–22.

Gwadz, Marya V., Karla Gostnell, Carol Smolenski, Brian Willis, David Nish, Theresa C. Nolan, Maya Tharaken, and Amanda S. Ritchie. "The Initiation of Homeless Youth into the Street Economy." *Journal of Adolescence* 32, no. 2 (2009): 357–77.

Hahna, R. A., B. I. Truman, and D. R. Williams. "Civil Rights as Determinants of Public Health and Racial and Ethnic Health Equity: Health Care, Education, Employment, and Housing in the United States." *Population Health* 4 (2018): 17–24. https://doi.org/10.1016/j.ssmph.2017.10.006.

Hammond, Gretchen Clark, and Mandy McGlone. "Entry, Progression, Exit, and Service Provision for Survivors of Sex Trafficking: Implications for Effective Interventions." *Global Social Welfare* 1, no. 4 (2014): 157–68. https://doi.org/10 .1007/s40609-014-0010-0.

Hampton, Michelle D., and Michelle Lieggi. "Commercial Sexual Exploitation of Youth in the United States: A Qualitative Systematic Review." *Trauma, Violence, & Abuse*, November 2017, 1–14. https://doi.org/10.1177/1524838017742168.

Hannan, Madeline, Kathryn Martin, Kimberly Caceres, and Nina Aledort. "Children at Risk: Foster Care and Human Trafficking." In Chisolm-Straker and Stoklosa, *Human Trafficking Is a Public Health Issue*, 105–21.

Harper, Zoe, and Sara Scott. *Meeting the Needs of Sexually Exploited Young People in London*. London: Corporation of London's Bridge House Trust, 2005. http://www.barnardos.org.uk/full_london_report.pdf.

Hartman, Micah, Anne B. Martin, Nathan Espinosa, Aaron Catlin, and the National Health Expenditure Accounts Team. "National Health Spending in 2016: Spending and Enrollment Growth Slow after Initial Coverage Expansions." *Health Affairs* 37, no. 1 (2018): 150–60. https://doi.org/10.1377/hlthaff.2017.1299.

Hayes-Smith, Justin, and Rachel B. Whaley. "Community Characteristics and Methamphetamine Use: A Social Disorganization Perspective." *Journal of Drug Issues* 39, no. 3 (2009): 547–76. https://doi.org/10.1177/002204260903900305.

Haynes, Dina Francesca. "(Not) Found Chained to a Bed in a Brothel: Conceptual, Legal, and Procedural Failures to Fulfill the Promise of the Trafficking Victims Protection Act." *Georgetown Immigration Law Journal* 21 (2013): 337–82.

Hemenway, David. "The Public Health Approach to Motor Vehicles, Tobacco, and Alcohol, with Applications to Firearms Policy." *Journal of Public Health Policy* 22, no. 4 (2001): 381–402.

———. "The Public Health Approach to Reducing Firearm Injury and Violence." *Stanford Law and Policy Review* 17 (2006): 635–56.

Hemmings, Stacey, Sharon Jakobowitz, Melanie Abas, Debra Bick, Louise M. Howard, Nicky Stanley, Cathy Zimmerman, and Sian Oram. "Responding to the Health Needs of Survivors of Human Trafficking: A Systematic Review." *BMC Health Services Research* 16, no. 320 (2016). https://doi.org/10.1186/s12913-016-1538-8.

Hollen, Vera, and Glorimar Ortiz. "Mental Health and Substance Use Comorbidity among Adolescents in Psychiatric Inpatient Hospitals: Prevalence and Covariates." *Journal of Child & Adolescent Substance Abuse* 24, no. 1 (2015): 102–12. https://doi.org/10.1080/1067828X.2013.768575.

Holtgrave, David R., Katherine A. Wunderink, Donna M. Vallone, and Cheryl G. Healton. "Cost-Utility Analysis of the National Truth Campaign to Prevent Youth Smoking." *American Journal of Preventive Medicine* 36, no. 5 (2009): 385–88. https://doi.org/10.1016/j.amepre.2009.01.020.

Hopper, Elizabeth. "Polyvictimization and Developmental Trauma Adaptation in Sex Trafficked Youth." *Journal of Child & Adolescent Trauma* 10, no. 2 (2017): 161–73. https://doi.org/10.1007/s40653-016-0114-z.

———. "Trauma-Informed Psychological Assessment of Human Trafficking Survivors." *Women & Therapy* (2017) 40, no. 1–2 (2017): 12–30. https://doi.org/10.1080/02703149.2016.1205905.

Hopper, Elizabeth, Ellen Bassuk, and Jeffery Olivet. "Shelter from the Storm: Trauma-Informed Care in Homeless Services Settings." *Open Health Services and Policy Journal* 3 (2010): 80–100.

Hornor, Gail, and Jennifer Sherfield. "Commercial Sexual Exploitation of Children: Health Care Use and Case Characteristics." *Journal of Pediatric Health Care* 32, no. 3 (2018): 250–62. https://doi.org/10.1016/j.pedhc.2017.11.004.

Human Rights First. "Human Trafficking by the Numbers." January 2017. http://
www.humanrightsfirst.org/sites/default/files/TraffickingbytheNumbers.pdf.

Human Rights Watch. *"I Wanted to Lie Down and Die": Trafficking and Torture of
Eritreans in Sudan and Egypt.* New York: Human Rights Watch Publications, 11
February 2014. https://www.hrw.org/report/2014/02/11/i-wanted-lie-down
-and-die/trafficking-and-torture-eritreans-sudan-and-egypt.

Human Trafficking Pro Bono Legal Center and National Disability Rights Network.
*Trafficking of Persons with Disabilities.* 2017. http://iofa.org/wp-content/uploads
/2017/09/Trafficking-Disability-Fact-Sheet-Disability-Adovcates-Investigators
....pdf.

Ijadi-Maghsoodi, Roya, Eraka Bath, Mekeila Cook, Lauren Textor, Elizabeth Barnert.
"Commercially Sexually Exploited Youths' Health Care Experiences, Barriers,
and Recommendations: A Qualitative Analysis." *Child Abuse & Neglect* 76 (2018):
334–41. https://doi.org/10.1016/j.chiabu.2017.11.002.

Ijadi-Maghsoodi, Roya, Mekeila Cook, Elizabeth S. Barnert, Shushanik Gaboian,
and Eraka Bath. "Understanding and Responding to the Needs of Commercially
Sexually Exploited Youth: Recommendations for the Mental Health Provider."
*Child and Adolescent Psychiatric Clinics of North America* 25, no. 1 (2016): 107–22.
https://doi.org/10.1016/j.chc.2015.08.007.

INFO Project and Johns Hopkins Bloomberg School of Public Health. "What Is
Monitoring and Evaluation?" *INFO Reports* 11 (March 2007). http://info.k4health
.org/inforeports/continuing_client/1.shtml (site discontinued).

Institute of Medicine and National Research Council. *Confronting Commercial Sexual
Exploitation and Sex Trafficking of Minors in the United States.* Washington, DC:
National Academies Press, 2013. https://www.ojjdp.gov/pubs/243838.pdf.

Inter-Agency Coordination Group against Trafficking in Persons. *The Gender
Dimensions of Human Trafficking.* Vienna: ICAT, September 2017. http://icat
.network/sites/default/files/publications/documents/ICAT-IB-04-V.1.pdf.

International Labour Office. *ILO Global Estimate of Forced Labour: Results and
Methodology.* Geneva: International Labour Organization, 2012. http://www.ilo
.org/wcmsp5/ groups/public/---ed_norm/---declaration/documents/publication
/wcms_182004.pdf.

———. *Profits and Poverty: The Economics of Forced Labour.* Geneva: International
Labour Organization, 2014. http://www.ilo.org /wcmsp5/groups/public/---ed
_norm/---declaration/documents/publication/wcms_243391.pdf.

———. *Unbearable to the Human Heart: Child Trafficking and Action to Eliminate It.*
Geneva: International Labour Organization, 2002. https://www.un.org/ruleoflaw
/files/childtrafficking.pdf.

International Labour Office and Walk Free Foundation. *Global Estimates of Modern
Slavery: Forced Labour and Forced Marriage.* Geneva: International Labour
Organization, 2017. http://www.ilo.org/wcmsp5/groups/public/---dgreports
/---dcomm/documents/publication/wcms_575479.pdf.

International Labour Organization. "Child Labour Statistics." https://www.ilo.org
/ipec/ChildlabourstatisticsSIMPOC/lang--en/index.htm.

———. "Fishing and Aquaculture." IPEC. Accessed 31 August 2018. https://www.ilo
.org/ipec/areas/Agriculture/WCMS_172419/lang--en/index.htm.

———. "Forced Labour, Modern Slavery, and Human Trafficking." Accessed 20 Feb 2019. http://www.ilo.org/global/topics/forced-labour/lang--en/index.htm.

———. "Gender and Child Labour in Agriculture." IPEC. Accessed 30 August 2018. https://www.ilo.org/ipec/areas/Agriculture/WCMS_172261/lang--en/index.htm.

———. "New ILO Global Estimate of Forced Labour: 20.9 Million Victims." ILO Newsroom. Last modified 1 June 2012. http://www.ilo.org/global/about-the-ilo /newsroom/news/WCMS_182109/lang--en/index.htm.

International Youth Foundation, The International Award Association, The International Federation of Red Cross and Red Crescent Societies, UN Children's Fund, World Alliance of YMCAs, World Association of Girl Guides and Girl Scouts, World Organization of the Scout Movement, and World YMCA. *Children & Young People: Participating in Decision-Making*. Accessed 27 August 2018. https://www .unicef.org/violencestudy/pdf/call_action.pdf.

Irazola, Seri, Erin Williamson, Catherine Chen, Ashley Garrett, and Heather J. Clawson. *Trafficking of US Citizens and Legal Permanent Residents: The Forgotten Victims and Survivors*. Washington, DC: ICF International, 2008. http://thehill .com/sites/default/files/ICFI_TraffickingofUSCitizens_0.pdf.

Isaac, Reena, Jennifer Solak, and Angelo Giardino. "Health Care Providers' Training Needs Related to Human Trafficking: Maximizing the Opportunity to Effectively Screen and Intervene." *Human Trafficking* 2, no. 1 (2011): 1–32.

Isaacs, Stephen. "Where the Public Good Prevailed: Government's Public Health Successes." *American Prospect*, 3 June 2001. http://www.prospect.org/cs /articles?article=where_the_public_good_prevailed.

Iyengar, Radha. "I'd Rather be Hanged for a Sheep than a Lamb: The Unintended Consequences of 'Three-Strikes' Laws." National Bureau of Economic Research Working Paper No. 13784, 2008. http://www.nber.org/papers/w13784.pdf.

Jennings, Ann. *Models for Developing Trauma-Informed Behavioral Health Systems and Trauma-Specific Services*. Draft. Prepared for Abt Associates. Accessed 23 October 2017. https://www.theannainstitute.org/MDT2.pdf.

Jennings, Ray. *Participatory Development as New Paradigm: The Transition of Development Professionalism*. Washington, DC: USAID, October 2000. http://pdf.usaid .gov/pdf_docs/Pnacq066.pdf.

Jobe, Alison. *The Causes and Consequences of Re-trafficking: Evidence from the IOM Human Trafficking Database*. Geneva: International Organization for Migration, 2010. https://publications.iom.int/system/files/pdf/causes_of _retrafficking.pdf.

Johnson, Nicole L., and Dawn M. Johnson. "Factors Influencing the Relationship between Sexual Trauma and Risky Sexual Behavior in College Students." *Journal of Interpersonal Violence*, 28, no. 11 (2013): 2315–31. https://doi.org/10.1177 /0886260512475318.

Jones, Risé, Emalee G. Flaherty, Helen J. Binns, Lori Lyn Price, Eric Slora, Dianna Abney, Donna L. Harris, Katherine Kaufer Christoffel, and Robert D. Sege. "Clinicians' Description of Factors Influencing Their Reporting of Suspected Child Abuse: Report of the Child Abuse Reporting Experience Study Research Group." *Pediatrics* 122, no. 2 (2008): 259–66. https://doi.org/10.1542/peds .2007-2312.

Jones, Samuel Vincent. "The Invisible Man: The Conscious Neglect of Men and Boys in the War on Human Trafficking." *Utah Law Review*, 2010, 1143–88.

Jukes, Matthew C. H., Lesley J. Drake, and Donald A. P. Bundy. *School Health, Nutrition and Education for All: Leveling the Playing Field*. Cambridge, MA: CABI Publishing, 2008.

Kangaspunta, Kristiina. *The Social Etiology of Human Trafficking, Their Global Distribution and Differences, Setting the Scene*. Paper presentation at the Pontifical Academy of Social Sciences, Vatican City, 17–21 April 2015. http://www.end slavery.va/content/endslavery/en/publications/acta_20/kangaspunta.pdf.

Kapur, Ratna. "The Citizen and the Migrant: Postcolonial Anxieties, Law, and the Politics of Exclusion/Inclusion." *Theoretical Inquiries in Law* 8, no. 2 (2007): 537–69.

Kara, Siddharth. *Sex Trafficking: Inside the Business of Modern Slavery*. New York: Columbia University Press, 2010.

Keating, Lisa M., Michelle A. Tomishima, Sharon Foster, and Michael Alessandri. "The Effects of a Mentoring Program on At-Risk Youth." *Adolescence* 37, no. 148 (Winter 2002): 717–34.

Kelly, Heath. "The Classical Definition of a Pandemic Is Not Elusive." *Bulletin of the World Health Organization* 89, no. 7 (2011): 540–41. https://doi.org/10.2471/BLT .11.088815.

Kempe, C. Henry, Frederic N. Silverman, Brandt F. Steele, William Droegemueller, and Henry K. Silver. "The Battered Child Syndrome." *Journal of the American Medical Association* 181, no. 1 (1962): 17–24. https://doi.org/10.1001/jama.1962 .03050270019004.

Kessler, Glenn. "Why You Should Be Wary of Statistics on 'Modern Slavery' and 'Trafficking.'" *Washington Post*, 24 April 2015. https://www.washingtonpost.com /news/fact-checker/wp/2015/04/24/why-you-should-be-wary-of-statistics-on -modern-slavery-and-trafficking/?utm_term=.c1110adc87cb.

Kidd, Sean A. "The Need for Improved Operational Definition of Suicide Attempts: Illustrations from the Case of Street Youth." *Death Studies* 27, no. 5 (2003): 449–55.

———. "Youth Homelessness and Social Stigma." *Journal of Youth and Adolescents* 36 (2007): 291–99. https://doi.org/10.1007/s10964-006-9100-3.

Kidd, Sean A., and Kathryn Scrimenti. "Evaluating Child and Youth Homelessness." *Evaluation Review*, 28, no. 4 (2004): 325–41.

Kirk, Lucy, Samantha Terry, Kamalini Lokuge, and Jessica L. Watterson. "Effectiveness of Secondary and Tertiary Prevention for Violence against Women in Low and Low-Middle Income Countries: A Systematic Review." *BMC Public Health* 17, no. 622 (2017). https://doi.org/10.1186/s12889-017-4502-6.

Klatt, Thimna, Della Cavner, and Vincent Egan. "Rationalising Predictors of Child Sexual Exploitation and Sex-Trading." *Child Abuse & Neglect* 38, no. 2 (2014): 252–60. https://doi.org/10.1016/j.chiabu.2013.08.019.

Kliner, Merav, and Laura Stroud. "Psychological and Health Impact of Working with Victims of Sex Trafficking." *Journal of Occupational Health* 54, no. 1 (2012): 9–15. https://doi.org/10.1539/joh.11-0125-OA.

Knight, Will. "Robot Camel-Jockeys Take to the Track." *New Scientist*, 21 July 2005.

https://www.newscientist.com/article/dn7705-robot-camel-jockeys-take-to
-the-track/.

Knox, Becca. *Big Surprise: Tobacco Company Prevention Campaigns Don't Work; Maybe It's because They Are Not Supposed To.* Campaign for Tobacco-Free Kids. 10 April 2018. https://www.tobaccofreekids.org/assets/factsheets/0302.pdf.

Kogan, Michael D., Paul W. Newacheck, Stephen J. Blumberg, Reem M. Ghandour, Gopal K. Singh, Bonnie B. Strickland, and Peter C. van Dyck. "Underinsurance among Children in the United States." *New England Journal of Medicine* 363, no. 9 (2010): 841–51. https://doi.org/10.1056/NEJMsa0909994.

Kruse, Douglas, and Lisa Schur. "Employment of People with Disabilities following the ADA." *Industrial Relations* 42, no. 1 (2003): 31–66. https://doi.org/10.1111 /1468-232X.00275.

Laczko, Frank, and Marco A. Gramegna. "Developing Better Indicators of Human Trafficking." *Brown Journal of World Affairs* 10, no. 1 (2003): 179–94.

Lalor, Kevin, and Rosaleen McElvaney. "Child Sexual Abuse, Links to Later Sexual Exploitation/High-Risk Sexual Behavior, and Prevention/Treatment Programs." *Trauma, Violence, & Abuse* 11, no. 4 (2010): 159–77. https://doi.org/10.1177 /1524838010378299.

Lamont, Alister. *Effects of Child Abuse and Neglect for Adult Survivors.* Melbourne: Australian Institute of Family Studies, January 2014.

Lampert, Allison. "U.N. Agency Urges Mandatory Training to Combat Human Trafficking on Flights." 23 April 2018. Reuters. https://www.reuters.com/article /us-un-aviation-trafficking/u-n-agency-urges-mandatory-training-to-combat -human-trafficking-on-flights-idUSKBN1HU1SC.

Lane, Wendy, and Howard Dubowitz. "Primary Care Pediatricians' Experience, Comfort, and Competence in the Evaluation and Management of Child Maltreatment: Do We Need Child Abuse Experts?" *Child Abuse & Neglect* 33, no. 3 (2009): 76–83. https://doi.org/10.1016/j.chiabu.2008.09.003.

Langum, David J. *Crossing over the Line: Legislating Morality and the Mann Act.* Chicago: University of Chicago Press, 1994.

Lansdown, Gerison. *Promoting Children's Participation in Democratic Decision-Making.* Florence: UNICEF Innocenti Research Centre, 2001. https://www.unicef-irc.org /publications/pdf/insight6.pdf.

Larkin, Michelle A., and Angela K. McGowan. "Introduction: Strengthening Public Health." *Journal of Law, Medicine & Ethics* 36 (2008): 4–5. https://doi.org/10.1111 /j.1748-720X.2008.00311.x.

Lawson, Tamara F. "A Shift toward Gender Equality in Prosecutions: Realizing Legitimate Enforcement of Crimes Committed against Women in Municipal and International Criminal Law." *Southern Illinois University Law Journal* 33 (2009): 181–215.

Layne, Christopher, Ernestine C. Briggs, and Christine A. Courtois. "Introduction to the Special Section: Using the Trauma History Profile to Unpack Risk Factors Caravan and Their Consequences." *Psychological Trauma: Theory, Research, Practice, and Policy* 6, no. S1 (2014): S1–S8.

Leder, Mary Ranee, S. Jean Emans, Janet P. Hafler, and Leonard A. Rappaport. "Addressing Sexual Abuse in the Primary Care Setting." *Pediatrics* 104, no. 2 (1999): 270–75.

Lederer, Laura J. "Ending Demand: An Annotated List of Books, Articles, Organizations, and Projects Addressing the Demand Side of Human Trafficking." *The
Protection Project: Journal of Human Rights and Civil Society* 5 (2012): 131–209.
http://www.protectionproject.org/wp-content/uploads/2012/11/TPP-J-HR
-Civ-Socy_Vol-5_2012-w-cover1.pdf.

———. "Sold for Sex: The Link between Street Gangs and Trafficking in Persons." *The
Protection Project: Journal of Human Rights and Civil Society* 4 (2011): 1–20. https://
www.globalcenturion.org/wp-content/uploads/2010/02/Sold-for-Sex-The-Link
-between-Street-Gangs-and-Trafficking-in-Persons-1.pdf.

Lederer, Laura J., and Christopher A. Wetzel. "The Health Consequences of Sex
Trafficking and Their Implications for Identifying Victims in Healthcare Facilities." *Annals of Health Law* 23, no. 1 (2014): 61–91.

Leichtman, Ahron. "The Top Ten Ways to Attack the Tobacco Industry and Win the
War against Smoking." *St. Louis University Public Law Review* 13, no. 2 (1994):
729–47.

Leidholdt, Dorchen. "Human Trafficking and Domestic Violence: A Primer for
Judges." *Judges' Journal* 52, no. 1 (2013): 16–21.

Levensky, Eric R., Alyssa Forcehimes, William T. O'Donohue, and Kendra Beitz.
"Motivational Interviewing: An Evidence-Based Approach to Counseling Helps
Patients Follow Treatment Recommendations." *American Journal of Nursing* 107,
no. 10 (2007): 50–58. https://doi.org/10.1097/01.NAJ.0000292202.06571.24.

Levy, Alexandra F. *United States Federal Courts' Continuing Failure to Order Mandatory
Criminal Restitution for Human Trafficking Victims*. Washington, DC: Human
Trafficking Pro Bono Legal Center and Wilmer Hale LLP, 2018. http://www
.htlegalcenter.org/wp-content/uploads/2018-Mandatory-Restitution-Report.pdf.

Levy, Alexandra F., and Martina E. Vandenberg. "Breaking the Law: The Failure to
Award Mandatory Criminal Restitution to Victims in Sex Trafficking Cases." *Saint
Louis University Law Journal* 60, no. 1 (2015): 43–72.

Levy, Alexandra F., Martina E. Vandenberg, and Lyric Chen. *When "Mandatory" Does
Not Mean Mandatory: Failure to Obtain Criminal Restitution in Federal Prosecution of
Human Trafficking Cases in the United States*. Washington, DC: Human Trafficking
Pro Bono Legal Center and Wilmer Hale LLP, 2014. http://www.htprobono.org
/wp-content/uploads/2014/09/HTProBono-Trafficking-Restitution-Report.pdf.

Lillie, Michelle. "Gang Involvement with Human Trafficking." Human Trafficking
Search. 2013. http://humantraffickingsearch.org/gang-involvement-with-human
-trafficking/.

———. "How Street Traffickers Recruit Young Girls." Human Trafficking Search. 2014.
http://humantraffickingsearch.org/how-street-traffickers-recruit-young-girls/.

———. *An Unholy Alliance: The Connection between Foster Care and Human Trafficking*.
Human Trafficking Search. 2015. http://humantraffickingsearch.org/wp-content
/uploads/2017/09/An-Unholy-Alliance_The-Connection-Between-Foster-Care
-and-Human-Trafficking.pdf.

Lillywhite, Ralph, and Paula Skidmore. "Boys Are Not Sexually Exploited? A Challenge to Practitioners." *Child Abuse Review* 15 (2006): 351–61.

Lim, Lin Lean, ed. *The Sex Sector: The Economic and Social Bases of Prostitution in
Southeast Asia*. Geneva: International Labour Organization, 1998.

Limoncelli, Stephanie. "The Trouble with Trafficking: Conceptualizing Women's Sexual Labor and Economic Human Rights." *Women's Studies International Forum* 32 (2009): 261–69. https://doi.org/10.1016/j.wsif.2009.05.002.

Link, Bruce G., and Jo C. Phelan. "Fundamental Sources of Health Inequalities." In *Policy Challenges in Modern Health Care*, edited by David Mechanic, Lynn B. Rogut, David C. Colby, and James R. Knickman, 71–84. New Brunswick, NJ: Rutgers University Press, 2005.

Littrell, Jeneé. *Human Trafficking in America's Schools*. Washington, DC: US Department of Education, 2015. https://humantraffickinghotline.org/sites/default/files/Human%20Trafficking%20in%20Americas%20Schools%20-%20DoEd.pdf.

Lloyd, Rachel. "At What Cost: The Road to Anti-Trafficking Is Paved with Good Intentions." Girls Educational & Mentoring Services. 4 December 2013. http://www.gems-girls.org/shifting-perspective/at-what-cost-the-road-to-anti-trafficking-is-paved-with-good-intentions.

———. *From Victim to Survivor, From Survivor to Leader: The Importance of Leadership Programming and Opportunities for Commercially Sexually Exploited and Trafficked Young Women & Girls*. Girls Education & Mentoring Services. Accessed 27 August 2018. http://www.gems-girls.org/WhitePaper.pdf.

Logan, T. K., Robert Walker, and Gretchen Hunt. "Understanding Human Trafficking in the United States." *Trauma Violence Abuse* 10, no. 1 (2009): 3–30. https://doi.org/10.1177/1524838008327262.

Lutnick, Alexandra. *Domestic Minor Sex Trafficking: Beyond Victims and Villains*. New York: Columbia University Press, 2016.

Macias-Konstantopoulos, Wendy, and Zheng B. Ma. "Physical Health of Human Trafficking Survivors: Unmet Essentials." In Chisolm-Straker and Stoklosa, *Human Trafficking Is a Public Health Issue*, 185–210.

Macy, Rebecca J., and L. M. Graham. "Identifying Domestic and International Sex-Trafficking Victims during Human Service Provision." *Trauma, Violence, & Abuse* 13, no. 2 (2012): 39–76. https://doi.org/10.1177/1524838012440340.

Macy, Rebecca J., and Natalie Johns. "Aftercare Services for International Sex Trafficking Survivors: Informing U.S. Service and Program Development in an Emerging Practice Area." *Trauma, Violence, & Abuse* 12, no. 2 (2011): 87–98. https://doi.org/10.1177/1524838010390709.

Maddock, Jay, Christine Maglione, and Jodi D. Barnett. "Statewide Implementation of the 1% or Less Campaign." *Health Education and Behavior* 34, no. 6 (2006): 953–63. https://doi.org/10.1177/1090198106290621.

Makoul, Gregory, Amanda Zick, and Marianne Green. "An Evidence-Based Perspective on Greetings in Medical Encounters." *JAMA Internal Medicine* 167, no. 11 (2007): 1172–76. https://doi.org/10.1001/archinte.167.11.1172.

Malloch, Margaret, and Paul Rigby. "Contexts and Complexities." In *Human Trafficking: The Complexities of Exploitation*, edited by Margaret Malloch and Paul Rigby. Edinburgh: Edinburgh University Press 2016.

Mandela, Nelson. *In His Own Words*. New York: Little, Brown, 2003.

Maney, Gregory, Tineka Brown, Taylor Gregory, Rafia Mallick, Steven Simoneschi, Charisse Wheby, and Nicole Wiktor. *Meeting the Service Needs of Human Trafficking Survivors in the New York City Metropolitan Area: Assessment and Recommendations*.

Hempstead, NY: Hofstra University, 2011. https://lifewaynetwork.org/wp-content /uploads/2011/11/Hofstra-University-LifeWay-Network-Report-2011.pdf.

Mariano, Willoughby. "Despite Millions Spent, Human Trafficking's Scope Is Unknown." *Atlanta Journal-Constitution*, 31 December 2012. https://www.ajc .com/news/despite-millions-spent-human-trafficking-scope-unknown/NkzRkI8 WkvrNcaJSibMWRJ/.

Mariner, Wendy K. "Law and Public Health: Beyond Emergency Preparedness." *Journal of Health Law* 38, no. 2 (2005): 247–85.

———. "Mission Creep: Public Health Surveillance and Medical Privacy." *Boston University Law Review* 87, no. 2 (2007): 347–95.

Marlegna, Barvara, Richard L. Berg, James G. Linneman, Robert J. Brison, and William Pickett. "Changing the Child Labor Laws for Agriculture: Impact on Injury." *American Journal of Public Health* 97, no. 2 (2007): 276–82. https://doi .org/10.2105/AJPH.2005.078923.

Martinez, Omar, and Guadalupe Kelle. "Sex Trafficking of LGBT Individuals: A Call for Service Provision, Research, and Action." *International Law News* 42, no. 4 (2013).

Maslow, Abraham H. "A Theory of Human Motivation." *Psychological Review* 50 (1943): 370–96.

McClain, Natalie, and Stacy Garrity. "Sex Trafficking and the Exploitation of Adolescents." *Journal of Obstetric Gynecologic & Neonatal Nursing* 40, no. 2 (2011): 243–52. https://doi.org/10.1111/j.1552-6909.2011.01221.x.

McLearn, Kathryn Taaffe, Diane Colasanto, and Cathy Schoen. *Mentoring Makes a Difference: Findings from The Commonwealth Fund 1998 Survey of Adults Mentoring Young People*. Commonwealth Fund. July 1998. https://www.commonwealthfund .org/sites/default/files/documents/___media_files_publications_fund_report_1998 _jul_mentoring_makes_a_difference_findings_from_the_commonwealth_fund _1998_survey_of_adults_mentoring_yo_mclearn_mentoring_pdf.pdf.

Mehlman-Orozco, Kimberly. "The Plight of Sex-Trafficking Survivors." *Gay & Lesbian Review Worldwide*, November–December 2016. http://www.glreview.org /wp-content/uploads/DigitalEditions/23.6/files/assets/common/downloads /page0005.pdf.

———. "What Happens after a Human Trafficking Victim Is Rescued?" *The Hill* (blog), 29 July 2016. http://thehill.com/blogs/congress-blog/judicial/289709-what -happens-after-a-human-trafficking-victim-is-rescued.

Mercy, James A., Mark L. Rosenberg, Kenneth E. Powell, Claire V. Broome, and William L. Roper. "Public Health Policy for Preventing Violence." *Health Affairs* 12, no. 4 (Winter 1993): 7–29. https://doi.org/10.1377/hlthaff.12.4.7.

Miko, Francis T. "Trafficking in Women and Children: The U.S. and International Response." In *Trafficking in Women and Children: Current Issues and Developments*, edited by Anna M. Troubnikoff, 1–30. New York: Nova Science, 2003.

Miller, Cari L., Sarah J. Fielden, Mark W. Tyndall, Ruth Zhang, Kate Gibson, and Kate Shannon. "Individual and Structural Vulnerability among Female Youth Who Exchange Sex for Survival." *Journal of Adolescent Health* 49, no. 1 (2011): 36–41. https://doi.org/10.1016/j.jadohealth.2010.10.003.

Miller, Elizabeth, Michele R. Decker, Jay G. Silverman, and Anita Raj. "Migration,

Sexual Exploitation, and Women's Health: A Case Report from a Community Health Center." *Violence Against Women* 13, no. 5 (2007): 486–97. https://doi.org /10.1177/1077801207301614.

Moore, Alexandra Schultheis, and Elizabeth Swanson Goldberg. "Victims, Perpetrators, and the Limits of Human Rights Discourse in Post-Palermo Fiction about Sex Trafficking." *International Journal of Human Rights* 19, no. 1 (2015): 16–31. https:// doi.org/10.1080/13642987.2014.980404.

Moossy, Robert. "Sex Trafficking: Identifying Cases and Victims." *National Institute of Justice Journal* 262 (2009). https://www.nij.gov/journals/262/pages/sex-trafficking .aspx.

Morens, David M., Gregory K. Folkers, and Anthony S. Fauci. "What Is a Pandemic?" *Journal of Infectious Diseases* 200, no. 7 (2009): 1018–21. https://doi.org/10.1086 /644537.

Morisano, Dominique, Thomas F. Babor, and Katherine A. Robaina. "Co-Occurrence of Substance Use Disorders with Other Psychiatric Disorders: Implications for Treatment Services." *Nordic Studies on Alcohol and Drugs* 31 (2017): 1–24.

Mount Sinai Adolescent Health Center. *Blueprint for Adolescent and Young Adult Healthcare*. New York: Mount Sinai Adolescent Health Center, December 2016. https://teenhealthcare.org/wp-content/uploads/2017/08/MSAHC-Blueprint -Guide_v13-PrintReducedSize3_RELEASE_compressed.pdf.

Muftic, Lisa R., and Mary A. Finn. "Health Outcomes among Women Trafficked for Sex in the United States: A Closer Look." *Journal of Interpersonal Violence* 28, no. 9 (2013): 1859–85. https://doi.org/10.1177/0886260512469102.

Muraya, Dorothy, and Deborah Fry. "Aftercare Services for Child Victims of Sex Trafficking: A Systematic Review of Policy and Practice." *Trauma, Violence, & Abuse* 17, no. 2 (2016): 204–20. https://doi.org/10.1177/1524838015584356.

Murphy, Laura T. *Labor and Sex Trafficking among Homeless Youth: A Ten City Study Full Report*. Loyola University New Orleans and Modern Slavery Research Project. 2016. https://nspn.memberclicks.net/assets/docs/NSPN/labor%20and%20sex %20trafficking%20among%20homeless%20youth.pdf.

Nack, Marisa. "The Next Step: The Future of New York State's Human Trafficking Law." *Journal of Law and Policy* 18, no. 2 (2010): 839–40.

Nadon, Susan M., Catherine Koverola, and Eduard H. Schludermann. "Antecedents to Prostitution—Childhood Victimization." *Journal of Interpersonal Violence* 13, no. 2 (1998): 206–21. https://doi.org/10.1177/088626098013002003.

Nag, Moni. "Sexual Behaviour in India with Risk of HIV/AIDS Transmission." *Health Transition Review* 5, no. S1 (1995): 293–305.

Nagle, Luz Estella. "Selling Souls: The Effect of Globalization on Human Trafficking and Forced Servitude." *Wisconsin International Law Journal* 26 (2008): 131–62.

Nam, Jennifer S. "The Case of the Missing Case: Examining the Civil Right of Action for Human Trafficking Victims." *Columbia Law Review* 107 (November 2007): 1655–74.

Napolitano, Kara. "At Greater Risk: Human Trafficking and the Child Welfare System." Laboratory to Combat Human Trafficking. 8 December 2016. http:// combathumantrafficking.org/2016/12/at-greater-risk-human-trafficking-and -the-child-welfare-system/.

National Alliance to End Homelessness. *Homeless Youth and Sexual Exploitation: Research Findings and Practice Implications.* Washington, DC: NAEH, 2009. https://b.3cdn.net/naeh/c0103117f1ee8f2d84_e8m6ii5q2.pdf.

National Center for Homeless Education. *Sex Trafficking of Minors: What Schools Need to Know to Recognize and Respond to the Trafficking of Students.* 2014. https://nche.ed.gov/downloads/briefs/trafficking.pdf.

National Center for Zoonotic, Vector-Borne, and Enteric Diseases. *Confronting Infectious Diseases in an Interconnected World: People, Animals, and the Environment.* Atlanta, GA: Center for Disease Control, 2009. http://www.onehealthinitiative.com/publications/d%20%20Confronting%20Infectious%20Diseases.pdf.

National Conference of State Legislatures. "Issue in Focus: Substance Abusing Offenders." *Bulletin* 1 (February 2010). http://www.ncsl.org/portals/1/Documents/cj/bulletinFeb-2010.pdf.

———. "Shaken Baby Syndrome Prevention Legislation." Last modified January 2014. http://www.ncsl.org/research/human-services/shaken-baby-syndrome-prevention-legislation.aspx (site discontinued).

National Human Trafficking Hotline. "Mission." About Us. Accessed 7 February 2018. https://humantraffickinghotline.org/mission.

National Human Trafficking Resource Center. *Labor Trafficking Cases by Industry in the United States.* Human Trafficking Hotline. Accessed 30 June 2017. https://humantraffickinghotline.org/sites/default/files/Labor%20Trafficking%20Cases%20by%20Industry%20in%20the%20US%20Fact%20Sheet%20FINAL_1.pdf.

National Network for Youth. *Human Trafficking and the Runaway and Homeless Youth Population.* Accessed 26 July 2018. https://www.1800runaway.org/wp-content/uploads/2015/05/Homeless-Youth-and-Human-Trafficking.pdf.

National Sexual Violence Resource Center. *Assisting Trafficking Victims: A Guide for Victim Advocates.* 2012. https://www.nsvrc.org/sites/default/files/publications_nsvrc_guides_human-trafficking-victim-advocates.pdf.

National Society for the Prevention of Cruelty to Children. *Vicarious Trauma: The Consequences of Working with Abuse.* August 2013. https://www.nspcc.org.uk/globalassets/documents/information-service/research-briefing-vicarious-trauma-consequences-working-with-abuse.pdf.

Newacheck, Paul W., Jeffery J. Stoddard, Dana C. Hughes, and Michelle Pearl. "Health Insurance and Access to Primary Care for Children." *New England Journal of Medicine* 338, no. 8 (1998): 513–18. https://doi.org/10.1056/NEJM199802193380806.

Nir, Sarah Maslin. "The Price of Nice Nails: Manicurists Are Routinely Underpaid and Exploited, and Endure Ethic Bias and Other Abuse, the New York Times Has Found." *New York Times*, 7 May 2015. https://www.nytimes.com/2015/05/10/nyregion/at-nail-salons-in-nyc-manicurists-are-underpaid-and-unprotected.html.

Normandin, Patricia A. "Child Human Trafficking: See, Pull, Cut the Thread of Abuse." *Journal of Emergency Nursing* 43, no. 6 (2017): 588–90. https://doi.org/10.1016/j.jen.2017.07.014.

Obama, Barack. Presidential Proclamation—National Slavery and Human Trafficking Prevention Month, 2017. 28 December 2016. https://obamawhitehouse.archives

.gov/the-press-office/2016/12/28/presidential-proclamation-national-slavery
-and-human-trafficking.

———. Remarks by the President to the Clinton Global Initiative. Sheraton New York
Hotel and Towers, 25 September 2012. http://www.whitehouse.gov/the-press
-office/2012/09/25/remarks-president-clinton-global-initiative.

Office of Justice Programs. *Substance Abuse Needs*. Human Trafficking Task Force
e-Guide, Office for Victims of Crime Training and Technical Assistance Center.
Accessed 8 August 2018. https://www.ovcttac.gov/taskforceguide/eguide/4
-supporting-victims/44-comprehensive-victim-services/mental-health-needs
/substance-abuse-needs/.

———. *The Victim as a Witness*. Human Trafficking Task Force e-Guide, Office for
Victims of Crime Training and Technical Assistance Center. Accessed 31 December 2018. https://www.ovcttac.gov/taskforceguide/eguide/5-building-strong-cases
/54-landing-a-successful-prosecution/the-victim-as-a-witness/.

———. *Victim-Centered Approach*. Human Trafficking Task Force e-Guide, Office for
Victims of Crime Training and Technical Assistance Center. Accessed 26 October
2016. https://www.ovcttac.gov/taskforceguide/eguide/1-understanding-human
-trafficking/13-victim-centered-approach/.

———. *Victims with Physical, Cognitive, or Emotional Disabilities*. Human Trafficking
Task Force e-Guide, Office for Victims of Crime Training and Technical Assistance
Center. Accessed 8 August 2018. https://www.ovcttac.gov/taskforceguide/eguide
/4-supporting-victims/45-victim-populations/victims-with-physical-cognitive-or
-emotional-disabilities/.

Office of Juvenile Justice and Delinquency Prevention. "Child Labor Trafficking."
*Literature Review: A Product of the Model Programs Guide*, December 2016. https://
www.ojjdp.gov/mpg/litreviews/child-labor-trafficking.pdf.

———. "Commercial Sexual Exploitation of Children and Sex Trafficking." *Literature
Review: A Product of the Model Programs Guide*, August 2014. https://www.ojjdp
.gov/mpg/litreviews/CSECSexTrafficking.pdf.

Office of Planning, Research & Evaluation. "Evaluation of Domestic Victims of
Human Trafficking Program: 2016–2020—Overview." Administration for
Children & Families. 9 December 2016. https://www.acf.hhs.gov/opre/resource
/evaluation-of-domestic-victims-of-human-trafficking-program-2016–2020
-overview.

Office on Trafficking in Persons, Administration for Children and Families. "CDC
Adds New Human Trafficking Data Collection Fields for Health Care Providers."
US Department of Health and Human Services. 14 June 2018. https://www.acf
.hhs.gov/otip/news/icd-10.

———. "Human Trafficking Data Collection Project." US Department of Health and
Human Services. Last modified 26 December 2017. https://www.acf.hhs.gov/otip
/research-policy/data-collection.

———. "The Power of Framing Human Trafficking as a Public Health Issue." US
Department of Health and Human Services. 11 January 2016. https://www.acf.hhs
.gov/otip/resource/publichealthlens.

Office on Trafficking in Persons and Office on Women's Health. *Human Trafficking
Data Element Worksheet*. US Department of Health and Human Services. Draft last

accessed 12 September 2018. https://www.acf.hhs.gov/sites/default/files/end trafficking/data_element_worksheet.pdf.

Ogolla, Christopher. "Will the Use of Racial Statistics in Public Health Surveillance Survive Equal Protection Challenges? A Prolegomenon for the Future." *North Carolina Central Law Review* 31, no. 1 (2008): 1–32.

O'Haver, Hanson, "How 'If You See Something, Say Something' Became Our National Motto." *Washington Post*, 23 September 2016. https://www.washington post.com/posteverything/wp/2016/09/23/how-if-you-see-something-say-some thing-became-our-national-motto/?utm_term=.a831bfd11858

Okech, David Y., Joon Choi, Jennifer Elkins, and Abigail C. Burns. "Seventeen Years of Human Trafficking Research in Social Work: A Review of the Literature." *Journal of Evidence-Informed Social Work* 15, no. 2 (2018): 103–22.

Okech, David Y., Nathan Hansen, Waylon Howard, John K. Anarfi, and Abigail C. Burns. "Social Support, Dysfunctional Coping, and Community Reintegration as Predictors of PTSD among Human Trafficking Survivors." *Behavioral Medicine* 44, no. 3 (2018): 209–18. https://doi.org/10.1080/08964289.2018.1432553

Olafson, Erna. "Child Sexual Abuse: Demography, Impact, and Interventions." *Journal of Child & Adolescent Trauma* 4, no. 1 (2011): 8–21. https://doi.org/10.1080 /19361521.2011.545811.

Optional Protocol to the Convention on the Rights of the Child on the Sale of Children, Child Prostitution and Child Pornography. UN General Assembly Resolution 54/263, Annex II, UN Doc. A/54/49 (2000).

Oram, Siân, Heidi Stöckl, Joanna Busza, Louise M. Howard, and Cathy Zimmerman. "Prevalence and Risk of Violence and the Physical, Mental, and Sexual Health Problems Associated with Human Trafficking: Systematic Review." *PLOS Medicine* 9, no. 5 (2012). https://doi.org/10.1371/journal.pmed.1001224.

Oram, Siân, and Cathy Zimmerman. "The Health of Persons Trafficked for Forced Labour." *Global Eye on Human Trafficking*, no. 4 (2008): 4. Accessed 8 February 2018. https://www.iom.int/jahia/webdav/site/myjahiasite/shared/shared/main site/projects/showcase_pdf/global_eye_fourth_issue.pdf.

Orentlitcher, David. "Diversity: A Fundamental American Value." *Missouri Law Review* 70 (2005): 777–812.

Orgera, Kendal, and Samantha Artiga. *Disparities in Health and Health Care: Five Key Questions and Answers*. Washington, DC: Kaiser Family Foundation, August 2018. http://files.kff.org/attachment/Issue-Brief-Disparities-in-Health-and-Health -Care-Five-Key-Questions-and-Answers.

Pack, Margaret. "Discovering an Integrated Framework for Practice: A Qualitative Investigation of Theories Used by Social Workers Working as Sexual Abuse Therapists." *Journal of Social Work Practice* 25, no. 1 (2011): 79–93. https://doi.org /10.1080/02650533.2010.530646.

———. "Vicarious Traumatization and Resilience: An Ecological Systems Approach to Sexual Abuse Counsellors' Trauma and Stress." *Sexual Abuse in Australia and New Zealand* 5, no. 2 (2013): 69–76.

Palmer, Wayne, and Antje Missbach. "Trafficking within Migrant Smuggling Oper-ations: Are Underage Transporters 'Victims' or 'Perpetrators'?" *Asian and Pacific*

*Migration Journal* 26, no. 3 (2017): 287–307. https://doi.org/10.1177/01171968
17726627.

Papalia, Nina L., Stefan Luebbers, James R. P. Ogloff, Margaret Cutajar, Paul E.
Mullen, and Emily Mann. "Further Victimization of Child Sexual Abuse Victims:
A Latent Class Typology of Re-victimization Trajectories." *Child Abuse & Neglect*
66 (2017): 112–29.

Participatory Epidemiology. "About Participatory Epidemiology." Accessed 18 June
2018. http://www.participatoryepidemiology.info/about-participatory-epidemiology
/index.html (site discontinued).

Petriliggieri, Francesca. "Poverty Is the Root Cause of Human Trafficking." In *Human
Trafficking*, edited by Dedria Bryfonski. Farmington Hills, MI: Greenhaven Press,
2013.

Phillips, Jasmine. "Black Girls and the (Im)Possibilities of a Victim Trope: The
Intersectional Failures of Legal and Advocacy Interventions in the Commercial
Sexual Exploitation of Minors in the United States." *UCLA Law Review* 62 (2015):
1642–75.

Pierce, Sarah. "Turning a Blind Eye: U.S. Corporate Involvement in Modern Day
Slavery." *Journal of Gender, Race and Justice* 14 (2011): 577–600.

Pinheiro, Paulo Sérgio. *World Report on Violence against Children.* Geneva: United
Nations, 2006.

Pinto, Antonio, Alfonso Reginelli, Fabio Pinto, Giacomo Sica, Mariano Scaglione,
Ferco H. Berger, and Luigia Brunese. "Radiological and Practical Aspects of Body
Packing." *British Journal of Radiology* 87, no. 1036 (2014). https://doi.org/10.1259
/bjr.20130500.

Pocock, Nicola S., Ligia Kiss, Siân Oram, and Cathy Zimmerman. "Labour Trafficking
among Men and Boys in the Greater Mekong Subregion: Exploitation, Violence,
Occupational Health Risks and Injuries." *PLOS ONE* 11, no. 12 (December 2016):
e0168500. https://doi.org/10.1371/journal.pone.0168500.

Polaris Project. *Analysis of State Human Trafficking Laws.* Washington, DC: Polaris
Project, August 2013. https://polarisproject.org/sites/default/files/2013-State
-Ratings-Analysis.pdf.

———. *How Does Your State Rate on Human Trafficking Laws in 2012?* Washington, DC:
Polaris Project, July 2012. https://polarisproject.org/sites/default/files/2012
-State-Ratings.pdf.

———. "On-Ramps, Intersections, and Exit Routes: A Roadmap for Systems and
Industries to Prevent and Disrupt Human Trafficking—Transportation Industry."
*Polaris Project*, July 2018. https://polarisproject.org/sites/default/files/A%20
Roadmap%20for%20Systems%20and%20Industries%20to%20Prevent%20
and%20Disrupt%20Human%20Trafficking.pdf.

———. *Sex Trafficking and LGBTQ Youth.* Polaris Project. Accessed 27 August 2018.
https://polarisproject.org/sites/default/files/LGBTQ-Sex-Trafficking.pdf.

———. *Shelter Beds for Human Trafficking Survivors in the United States.* Washington,
DC: Polaris Project, 2012. http://www.ccasa.org/wp-content/uploads/2014/01
/Shelter-Beds-For-Human-Trafficking-Survivors.pdf.

Popkin, Susan J., Tama Leventhal, and Gretchen Weismann. "Girls in the 'Hood: How

Safety Affects the Life Chances of Low-Income Girls." *Urban Affairs Review* 45, no. 6 (2010): 715-44. https://doi.org/10.1177/1078087410361572.

Poucki, Sasha, and Nicole Bryan. "Vulnerability to Human Trafficking among the Roma Population in Serbia: The Role of Social Exclusion and Marginalization." *Journal of Intercultural Studies* 35 (2014): 145-62.

Powell, Clydette, Kirsten Dickins, and Hanni Stoklosa. "Training US Health Care Professionals on Human Trafficking: Where Do We Go from Here?" *Medical Education Online* 22, no. 1 (2017): 1-12.

Prentice, Andrew M., M. Eric Gershwin, Ulrich E. Shaible, Gerald T. Keusch, Cesar G. Victora, and Jeffrey I. Gordon. "New Challenges in Studying Nutrition-Disease Interactions in the Developing World." *Journal of Clinical Investigation* 118, no. 4 (2008): 1322-29. https://doi.org/10.1172/JCI34034.

Prentice, Julia C., and Steven D Pizer. "Delayed Access to Health Care and Mortality." *Health Services Research* 42, no. 2 (2007): 644-62.

The Protection Project. *Human Rights Report: Poland.* http://www.protectionproject.org/human_rights_reports/report_documents/poland.doc (site discontinued).

Protocol to Prevent, Suppress and Punish Trafficking in Persons, Especially Women and Children, Supplementing the United Nations Convention Against Transnational Organized Crime. UN General Assembly Resolution 55/25, Annex II, UN Doc. A/RES/45/49 (2000).

Puzio, Dorothy. "An Overview of Public Health in the New Millennium: Individual Liberty vs. Public Safety." *Journal of Law and Health* 18 (2003-4): 173-98.

Rafferty, Yvonne. "The Impact of Trafficking on Children: Psychological and Social Policy Perspectives." *Society for Research in Child Development* 2, no. 1 (March 2008): 13-18. https://doi.org/10.1111/j.1750-8606.2008.00035.x.

Raghavan, Chitra, and Doychak, Kendra. "Trauma-coerced Bonding and Victims of Sex Trafficking: Where Do We Go from Here?" *International Journal of Emergency Mental Health and Human Resilience* 17, no. 2 (2015): 583-87.

Raider, Melvyn C., William Steele, Margaret Delillo-Storey, Jacqueline Jacobs, and Caelan Kuban. "Structured Sensory Therapy (SITCAPART) for Traumatized Adjudicated Adolescents in Residential Treatment." *Residential Treatment for Children & Youth* 25, no. 2 (2008): 167-85. https://doi.org/10.1080/08865710802310178.

Raney, Rebecca Fairley. "Unseen Victims of Sex Trafficking: While Most People Think of Women and Girls as the Victims of Human Trafficking, Men and Boys Are Also at Risk." *Monitor on Psychology* 48 no. 4 (2017) 22-23.

Raphael, Jody, Katie Feifer, Jayne Bigelsen, Michelle Dempsey, and Shea Rhodes. *What We Know about Sex Trafficking, Prostitution, and Sexual Exploitation in the U.S.* New York: World Without Exploitation, February 2017. https://endsexualexploitation.org/wp-content/uploads/Research-Summary_What-we-know-about-trafficking-prostitution-and-exploitation-in-US-.pdf.

Raphael, Jody, Jessica Ashley Reichert, and Mark Powers. "Pimp Control and Violence: Domestic Sex Trafficking of Chicago Women and Girls." *Journal Women & Criminal Justice* 20, no. 1-2 (2012): 89-104. https://doi.org/10.1080/08974451003641065.

Ravi, Anita, Megan R. Pfeiffer, Zachary Rosner, and Judy A. Shea. "Trafficking and

Trauma Insight and Advice for the Healthcare System from Sex-trafficked Women Incarcerated on Rikers Island." *Medical Care* 55, no. 12 (2017): 1017–22. https://journals.lww.com/lww-medicalcare/Fulltext/2017/12000/Trafficking_and_Trauma_Insight_and_Advice_for_the.6.aspx.

Reavis, James, Jan Looman, Kristina Franco, and Briana Rojas. "Adverse Childhood Experiences and Adult Criminality: How Long Must We Live before We Possess Our Own Lives?" *Permanente Journal* 17, no. 2 (2013): 44–48.

Reichert, Jessica, and Amy Sylwestrzak. *National Survey of Residential Programs for Victims of Sex Trafficking.* Chicago: Illinois Criminal Justice Information Authority, 2013. http://www.icjia.state.il.us/assets/pdf/ResearchReports/NSRHVST_101813.pdf.

Reid, Joan A. "Doors Wide Shut: Barriers to the Successful Delivery of Victim Services for Domestically Trafficked Minors in a Southern U.S. Metropolitan Area." *Women & Criminal Justice* 20, no. 1–2 (2010): 147–66. https://doi.org/10.1080/08974451003641206.

———. "Human Trafficking of Minors and Childhood Adversity in Florida." *American Journal of Public Health* 107, no. 2 (2017): 306–11. https://doi.org/10.2105/AJPH.2016.303564.

———. "Sex Trafficking of Girls with Intellectual Disabilities: An Exploratory Mixed Methods Study." *Sexual Abuse* 30, no. 2 (2018): 107–31.

Reinhard, Ashley, Ina Whitacre, Ashley M. Hervey, and Gina M. Berg. "Knowledge and Attitudes of Physicians in Kansas Regarding Domestic Minor Sex Trafficking." *Kansas Journal of Medicine,* 5 no. 4 (2012): 142–53.

Rew, Lynn, Tiffany Whittaker, Margarette Tylor-Seehafer, and Lorie Smith. "Sexual Health Risks and Protective Resources in Gay, Lesbian, Bisexual and Heterosexual Homeless Youth." *Journal for Specialists in Pediatric Nursing* 10, no. 1 (2005): 11–20.

Rhodan, Maya. "Deportation Fears Silence Some Domestic Violence Victims." *Time,* 30 May 2017. http://time.com/4798422/domestic-violence-deportation-immigration.

Richards, Tiffany A. "Health Implications of Human Trafficking." *Nursing for Women's Health* 18, no. 2 (2014): 155–62. https://doi.org/10.1111/1751-486X.12112.

Robinson, Paul H., and John M. Darley. "Does Criminal Law Deter? A Behavioural Science Investigation." *Oxford Journal of Legal Studies* 24, no. 2 (2004): 173–205. https://doi.org/10.1093/ojls/24.2.173.

———. "The Role of Deterrence in the Formulation of Criminal Law Rules: At Its Worst When Doing Its Best." *Georgetown Law Journal* 91 (2003): 950–1002.

Roe-Sepowitz, Dominique, James Gallagher, Markus Risinger, and Kristine Hickle. "The Sexual Exploitation of Girls in the United States: The Role of Female Pimps." *Journal of Interpersonal Violence* 30, no. 16 (2015): 2814–30. https://doi.org/10.1177/0886260514554292.

Romer, Daniel, Ellen Peters, Andrew A. Strasser, and Daniel Langleben. "Desire versus Efficacy in Smokers' Paradoxical Reactions to Pictorial Health Warnings for Cigarettes." *PLOS ONE* 8, no. 1 (January 2013). https://doi.org/10.1371/journal.pone.0054937.

Rosenberg, Mark L., and Mary Ann Fenley, eds. *Violence in America: A Public Health Approach.* New York: Oxford University Press, 1991.

Rotherham-Borus, Mary Jane, Heino Meyer-Bahlburg, Cheryl Koopman, Margaret Rosario, Theresa Exner, Ronald Henderson, Marjory Mattieu, and Rhoda Gruen. "Lifetime Sexual Behaviors among Runaway Males and Females." *Journal of Sex Research* 29, no. 1 (1992): 15–29. https://doi.org/10.1080/00224499209551631.

Rothman, Emily F., Deinera Exner, and Allyson L. Baughman. "The Prevalence of Sexual Assault against People Who Identify as Gay, Lesbian, or Bisexual in the United States: A Systemic Review." *Trauma, Violence, & Abuse* 12, no. 2 (2011): 55–66.

Rothman, Emily F., Hanni Stoklosa, Susie B. Baldwin, Makini Chisolm-Straker, Rumi Kato Price, and Holly G. Atkinson. "Public Health Research Priorities to Address US Human Trafficking." *American Journal of Public Health* 107, no. 7 (July 2017): 1045–47. https://doi.org/10.2105/AJPH.2017.303858.

Ruttenberg, Hattie. "The Limited Promise of Public Health Methodologies to Prevent Youth Violence." *Yale Law Journal* 103, no. 7 (1994): 1885–1912.

Sabella, Donna. "The Role of the Nurse in Combating Human Trafficking." *American Journal of Nursing* 111, no. 2 (2011): 28–37. https://doi.org/10.1097/01.NAJ .0000394289.55577.b6.

Sadruddin, Hussein, Natalia Walter, and Jose Hidalgo. "Human Trafficking in the United States: Expanding Victim Protection beyond Prosecution Witnesses." *Stanford Law and Policy Review* 16, no. 2 (2005): 379–415.

Sale, Elizabeth, Nikki Bellamy, J. Fred Springer, and Min Qi Wang. "Quality of Provider-Participant Relationships and Enhancement of Adolescent Social Skills." *Journal of Primary Prevention* 29, no. 3 (2008): 263–78. https://doi.org/10.1007 /s10935-008-0138-8.

Salston, MaryDale, and Charles R. Figley. "Secondary Traumatic Stress Effects of Working with Survivors of Criminal Victimization." *Journal of Traumatic Stress* 16, no. 2 (2003): 167–74. https://doi.org/10.1023/A:1022899207206.

Sar, Vedat. "Developmental Trauma, Complex PTSD, and the Current Proposal of DSM-5." *European Journal of Psychotraumatology* 5, no. 2 (2011): 1–9. https://doi .org/10.3402/ejpt.v2i0.5622.

Schmitt, Valerie. "How Your Community Can Stop the Trafficking of Homeless LGBTQ Youth." *Polaris Project* (blog), 6 May 2016. https://polarisproject.org /blog/2016/05/06/how-your-community-can-stop-trafficking-homeless -lgbtq-youth.

Schneider, Stephanie, Steven Grilli, and Jennifer Schneider. "Evidence-Based Treatments for Traumatized Children and Adolescents." *Current Psychiatry Reports* 15, no. 1 (2013): 332–41. https://doi.org/10.1007/s11920-012-0332-5.

Schoen, Cathy, Karen Davis, Karen Scott Collins, Linda Greenberg, Catherine Des Roches, and Melinda Abrams. *The Commonwealth Fund Survey of the Health of Adolescent Girls.* Washington, DC: Commonwealth Fund, November 1997. http://www.commonwealthfund.org/publications/fund-reports/1997/nov/the -commonwealth-fund-survey-of-the-health-of-adolescent-girls.

Scullion, Dianne. "Gender Perspectives on Child Trafficking: A Case Study of Child Domestic Workers." In *Gender and Migration in 21st Century Europe*, edited by Helen Stalford, Samantha Currie, and Samantha Velluti, 45–62. London: Rout-ledge, 2016.

Shahinian, Gulnara. "Victims and Traffickers, New Relationship and Gender Roles." Accessed 20 February 2019. http://docplayer.net/41695510-Victims-and-traffickers -new-relationship-and-gender-roles.html.

Shared Hope International. *National State Survey Law: Mandatory Restitution/Civil Remedies*. Arlington, VA: Shared Hope International, 2017. http://sharedhope .org/wp-content/uploads/2016/03/NSL_Survey_Mandatory-Restitution_Civil -Remedies.pdf.

Shared Hope International, ECPAT-USA, and The Protection Project of the Johns Hopkins University School of Advanced International Studies. *U.S. Mid-Term Review on the Commercial Exploitation of Children in America*. Arlington, VA: Shared Hope International, 2006. https://sharedhope.org/wp-content/uploads/PIC/US _MTR_of_CSEC.pdf.

Shaw, Jon A., John E. Lewis, Harvey A. Chitiva, and Andrew R. Pangilinan. "Adolescent Victims of Commercial Sexual Exploitation versus Sexually Abused Adolescents." *Journal of the American Academy of Psychiatry and the Law* 45 (2017): 325-31.

Shen, Anqi. "Female Perpetrators in Internal Child Trafficking in China: An Empirical Study." *Journal of Human Trafficking* 2, no. 1 (2016): 63-77. https://doi.org/10.1080 /23322705.2016.1136537.

Sidner, Sarah. "Old Mark of Slavery Is Being Used on Sex Trafficking Victims." CNN, 14 March 2017. http://www.cnn.com/2015/08/31/us/sex-trafficking-branding /index.html.

Siegel, Michael, and Lynne Doner Lotenberg. *Marketing Public Health: Strategies to Promote Social Change*. 2nd ed. Sudbury, MA: Jones & Bartlett, 1998.

Silbert, Mimi H., and Ayala M. Pines. "Sexual Child Abuse as an Antecedent to Prostitution." *Child Abuse & Neglect* 5, no. 4 (1981): 407-11. https://doi.org/10 .1016/0145-2134(81)90050-8.

———. "Victimization of Street Prostitutes." *Victimology* 7 (1982): 122-33.

Silverman, Jay G., Michele R. Decker, Jhumka Gupta, Ayonija Maheshwari, George R. Seage, and Anita Raj. "Syphilis and Hepatitis B Co-infection among HIV-Infected, Sex-Trafficked Women and Girls, Nepal." *Emerging Infectious Diseases* 14, no. 6 (2008): 932-34. https://doi.org/10.3201/eid1406.080090.

Silverman, Jay G., Michele R. Decker, Jhumka Gupta, Ayonija Maheshwari, Brian M. Willis, and Anita Raj. "HIV Prevalence and Predictors of Infection in Sex-Trafficked Nepalese Girls and Women." *Journal of the American Medical Association* 298, no. 5 (2007): 536-42. https://doi.org/10.1001/jama.298.5.536.

Smink, Jay. "Mentoring: An Effective Strategy for Youth Development." In *Helping Students Graduate: A Strategic Approach to Dropout Prevention*, edited by Jay Smink and Franklin P. Schargel, 139-53. New York: Routledge, 2013.

Smith, Bryan, Gary Bell, Getty Images, and Diana Emmanuelli. "The Mankiller Lurking in the Ocean That Should Terrify You More Than Sharks." *Men's Health*, 13 April 2015. https://www.menshealth.com/trending-news/a19537424/death-by -jellyfish/.

Smith, Linda, and Samantha H. Vardaman. "A Legislative Framework for Combating Domestic Minor Sex Trafficking." *Regent University Law Review* 23 (2011): 265-96.

Snyder, Leslie B., Mark A. Hamilton, Elizabeth W. Mitchell, James Kiwanuka-Tondo, Fran Fleming-Melici, and Dwayne Proctor. "A Meta-Analysis of the Effect of

Mediated Health Communication Campaigns on Behavior Change in the United States." *Journal of Health Communication* 9, no. S1 (2004): S71–96. https://doi.org /10.1080/10810730490271548.

Soohoo, Cynthia. *Criminalization of Trafficking Victims*. New York: International Women's Human Rights Clinic, April–May 2015. http://www.law.cuny.edu /academics/clinics/iwhr/publications/Criminalization-of-Trafficking-Victims.pdf.

Soroptimist International of the Americas. *Designing a Club Mentoring Program for Girls*. Philadelphia: Soroptimist International of the Americas, December 2004. http://www.soroptimist.org/members/program/ProgramDocs/ModelProgram Kits/Mentoring1204.pdf (site discontinued).

Southern Poverty Law Center. "$20 Million Settlement Agreement Reached in Labor Trafficking Cases Coordinated by SPLC on Behalf of Exploited Indian Guest Workers." 13 July 2015. https://www.splcenter.org/news/2015/07/14/20-million -settlement-agreement-reached-labor-trafficking-cases-coordinated-splc-behalf.

Spires, Robert W. *Preventing Human Trafficking: Education and NGOs in Thailand*. New York: Routledge, 2016.

Starks, Victoria. "The U.S. Government's Recent Initiatives to Prevent Contractors from Engaging in Trafficking in Person: Analysis of Federal Acquisition Regulation Subpart 22.17." *Public Contract Law Journal* 37 (2008): 879–903.

Stoklosa, Hanni. *Background Paper for Exploring the Development of a U.S. Department of Labor Research Strategy on Child Labor and Forced Labor in International Settings: A Workshop*. Washington DC: National Academies of Sciences, Engineering, and Medicine, 2016. http://nationalacademies.org/hmd/~/media/Files/Activity%20 Files/Global/ViolenceForum/2016-OCT-18/Background%20Paper.pdf.

Stoklosa, Hanni, Aimee Grace, and Nicole Littenberg. "Medical Education on Human Trafficking." *AMA Journal of Ethics* 15, no. 10 (October 2015): 914–21. http://journalofethics.ama-assn.org/2015/10/medu1-1510.html.

Stoltz, Jo-Anne M., Kate Shannon, Thomas Kerr, Ruth Zhang, Julio S. Montaner, and Evan Wood. "Associations between Childhood Maltreatment and Sex Work in a Cohort of Drug-Using Youth." *Social Science and Medicine* 65, no. 6 (2007): 1214–21. https://doi.org/10.1016/j.socscimed.2007.05.005.

Stoto, Michael A. "Public Health Surveillance in the Twenty-First Century: Achieving Population Health Goals While Protecting Individuals' Privacy and Confidentiality." *Georgetown Law Journal* 96 (2008): 703–19.

Strand, Virginia C., Teresa L. Sarmiento, and Lina E. Pasquale. "Assessment and Screening Tools for Trauma in Children and Adolescents: A Review." *Trauma, Violence, & Abuse* 6, no. 1 (2005): 55–78. https://doi.org/10.1177/1524838004272559.

Stransky, Michelle, and David Finkelhor. *How Many Juveniles Are Involved in Prostitution in the U.S.?* Durham, NH: Crimes Against Children Research Center, 2008.

Stratford, Dale, Tedd V. Ellerbrock, J. Keith Akins, and Heather L. Hall. "Highway Cowboys, Old Hands, and Christian Truckers: Risk Behavior for Human Immunodeficiency Virus Infection among Long-haul Truckers in Florida." *Social Science and Medicine* 50, no. 5 (2000): 737–49.

Stuber, Jennifer, Sandro Galea, and Bruce G. Link. "Smoking and the Emergence of a Stigmatized Social Status." *Social Science and Medicine* 67, no. 3 (2008): 420–30. https://doi.org/10.1016/j.socscimed.2008.03.010.

Substance Abuse and Mental Health Service Administration. "Trauma-Informed Approach and Trauma-Specific Interventions." Last modified 27 April 2018. http://www.samhsa.gov/nctic/trauma-interventions.

Surko, Michael, Ken Peake, Irwin Epstein, and Daniel Medeiros. "Multiple Risks, Multiple Worries, and Adolescent Coping: What Clinicians Need to Ask About." *Social Work in Mental Health* 3, no. 3 (2005): 261–85. https://doi.org/10.1300/J200v03n03_03.

Surtees, Rebecca. "Traffickers and Trafficking in Southern and Eastern Europe: Considering the Other Side of Human Trafficking." *European Journal of Criminology* 5, no. 1 (2008): 39–68. https://doi.org/10.1177/1477370807084224.

Surtees, Rebecca, and Sarah Craggs. *Beneath the Surface: Methodological Issues in Research and Data Collection with Assisted Trafficking Victims*. Geneva: International Organization for Migration and the NEXUS Institute, 2010. http://publications.iom.int/system/files/pdf/beneath_the_surface.pdf.

Taddeo, Danielle, Maud Egedy, and Jean-Yves Frappier. "Adherence to Treatment in Adolescents." *Paediatrics & Child Health* 13, no. 1 (2008): 19–24.

Task Force on Trafficking of Women and Girls. *Report of the Task Force on Trafficking of Women and Girls*. Washington, DC: American Psychological Association, 2014. http://www.apa.org/pi/women/programs/trafficking/report.aspx.

Tervalon, Melanie, and Jann Murray-Garcia. "Cultural Humility versus Cultural Competence: A Critical Distinction in Defining Physician Training Outcomes in Multicultural Education." *Journal of Health Care of the Poor and Underserved* 9, no. 2 (1998): 117–25. https://doi.org/10.1353/hpu.2010.0233.

Texas Human Trafficking Prevention Task Force. *Introduction to Human Trafficking: A Guide for Texas Education Professionals*. July 2014. https://humantraffickinghotline.org/sites/default/files/Intro%20to%20HT%20for%20Educational%20Professionals%20-%20TX%20Dept%20of%20Ed.pdf.

TheCode.Org. "Members of the Code." http://www.thecode.org/who-have-signed/.

Tierney, Joseph P., Jean Baldwin Grossman, and Nancy Resch. *Making a Difference: An Impact Study of Big Brothers Big Sisters*. Public/Private Ventures. September 2000. https://www.issuelab.org/resources/11972/11972.pdf.

Todres, Jonathan. "Assessing Public Health Strategies for Advancing Child Protection: Human Trafficking as a Case Study." *Journal of Law and Policy* 21 (2013): 93–112.

———. "Can Mandatory Reporting Laws Help Child Survivors of Human Trafficking?" *Wisconsin Law Review Forward*, 2016, 69–78.

———. "A Child Rights Framework for Addressing Trafficking of Children." *Michigan State International Law Review* 22, no. 2 (2013): 557–93.

———. "Human Rights, Labor, and the Prevention of Human Trafficking: A Response to *A Labor Paradigm for Human Trafficking*." *UCLA Law Review Discourse* 60 (2013): 142–58.

———. "Human Trafficking and Film: How Popular Portrayals Influence Law and Public Perception." *Cornell Law Review Online* 101 (2015): 1–24.

———. "The Importance of Realizing 'Other' Rights to Prevent Sex Trafficking." *Cardozo Journal of Law and Gender* 12 (2006): 885–907.

———. "Law, Otherness, and Human Trafficking." *Santa Clara Law Review* 49 (2009): 605–72.

———. "Mainstreaming Children's Rights in Post-Disaster Settings." *Emory International Law Review* 25 (2011): 1233–61.

———. "Moving Upstream: The Merits of a Public Health Law Approach to Human Trafficking." *North Carolina Law Review* 89, no. 2 (2011): 447–506.

———. "The Private Sector's Pivotal Role in Combating Human Trafficking." *California Law Review Circuit* 3 (2012): 80–98.

———. "Taking Prevention Seriously: Developing a Comprehensive Response to Child Trafficking and Sexual Exploitation." *Vanderbilt Journal of Transnational Law* 43, no. 1 (2010): 1–56.

———. "Widening Our Lens: Incorporating Essential Perspectives in the Fight against Human Trafficking." *Michigan Journal of International Law* 33 (2011): 53–76.

Todres, Jonathan, and Leslie E. Wolf. "The Complexities of Conducting Research on Child Trafficking." *JAMA Pediatrics* 171, no. 1 (2017): 9–10.

Tomasiewicz, Meaghan L. *Sex Trafficking of Transgender and Gender Nonconforming Youth in the United States.* Chicago: Loyola University, May 2018. https://ecommons.luc.edu/chrc/16/.

Toney-Butler, Tammy J., and Olivia Mittel. *Human Trafficking.* Treasure Island, FL: StatPearls. Last updated 1 June 2018. https://www.ncbi.nlm.nih.gov/books/NBK 430910/.

Tonmyr, Lil, and Wendy Hovdestad. "Public Health Approach to Child Maltreatment." *Paediatrics & Child Health* 18, no. 8 (2013): 411–13.

Tourtchaninova, Maria, and Minouche Kandel. *Mayor's Task Force on Anti-Human Trafficking: Human Trafficking in San Francisco Report.* San Francisco, CA: City and County of San Francisco Department on the Status of Women, 8 November 2018. https://sfgov.org/dosw/sites/default/files/2016%20Human% 20Trafficking%20 in%20San%20Francisco%20Report_2.pdf.

Tracy, Erin E., and Wendy Macias-Konstantopoulos. "Identifying and Assisting Sexually Exploited and Trafficked Patients Seeking Women's Health Care Services." *Obstetrics & Gynecology* 130, no. 2 (2017): 443–53. https://doi.org/10.1097 /AOG.0000000000002144.

Trickett, Penelope, Frank Putnam, and Jennie Noll. *Longitudinal Study on Childhood Sexual Abuse Summary.* PTSD Association of Canada. August 2005. http://www .ptsdassociation.com/longitudinal/2015/7/15/longitudinal-study-on-childhood -sexual-abuse.

Tripp, Tara M., and Jennifer McMahon-Howard. "Perception vs. Reality: The Relationship between Organized Crime and Human Trafficking in Metropolitan Atlanta." *American Journal of Criminal Justice* 41 (2016): 732–64. https://doi.org /10.1007/s12103-015-9315-5.

Truckers Against Trafficking. "Labor Trafficking: Spotting Labor Trafficking Out on the Road." Accessed 13 September 2018. http://truckersagainsttrafficking.org /labor-trafficking/.

Turner-Moss, Eleanor, Cathy Zimmerman, Louise M. Howard, and Siân Oram. "Labour Exploitation and Health: A Case Series of Men and Women Seeking Post-Trafficking Services." *Journal of Immigrant and Minority Health* 16, no. 3 (2014): 473–80. https://doi.org/10.1007/s10903-013-9832-6.

Twis, Mary K., and Beth Anne Shelton. "Systematic Review of Empiricism and Theory in Domestic Minor Sex Trafficking Research." *Journal of Evidence-Informed Social Work* 15, no. 4 (2018): 432–56.

UNICEF Innocenti Research Centre. *Child Trafficking in Europe: A Broad Vision to Put Children First*, Florence: UNICEF Innocenti Research Centre, 2008.

United Nations. "Background Paper of the Secretary-General." In *Improving the Coordination of Efforts Against Trafficking in Persons*. 29 April 2009. http://www.un.org /ga/president/63/letters/SGbackgroundpaper.pdf.

United Nations Children's Fund (UNICEF). "Children with Disabilities." Our Priorities. Accessed 31 July 2018. http://www.unicef.cn/en/child-protection /children-with-disabilities/.

———. *Reversing the Trend: Child Trafficking in East and South-East Asia*. Bangkok: UNICEF East Asia and Pacific Regional Office, August 2009. https://www.unicef .org/protection/Unicef_EA_SEA_Trafficking_Report_Aug_2009_low_res.pdf.

UN Commission on Human Rights. "Integration of the Human Rights of Women and the Gender Perspective: Violence Against Women Rep. of the Special Rapporteur on Violence Against Women, Its Causes and Consequences." UN Doc. E/CN.4/ 2000/68. 29 February 2000.

UN Convention on the Rights of the Child. UN General Assembly Resolution 44/25. UN Doc. A/RES/44/25 (1989).

UN General Assembly. "Report of the Economic & Social Council for 1997." 18 September 1997. UN Doc. A/53/2. http://www.un.org/documents/ga/docs/52 /plenary/a52-3.htm.

UN Global Initiative to Fight Human Trafficking. *Human Trafficking and Business: Good Practices to Prevent and Combat Human Trafficking*. 2010. https://www.ilo .org/wcmsp5/groups/public/---ed_norm/---declaration/documents/publication /wcms_142722.pdf.

UN Inter-Agency Project on Human Trafficking. *Targeting Endemic Vulnerability Factors to Human Trafficking*. Bangkok: United Nations, 21 December 2007. http:// un-act.org/publication/view/siren-gms-02-targeting-endemic-vulnerability -factors-human-trafficking/.

UN Office for the Coordination of Humanitarian Affairs. "Case Studies." *Ending Protracted Internal Displacement*. Accessed 17 August 2018. https://www.unocha .org/ending-protracted-internal-displacement/case-studies.

UN Office on Drugs and Crime. *Anti-Human Trafficking Manual for Criminal Justice Practitioners*. New York: United Nations, 2009. https://www.unodc.org/docu ments/human-trafficking/TIP_module4_Ebook.pdf.

———. *Global Report on Trafficking in Persons*. Vienna: UN Office on Drugs and Crime, February 2009. https://www.unodc.org/documents/Global_Report_on_TIP.pdf.

———. *Global Report on Trafficking in Persons 2014*. Vienna: United Nations, November 2014. http://www.unodc.org/res/cld/bibliography/global-report-on-trafficking -in-persons_html/GLOTIP_2014_full_report.pdf.

———. *Human Trafficking Indicators*. Accessed 19 June 2018. https://ec.europa.eu /anti-trafficking/sites/antitrafficking/files/unodc_indicators_en_1.pdf.

———. *The Role of Recruitment Fees and Abusive and Fraudulent Recruitment Practices of Recruitment Agencies in Trafficking in Persons.* Vienna: UN Office on Drugs and Crime, 2015. https://www.unodc.org/documents/human-trafficking/2015 /Recruitment_Fees_Report-Final-22_June_2015_AG_Final.pdf.

———. *Toolkit to Combat Trafficking in Persons: New York: United Nations.* Vienna: United Nations, 2008. https://www.unodc.org/documents/human-trafficking /HT_Toolkit08_English.pdf.

———. "UNODC Launches Global Initiative to Fight Human Trafficking." 26 March 2007. http://www.unodc.org/unodc/en/press/releases/2007-03-26.html.

UN Treaty Collection. "Status of Ratifications: Optional Protocol to the Convention on the Rights of the Child on the Sale of Children, Child Prostitution and Child Pornography." Human Rights. Accessed 8 August 2018. https://treaties.un.org /Pages/ViewDetails.aspx?src=TREATY&mtdsg_no=IV-11-c&chapter=4& clang=_en.

———. "Status of Ratifications: Protocol to Prevent, Suppress and Punish Trafficking in Persons, Especially Women and Children, supplementing the United Nations Convention against Transnational Organized Crime." Penal Matters. Accessed 8 August 2018. https://treaties.un.org/pages/ViewDetails.aspx? src=TREATY &mtdsg_no=XVIII-12-a&chapter=18&clang=_en.

Upadhyay, Shraddha. "Human Trafficking: Focused on Trafficking in Child." *Indian Social Science Journal* 4, no. 2 (2015): 43–56.

US Department of Education. *Human Trafficking of Children in the United States: A Fact Sheet for Schools.* Washington, DC: Office of Safe and Healthy Students, 2012. http://rems.ed.gov/docs/ED_HumanTrafficking_FactSheet.pdf.

US Department of Health and Human Services. *Coordination, Collaboration, Capacity: Federal Strategic Action Plan on Services for Victims of Human Trafficking in the United States 2013-2017.* Washington DC: Department of Justice, Health and Human Services, and Homeland Security, January 2014. https://www.ovc.gov /pubs/FederalHumanTraffickingStrategicPlan.pdf.

———. *Fact Sheet: Labor Trafficking.* Administration for Children and Families. 6 August 2012. http://www.acf.hhs.gov/programs/orr/resource/fact-sheet-labor -trafficking-english.

———. *Guidance to States and Services on Addressing Human Trafficking of Children and Youth in the United States.* Administration for Children, Youth and Families. Accessed 16 April 2018. https://www.acf.hhs.gov/sites/default/files/cb/acyf _human_trafficking_guidance.pdf.

———. *Resources: Health Care Provider Brochure.* Administration for Children and Families. Accessed 23 July 2012. https://www.acf.hhs.gov/sites/default/files/orr /health_care_provider_brochure.pdf.

———. *School-Based Obesity Prevention Strategies for State Policymakers.* Division of Adolescent and School Health, National Center for Chronic Disease Prevention and Health Promotion, and Centers for Disease Control and Prevention. Accessed 27 August 2018. http://www.cdc.gov/healthyYouth/policy/pdf/obesity_prevention _strategies.pdf.

———. *Services Available to Victims of Human Trafficking: A Resource Guide for Social Service Providers.* The Campaign to Rescue & Restore Victims of Human Trafficking. 2012. https://www.acf.hhs.gov/sites/default/files/orr/traffickingservices_0.pdf.

———. *Surgeon General's Call to Action to Prevent & Decrease Overweight & Obesity.* Rockville, MD: GPO, 2001.

———. "Trauma-Informed Practice." Child Welfare Information Gateway. Accessed 27 August 2018. https://www.childwelfare.gov/topics/responding/trauma/.

US Department of Justice. *Facts about the Department of Justice's Anti-Trafficking Efforts.* July 2008. http://www.justice.gov/olp/pdf/myths-and-facts.pdf (site discontinued).

———. *The National Strategy for Child Exploitation Prevention and Interdiction: A Report to Congress.* April 2016. https://www.justice.gov/psc/file/842411/download.

———. *National Strategy to Combat Human Trafficking.* January 2017. https://www .justice.gov/humantrafficking/page/file/922791/download.

———. *OJJDP FY 2017 Internet Crimes Against Children Task Force Program Support.* Office of Juvenile Justice and Delinquency Protection. 2017. https://www.ojjdp .gov/grants/solicitations/FY2017/ICACProgramSupport.pdf.

———. *Report of the Attorney General's National Task Force on Children Exposed to Violence.* Washington, DC: US Department of Justice, 2012. https://www.justice .gov/defendingchildhood/cev-rpt-full.pdf.

US Department of Labor. "New Research and App to Combat Child Labor and Modern Slavery." 20 September 2017. https://www.dol.gov/newsroom/releases /ilab/ilab20170920.

US Department of State. *Assisting Male Survivors of Human Trafficking.* June 2017. https://www.state.gov/documents/organization/272323.pdf.

———. "Global Law Enforcement Data." Office to Monitor and Combat Trafficking in Persons. Accessed 27 August 2018. https://www.state.gov/j/tip/rls/tiprpt/2016 /258694.htm.

———. "Identify and Assist a Human Trafficking Victim." Office to Monitor and Combat Trafficking in Persons. Accessed 27 August 2018. https://www.state.gov /j/tip/id/.

———. *Trafficking in Persons Report 2010.* Washington, DC: US Department of State, 2010. https://www.state.gov/documents/organization/142979.pdf.

———. *Trafficking in Persons Report 2011.* Washington, DC: US Department of State, 2011. https://www.state.gov/documents/organization/164452.pdf.

———. *Trafficking in Persons Report 2012.* Washington, DC: US Department of State, 2012. https://www.state.gov/documents/organization/192587.pdf.

———. *Trafficking in Persons Report 2016.* Washington, DC: US. Department of State, 2016. https://www.state.gov/documents/organization/258876.pdf.

———. *Trafficking in Persons Report 2017.* Washington, DC: US Department of State, 2017. https://www.state.gov/documents/organization/271339.pdf.

———. *U.S. Government Entities Combating Human Trafficking.* Washington, DC: Office to Monitor and Combat Human Trafficking, June 2017. https://www.state.gov/j /tip/rls/fs/2017/272160.htm.

US Department of Transportation. *DOT Trains Employees on Human Trafficking Awareness.* 30 March 2017. https://www.transportation.gov/stophumantrafficking.

US Government Accountability Office. *Human Trafficking: A Strategic Framework Could Help Enhance the Interagency Collaboration Needed to Effectively Combat Trafficking Crimes.* Washington, DC: GAO, July 2007. http://www.gao.gov/new

.items/d07915.pdf.University of Kansas Anti-Slavery and Human Trafficking Initiative. "Research: The ASHTI Prevention Strategies Model." Accessed 27 August 2018. http://ipsr.ku.edu/ASHTI/model.html.

Valera, Roberto, Robert G. Sawyer, and Glenn R. Schiraldi. "Perceived Health Needs of Inner-City Street Prostitutes: A Preliminary Study." *American Journal of Health Behavior* 25, no. 1 (2001): 50–59.

Van Bueren, Geraldine. *The International Law on the Rights of the Child*. The Hague: Kluwer Law International, 1995.

Vasudevan, Vinod, Shashi S. Nambisan, Ashok K. Singh, and Traci Pearl. "Effectiveness of Media and Enforcement Campaigns in Increasing Seat Belt Usage Rates in a State with a Secondary Seat Belt Law." *Traffic Injury Prevention* 10, no. 4 (2009): 330–39. https://doi.org/10.1080/15389580902995190.

Verité. *Help Wanted: Hiring, Human Trafficking and Modern-Day Slavery in the Global Economy*. Amherst, MA: Verité, 2016. https://www.verite.org/wp-content/uploads /2016/11/Help_Wanted_2010.pdf.

———. *Tool 2: Understand the Role of Labor Brokers in the Human Trafficking and Forced Labor of Migrant Workers*. Amherst, MA: Verité, 2011. http://digitalcommons.ilr .cornell.edu/cgi/viewcontent.cgi?article=2235&context=globaldocs.

———. *Why Modern Slavery Persists in Global Supply Chains*. Accessed 20 August 2018. https://www.verite.org/why-modern-slavery-persists-in-global-supply-chains/.

Veugelers, Paul J., and Angela L. Fitzgerald. "Effectiveness of School Programs in Preventing Childhood Obesity: A Multilevel Comparison." *American Journal of Public Health* 95, no. 3 (2005): 432–35. https://doi.org/10.2105/AJPH.2004.045898.

Viuhko, Minna. "Hardened Professional Criminals, or Just Friends and Relatives? The Diversity of Offenders in Human Trafficking." *International Journal of Comparative and Applied Criminal Justice* 42, no. 2–3 (2018): 177–93. https://doi.org /10.1080/01924036.2017.1391106.

Wagle, Udaya. "The Policy Science of Democracy: The Issues of Methodology and Citizen Participation." *Policy Sciences* 33, no. 2 (2000): 207–23.

Wagner, Lisa, Linda Carlin, Ana Cauce, and Adam Tenner. "A Snapshot of Homeless Youth in Seattle: Their Characteristics, Behaviors and Beliefs about HIV Protective Strategies." *Journal of Community Health* 26, no. 3 (2001): 219–32.

Walden, Inara, and Liz Wall. *Reflecting on the Primary Prevention of Violence against Women*. Melbourne: Australian Institute of Families Studies and Australian Center for the Study of Sexual Assault, 2014. https://aifs.gov.au/sites/default/files /publication-documents/i19.pdf.

Walters, Jennifer H., Kathleen Krieger, Marianne Kluckman, Rose Feinberg, Steve Orme, Nakisa Asefnia, and Deborah Gibbs. *Evaluation of Domestic Victims of Human Trafficking Demonstration Projects*. Research Triangle Park, NC: RTI International, August 2017. https://www.acf.hhs.gov/sites/default/files/opre /sc1_final_report_508_compliantb.pdf.

Weinred, Linda, Kenneth Fletcher, Lucy Candib, and Gonzalo Bacigalupe. "Physicians' Perceptions of Adult Patients' History of Child Abuse in Family Medicine Settings." *Journal of the American Board of Family Medicine* 20, no. 4 (2007): 417–19. https://doi.org/10.3122/jabfm.2007.04.060208.

Weitzer, Ronald. "New Directions in Research on Human Trafficking." *Annals of the*

American Academy of Political and Social Science 653 (May 2014): 6–24. https://doi.org/10.1177/0002716214521562.

Welsh, Brandon C. "Public Health and the Prevention of Juvenile Criminal Violence." Youth Violence & Juvenile Justice 3, no. 1 (2005): 23–40. https://doi.org/10.1177/1541204004270911.

Wickrama, K. A. S., Rand D. Conger, Lori E. Wallace, and Glen H. Elder Jr. "Linking Early Risks to Impaired Physical Health of Young Adults: A Perspective on the Transition to Adulthood." Journal of Health and Social Behavior 44 (2003): 61–74.

Wickrama, Thulitha, K. A. S. Wickrama, and Diana L. Baltimore. "Adolescent Precocious Development and Young Adult Health Outcomes." Advances in Life Course Research 15, no. 4 (2010): 121–31. https://doi.org/10.1016/j.alcr.2010.08.003.

Williamson, Erin, Heather J. Clawson, and Catherine Chen. Where Is the Research on Human Trafficking and the Evaluation of Anti-Trafficking Efforts? Fairfax, VA: ICF International, 2008. http://www.icfi.com/Docs/research-human-trafficking.pdf (site discontinued).

Williamson, Erin, Nicole M. Dutch, and Heather. J. Clawson. Evidence-Based Mental Health Treatment for Victims of Human Trafficking. Washington, DC: US Department of Health and Human Services, Office of the Assistant Secretary for Planning and Evaluation, 2010. https://aspe.hhs.gov/basic-report/evidence-based-mental-health-treatment-victims-human-trafficking.

Willis, Brian M., and Barry S. Levy. "Child Prostitution: Global Health Burden, Research Needs, and Interventions." Lancet 359 (2002): 1417–22. https://doi.org/10.1016/S0140-6736(02)08355-1.

Wing, Kenneth R., Wendy K. Mariner, George J. Annas, and Daniel S. Strouse. Public Health Law. Newark, NJ: LexisNexis, 2007.

Wisdom, Jennifer P., Gregory N. Clarke, and Clark A. Green. "What Teens Want: Barriers to Seeking Care for Depression." Administration and Policy in Mental Health and Mental Health Services Research 33, no. 2 (2006): 133–45. https://doi.org/10.1007/s10488-006-0036-4.

Witte, Kim, and Mike Allen. "A Meta-Analysis of Fear Appeals: Implications for Effective Public Health Campaigns." Health Education and Behavior 27, no. 2 (2000): 591–615. https://doi.org/10.1177/109019810002700506.

Wolf, Joan B. "Is Breast Really Best? Risk and Total Motherhood in the National Breastfeeding Awareness Campaign." Journal of Health Politics, Policy and Law 32, no. 4 (2007): 595–636. https://doi.org/10.1215/03616878-2007-018.

Wolfteich, Paula, and Brittany Loggins. "Evaluation of the Children's Advocacy Center Model: Efficiency, Legal and Revictimization Outcomes." Child and Adolescent Social Work Journal 24, no. 4 (2007): 333–52. https://doi.org/10.1007/s10560-007-0087-8.

Wong, J. C., Leung P. Hong, and Stewart P. Yin. "Human Trafficking: An Evaluation of Canadian Medical Students Awareness and Attitudes." Education for Health 24, no. (2011): 2059–71.

World Health Assembly. Prevention of Violence: Public Health Priority. Geneva: World Health Organization, 1996. http://apps.who.int/iris/handle/10665/179463.

World Health Organization. "Childhood Maltreatment." WHO News, 30 September 2016. http://www.who.int/news-room/fact-sheets/detail/child-maltreatment.

————. *Integrated Health Services: What and Why?* Technical Brief no. 1 (2008). http://
www.who.int/healthsystems/service_delivery_techbrief1.pdf.

————. *Making Health Services Adolescent Friendly: Developing National Quality Standards for Adolescent Friendly Health Services.* Geneva: WHO, 2012. http://apps.who
.int/iris/bitstream/10665/75217/1/9789241503594_eng.pdf.

————. "The Public Health Approach." Violence Prevention Alliance. 2018. http://
www.who.int/violenceprevention/approach/public_health/en/.

————. *Report of the International Consultation, 29–30 October 2008, Lyon, France:
Cities and Public Health Crises.* Lyon: WHO, 2009. http://www.who.int/ihr/lyon
/FRWHO_HSE_IHR_LYON_2009.5.pdf.

————. "What Are the Health Risks Related to Overcrowding?" Water Sanitation
Hygiene. Accessed 14 November 2017. http://www.who.int/water_sanitation
_health/emergencies/qa/emergencies_qa9/en/.

————. *World Health Statistics: Monitoring Health for the Sustainable Development Goals.*
Geneva: WHO, 2017. http://apps.who.int/iris/bitstream/handle/10665/255336
/9789241565486-eng.pdf;jsessionid=DCE03FEA10585D3DD3BE12D6088B9
A13?sequence=1.

Wright, Ellie, and Jon Ord. "Youth Work and the Power of 'Giving Voice': A Reframing
of Mental Health Services for Young People." *Youth & Policy* 115 (2015): 63–84.

Wulfhorst, Ellen. "Human Traffickers Preying More on Children, Men, Laborers:
Global Study." 21 December 2016. Reuters. https://www.reuters.com/article
/us-un-trafficking-victims-idUSKBN14A1IP?il=0.

Yates, Gary L., Richard G. MacKenzie, Julia Pennbridge, and Avon Swofford. "A Risk
Profile Comparison of Homeless Youth Involved in Prostitution and Homeless
Youth Not Involved." *Journal of Adolescent Health* 12, no. 7 (1991): 545–48.

Zablocki, Mark, and Michael P. Krezmien. "Drop-Out Predictors among Students
with High-Incidence Disabilities: A National Longitudinal and Transitional Study
2 Analysis." *Journal of Disability Policy Studies* 24, no. 1 (2012): 53–64. https://doi
.org/10.1177/1044207311427726.

Zerk, Danielle M., Peter G. Mertin, and Michael Proeve. "Domestic Violence and
Maternal Reports of Young Children's Functioning." *Journal of Family Violence* 24,
no. 7 (2009): 423–32. https://doi.org/10.1007/s10896-009-9237-4.

Zhang, Sheldon X., Michael W. Spiller, Brian Karl Finch, and Yang Qin. "Estimating
Labor Trafficking among Unauthorized Migrant Workers in San Diego." *Annals of
the American Academy of Political and Social Science* 653 (2014): 65–86. https://doi
.org/10.1177/0002716213519237.

Zimmerman, Cathy, and Rosilyne Borland, eds. *Caring for Trafficked Persons: Guidance for Health Providers.* Geneva: International Organization for Migration, 2009.
http://publications.iom.int/system/files/pdf/ct_handbook.pdf.

Zimmerman, Cathy, Mazeda Hossain, and Charlotte Watts. "Human Trafficking
and Health: A Conceptual Model to Informal Policy, Intervention and Research."
*Social Science & Medicine* 73, no. 2 (2011): 327–35. https://doi.org/10.1016/j
.socscimed.2011.05.028.

Zimmerman, Cathy, Mazeda Hossain, Katherine Yun, Vasil Gajdadziev, Natalia
Guzun, Maria Tchomarova, and Rosa Angela Ciarrocchi. "The Health of Trafficked Women: A Survey of Women Entering Posttrafficking Services in Europe."

*American Journal of Public Health* 98, no. 1 (2008): 55–59. https://doi.org/10.2105
/AJPH.2006.108357.

Zimmerman, Cathy, Mazeda Hossain, Katherine Yun, Brenda Roche, Linda Morrison, and Charlotte Watts. *Stolen Smiles: A Summary Report on the Physical and Psychological Health Consequences of Women and Adolescents Trafficked in Europe.* London: London School of Hygiene & Tropical Medicine, 2006. https://www.icmec.org /wp-content/uploads/2015/10/Stolen-Smiles-Physical-and-Psych-Consequences -of-Traffic-Victims-in-Europe-Zimmerman.pdf.

Zimmerman, Cathy, and Ligia Kiss. "Human Trafficking and Exploitation: A Global Health Concern." *PLOS Medicine* 14, no. 11 (2017): e1002437. https://doi.org/10 .1371/journal.pmed.1002437.

Zimmerman, Cathy, Lori Michau, Mazeda Hossain, Ligia Kiss, Rosalyne Borland, and Charlotte Watts. "Rigged or Rigorous? Partnerships for Research and Evaluation of Complex Social Problems: Lessons from the Field of Violence against Women and Girls." *Journal of Public Health Policy* 37, no. 1 (2016): 95–109. https://doi.org /10.1057/s41271-016-0006-3.

Zimmerman, Cathy, and Charlotte Watts. "Documenting the Effects of Trafficking in Women." In *Public Health and Human Rights: Evidence-Based Approaches*, edited by Chris Beyrer and Hank Pizer, 143–76. Baltimore: Johns Hopkins University Press, 2007.

Zimmerman, Cathy, Katherine Yun, Inna Shvab, Charlotte Watts, Luca Trappolin, Mariangela Treppete, Franca Bimbi, Brad Adams, Sae-tang Jiriporn, Ledia Beci, Marcia Albrecht, Julie Bindel, and Linda Regan. *The Health Risks and Consequences of Trafficking in Women and Adolescents: Findings from a European Study.* London: London School of Hygiene & Tropical Medicine, 2003. https://www.icmec.org /wp-content/uploads/2015/10/Health-Risks-and-Consequences-of-Traffic-in -Europe-Zimmerman-2003.pdf.

Zong, Jie, Jeanne Batalova, and Jeffrey Hallock. "Frequently Requested Statistics on Immigrants and Immigration in the United States." Migration Policy Institute. 8 February 2018. http://www.migrationpolicy.org/article/frequently-requested -statistics-immigrants-and-immigration-united-states#Unauthorized%20 Immigration.

Page numbers in *italics* refer to figures and tables.

clinicians. *See* medical personnel

Clinton, Bill, 59

community-level risk factors, 93–94, 131–32

community participation in prevention efforts, 104

compassion fatigue, 192

complex PTSD, 47

comprehensive responses: education for, 210–12; as ensuring integration, 209–10; as involving all sectors, 207–9; sustained commitment to, 212–15

*Confronting Commercial Sexual Exploitation and Sex Trafficking of Minors in the United States* report, 190

consequences of child maltreatment, 121

consequences of trafficking: developmental, 49–50, 51, 145; educational, 39–40, 50–51, 132–33; financial, 51–52; housing, 52–54; intimate partner violence, 49; legal, 39–40, 55–56; overview of, 57; to physical health, 6–7, 40–44, 175–76, 179; to psychological and mental health, 7, 43–44, 46–48, 117, 175–76, 179; to sexual and reproductive health, 7, 44–46, 108; as significant and lasting, 38–39; substance abuse, 48–49

coordination of efforts between stakeholders, 106–7, 186, 203–4, 205, 209–10. *See also* partnerships

Courtney's House, 174

Crenshaw, Kimberlé, 128. *See also* intersectionality

crime of human trafficking: elements of, 5–6, 26–27; hidden nature of, 21–22. *See also* public health approach

criminalization of youth, 55–56, 71–72, 126

criminal justice framework, 60, 75–77, 248n4

cultural norms, 133–34

data collection: building system of, 86–87; on organizations in cities, 205; quality of, 20–21, 25; of sensitive data, 111

debt collectors, 31

definitional issues, 22–24, 26–27

definition of human trafficking, 5, 26–27

demand side of trafficking, 32–33, 35–36, 93–94, 98–99, 112–14

dental services, 185

deportation proceedings, 55

developmental issues, 49–50, 51, 145

direct services to victims, 66–67

disabilities, youth with, 124–25

discrimination: disability-based, 124; as risk factor, 133; as risk of public health campaigns, 108; against transgender youth, 123

diversion programs, 72

Dottridge, Mike, 105, 174

drivers of child trafficking, 35–36

ECPAT-USA, 75, 110

education: for at-risk children, 84–85, 92; for comprehensive, integrated response, 210–12; in social marketing and advertising campaigns, 99–100, 101–2

educational issues, 39–40, 50–51, 132–33

Education Department, *Human Trafficking of Children in the United States*, 70

emergency room personnel, 141, 189

emergency shelters, 53, 85, 173, 212–13

emotional health issues. *See* psychological and emotional health issues

empathy, 192

employment issues, 213

empowering youth, 149–50

enforcers, 31

engagement of youth, 144–45, 175

environmental hazard exposure, 42, 160

ethics: in public health approach, 215–17; in social marketing and advertising campaigns, 102

evaluation: of anti-trafficking programs, 66, 88; of child maltreatment, 140, 164–65, 182; importance of, 83–84; of public health practices, 86, 88–89; of responses, 75–76; of sex trafficking risk, 139; of social marketing and advertising campaigns, 102; of victim

identification training programs, 68–69; by youth, 144, 175
evidence-based responses, 83–90, 201–2
exit strategies, 186, 187
exploitation, trafficking as form of, 28–29

facilitators, 32–33
family: risk factors in, 129; therapy for, 186; trafficking by, 150–51
federal legal framework, 63–70
females: as at-risk for exploitation, 122; as recruiters, 84–85; sexualization and objectification of, 99, 134
financial issues, 51–52
financial support of state and local programs, 67
Finkelhor, David, 20–21
follow-up visits, 161–62
forced abortions, 45
forced labor, 23
forced marriages, 19–20
foster care system, 125
Freeman-Longo, Robert, 86, 98

gang involvement, 127
GEMS, 174, 216
gender: as risk factor, 122–23; of traffickers, 84–85; of victims, 85. *See also* females; male victims
globalization of trade and commerce, 28
Global Slavery Index, 22–23
governments: coordination of prevention efforts between public and, 106–7; criminalization of human trafficking and, 60–61
guides and crew members, 30
Guth, Andrew, 25

harm: as created by human beings, 102–3; efforts to address, 112–13; magnitude of, 21, 37; types of, 39–40. *See also* consequences of trafficking
Health and Human Services (HHS) Department: *Evidence-Based Mental Health Treatment for Victims of Human Trafficking,* 184; Federal Strategic Action Plan on Services for Victims of Human Trafficking in the United States, 54; Human Trafficking Data Collection Project, 87; Street Outreach Program, 69
health care services: barriers to access to, 43, 132; trauma-focused, 181, 183–84; trauma-informed, 180–81; youth-friendly, 177–80. *See also* health care system
health care system: barriers to identification in, 163–65; eligibility for, 74; holistic approach by, 145, 152, 162–63; identification in, 3–4, 136–39, 142–48; interactions with, 140–42; overview of, 1–5; training of staff in, 188–91. *See also* health care services; medical personnel
health consequences: physical, 6–7, 40–44, 175–76, 179; psychological and emotional, 7, 46–48, 175–76, 179; sexual and reproductive, 7, 44–46
Health Squad app, 161–62
HEAL Trafficking, 75
HHS. *See* Health and Human Services (HHS) Department
histories, taking: ending on positive note, 159; immigration status and, 159; labor trafficking and, 157–58; sex trafficking and, 158; standard, 152–53, *154–56,* 157; trauma experiences and, 182–83
HIV/AIDS, 45, 108
homeless youth: as at-risk, 53, 120–21, 123; connecting with services, 166; mentoring programs and, 93; stigma and, 133
homicide, 44
housing: case management and, 173–74; insecurity of, 52–54, 120–21; shelters, 53, 85, 173, 212–13. *See also* homeless youth
human trafficking: definitions of, 22–23, 24; elements of crime of, 5, 26–27; overview of, 2–3; reach of, 5–6; spectrum of, 29, 162; use of term, xii. *See also* consequences of trafficking; identification of trafficking victims; responses to human trafficking; risk factors for trafficking

pregnancy, risk of, 44–45
prescription medications, 177
President's Interagency Trafficking Task Force, 70
Preventing Sex Trafficking and Strengthening Families Act of 2014, 66–67
prevention: in international law, 61–62; as overlooked, 9; in public health approach, 90–97, 198–99; in state law, 72–74; in US federal law, 68–70
private sector, 33–34, 110, 208–9, 213
program implementation, 86
program monitoring and evaluation, 88–89, 102, 144. *See also* evaluation
prosecution: in international law, 60–61; in state law, 71; in US federal law, 63–65
protection and assistance: in international law, 61; in state law, 71–72; in US federal law, 65–68
protective factors, 135
PROTECT Our Children Act of 2008, 70
Protocol to Prevent, Suppress and Punish Trafficking in Persons, Especially Women and Children, Supplementing the United Nations Convention Against Transnational Organized Crime (Trafficking Protocol): adoption and mandates of, 8, 58–59; anchoring effect of, 77; components of, 60–62; definition of child trafficking in, 26
providers. *See* medical personnel
psychological and emotional health issues, 7, 43–44, 46–48, 175–76, 179. *See also* substance use and abuse; trauma
PTSD (post-traumatic stress disorder), 46–48, 117
public health, scale of problem and allocation of resources for, 18
public health approach: benefits of, 81–83, 115–16; causes addressed in, 97–103; to criminal activity, 197; ethics in, 215–17; evidence-based research in, 83–90; monitoring and evaluation in, 88–89; moving upstream example of, 195–96; partnerships in, 103–7; pre-

vention emphasis of, 90–97; risk group identification in, 87–88, 118; stigma as risk of, 108, 110, 215; success in, 91, 195–96; surveillance methods of, 86–87, 110–11. *See also* public health toolkit
public health campaigns. *See* social marketing and advertising campaigns
public health perspective: challenges unveiled by, 111–15; overview of, 107–8; potential risks unveiled by, 108–11
public health toolkit: anticipation of unintended consequences in, 204, 206–7; causes addressed in, 200–201; community partnerships in, 202–3; coordination among stakeholders in, 203–4, 205; evidence-based research in, 201–2; overview of, 198; prevention emphasis in, 198–99; socio-ecological model in, 199–200
purchasers, 32
purpose, as element of human trafficking, 5, 26–27

recruiters, 30, 31, 84–85, 130–31
referral systems, 185, 186–87
relationship-based services, 147–48, 217
relationship-level risk factors, 93, 129–31
research: biases in, 24; ethics in, 215; evidence-based responses and, 83–90, 201–2; involving children, 40, 88
resilience: of providers, 193; of survivors, 56–57
resources: for comprehensive, integrated approach, 213–14; for public health, 18; for state and local programs, 67; for training, 191
responses to human trafficking: assessment of, 75–76; constraints embedded in, 76–78; evidence-based, 83–90, 201–2; optimizing, 81; overview of, 8–9; scale of problem and allocation of resources in, 18; US as leader in, 59. *See also* comprehensive responses; criminal justice framework; health care services; legal framework; public health approach; services

restitution, 52, 67–68, 212
retributive justice model, 248n4
Rigby, Paul, 201
risk factors for trafficking: community-level, 93–94, 131–32; exploration of, 86, 88; individual-level, 92, 119–29; interaction among, 127–29, 134; overview of, 40, 117–19, 134–35; public health approach to, 197; relationship-level, 93, 129–31; societal-level, 94–95, 132–34; socio-ecological model of, *96.* *See also* vulnerability to trafficking
risk group identification, 86, 87–88
risks of public health programs, 108–11, 215
road safety, 109, 115
romantic partners, 130–31

safe harbor laws, 55–56, 67, 71–72
scale of problem: biases and political agendas in determining, 24; commitment of resources and, 214; definitional issues in determining, 22–23; hidden nature of crime and, 21–22; importance of estimates of, 25–26; methodological issues in determining, 23–24; overview of, 18–20; quality of data collection and, 20–21
school lunch/nutrition programs, 88–89, 95–96
screening for sex trafficking risk, 139
secondhand smoke, 113
self-identification as survivors or victims, 73, 138, 163, 165
services: adolescent-friendly, 142–48, 177–80; for children, 74; connecting youth with, 166–68; direct to victims, 66–67; judgment-free, 145–46, 151, 152, 166; for LGBTQ youth, 53; MSAHC case example of, 169–71; multidisciplinary approach to, 38–39, 173, 184–88; overview of, 193–94; principles for, 143; relationship-based, 147–48; stigma-free, 145–46; trauma-informed, 147, 180–81; unintended consequences of, 89; walk-in, 183; wraparound, 38–39. *See also* health care services; treatment

sex tourism, 64–65
sex trafficking: early bias toward focus on, 77–78; gangs and, 127; health consequences of, 7, 44–46, 108, 175–76; overview of, 2–3; taking histories and, 158; US federal law on, 63–65
sexual abuse, 98, 121
sexual and reproductive health issues, 7, 44–46, 108, 175–76
sexually transmitted infections, 45, 108
Shared Hope International, 75
shelters, 53, 85, 173, 212–13
Signal International, 52
signs of trafficking, 1–2, 158
slavery, 28
smart phone apps, 208–9
smuggling, 27
Snyder, Leslie, 100
social marketing and advertising campaigns: assessment of, 102; attitudes and, 97–99; criminal sanctions in, 76; education in, 99–100, 101–2; effectiveness of, 114; ethics in, 102; mobilization for action in, 101; overview of, 102–3; strategies of, 100–101
societal attitudes, 98–99
societal-level risk factors, 94–95, 132–34
socio-ecological model: drivers of trafficking and, 36; overview of, 91–92, 119, 199–200; program using, 92–95. *See also* risk factors for trafficking
State Department, *Trafficking in Persons Report,* 8, 69
state legal framework, 71–74
stigma: as risk factor, 133; as risk of public health campaigns, 108, 110, 215; services without, 145–46
Stransky, Michelle, 20–21
Street Outreach Program, 69
substance use and abuse, 46–47, 48–49, 126–27, 166–67
success, in public health approach, 91, 195–96
suicide and suicidal ideation, 43–44
supply-and-demand model of trafficking, 35–36, 112–14
support for medical personnel, 192–93
surveillance methods, 86–87, 110–11

survivor-led and survivor-informed approaches, 174–75, 202–3

survivors: agency of, 206; definition of, xi–xii, 32; needs and priorities of, 108–9; resilience of, 56–57; retraumatizing, 216; self-identification as, 73, 138, 163, 165

sustaining commitment to services, 212–15

tattoos and scarring, 42–43, 160

terminology, xi–xii

three P's framework, 59–62, 63, 76

traffickers, 30–32

Trafficking Victims Protection Act of 2000 (TVPA), 8, 59, 70, 71

Trafficking Victims Protection Reauthorization Acts of 2008 and 2013, 89

training: for comprehensive, integrated response, 210–12; of health care professionals, 139–40, 141, 188–91; in identification of victims, 3, 14, 34, 68–69; in motivational interviewing, 178; at MSAHC, 178, 179; surveillance and, 86–87

transgender youth, 123–24

transportation: bystanders in transportation sector, 34; to health services, 177–78; of minors in interstate or foreign commerce, 64–65

Transportation Department, training of personnel of, 210–11

transporters, 30

trauma: brain development and, 47–48; consequences of, 176; definition of, 146–47; developing radar for, 182–83; disability due to, 125; PTSD and, 47, 117; services focused on, 181, 183–84; services informed by, 147, 180–81; signs of, 162; vicarious, 192

trauma-focused cognitive behavioral therapy, 183–84

travel industry, 110

treaties related to child trafficking, 8. *See also* Sale of Children Protocol; Trafficking Protocol

treatment: case management, 172–74; core components of, 171–72; multi-

faceted, 109–10, 184–88; role of survivors in, 174–75, 202–3; trauma-focused, 181, 183–84. *See also* health care services; services

truckers and trafficking, 93–94

trust: building, 151–52, 153, 161, 166; trauma-informed practices and, 181

TVPA (Trafficking Victims Protection Act of 2000), 8, 59, 70, 71

unintended consequences of programs, 89, 204, 206–7

United Arab Emirates, trafficking for camel racing in, 208

United Nations (UN), 60, 248n16

*United States v. Webster,* 52

US legal framework: federal, 63–70; state, 71–74

vicarious trauma, 192

victim-centered approach, 8–9, 77

victims: arrests of, 55–56, 71–72, 126; definition of, 32; direct services to, 66–67; rescuing of, 206; self-identification as, 73, 138, 163, 165; stereotypes of and misperceptions about, 190; use of term, xii; working with, 187, 191–93. *See also* assistance to victims; identification of trafficking victims; male victims; survivors; treatment

violence: forced labor and, 42; human trafficking as form of, 8; by intimate partners, 49, 113; physical health issues and, 40–41, 160; public health approach to, 112; reactive approach to, 90; by recruiter boyfriends, 130–31; scientific approach to prevention of, 83; sexual, 44, 45–46; socio-ecological model and, 119

vulnerability to trafficking: "changing points" and, 105, 174–75; housing insecurity and, 52–54; identification of, 105; programs to reduce, 69; substance use and abuse and, 46–47; supply-and-demand model and, 35, 36. *See also* at-risk children; risk factors for trafficking

Wickrama, Thulitha, 49–50
wraparound services, 38–39

youth: criminalization of, 55–56; with disabilities, 124–25; empowering, 149–50; engagement of, 144–45, 175; LGBTQ, 44, 53, 123–24; manipulation of, to serve adult agendas, 106; medical personnel and, 148, 150–52; services for, 142–48, 166–68, 177–80. *See also* children; homeless youth